4/2007

# BSD
# HACKS™

*Dru Lavigne*

**O'REILLY®**

Beijing · Cambridge · Farnham · Köln · Paris · Sebastopol · Taipei · Tokyo

# BSD Hacks™

by Dru Lavigne

Copyright © 2004 O'Reilly Media, Inc. All rights reserved.
Printed in the United States of America.

Published by O'Reilly Media, Inc., 1005 Gravenstein Highway North,
Sebastopol, CA 95472.

O'Reilly books may be purchased for educational, business, or sales promotional use. Online editions are also available for most titles (*safari.oreilly.com*). For more information, contact our corporate/institutional sales department: (800) 998-9938 or *corporate@oreilly.com*.

| | | | |
|---|---|---|---|
| **Editor:** | chromatic | **Production Editor:** | G. d'Entremont |
| **Series Editor:** | Rael Dornfest | **Cover Designer:** | Hanna Dyer |
| **Executive Editor:** | Dale Dougherty | **Interior Designer:** | David Futato |

**Printing History:**

| | |
|---|---|
| May 2004: | First Edition. |

RepKover. This book uses RepKover™, a durable and flexible lay-flat binding.

ISBN: 0-596-00679-9

[C]

# Contents

# Credits

## About the Author

Dru Lavigne is the author of ONLamp.com's FreeBSD Basics column and has been an avid BSD user since FreeBSD 2.2.1. As an IT instructor, she specializes in networking, routing, and security. She is also responsible for ISECOM's Protocol Database, which can be found at *http://www.isecom.org*.

## Contributors

The following people contributed their hacks, writing, and inspiration to this book:

- John Richard, known locally as JR, is a system administrator in Kingston, Ontario, Canada. His trademark in the field is his insistence on a FreeBSD box as the primary firewall on a network. He has enjoyed working with the author in the past at a private college in Kingston. In his spare time, he experiments with FreeBSD and rides his Harley-Davidson.

  [Hack #64]

- Joe Warner is a Technical Analyst for Siemens Medical Solutions Health Services Corporation and has been using FreeBSD as a server and desktop since October of 2000. Joe has lived in Salt Lake City, Utah for most of his life and enjoys *BSD, computing, history, and *The Matrix*.

  [Hacks #35 and #59]

- Dan Langille (*http://www.langille.org/*) runs a consulting group in Ottawa, Canada. He has fond memories of his years in New Zealand, where the climate is much more conducive to year-round mountain biking. He lives in a house ruled by felines.

  [Hack #41]

- Robert Bernier's professional career has included engineering, accident investigation, and Olympic trials. In the 1980s, his interest returned to IT when he realized he wouldn't have to use a punch card anymore. Eventually he discovered Linux and by the mid-1990s had developed a passion for all things open source. Today, Robert teaches at the local community college and writes for a number of IT publications based in North America and Europe.

  [Hack #12]

- Kirk Russell (*kirk@qnx.com*) is a kernel tester at QNX Software Systems (*http://www.qnx.com/*).

  [Hack #36]

- Karl Vogel is a system administrator for the C-17 Program Office. He's worked at Wright-Patterson Air Force Base for 22 years and has a BS in Mechanical & Aerospace Engineering from Cornell University.

  [Hack #32]

- Howard Owen discovered computers by reading about Conway's "Life" in Life magazine. It took many years from that discovery to the time he could actually make a living with the godforsaken things. Once that happened, however, Howard turned into a "major geek." He has worked as a sysadmin, systems engineer, and systems architect. He is currently employed by IBM in Silicon Valley supporting Linux, but he still runs FreeBSD and OpenBSD at home.

  [Hacks #61 and #62]

- Daniel Harris is a student and occasional consultant in West Virginia. He is interested in computer networking, documentation, and security; he also enjoys writing, armchair politics, and amateur radio.

  [Hack #55]

- Andrew Gould, CPA, performs financial and clinical data analysis for a hospital in Texas. His primary tool for data integration is a PostgreSQL database server running on FreeBSD. Andrew has been using FreeBSD at both work and home for four years. Andrew has a BS in Education and a BBA in Accounting from the University of Texas at Austin.

  [Hacks #17, #40, #44, and #68]

- Jim Mock is a FreeBSD admin and developer turned Mac OS X user and developer. He's a FreeBSD committer, as well as an OpenDarwin committer, and he currently maintains 50+ DarwinPorts. Jim is also a member of the DarwinPorts Port Manager team. He can be reached at *jim@bsdnews.org* or through his personal site at *http://soupnazi.org/*.

  [Hack #88]

- Avleen Vig is a systems administrator at EarthLink (*http://www.earthlink.net/*), where he maintains the company's web, mail, news, and other Internet services for over 8 million users. He spends his spare time with his newborn son, contributing to the various Internet and Unix communities, and enjoying life. After seizing the day in 2001 and moving to LA from London, he's waiting to see where life will take him next.

  [Hack #69]

- Alexandru Popa is a CCNA studying for a CCNP, and is actively involved in the FreeBSD community in his spare time. At the time of this writing, he was studying Computer Science at the Politechnica University of Bucharest. He also maintains *cvsup.ro.freebsd.org* out of a basement in a deserted building, using a large hamster array for power. He can be contacted at *alex@bsdnews.org*.

  [Hack #70]

- Jens Schweikhardt is a German software engineer and Internet wizard who is constantly looking for interesting things to do. As a seven-time IOCCC winner, he is well-known for taking C compilers to their limits. He contributes to Unix standardization and, of course, to God's Own Operating System. When not hacking, Jens has been caught writing romantic poetry and riding his Italian Moto Guzzi around the Swabian hills and valleys. If he were given one modest wish, it would be clear skies when he goes stargazing with his telescope.

  [Hack #78]

- Matthew Seaman is 38 years old and a former scientist and academic (Oxford University postgraduate). He is now a specialist in computer system administration, network architecture, and infrastructure design.

  [Hacks #49, #50, and #97]

- Nathan Rosenquist first tried FreeBSD in 1996, and has been using Unix ever since. During the day, he can be found developing Perl-based web applications and business automation software. He lives in Shadow Hills, California with his girlfriend Carrie and their dog Nutmeg.

  [Hack #39]

- Adrian Mayo (*http://unix.1dot1.com/*) has worked with computers for 20 years, specializing in the design of safety and mission-critical software for the aerospace and medical industries. He has gained exposure to BSD Unix through Apple's Mac OS X operating system. He is Editor for the news and support site *http://www.osxfaq.com*, writing most of the technical content, including the Unix tutorials and Daily Unix tips.

  [Hacks #14, #15, and #16]

- Sebastian Stark (*seb@biskalar.de*) works as a system administrator at the Max Planck Institute for Biological Cybernetics in Germany. He manages a bunch of workstations, as well as a computer cluster that is used for machine-learning research.

  [Hack #52]

- Marlon Berlin (*marlon@biskalar.de*) studies linguistics, comparative literature, and mathematics in Berlin. He works for DNS:NET, a German ISP, as a systems developer.

  [Hack #52]

- David Maxwell (*david@netbsd.org*) is a NetBSD Developer and member of the NetBSD Security-Officer team. He attended Unix Unanimous in Toronto since the first meeting in the early '80s, and still visits when he can. He was an avid Amiga user, and relishes a good (or bad) pun when he can muster one. David currently works at Integrated Device Technology, Inc. (IDT).

  [Hacks #10, #53, #73, #75, and #76]

- Julio Merino Vidal is studying Informatics Engineering at the UPC University of Barcelona, Spain. He has been a NetBSD developer since November 2002, working on the NetBSD Packages Collection (*http://www.pkgsrc.org/*) and translating the web site to Spanish. He also maintains his own free software projects, including Buildtool (*http://buildtool.sourceforge.net/*). You can contact him at *jmmv@NetBSD.org*.

  [Hacks #27 and #87]

- Jan L. Peterson (*jlp@peterson.ath.cx*) is a professional system administrator with 16 years of experience working with multiple Unix versions (and the occasional Windows machine). Laid off from his last job when the company was acquired by a direct competitor, he has spent the last couple of years as a consultant. More about Jan can be found at *http://www.peterson.ath.cx/~jlp/*.

  [Hack #74]

- Michael Vince was born in 1977. His initial interest in computers was video games, but he soon ventured into many other areas, such as programming, Unix, the Web, and networks. Having completed a Diploma in Computer Systems and a CCNA, he is an IT administrator for software companies and has been involved in large software projects that put his development skills to good use. A tech news junkie, he is always interested in the future of computing. He also enjoys staying up late solving difficult problems that require complex regular expressions in Perl, going to the gym, and hanging out in cafes. He is currently working on a software product called Ezmin.

[Hack #64]

- Daniel Carosone has been involved with NetBSD as a user, advocate, and developer for over 10 years. He is a member of the NetBSD Security Officer team, which provides leadership for security matters within the project and coordinates responses to public incidents and vulnerabilities. He is Chief Technologist for e-Secure, specializing in security consulting and management services to financial, government, and telecommunications organizations. He promotes security awareness through conference presentations and university lectures. He lives in Melbourne, Australia, and—when not working too hard—enjoys hiking, driving, and astronomy.

[Hack #60]

- Aaron Crandall, BSEE, has used OpenBSD since 2.7. He currently works for the Oregon Graduate Institute running computers as a part-time Master's student. He's built and given away more OpenBSD firewalls than he can count. Contact him at *aaron.crandal@cse.ogi.edu*.

[Hack #45]

- chromatic is the Technical Editor of the O'Reilly Network. In practice, that means he edits ONLamp.com (open source administration and development) and, occasionally, books like this one. Outside of work, he enjoys cooking and somehow produces a whole slew of weird software hacks like SDL Parrot, tiny mail tools, and that Perl 6 thing. Wade through the disarray of his web site at *http://wgz.org/chromatic/*.

[Hack #92]

- Brett Warden, BSEE, specializes in Perl programming and embedded systems. He lives in the Northwest with his wife, son, and two antisocial cats. He's currently keeping an eye out for contracting and permanent positions. You can find a collection of odd projects at *http://www.wgz.org/bwarden/*.

[Hack #65]

## Acknowledgments

I would like to thank the many BSD and open source users who so willingly shared their experiences, ideas, and support. You serve as a constant reminder that BSD is more than an operating system—it is a community.

I would also like to thank all of my students and the readers of the FreeBSD Basics column. Your questions and feedback fuel my curiosity; may this book return that favor.

Thanks to David Lents and Rob Flickenger for reviews and advice. Special thanks to Jacek Artymiak for his invaluable input from the OpenBSD and NetBSD perspectives. And finally, special thanks to chromatic. A writer couldn't have asked for a better editor.

# Preface

"What was it about UNIX that won my heart?…UNIX is mysterious when you first approach. A little intimidating, too. But despite an unadorned and often plain presentation, the discerning suitor can tell there's lot going on under the surface."

—Thomas Scoville, *http://unix.oreilly.com/news/unix_love_0299.html*

When the above-mentioned article was first published, I was still very much a BSD newbie. My spare hours were spent struggling with kernel recompiles, PPP connectivity (or lack thereof), rm and chmod disasters, and reading and rereading every bit of the then available documentation. Yet, that article gave voice to my experience, for, like the quoted author, I had stumbled upon operating system love. In other words, I was discovering how to hack on BSD.

Since then, I've learned that there is an unspoken commonality between the novice Unix user and the seasoned guru. It doesn't matter whether you've just survived your first successful installation or you've just executed a complex script that will save your company time and money, the feeling is the same. It's the excitement of venturing into unknown territory and discovering something new and wonderful. It's that sense of accomplishment that comes with figuring something out for yourself, with finding your own solution to the problem at hand.

This book contains 100 hacks written by users who love hacking with BSD. You'll find hacks suited to both the novice user and the seasoned veteran, as well as everyone in between. Read them in any order that suits your purpose, but keep the "onion principle" in mind. While each hack does present at least one practical solution to a problem, that's just the outer layer. Use your imagination to peel away deeper layers, exposing new solutions as you do so.

# Why BSD Hacks?

The term *hacking* has an unfortunate reputation in the popular press, where it often refers to someone who breaks into systems or wreaks havoc with computers. Among enthusiasts, on the other hand, the term *hack* refers to a "quick-n-dirty" solution to a problem or a clever way to do something. The term *hacker* is very much a compliment, praising someone for being *creative* and having the technical chops to get things done. O'Reilly's Hacks series is an attempt to reclaim the word, document the ways people are hacking (in a good way), and pass the hacker ethic of creative participation on to a new generation of hackers. Seeing how others approach systems and problems is often the quickest way to learn about a new technology.

*BSD Hacks* is all about making the most of your BSD system. The BSDs of today have a proud lineage, tracing back to some of the original hackers—people who built Unix and the Internet as we know it today. As you'd expect, they faced many problems and solved problems both quickly and elegantly. We've collected some of that wisdom, both classic and modern, about using the command line, securing systems, keeping track of your files, making backups, and, most importantly, how to become your own BSD guru along the way.

## How to Use this Book

One of the beauties of Unix is that you can be very productive with surprisingly little knowledge. Even better, each new trick you learn can shave minutes off of your day. We've arranged the chapters in this book by subject area, not by any suggested order of learning. Skip around to what interests you most or solves your current problem. If the current hack depends on information in another hack, we'll include a link for you to follow.

Furthermore, the "See Also" sections at the end of individual hacks often include references such as man fortune. These refer to the manual pages installed on your machine. If you're not familiar with these manpages, start with "How'd He Know That?" [Hack #89].

## How This Book Is Organized

To master BSD, you'll have to understand several topics. We've arranged the hacks loosely into chapters. They are:

Chapter 1, *Customizing the User Environment*
Though modern BSDs have myriad graphical applications and utilities, the combined wisdom of 35 years of command-line programs is just a shell away. This chapter demonstrates how to make the most of the command line, customizing it to your needs and preferences.

Chapter 2, *Dealing with Files and Filesystems*

What good is knowing Unix commands if you have no files? You have to slice, dice, and store data somewhere. This chapter explains techniques for finding and processing information, whether it's on your machine or on a server elsewhere.

Chapter 3, *The Boot and Login Environments*

The best-laid security plans of administrators often go out the window when users enter the picture. Keeping the bad guys off of sensitive machines requires a two-pronged approach: protecting normal user accounts through good password policies and protecting the boxes physically. This chapter explores several options for customizing and securing the boot and login processes.

Chapter 4, *Backing Up*

After you start creating files, you're bound to run across data you can't afford to lose. That's where backups come in. This chapter offers several ideas for various methods of ensuring that your precious data will persist in the face of tragedy.

Chapter 5, *Networking Hacks*

Unless you're a die-hard individualist, you're likely connected to a network. That fact presents several new opportunities for clever hacks as well as mystifying failures. This chapter illuminates ways to take advantage of your network connection.

Chapter 6, *Securing the System*

Security is as much a mindset as it is a process. Knowing the tools at your disposal will help. This chapter delves into multiple tools and ideas for increasing the security of your systems, whether keeping out the bad guys or staying on top of updates.

Chapter 7, *Going Beyond the Basics*

With years and years of refinement, the BSDs provide powerful and maintainable environments. Are you taking full advantage of everything your system has to offer? This chapter pushes the envelope of what you can accomplish.

Chapter 8, *Keeping Up-to-Date*

No bragging about BSD is complete without mentioning the ports or packages system that keeps thousands of applications right at your fingertips. Keeping up-to-date could never be easier, could it? This chapter tackles the subject of installing and updating software, including the core system.

Chapter 9, *Grokking BSD*

You cannot be a true BSD master until you grok the Unix mindset. How did the gurus become gurus? Is the true path still open? This chapter reveals some secrets of the masters and has a little fun along the way.

## Conventions Used in This Book

This book uses the following typographical conventions:

*Italic*

> Indicates new terms, URLs, email addresses, filenames, pathnames, and directories.

`Constant width`

> Indicates commands, options, switches, variables, attributes, functions, user and group names, the contents of files, and the output from commands.

**`Constant width bold`**

> In code examples, shows commands or other text that should be typed literally by the user.

`Constant width italic`

> Shows text that should be replaced with user-supplied values.

*Color*

> The second color is used to indicate a cross-reference within the text.

 This icon signifies a tip, suggestion, or general note.

 This icon indicates a warning or caution.

The thermometer icons, found next to each hack, indicate the relative complexity of the hack:

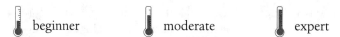

beginner          moderate          expert

## Using Code Examples

This book is here to help you get your job done. In general, you may use the code in this book in your programs and documentation. You do not need to contact us for permission unless you're reproducing a significant portion of the code. For example, writing a program that uses several chunks of code from this book does not require permission. Selling or distributing a CD-ROM of examples from O'Reilly books does require permission. Answering a question by citing this book and quoting example code does not require permission. Incorporating a significant amount of example code from this book into your product's documentation does require permission.

We appreciate, but do not require, attribution. An attribution usually includes the title, author, publisher, and ISBN, for example: "*BSD Hacks* by Dru Lavigne. Copyright 2004 O'Reilly Media, Inc., 0-596-00679-9."

If you feel your use of code examples falls outside fair use or the permission given here, feel free to contact us at *permissions@oreilly.com*.

## We'd Like to Hear from You

Please address comments and questions concerning this book to the publisher:

> O'Reilly Media, Inc.
> 1005 Gravenstein Highway North
> Sebastopol, CA 95472
> (800) 998-9938 (in the United States or Canada)
> (707) 829-0515 (international or local)
> (707) 829-0104 (fax)

We have a web page for this book, where we list errata, examples, and any additional information. You can access this page at:

> *http://www.oreilly.com/catalog/bsdhks*

To comment or ask technical questions about this book, send email to:

> *bookquestions@oreilly.com*

For more information about our books, conferences, Resource Centers, and the O'Reilly Network, see our web site at:

> *http://www.oreilly.com/*

# Customizing the User Environment

## Hacks 1-12

Users of open source (*http://opensource.org*) Unix operating systems are an interesting breed. They like to poke under the surface of things, to find out how things work, and to figure out new and interesting ways of accomplishing common computing tasks. In short, they like to "hack."

While this book concentrates on the BSDs, many of the hacks apply to any open source operating system. Each hack is simply a demonstration of how to examine a common problem from a slightly different angle. Feel free to use any of these hacks as a springboard to your own customized solution. If your particular operating system doesn't contain the tool used in the solution, use a tool that does exist, or invent your own!

This chapter provides many tools for getting the most out of your working environment. You'll learn how to make friends with your shell and how to perform your most common tasks with just a few keystrokes or mouse clicks. You'll also uncover tricks that can help prevent command-line disasters. And, above all, you'll discover that hacking BSD is fun. So, pull your chair up to your operating system of choice and let's start hacking.

### HACK #1 Get the Most Out of the Default Shell

Become a speed daemon at the command line.

For better or for worse, you spend a lot of time at the command line. If you're used to administering a Linux system, you may be dismayed to learn that bash is not the default shell on a BSD system, for either the superuser or regular user accounts.

Take heart; the FreeBSD superuser's default tcsh shell is also brimming with shortcuts and little tricks designed to let you breeze through even the most tedious of tasks. Spend a few moments learning these tricks and you'll feel right at home. If you're new to the command line or consider yourself a terrible typist, read on. Unix might be a whole lot easier than you think.

> NetBSD and OpenBSD also ship with the C shell as their default shell. However, it is not always the same tcsh, but often its simpler variant, csh, which doesn't support all of the tricks provided in this hack.
>
> However, both NetBSD and OpenBSD provide a tcsh package in their respective package collections.

## History and Auto-Completion

I hate to live without three keys: up arrow, down arrow, and Tab. In fact, you can recognize me in a crowd, as I'm the one muttering loudly to myself if I'm on a system that doesn't treat these keys the way I expect to use them.

tcsh uses the up and down arrow keys to scroll through your command history. If there is a golden rule to computing, it should be: "You should never have to type a command more than once." When you need to repeat a command, simply press your up arrow until you find the desired command. Then, press Enter and think of all the keystrokes you just saved yourself. If your fingers fly faster than your eyes can read and you whiz past the right command, simply use the down arrow to go in the other direction.

The Tab key was specifically designed for both the lazy typist and the terrible speller. It can be painful watching some people type out a long command only to have it fail because of a typo. It's even worse if they haven't heard about history, as they think their only choice is to try typing out the whole thing all over again. No wonder some people hate the command line!

Tab activates auto-completion. This means that if you type enough letters of a recognizable command or file, tcsh will fill in the rest of the word for you. However, if you instead hear a beep when you press the Tab key, it means that your shell isn't sure what you want. For example, if I want to run sockstat and type:

    % so

then press my Tab key, the system will beep because multiple commands start with so. However, if I add one more letter:

    % soc

and try again, the system will fill in the command for me:

    % sockstat

## Editing and Navigating the Command Line

There are many more shortcuts that can save you keystrokes. Suppose I've just finished editing a document. If I press my up arrow, my last command will be displayed at the prompt:

```
% vi mydocs/today/verylongfilename
```

I'd now like to double-check how many words and lines are in that file by running this command:

```
% wc mydocs/today/verylongfilename
```

I could pound on the backspace key until I get to the vi portion of the command, but it would be much easier to hold down the Ctrl key and press a. That would bring me to the very beginning of that command so I could replace the vi with wc. For a mnemonic device, remember that just as a is the first letter of the alphabet, it also represents the first letter of the command at a tcsh prompt.

I don't have to use my right arrow to go to the end of the command in order to press Enter and execute the command. Once your command looks like it should, you can press Enter. It doesn't matter where your cursor happens to be.

Sometimes you would like your cursor to go to the end of the command. Let's say I want to run the word count command on two files, and right now my cursor is at the first c in this command:

```
% wc mydocs/today/verylongfilename
```

If I hold down Ctrl and press e, the cursor will jump to the end of the command, so I can type in the rest of the desired command. Remember that e is for end.

Finally, what if you're in the middle of a long command and decide you'd like to start from scratch, erase what you've typed, and just get your prompt back? Simply hold down Ctrl and press u for undo.

 If you work in the Cisco or PIX IOS systems, all of the previous tricks work at the IOS command line.

Did you know that the cd command also includes some built-in shortcuts? You may have heard of this one: to return to your home directory quickly, simply type:

```
% cd
```

That's very convenient, but what if you want to change to a different previous directory? Let's say that you start out in the */usr/share/doc/en_US. ISO8859-1/books/handbook* directory, then use cd to change to the */usr/ X11R6/etc/X11* directory. Now you want to go back to that first directory. If you're anything like me, you really don't want to type out that long directory path again. Sure, you could pick it out of your history, but chances are you originally navigated into that deep directory structure one directory at a time. If that's the case, it would probably take you longer to pick each piece out of the history than it would be to just type the command manually.

Fortunately, there is a very quick solution. Simply type:

```
% cd -
```

Repeat that command and watch as your prompt changes between the first and the second directory. What, your prompt isn't changing to indicate your current working directory? Don't worry, "Useful tcsh Shell Configuration File Options" [Hack #2] will take care of that.

## Learning from Your Command History

Now that you can move around fairly quickly, let's fine-tune some of these hacks. How many times have you found yourself repeating commands just to alter them slightly? The following scenario is one example.

Remember that document I created? Instead of using the history to bring up my previous command so I could edit it, I might have found it quicker to type this:

```
% wc !$
wc mydocs/today/verylongfilename
     19        97       620 mydocs/today/verylongfilename
```

The !$ tells the shell to take the last parameter from the previous command. Since that command was:

```
% vi mydocs/today/verylongfilename
```

it replaced the !$ in my new command with the very long filename from my previous command.

The ! (or bang!) character has several other useful applications for dealing with previously issued commands. Suppose you've been extremely busy and have issued several dozen commands in the last hour or so. You now want to repeat something you did half an hour ago. You could keep tapping your up arrow until you come across the command. But why search yourself when ! can search for you?

For example, if I'd like to repeat the command mailstats, I could give !
enough letters to figure out which command to pick out from my history:

    $ !ma

! will pick out the most recently issued command that begins with ma. If I
had issued a man command sometime after mailstats command, tcsh would
find that instead. This would fix it though:

    % !mai

If you're not into trial and error, you can view your history by simply typing:

    % history

If you're really lazy, this command will do the same thing:

    % h

Each command in this history will have a number. You can specify a command by giving ! the associated number. In this example, I'll ask tcsh to
reissue the mailstats command:

```
% h
  165  16:51  mailstats
  166  16:51  sockstat
  167  16:52  telnet localhost 25
  168  16:54  man sendmail

% !165
```

## Silencing Auto-Complete

The last tip I'll mention is for those of you who find the system bell irritating. Or perhaps you just find it frustrating typing one letter, tabbing, typing
another letter, tabbing, and so on until auto-complete works. If I type:

    % ls -l b

then hold down the Ctrl key while I press d:

    backups/  bin/   book/   boring.jpg
    ls -l b

I'll be shown all of the b possibilities in my current directory, and then my
prompt will return my cursor to what I've already typed. In this example, if I
want to view the size and permissions of *boring.jpg*, I'll need to type up to here:

    % ls -l bor

before I press the Tab key. I'll leave it up to your own imagination to decide
what the d stands for.

## See Also

• man tcsh

H A C K
#2
# Useful tcsh Shell Configuration File Options
Make the shell a friendly place to work in.

Now that you've had a chance to make friends with the shell, let's use its configuration file to create an environment you'll enjoy working in. Your prompt is an excellent place to start.

## Making Your Prompt More Useful

The default tcsh prompt displays % when you're logged in as a regular user and hostname# when you're logged in as the superuser. That's a fairly useful way to figure out who you're logged in as, but we can do much better than that.

Each user on the system, including the superuser, has a *.cshrc* file in his home directory. Here are my current prompt settings:

```
dru@~:grep prompt ~/.cshrc
if ($?prompt) then
        set prompt = "%B%n@%~%b: "
```

That isn't the default tcsh prompt, as I've been using my favorite customized prompt for the past few years. The possible prompt formatting sequences are easy to understand if you have a list of possibilities in front of you. That list is buried deeply within man cshrc, so here's a quick way to zero in on it:

```
dru@~:man cshrc
/prompt may include
```

Here I've used the / to invoke the manpage search utility. The search string prompt may include brings you to the right section, and is intuitive enough that even my rusty old brain can remember it.

If you compare the formatting sequences shown in the manpage to my prompt string, it reads as follows:

```
set prompt = "%B%n@%~%b: "
```

That's a little dense. Table 1-1 dissects the options.

*Table 1-1. Prompt characters*

| Character | Explanation |
| --- | --- |
| " | Starts the prompt string. |
| %B | Turns on bold. |
| %n | Shows the login name in the prompt. |
| @ | I use this as a separator to make my prompt more visually appealing. |

*Table 1-1. Prompt characters (continued)*

| Character | Explanation |
| --- | --- |
| %~ | Shows the current working directory. It results in a shorter prompt than %/, as my home directory is shortened from /usr/home/myusername to ~ |
| %b | Turns off bold. |
| : | Again, this is an extra character I use to separate my prompt from the cursor. |
| " | Ends the prompt string. |

With this prompt, I always know who I am and where I am. If I also needed to know what machine I was logged into (useful for remote administration), I could also include %M or %m somewhere within the prompt string.

## Switching to the Superuser

The superuser's *.cshrc* file (in */root*, the superuser's home directory) has an identical prompt string. This is very fortunate, as it reveals something you might not know about the su command, which is used to switch users. Right now I'm logged in as the user dru and my prompt looks like this:

```
dru@/usr/ports/net/ethereal:
```

Watch the shell output carefully after I use su to switch to the root user:

```
dru@/usr/ports/net/ethereal: su
Password:
dru@/usr/ports/net/ethereal:
```

Things seem even more confusing if I use the whoami command:

```
dru@/usr/ports/net/ethereal: whoami
dru
```

However, the id command doesn't lie:

```
dru@/usr/ports/net/ethereal: id
uid=0(root) gid=0(wheel) groups=0(wheel), 5(operator)
```

It turns out that the default invocation of su doesn't actually log you in as the superuser. It simply gives you superuser privileges while retaining your original login shell.

If you really want to log in as the superuser, include the login (-1) switch:

```
dru@/usr/ports/net/ethereal: su -l
Password:
root@~: whoami
root
root@~: id
uid=0(root) gid=0(wheel) groups=0(wheel), 5(operator)
```

I highly recommend you take some time to experiment with the various formatting sequences and hack a prompt that best meets your needs. You can add other features, including customized time and date strings and command history numbers [Hack #1], as well as flashing or underlining the prompt.

## Setting Shell Variables

Your prompt is an example of a shell variable. There are dozens of other shell variables you can set in *.cshrc*. My trick for finding the shell variables section in the manpage is:

```
dru@~:man cshrc
/variables described
```

As the name implies, shell variables affect only the commands that are built into the shell itself. Don't confuse these with environment variables, which affect your entire working environment and every command you invoke.

If you take a look at your ~/.cshrc file, environment variables are the ones written in uppercase and are preceded with the setenv command. Shell variables are written in lowercase and are preceded with the set command.

You can also enable a shell variable by using the set command at your command prompt. (Use unset to disable it.) Since the variable affects only your current login session and its children, you can experiment with setting and unsetting variables to your heart's content. If you get into trouble, log out of that session and log in again.

If you find a variable you want to keep permanently, add it to your ~/.cshrc file in the section that contains the default set commands. Let's take a look at some of the most useful ones.

If you enjoyed Ctrl-d from "Get the Most Out of the Default Shell" [Hack #1], you'll like this even better:

```
set autolist
```

Now whenever you use the Tab key and the shell isn't sure what you want, it won't beep at you. Instead, the shell will show you the applicable possibilities. You don't even have to press Ctrl-d first!

The next variable might save you from possible future peril:

```
set rmstar
```

I'll test this variable by quickly making a *test* directory and some files:

```
dru@~:mkdir test
dru@~:cd test
dru@~/test:touch a b c d e
```

Then, I'll try to remove the files from that *test* directory:

```
dru@~/test:rm *
Do you really want to delete all files? [n/y]
```

Since my prompt tells me what directory I'm in, this trick gives me one last chance to double-check that I really am deleting the files I want to delete.

If you're prone to typos, consider this one:

```
set correct=all
```

This is how the shell will respond to typos at the command line:

```
dru@~:cd /urs/ports
CORRECT>cd /usr/ports (y|n|e|a)?
```

Pressing y will correct the spelling and execute the command. Pressing n will execute the misspelled command, resulting in an error message. If I press e, I can edit my command (although, in this case, it would be much quicker for the shell to go with its correct spelling). And if I completely panic at the thought of all of these choices, I can always press a to abort and just get my prompt back.

If you like to save keystrokes, try:

```
set implicitcd
```

You'll never have to type cd again. Instead, simply type the name of the directory and the shell will assume you want to go there.

## Create Shell Bindings

Train your shell to run a command for you whenever you press a mapped key.

Have you ever listened to a Windows power user expound on the joys of hotkeys? Perhaps you yourself have been known to gaze wistfully at the extra buttons found on a Microsoft keyboard. Did you know that it's easy to configure your keyboard to launch your most commonly used applications with a keystroke or two?

One way to do this is with the bindkey command, which is built into the tcsh shell. As the name suggests, this command binds certain actions to certain keys. To see your current mappings, simply type bindkey. The output is several pages long, so I've included only a short sample. However, you'll recognize some of these shortcuts from "Get the Most Out of the Default Shell" [Hack #1].

```
Standard key bindings
"^A"           -> beginning-of-line
"^B"           -> backward-char
```

```
"^E"              ->  end-of-line
"^F"              ->  forward-char
"^L"              ->  clear-screen
"^N"              ->  down-history
"^P"              ->  up-history
"^U"              ->  kill-whole-line

Arrow key bindings
down              ->  history-search-forward
up                ->  history-search-backward
left              ->  backward-char
right             ->  forward-char
home              ->  beginning-of-line
end               ->  end-of-line
```

The ^ means hold down your Ctrl key. For example, press Ctrl and then l, and you'll clear your screen more quickly than by typing clear. Notice that it doesn't matter if you use the uppercase or lowercase letter.

## Creating a Binding

One of my favorite shortcuts isn't bound to a key by default: complete-word-fwd. Before I do the actual binding, I'll first check which keys are available:

```
dru@~:bindkey | grep undefined
```

```
"^G"              ->  is undefined
"\305"            ->  is undefined
"\307"            ->  is undefined
<snip>
```

Although it is possible to bind keys to numerical escape sequences, I don't find that very convenient. However, I can very easily use that available Ctrl-g. Let's see what happens when I bind it:

```
dru@~:bindkey "^G" complete-word-fwd
```

When I typed in that command, I knew something worked because my prompt returned silently. Here's what happens if I now type ls -l /etc/, hold down the Ctrl key, and repeatedly press g:

```
ls -l /etc/COPYRIGHT
ls -l /etc/X11
ls -l /etc/aliases
ls -l /etc/amd.map
```

I now have a quick way of cycling through the files in a directory until I find the exact one I want. Even better, if I know what letter the file starts with, I can specify it. Here I'll cycle through the files that start with a:

```
ls -l /etc/a
ls -l /etc/aliases
```

```
ls -l /etc/amd.map
ls -l /etc/apmd.conf
ls -l /etc/auth.conf
ls -l /etc/a
```

Once I've cycled through, the shell will bring me back to the letter a and beep.

If you prefer to cycle backward, starting with words that begin with z instead of a, bind your key to complete-word-back instead.

When you use bindkey, you can bind any command the shell understands to any understood key binding. Here's my trick to list the commands that tcsh understands:

```
dru@~ man csh
/command is bound
```

And, of course, use bindkey alone to see the understood key bindings. If you just want to see the binding for a particular key, specify it. Here's how to see the current binding for Ctrl-g:

```
dru@~:bindkey "^G"
"^G"    ->    complete-word-fwd
```

## Specifying Strings

What's really cool is that you're not limited to just the commands found in man csh. The s switch to bindkey allows you to specify any string. I like to bind the lynx web browser to Ctrl-w:

```
dru@~:bindkey -s "^W" "lynx\n"
```

I chose w because it reminds me of the World Wide Web. But why did I put \n after the lynx? Because that tells the shell to press Enter for me. That means by simply pressing Ctrl-w, I have instant access to the Web.

Note that I overwrite the default binding for Ctrl-w. This permits you to make bindings that are more intuitive and useful for your own purposes. For example, if you never plan on doing whatever ^J does by default, simply bind your desired command to it.

There are many potential key bindings, so scrolling through the output of bindkeys can be tedious. If you only stick with "Ctrl letter" bindings, though, it's easy to view your customizations with the following command:

```
dru@~:bindkey | head -n 28
```

As with all shell modifications, experiment with your bindings first by using bindkey at the command prompt. If you get into real trouble, you can always log out to go back to the defaults. However, if you find some bindings you want to keep, make them permanent by adding your bindkey statements to your *.cshrc* file. Here is an example:

```
dru@~:cp ~/.cshrc ~/.cshrc.orig
dru@~:echo 'bindkey "^G" complete-word-fwd' >> ~/.cshrc
```

Notice that I backed up my original *.cshrc* file first, just in case my fingers slip on the next part. I then used >> to append the echoed text to the end of *.cshrc*. If I'd used > instead, it would have replaced my entire *.cshrc* file with just that one line. I don't recommend testing this on any file you want to keep.

Along those lines, setting:

```
set noclobber
```

will prevent the shell from clobbering an existing file if you forget that extra > in your redirector. You'll know you just prevented a nasty accident if you get this error message after trying to redirect output to a file:

```
.cshrc: File exists.
```

### See Also

- `man tcsh`
- "Useful tcsh Shell Configuration File Options" [Hack #2]

## HACK #4  Use Terminal and X Bindings

Take advantage of your terminal's capabilities.

It's not just the tcsh shell that is capable of understanding bindings. Your FreeBSD terminal provides the kbdcontrol command to map commands to your keyboard. Unfortunately, neither NetBSD nor OpenBSD offer this feature. You can, however, remap your keyboard under X, as described later.

### Creating Temporary Mappings

Let's start by experimenting with some temporary mappings. The syntax for mapping a command with kbdcontrol is as follows:

```
kbdcontrol -f number "command"
```

Table 1-2 lists the possible numbers, each with its associated key combination.

*Table 1-2. Key numbers*

| Number | Key combination |
| --- | --- |
| 1, 2,…12 | F1, F2,…F12 |
| 13, 14,…24 | Shift+F1, Shift+F2,…Shift+F12 |
| 25, 26,…36 | Ctrl+F1, Ctrl+F2,…Ctrl+F12 |

*Table 1-2. Key numbers (continued)*

| Number | Key combination |
|--------|-----------------|
| 37, 38,...48 | Shift+Ctrl+F1, Shift+Ctrl+F2,...Shift+Ctrl+F12 |
| 49 | Home |
| 50 | Up arrow |
| 51 | Page Up |
| 52 | Numpad - (Num Lock off) |
| 53 | Left arrow (also works in editor) |
| 54 | Numpad 5 (without Num Lock) |
| 55 | Right arrow |
| 56 | Numpad + (without Num Lock) |
| 57 | End |
| 58 | Down arrow (affects c history) |
| 59 | Page Down |
| 60 | Ins |
| 61 | Del |
| 62 | Left GUI key (Windows icon next to left Ctrl) |
| 63 | Right GUI key (Windows icon next to right Alt) |
| 64 | Menu (menu icon next to right Ctrl) |

Those last three key combinations may or may not be present, depending upon your keyboard. My Logitech keyboard has a key with a Windows icon next to the left Ctrl key; that is the left GUI key. There's another key with a Windows icon next to my right Alt key; this is the right GUI key. The next key to the right has an icon of a cursor pointing at a square containing lines; that is the Menu key.

Now that we know the possible numbers, let's map lynx to the Menu key:

```
% kbdcontrol -f 64 "lynx"
```

Note that the command must be contained within quotes and be in your path. (You *could* give an absolute path, but there's a nasty limitation coming up soon.)

If I now press the Menu key, lynx is typed to the terminal for me. I just need to press Enter to launch the browser. This may seem a bit tedious at first, but it is actually quite handy. It can save you from inadvertently launching the wrong application if you're anything like me and tend to forget which commands you've mapped to which keys.

Let's see what happens if I modify that original mapping somewhat:

```
% kbdcontrol -f 64 "lynx www.google.ca"
kbdcontrol: function key string too long (18 > 16)
```

When doing your own mappings, beware that the command and its arguments can't exceed 16 characters. Other than that, you can pretty well map any command that strikes your fancy.

## Shell Bindings Versus Terminal Bindings

Before going any further, I'd like to pause a bit and compare shell-specific bindings, which we saw in "Create Shell Bindings" [Hack #3], and the terminal-specific bindings we're running across here.

One advantage of using kbdcontrol is that your custom bindings work in any terminal, regardless of the shell you happen to be using. A second advantage is that you can easily map to any key on your keyboard. Shell mappings can be complicated if you want to map them to anything other than "Ctrl letter".

However, the terminal mappings have some restrictions that don't apply to the tcsh mappings. For example, shell mappings don't have a 16 character restriction, allowing for full pathnames. Also, it was relatively easy to ask the shell to press Enter to launch the desired command.

Terminal bindings affect only the current user's terminal. Any other users who are logged in on different terminals are not affected. However, if the mappings are added to *rc.conf* (which only the superuser can do), they will affect all terminals. Since bindings are terminal specific, even invoking su won't change the behavior, as the user is still stuck at the same terminal.

## More Mapping Caveats

There are some other caveats to consider when choosing which key to map. If you use the tcsh shell and enjoy viewing your history [Hack #1], you'll be disappointed if you remap your up and down arrows. The right and left arrows can also be problematic if you use them for navigation, say, in a text editor. Finally, if you're physically sitting at your FreeBSD system, F1 through F8 are already mapped to virtual terminals and F9 is mapped to your GUI terminal. By default, F10 to F12 are unmapped.

If you start experimenting with mappings and find you're stuck with one you don't like, you can quickly return all of your keys to their default mappings with this command:

```
% kbdcontrol -F
```

On the other hand, if you find some new mappings you absolutely can't live without, make them permanent. If you have superuser privileges on a FreeBSD system you physically sit at, you can carefully add the mappings to

*/etc/rc.conf*. Here, I've added two mappings. One maps lynx to the Menu key and the other maps startx to the left GUI key:

```
keychange="64 lynx"
keychange="62 startx"
```

Since the superuser will be setting these mappings, the mapped keys will affect all users on that system. If you want to save your own personal mappings, add your specific kbdcontrol commands to the end of your shell configuration file. For example, I've added these to the very end of my *~/.cshrc* file, just before the last line which says endif:

```
% kbdcontrol -f 64 "lynx"
% kbdcontrol -f 62 "startx"
```

## Making Mappings Work with X

This is all extremely handy, but what will happen if you try one of your newly mapped keys from an X Window session? You can press that key all you want, but nothing will happen. You won't even hear the sound of the system bell beeping at you in protest. This is because the X protocol handles all input and output during an X session.

You have a few options if you want to take advantage of keyboard bindings while in an X GUI. One is to read the documentation for your particular window manager. Most of the newer window managers provide a point and click interface to manage keyboard bindings. My favorite alternative is to try the xbindkeys_config application, which is available in the ports collection [Hack #84]:

```
# cd /usr/ports/x11/xbindkeys_config
# make install clean
```

This port also requires xbindkeys:

```
# cd /usr/ports/x11/xbindkeys
# make install clean
```

> Rather than building both ports, you could instead add this line to */usr/ports/x11/xbindkeys_config/Makefile*:
>
> ```
> BUILD_DEPENDS= xbindkeys:${PORTSDIR}/x11/xbindkeys
> ```
>
> This will ask the xbindkeys_config build to install both ports.

Once your builds are complete, open an xterm and type:

```
% xbindkeys --defaults ~/.xbindkeysrc
% xbindkeys_config
```

The GUI in Figure 1-1 will appear.

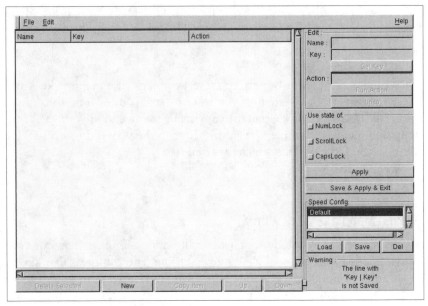

*Figure 1-1. The xbindkeys_config program*

Creating a key binding is a simple matter of pressing the New button and typing a useful name into the Name: section. Then, press Get Key and a little window will appear. Press the desired key combination, and voilà, the correct mapping required by X will autofill for you. Associate your desired Action:, then press the Save & Apply & Exit button.

Any keyboard mappings you create using this utility will be saved to a file called ~/.xbindkeysrc.

## See Also

- man `kbdcontrol`
- man `atkbd`
- The xbindkeys web site (*http://hocwp.free.fr/xbindkeys/xbindkeys.html*)

# Use the Mouse at a Terminal
Use your mouse to copy and paste at a terminal.

If you're used to a GUI environment, you might feel a bit out of your element while working at the terminal. Sure, you can learn to map hotkeys and to use navigational tricks, but darn it all, sometimes it's just nice to be able to copy and paste!

Don't fret; your mouse doesn't have to go to waste. In fact, depending upon how you have configured your system, the mouse daemon moused may already be enabled. The job of this daemon is to listen for mouse data in order to pass it to your console driver.

> Of course, if you're using screen **[Hack #12]**, you can also take advantage of its copy and paste mechanism.

## If X Is Already Installed

If you installed and configured X when you installed your system, moused is most likely started for you when you boot up. You can check with this:

```
% grep moused /etc/rc.conf
moused_port="/dev/psm0"
moused_type="auto"
moused_enable="YES"
```

Very good. moused needs to know three things:

- The mouse port (in this example, */dev/psm0*, the PS/2 port)
- The type of protocol (in this example, auto)
- Whether to start at boot time

If you receive similar output, you're ready to copy and paste.

To copy text, simply select it by clicking the *left* mouse button and dragging. Then, place the mouse where you'd like to paste the text and click the *middle* button. That's it.

> To select an entire word, double-click anywhere on that word. To select an entire line, triple-click anywhere on that line.

**Configuring a two-button mouse.** What if you don't have three mouse buttons? As the superuser, add the following line to */etc/rc.conf* (assuming it's not already there):

```
moused_flags="-m 2=3"
```

This flag tells moused to treat the second, or right, mouse button as if it were the third, or middle, mouse button. Now you can use the right mouse button to paste your copied text.

To apply that change, restart moused:

```
# /etc/rc.d/moused restart
Stopping moused.
Starting moused:.
```

Test your change by copying some text with the left mouse button and pasting with the right mouse button.

## If X Is Not Installed

You can achieve the same results on a system without X installed. You'll have to add the lines to */etc/rc.conf* manually, though.

The example I've given you is for a PS/2 mouse. If you're using another type of mouse, read the "Configuring Mouse Daemon" section of `man moused`. It gives explicit details on figuring out what type of mouse you have and what type of protocol it understands. It even includes a section on configuring a laptop system for multiple mice: one for when on the road and one for when the laptop is attached to the docking station.

For example, if you're using a USB mouse, the only difference is that the port is `/dev/usm0` instead of `/dev/psm0`.

A serial mouse physically plugged into `COM1` would be `/dev/cuaa0`. You may have to experiment with the type, as `auto` doesn't work with all serial mice. Again, the manpage is your best reference.

## See Also

- `man moused`
- Documentation on enabling mouse support in NetBSD at *http://www. netbsd.org/Documentation/wscons/*
- Documentation on enabling mouse support in OpenBSD at *http://www. openbsd.org/faq/faq7.html)*

HACK
# #6 Get Your Daily Dose of Trivia
Brighten your day with some terminal eye candy.

As the saying goes, all work and no play makes Jack a dull boy. But what's a poor Jack or Jill to do if your days include spending inordinate amounts of time in front of a computer screen? Well, you could head over to *http://www.thinkgeek.net/* to stock up on cube goodies and caffeine. Or, you could take advantage of some of the entertainments built into your operating system.

## A Fortune a Day

Let's start by configuring some terminal eye candy. Does your system quote you a cheery, witty, or downright strange bit of wisdom every time you log into your terminal? If so, you're receiving a fortune:

```
login: dru
Password:
```

```
Last login: Thu Nov 27 10:10:16 on ttyv7

"You can't have everything. Where would you put it?"
              -- Steven Wright
```

If you're not receiving a fortune, as the superuser type /stand/sysinstall. Choose Configure, then Distributions, and select games with your spacebar. Press Tab to select OK, then exit out of sysinstall when it is finished.

Then, look for the line that runs */usr/games/fortune* in your ~/.cshrc file:

```
% grep fortune ~/.cshrc
/usr/games/fortune
```

If for some reason it isn't there, add it:

```
% echo '/usr/games/fortune' >> ~/.cshrc
```

Don't forget to use both greater-than signs; you don't want to erase the contents of your .cshrc file! To test your change, use the source shell command, which re-executes the contents of the file. This can come in handy if you've updated an alias and want to take advantage of it immediately:

```
% source ~/.cshrc
Indifference will be the downfall of mankind, but who cares?
```

If you'd also like to receive a fortune when you log out of your terminal, add this line to the end of your .logout file. If you don't have one, and there isn't one by default, you can create it and add this line in one step:

```
% echo '/usr/games/fortune' > ~/.logout
```

Note that this time I used only one greater-than sign, as I was creating the file from scratch. If the file already exists, use two greater-than signs to append your new line to the end of the existing file.

Believe it or not, fortune comes with switches, some of which are more amusing than others. I'll leave it to you to peruse man fortune.

## Pursuing Trivia

I'm a trivia buff, so I love using the calendar command. Contrary to logic, typing calendar won't show me this month's calendar (that's the job of cal). However, I will get an instant dose of trivia, related to the current date:

```
% calendar
Nov 27        Alfred Nobel establishes Nobel Prize, 1895
Nov 27        Friction match invented, England, 1826
Nov 27        Hoosac Railroad Tunnel completed, 1873, in NW Massachusetts
Nov 28        Independence Day in Albania and Mauritania
Nov 28        Independence from Spain in Panama
Nov 28        Proclamation of the Republic in Chad
Nov 27        Jimi Hendrix (Johnny Allen Hendrix) is born in Seattle, 1942
```

Cool. I had forgotten it was the anniversary of the Hoosac tunnel, an event that put my hometown on the map.

It's an easy matter to automate the output provided by calendar. If you want to see your trivia when you log in or log out, simply add a line to your *.cshrc* or *.logout* file. Because the line you add is really just a path to the program, use the output of the which command to add that line for you:

```
% echo `which calendar` >> .cshrc
```

Again, don't forget to append with >>, or have noclobber set in your *.cshrc* file [Hack #2].

## Sundry Amusements

Of course, there are several other date and time related mini-hacks at your disposal. Here are two you might enjoy.

**The current time.** Ever wonder what time it is while you're working on the terminal? Sure, you could use date, but the output is so small and boring. Try this the next time you want to know what time it is:

```
% grdc
```

Whoa, you can see that one from across the room. That's not a bad idea if you want to send your cubicle buddy a hint.

I've been known to add */usr/games/grdc* to my *~/.logout*. When I log out, my terminal displays the time until I press Ctrl-c and log in again. That's sort of a built-in password protected screen saver for the terminal.

**The phase of the moon.** Have you ever read man  pom? It has one of the more useful descriptions I've seen:

> The pom utility displays the current phase of the moon. Useful for selecting software completion target dates and predicting managerial behavior.

Sounds like Dilbert had a hand in that one. If I add the line */usr/games/pom* to my *~/.cshrc*, I'll learn a bit about astronomy when I log in:

```
% pom
The Moon is Waxing Gibbous (53% of Full)
```

There's a one-liner to promote water cooler conversation.

## Adding Some Color to Your Terminal

Have you ever tried this command?

```
% vidcontrol show
```

| 0 |  | 8 grey |
|---|---|---|
| 1 | blue | 9 lightblue |
| 2 | green | 10 lightgreen |
| 3 | cyan | 11 lightcyan |
| 4 | red | 12 lightred |
| 5 | magenta | 13 lightmagenta |
| 6 | brown | 14 yellow |
| 7 | white | 15 lightwhite |

Gee, that reminds me of my old DOS days when I discovered *ansi.sys*. Yes, your terminal is capable of color and you're looking at your possible color schemes! (It likely looks much more exciting on your terminal, since it's not in color in this book.)

If you see some colors that appeal to you, add them to your terminal. For example, this command will set the foreground color to yellow and the background color as blue:

```
% vidcontrol yellow blue
```

Note that you can use only colors 1 through 7 as background colors; you'll receive a syntax error if you try to use colors 8–15 in your background. Try out the various combinations until you find one that appeals to your sense of taste. You can even add a border if you like:

```
% vidcontrol -b red
```

These settings affect only your own terminal. If you want, add the desired vidcontrol lines to your *~/.cshrc* file so your settings are available when you log into your terminal.

If you have problems finding your cursor, try:

```
% vidcontrol -c blink
```

or:

```
% vidcontrol -c destructive
```

Changing the cursor affects all virtual terminals on the system. If other users complain about your improvement, this will bring things back to normal:

```
% vidcontrol -c normal
```

## See Also

- man fortune
- man calendar
- man vidcontrol
- The games packages, in NetBSD and OpenBSD

## Lock the Screen

#7    Secure your unattended terminal from prying eyes.

If you work in a networked environment, the importance of locking your screen before leaving your workstation has probably been stressed to you. After all, your brilliant password becomes moot if anyone can walk up to your logged in station and start poking about the contents of your home directory.

If you use a GUI on your workstation, your Window Manager probably includes a locking feature. However, if you use a terminal, you may not be aware of the mechanisms available for locking your terminal.

As an administrator, you may want to automate these mechanisms as part of your security policy. Fortunately, FreeBSD's screen locking mechanism is customizable.

### Using lock

FreeBSD comes with lock (and it's available for NetBSD and OpenBSD). Its default invocation is simple:

```
% lock
Key: 1234
Again: 1234
lock /dev/ttyv6 on genisis. timeout in 15 minutes.
time now is Fri Jan 2 12:45:02 EST 2004
Key:
```

Without any switches, lock will request that the user input a key which will be used to unlock the terminal. This is a good thing, as it gives the user an opportunity to use something other than her login password. If the user tries to be smart and presses Enter (for an empty password), the lock program will abort.

Once a key is set, it is required to unlock the screen. If a user instead types Ctrl-c, she won't terminate the program. Instead, she'll receive this message:

```
Key: lock: type in the unlock key. timeout in 10:59 minutes
```

Did you notice that timeout value of 15 minutes? At that time, the screen will unlock itself, which sorta diminishes the usefulness of locking your screen. After all, if you run into your boss in the hall, your 5-minute coffee break might turn into a 25-minute impromptu brainstorming session.

To lock the terminal forever, or at least until someone types the correct key, use the -n switch. If the system is a personal workstation, -v is also handy;

this locks all of the virtual terminals on the system, meaning a passerby can't use Alt-F*n* to switch to another terminal.

As an administrator, you can assist users in using the desired switches by adding an alias to */usr/share/skel/dot.cshrc* [Hack #9]. This alias removes the timeout and locks all terminals:

```
alias lock    /usr/bin/lock -nv
```

## Using autologout

If you use the tcsh shell, you also have the ability either to lock your session or to be logged out of your session automatically after a set period of inactivity. As an administrator, you can set your policy by adding a line to */usr/share/skel/dot.cshrc*.

Do be aware, though, that a user can edit her own *~/.cshrc* file, which will negate your customized setting.

The autologout variable can accept two numbers. The first number represents the number of minutes of inactivity before logging out the user. The second number represents the number of minutes of inactivity before locking the user's screen. Once the screen is locked, the user must input the password to unlock it. If the screen is not unlocked in time, the user will be logged out once the shell has been idle for the logout period of minutes.

The manpage is pretty vague on how to set those two numbers. For example, if you try:

```
set autologout = 30 15
```

users will receive this error message when they try to log in:

```
set: Variable name must begin with a letter.
```

That's a deceptive error message, as this variable does accept numerals. The correct invocation is to enclose the two numbers between parentheses:

```
set autologout = (30 15)
```

This particular setting will log out a user after 15 minutes of inactivity. The user will know this happened as the terminal will resemble:

```
%
Password:
```

After 30 minutes of inactivity (or 15 minutes after the screen was locked), the user will be logged out and see this:

```
%
Password:auto-logout
```

Consider whether or not your users tend to run background jobs before globally implementing autologout. Also see "Use an Interactive Shell" [Hack #11], which allows users to reattach to their terminals.

## Enforcing Logout

What if you do want to enforce a logout policy that users can't change in their shell configuration files? Consider using idled, which can be installed from */usr/ports/sysutils/idled* or built from source. This utility was designed to log out users either after a configured period of inactivity or after they've been logged in for a certain amount of time.

Once you've installed idled, copy the template configuration file:

```
# cd /usr/local/etc/
# cp idled.cf.template idled.cf
```

Open */usr/local/etc/idled.cf* using your favorite editor. You'll find this file to be well commented and quite straightforward. You'll be able to configure the time before logout as well as when the user will receive a warning message. In addition, you can refuse logins, set session timeouts, and provide for exemptions.

## See Also

- `man lock`
- `man tcsh man idled`
- `man idled.cf`
- The idled web site (*http://www.darkwing.com/idled/*)

## Create a Trash Directory
HACK #8

Save "deleted" files until you're really ready to send them to the bit bucket.

One of the first things Unix users learn is that deleted files are really, really gone. This is especially true at the command line where there isn't any Windows-style recycling bin to rummage through should you have a change of heart regarding the fate of a removed file. It's off to the backups! (You do have backups, don't you?)

Fortunately, it is very simple to hack a small script that will send removed files to a custom trash directory. If you've never written a script before, this is an excellent exercise in how easy and useful scripting can be.

## Shell Scripting for the Impatient

Since a script is an executable file, you should place your scripts in a directory that is in your path. Remember, your path is just a list of directories where the shell will look for commands if you don't give them full pathnames. To see your path:

```
% echo $PATH
PATH=/sbin:/bin:/usr/sbin:/usr/bin:/usr/games:/usr/local/sbin:/usr/
local/bin:/usr/X11R6/bin:/home/dru/bin
```

In this output, the shell will look for executables in the *bin* subdirectory of dru's home directory. However, it won't look for executables placed directly in my home directory, or */home/dru*. Since *bin* isn't created by default, I should do that first:

```
% cd
% mkdir bin
```

As I create scripts, I'll store them in */home/dru/bin*, since I don't have permission to store them anywhere else. Fortunately, no one else has permission to store them in my *bin* directory, so it's a good match.

The scripts themselves contain at least three lines:

```
#!/bin/sh
# a comment explaining what the script does
the command to be executed
```

The first line indicates the type of script by specifying the program to use to execute the script. I've chosen to use a Bourne script because that shell is available on all Unix systems.

Your script should also have comments, which start with the # character. It's surprising how forgetful you can be six months down the road, especially if you create a lot of scripts. For this reason, you should also give the script a name that reminds you of what it does.

The third and subsequent lines contain the meat of the script: the actual command(s) to execute. This can range from a simple one-liner to a more complex set of commands, variables, and conditions. Fortunately, we can make a trash script in a simple one-liner.

## The Code

Let's start with this variant, which I found as the result of a Google search:

```
% more ~/bin/trash
#!/bin/sh
# script to send removed files to trash directory
mv $1 ~/.trash/
```

You should recognize the path to the Bourne shell, the comment, and the `mv` command. Let's take a look at that `$1`. This is known as a *positional parameter* and specifically refers to the first parameter of the trash command. Since the `mv` commands takes filenames as parameters, the command:

```
mv $1 ~/.trash/
```

is really saying, `mv` the first filename, whatever it happens to be, to a directory called *.trash* in the user's home directory (represented by the shell shortcut of ~). This move operation is our custom "recycle."

Before this script can do anything, it must be set as executable:

```
% chmod +x ~/bin/trash
```

And I must create that trash directory for it to use:

```
% mkdir ~/.trash
```

Note that I've chosen to create a hidden trash directory; any file or directory that begins with the `.` character is hidden from normal listings. This really only reduces clutter, though, as you can see these files by passing the -a switch to ls. If you also include the F switch, directory names will end with a /:

```
% ls -aF ~
.cshrc    .history    .trash/
bin/      images/     myfile
```

## Replacing rm with ~/bin/trash

Now comes the neat part of the hack. I want this script to kick in every time I use `rm`. Since it is the shell that executes commands, I simply need to make my shell use the `trash` command instead. I do that by adding this line to ~/.cshrc:

```
alias rm        trash
```

That line basically says: when I type `rm`, execute `trash` instead. It doesn't matter which directory I am in. As long as I stay in my shell, it will `mv` any files I try to `rm` to my hidden trash directory.

## Running the Code Safely

Whenever you create a script, always test it first. I'll start by telling my shell to reread its configuration file:

```
% source ~/.cshrc
```

Then, I'll make some test files to remove:

```
% cd
% mkdir test
% cd test
% touch test1
```

```
% rm test1

% ls ~/.trash
test1
```

Looks like the script is working. However, it has a flaw. Have you spotted it yet? If not, try this:

```
% touch a aa aaa aaaa
% rm a*

% ls ~/.trash
test1        a

% ls test
aa           aaa          aaaa
```

What happened here? I passed the shell more than one parameter. The a* was expanded to a, aa, aaa, and aaaa *before* trash could execute. Those four parameters were then passed on to the mv command in my script. However, trash passes only the first parameter to the mv command, ignoring the remaining parameters. Fortunately, they weren't removed, but the script still didn't achieve what I wanted.

You can actually have up to nine parameters, named $1 to $9. However, our goal is to catch all parameters, regardless of the amount. To do that, we use $@:

```
mv $@ ~/.trash/
```

Make that change to your script, then test it by removing multiple files. You should now have a script that works every time.

## Taking Out the Trash

You should occasionally go through your trash directory and really remove the files you no longer want. If you're really on your toes you may be thinking, "But how do I empty the trash directory?" If you do this:

```
% rm ~/.trash/*
```

your trash directory won't lose any files! This time you really do want to use rm, not trash. To tell your shell to use the real rm command, simply put a \ in front of it like so:

```
% \rm /trash/*
```

Voila, empty recycling bin.

## Hacking the Hack

One obvious extension is to keep versioned backups. Use the date command to find the time of deletion and append that to the name of the file in the trash command. You could get infinitely more complicated by storing a limited number of versions or deleting all versions older than a week or a month. Of course, you could also keep your important files under version control and leave the complexity to someone else!

## Customize User Configurations

**#9**    Now that you know how to set up a useful environment for yourself, it's time to share the wealth.

It's very easy for a system administrator to ensure that each newly created user starts out with the same configuration files. For example, every user can receive the same customized prompt, shell variables, or hotkeys.

Whenever you create a new user, several default (and hidden, or *dot*, files) are copied into the new user's home directory. In FreeBSD, the source of these files is */usr/share/skel/*. Any customizations you make to these files will be seen by all subsequently created users. Do note that you'll have to manually copy over any modified files to existing users.

It's useful to understand these files, as they apply to every user you create. Depending upon your needs, you'll probably end up removing some of the defaults, customizing others, and even adding a few of your own.

### Default Files

Let's take a quick tour of the default files:

```
% ls -l /usr/share/skel
total 24
drwxr-xr-x   2 root  wheel   512 Jul 28 16:09 ./
drwxr-xr-x  27 root  wheel   512 Jul 28 16:06 ../
-rw-r--r--   1 root  wheel   921 Jul 28 16:09 dot.cshrc
-rw-r--r--   1 root  wheel   248 Jul 28 16:09 dot.login
-rw-r--r--   1 root  wheel   158 Jul 28 16:09 dot.login_conf
-rw-------   1 root  wheel   371 Jul 28 16:09 dot.mail_aliases
-rw-r--r--   1 root  wheel   331 Jul 28 16:09 dot.mailrc
-rw-r--r--   1 root  wheel   797 Jul 28 16:09 dot.profile
-rw-------   1 root  wheel   276 Jul 28 16:09 dot.rhosts
-rw-r--r--   1 root  wheel   975 Jul 28 16:09 dot.shrc
```

Note that each starts with the word dot. However, when the files are copied into a user's home directory, the dots turn into literal dots (.). Also, the files in this directory are owned by root, but when a new user is created, the copied over files will change ownership as they are placed in that user's home directory.

**dot.cshrc.** Let's examine each default file, starting with *dot.cshrc*. ("Useful tcsh Shell Configuration File Options" **[Hack #2]** introduced several *.cshrc* hacks.) If you'd like new users to receive your customizations, simply replace *usr/share/skel/dot.cshrc* with your hacked version of *.cshrc*. Don't forget to rename the file as you copy it:

```
# cp /root/.cshrc /usr/share/skel/dot.cshrc
```

Here, I overwrote the default *dot.cshrc* by copying over the superuser's customized version of *.cshrc*. Although you could edit */usr/share/skel/dot.cshrc* directly, you may find it more convenient to have a customized copy stored elsewhere.

All isn't lost if you already have existing users whom you'd like to receive this file. First, find out what users already exist and have home directories. This is a quick way to do so:

```
# ls /usr/home
dru     test
```

Since this system has only two existing users, it's an easy matter to copy over my customized *.cshrc*. I'm also a lazy typist, so I use ~ instead of typing out /usr/home. Also note that I have to remember to manually change ownership:

```
# cp /root/.cshrc ~dru/
# chown dru ~dru/.cshrc
# cp /root/.cshrc ~test/
# chown test ~test/.cshrc
```

If your system already contains many users, you'll probably prefer to write a script. Here is an example:

```
#!/usr/bin/perl -w

# copydotfiles.pl
#    - copy default files to user directories
#    - change ownership of those files
# You may wish to change these constants for your system:

use constant HOMEDIR => '/usr/home';
use constant SKELDIR => '/usr/share/skel';
use constant PREFIX  => 'dot';

use strict;

use File::Copy;
use File::Spec::Functions;

die "Usage: $0 <files> <to> <copy>\n" unless @ARGV;

for my $user ( get_users() )
{
    for my $dotfile (@ARGV)
    {
```

```
            my $source = catfile( SKELDIR(),        PREFIX() . $dotfile );
            my $dest   = catfile( $user->{homedir},          $dotfile );

            if (-e $dest)
            {
                warn "Skipping existing dotfile $dest...\n";
                next;
            }

            copy( $source,      $dest )
                or die "Cannot copy $source to $dest: $!\n";
            chown( $user->{uid}, $dest );
        }
    }

    sub get_users
    {
        local *DIRHANDLE;
        opendir( DIRHANDLE, HOMEDIR() )
            or die "Cannot open home directory: $!\n";

        my @users;

        while (my $directory = readdir( DIRHANDLE ))
        {
            next if $directory =~ /^\./;

            my $path = File::Spec->catdir( HOMEDIR(), $directory );
            my $uid  = getpwnam( $directory );

            next unless -d $path;
            next unless $uid;

            push @users, { homedir => $path, uid => $uid };
        }

        return @users;
    }
```

This script first examines all of the users with home directories, returning a
list of those directories and the user IDs. It loops through that list, copying
each dot file you provided on the command line to that user's home directory and changing the ownership to the user.

If you run it as:

```
    # copydotfiles.pl .cshrc
```

all users will receive a new *.cshrc* file, unless one already exists.

**dot.login.** The next file, *dot.login*, is used only by the csh and tcsh shells. If
your users don't plan on using these shells, you can safely remove this file
from */usr/share/skel*. If your users do use those shells, consider whether there

are any commands you would like to run when users log in. Note that this file is read *after .cshrc*.

By default, the only uncommented line in this file is:

```
% grep -v '#' /usr/share/skel/dot.login

[ -x /usr/games/fortune ] && /usr/games/fortune freebsd-tips
```

Here, I used the reverse filter switch -v to the grep search utility to look for all the lines that do *not* begin with the # comment symbol.

The resulting line tells the shell to run the fortune program. If you chose to install the games distribution when you installed FreeBSD, your fortune appears just before the MOTD whenever you login. Have you ever noticed that you don't receive a fortune when you use su? That's because *.login* is only read when you log in, and the default invocation of su does not actually log you in.

Instead, it opens what is known as a *nonlogin shell*. You also get one of those every time you open an xterm. Basically, the only time you get a real login shell is when you type in your username and password at a login prompt.

Herein lies the difference between *.cshrc* and *.login*. Place what you would like to happen only when you log in into *.login*, and place what you would like to happen whenever you use the csh shell, even if it isn't a login shell, into *.cshrc*. If you don't see the need for a difference, you don't need */usr/share/skel/dot.login*.

**dot.login_conf.** Reading the default contents of *dot.login_conf* will give you an idea of its purpose and where to go for additional information:

```
% more /usr/share/skel/dot.login_conf
# $FreeBSD: src/share/skel/dot.login_conf,v 1.3 2001/06/10 17:08:53 ache Exp $
#
# see login.conf(5)
#
#me:\
#        :charset=iso-8859-1:\
#        :lang=de_DE.ISO8859-1:
```

Note that this file is commented by default, but shows the syntax a user can use to create a customized *.login.conf*. Usually such settings are set in the globally administrated */etc/login.conf* file, and individual users can override only *some* of those settings. If your users don't have a need or the know-how to configure those settings, you can safely remove this file from */usr/share/skel*.

**dot.mail_aliases and dot.mailrc.** The next two files work hand in hand and customize the behavior of man mail. Since it is quite rare to find users who still rely on the original mail program, you can safely remove those files.

**dot.profile.**  The *dot.profile* file is read by the Bourne, bash, and Korn shells. It is the *only* file read when a user logs into a Bourne shell, the first file read when a user logs into the Korn shell, and is optional for bash users.

If your users don't use the Bourne or Korn shells, there's not much sense populating their home directories with this file. Depending upon your slant, you may wish to keep this file in order to place path statements and environment variables for use with Bourne shell scripts. However, most users tend to place those directly into the script itself to allow for portability.

If your users wish to use the bash shell, which isn't installed by default, keep in mind that *.profile* allows a user to override the settings found in the global */etc/profile* file. You may find it easier to make your edits to the global file and then remove */usr/share/skel/dot.profile*. More sophisticated users can always create their own *~/.profile*. However, most bash users tend to make their modifications to *~/.bash_profile*.

**dot.rhosts.**  Did you happen to notice in the earlier long listing that this file has different permissions from most of the other files? If you read man rhosts, you'll see that this file is ignored if it is writable by any user other than the owner of the file.

So, when is this file used? It's used when a user types one of the r* commands: rsh, rcp, or rlogin. I won't show you how to set up this file or use those commands, as they were designed for use back in the days when networks were considered trusted. They've pretty well been replaced by ssh and scp, which provide a much safer way to log into remote systems and to transfer files. For this reason, I always remove */usr/share/skel/dot.rhosts* from my systems.

**dot.shrc.**  The last default file is *dot.shrc*. As you may have guessed, it is the rc file for sh, the Bourne shell. Again, if your users don't log into that shell, they won't miss this file.

## Missing (but Useful) Dot Files

Now that we've had the opportunity to look at the default files, it's time to consider any useful missing files.

**dot.logout.**  We've already seen that *~/.login* is read when a user logs into the csh or tcsh shells. Not surprisingly, *~/.logout* is read when a user logs out of their login shell. This is an excellent place to put commands you would like to execute as a user logs out. It could be something as simple as:

```
# more dot.logout
# this line clears your screen when you logout
```

```
clear
# add your own commands or scripts, one line at a time,
# which you would like to execute
# whenever you logout and leave your terminal
```

This *dot.logout* will clear the user's terminal, making it much neater for the next person who logs in. Notice that I commented this file, so the user is aware of its use. When creating your own dot files, use lots of comments. If you intend for your users to customize their own dot files, use comments that explain the syntax they can use when they do their modifications.

*dot.logout* can run any command or script that suits a user's needs. Here are some ideas to get your imagination rolling:

- A script that backs up the user's home directory
- A script that shows how much time the user spent online
- A script that displays other statistics, such as available disk space

**dot.xinitrc.** I also find it very useful to create a custom *dot.xinitrc*. By default, users receive the extremely lightweight twm window manager. Since I usually install KDE, this line ensures that each user will receive that window manager instead:

```
# more dot.xinitrc
exec startkde
```

You can also specify which programs you would like to launch when a user types startx and their *~/.xinitrc* file kicks in. For example, this is a popular line to add:

```
# more dot.xinitrc
exec xterm &
exec startkde
```

This starts an xterm in the background. Notice the & at the end of its line—this is to ensure that once xterm loads, it doesn't interfere with any other programs that are still loading. When you're creating your own *dot.xinitrc*, you can start any program you like. However, start your window manager *last*. Start your other programs, one line at a time, putting an & at the end of each line. The only line that does not have an & will be the very last line, the one that loads your window manager.

Since I prefer to start my browser instead of an xterm, here is my customized *dot.xinitrc*:

```
#to start another program when you "startx", type:
#exec path_to_program &
#before these lines
exec /usr/X11R6/bin/mozilla &
exec startkde
```

There are dozens of possibilities for customized dot files. Take stock of your own systems, and ask yourself: "What programs do my users use?" For example, if your users use bash, vim, screen, procmail, or fetchmail, why not start them off with a customized configuration file that contains comments on how to add their own customizations and URLs of where to go for further ideas? A little homework and creativity on your part can help your users get the most out of the utilities they use on a daily basis.

## Editing /usr/src/share/skel/Makefile

Let's end this hack by examining where the default dot files in *usr/share/skel* came from in the first place. You'll find the answer here:

```
% ls /usr/src/share/skel
./                dot.login            dot.profile
../               dot.login_conf       dot.rhosts
Makefile          dot.mail_aliases     dot.shrc
dot.cshrc         dot.mailrc
```

That *Makefile* controls the installation of those files:

```
# more /usr/src/share/skel/Makefile

#       @(#)Makefile       8.1 (Berkeley) 6/8/93
# $FreeBSD: src/share/skel/Makefile,v 1.8 2002/07/29 09:40:13 ru Exp $

FILES1= dot.cshrc dot.login dot.login_conf dot.mailrc dot.profile dot.shrc
FILES2=      dot.mail_aliases dot.rhosts
MODE1=       0644
MODE2=       0600

NOOBJ=       noobj

all clean cleandir depend lint tags:

install:
        ${INSTALL} -o ${BINOWN} -g ${BINGRP} -m ${MODE1} ${FILES1} \
            ${DESTDIR}${BINDIR}/skel
        ${INSTALL} -o ${BINOWN} -g ${BINGRP} -m ${MODE2} ${FILES2} \
            ${DESTDIR}${BINDIR}/skel

.include <bsd.prog.mk>
```

Even if you've never read a *Makefile* before, you'll find it's not too hard to figure out what's going on if you already know which results to expect. In this *Makefile*, FILES=1 is simply a list of files to install. Take a look at MODE1; it tells the chmod command what permissions to set on those files.

Similarly, FILES=2 is another list of files. Those two files had different permissions, which were defined by MODE2.

Move down to the install section. Don't worry so much about the syntax; rather, notice the pattern. The first set of files are installed and their mode is applied. Then the second set of files are installed with their mode.

It's an easy matter to customize this file to reflect the dot files you'd like to see installed. In this example, I only want to install my custom versions of *dot.cshrc*, *dot.login*, and *dot.xinitrc*. Since they all require the first mode, I'll remove any references to the second set of files:

```
# cd /usr/src/share/skel
# cp Makefile Makefile.orig
# vi Makefile

#         @(#)Makefile        8.1 (Berkeley) 6/8/93
# my customized dot files to be installed into /usr/share/skel

FILES1= dot.cshrc dot.login dot.xinitrc
MODE1=       0644

NOOBJ=       noobj

all clean cleandir depend lint tags:

install:
        ${INSTALL} -o ${BINOWN} -g ${BINGRP} -m ${MODE1} ${FILES1} \
            ${DESTDIR}${BINDIR}/skel

.include <bsd.prog.mk>
```

Now let's try a test run. I'll replace the default dot files found in */usr/src/share/skel* with my customized versions. I'll then remove the contents of */usr/share/skel* and see what happens when I run my customized *Makefile*:

```
# cd /usr/src/share/skel
# rm dot.*
# cp ~/mystuff/dot.* .

# rm /usr/share/skel/*
# ls /usr/share/skel

# make install
install -o root -g wheel -m 0644 dot.cshrc dot.login dot.xinitrc
    /usr/share/skel
# ls /usr/share/skel
dot.cshrc    dot.login    dot.xinitrc
```

I find it very handy to keep a copy of my customized *Makefile* and dot files in a separate directory, in this case *~/mystuff*. This ensures they are backed up. It's easy for me to grab those files whenever I want to customize a particular system.

It's especially important to use a separate location if you use cvsup to keep your system up-to-date. Otherwise, your next update will notice your modified src and happily replace those missing original source files. But don't worry; it won't touch your new /usr/share/skel.

Of course, sometimes this is a very useful trick in itself. If you ever mess up a file located somewhere within /usr/src, a quick cvsup will put everything back the way it was. See "Automate Updates" [Hack #80] for details on automating cvsup.

### The Other BSDs

The preceding discussion is based on FreeBSD, but it also applies to NetBSD and OpenBSD systems, save for a few tiny differences outlined here.

**NetBSD.** NetBSD administrators will find the skeleton home directory in /etc/skel. Specify a different location by passing the -k option to useradd.

**OpenBSD.** OpenBSD systems store the skeleton home directory in /etc/skel. Specify a different skeleton directory location by passing the -dotdir option to adduser.

### See Also

- man adduser
- The manpages returned by apropos user

## HACK #10 Maintain Your Environment on Multiple Systems

> The sign of a true Unix guru is the ability to perform a task quickly when confronted with an unfamiliar shell, keyboard, terminal, window manager, or operating system.

A large part of using Unix systems effectively involves configuring a comfortable environment using familiar tools available from the Unix shell prompt. It's much easier to perform a task quickly when all of the shortcuts your fingers have learned work on the first try.

Even something as simple as setting up your prompt the way you like it can steal significant time from your productivity if you need to do it on several hosts. If you're going to spend significant time in a Unix shell, it's worth getting organized. A bit of onetime effort will reward you later, every time you sit down at the keyboard.

## Enter unison

unison is a tool for maintaining synchronized copies of directories. I've used it to maintain a central repository of all of my dot files, shell scripts, signatures file, SpamAssassin configuration—basically any file I'd like to have available, regardless of which host I happen to be logged into.

You can install unison from the NetBSD pkgsrc collection:

```
# cd /usr/pkgsrc/net/unison
# make install clean
```

FreeBSD and OpenBSD ports also include *net/unison*.

Even better, this utility is available for most Unix and Windows platforms. See the main unison web site for details.

## Using unison

Whenever I configure a new Unix host or get a shell on another system, I install unison. Then, I create a directory to receive the files I've stored in the */usr/work/sync* directory at *host.example.com*. I call the local directory *~/sync*.

To synchronize those two directories:

```
% unison ~/sync ssh://username@host.example.com://usr/work/sync
p = /home/david/.unison; bn = .unison
Contacting server...
p = /home/david/sync; bn = sync
username@host.example.com's password:
```

After ssh prompts for a password or pass phrase, the unison exchange begins. On a first-time synchronization, unison will ask only one question: whether you wish to copy the remote directory to the local host.

```
Looking for changes
Warning: No archive files were found for these roots. This can happen
either because this is the first time you have synchronized these roots,
or because you have upgraded Unison to a new version with a different
archive format.
```

Update detection may take a while on this run if the replicas are large.

unison will assume that the last synchronized state of both replicas was completely empty. This means that any files that are different will be reported as conflicts, and any files that exist only on one replica will be judged as new and propagated to the other replica. If the two replicas are identical, then unison will report no changes:

```
Press return to continue.
Waiting for changes from server
Reconciling changes
```

```
local        host.example.com
      <---- dir        /  [f]
```

```
Proceed with propagating updates? [ ] y
Propagating updates
```

```
UNISON started propagating changes at 11:44:39 on 02 Feb 2004
[BGN] Copying
from //host.example.com//usr/work/sync
to /home/david/sync
bin
dotfiles
spamassassin
bin/randomsig2.pl
bin/sy
bin/testaspam
dotfiles/.c
dotfiles/.cshrc
dotfiles/.login
dotfiles/.muttrc
dotfiles/.profile
dotfiles/.tcshrc
dotfiles/.xinitrc
spamassassin/user_prefs
[...]
[END] Copying
UNISON finished propagating changes at 11:44:41 on 02 Feb 2004
Saving synchronizer state
Synchronization complete
```

I now have a populated ~/*sync* directory on the new system, organized into
subdirectories. Each subdirectory contains the files I find useful to carry
around with my various accounts on multiple Unix machines.

Notice also that although my preferred shell is tcsh, I maintain a *.cshrc* and
*.profile* for use on systems where tcsh is not available.

## Automating the Process

I've automated the process with a simple shell script called sy in my *bin*
directory. sy runs the unison command to synchronize the ~/*sync* directory.

```
#!/bin/sh
unison ~/sync ssh://username@host.example.com://usr/work/sync
```

## Creating Portable Files

Making good use of the *sync* directory requires some discipline. It's one
thing to be able to copy files easily; it's another thing to be able to use them
without modification on several hosts.

To take advantage of this hack, when you copy the dot files to your home directory and notice that something doesn't work exactly the way you like it to, make sure you *don't simply change it for the local host.*

Instead, update the dot files so that they use conditional if statements, shell backticks (e.g., `hostname`), or environment variables, to make them behave correctly on the new hosts without breaking them on the systems where you already use them. Then, copy the dot file back into your ~/*sync* directory and run the sy script. unison will prompt for a password or passphrase for the ssh connection, then ask you to verify that you want to update your files back to the main server.

The first few times you do this, you may introduce breakage when the new dot file is used on another host. With a bit of practice you'll learn how to avoid that. The most important trick is to test. Open a shell to the host and update the dot file, and then open a second shell to the host without closing the first one. If you broke anything that affects your ability to log in, you can fix it with the first shell and test again.

There's no need to resynchronize every other host you use for each file you change. I generally wait until I'm logged onto a given host and need a newer script, or need to make some additional changes to the local copy of the dot file. Then I synchronize, make the changes in the sync directory, test them locally, and resync them back to the main host.

Using this approach means that I don't have to reinvent the wheel every time I want to perform a procedure I've done before. Any process useful enough to be done a couple of times becomes a script in my toolkit, and is conveniently available anywhere I have a shell. With unison, I don't have to keep track of which files were modified on which end of the connection since my last update.

Keep in mind that using a tool like unison can provide a mechanism for someone to attempt to feed updates into your central file repository. When you log into a host and run the update, be conscious of whether unison asks for approval to send back changes. If you don't remember making those changes, you might be helping an attacker feed a Trojan horse into your *.login,* which could end up giving the attacker access to every system you use that script on. unison will ask for confirmation for every file change. Presumably, your central host is secure, but you need to be particularly conscious when permitting file uploads.

## See Also

- The unison home page (*http://www.cis.upenn.edu/~bcpierce/unison/*)

# Use an Interactive Shell
Save and share an entire login session.

How many times have you either struggled with or tried to troubleshoot another user through a thorny problem? Didn't you wish you had another set of eyes behind you so you could simply type your command set, point at the troublesome output, and say, "That's the problem." Well, if you can't bring another user to your output, you can still share that real-time output using an interactive shell.

## Recording All Shell Input and Output

There are actually several ways to share what is happening on your screen. Let's start by recording all of your input and output to a file. Then we'll see how we can also allow another user to view that output from another terminal.

Your BSD system comes with the script command which, not surprisingly, allows you to script your session. This command is extremely simple to use. Simply type script:

```
% script
Script started, output file is typescript
```

By default, script will create an output file named *typescript* in your current directory. If you prefer, you can specify a more descriptive name for your script file:

```
% script configure.firewall.nov.11.2003
Script started, output file is configure.firewall.nov.11.2003
```

Regardless of how you invoke the command, a new shell will be created. This means that you will see the MOTD and possibly a fortune, and your *.cshrc* will be reread.

You can now carry on as usual and all input and output will be written to your script file. When you are finished, simply press Ctrl-d. You will see this message:

```
Script done, output file is configure.firewall.nov.11.2003
```

If you've ended a script and decide later to append some more work to a previous session, remember the -a (append) switch:

```
% script -a configure.firewall.nov.11.2003
```

This will append your current scripting session to the named file.

I find script extremely useful, especially when I'm learning how to configure something for the first time. I can easily create a written record of which commands I used, which commands were successful, and which commands caused which error messages. It also comes in handy when I need to send an error message to a mailing list or a program's maintainer. I can simply copy or attach my script file into an email.

## Cleaning Up script Files

The script utility is a very quick and dirty way to record a session, and it does have its limitations. One of its biggest is that it records everything, including escape characters. For example, here is the first line from one of my script files:

```
[1mdru@~ [m: cd /s  [K/ysr/  [K  [K  [K  [K  [Kusr/ports/security/sn o rt
```

It's a bit hard to tell, but this is what script was recording:

```
cd /usr/ports/security/snort
```

This isn't really script's fault; it's ugly for several reasons. One, my customized prompt contains control characters. Those display as [1m and [m around my username. Second, I had problems typing that day. Instead of /usr, I typed /s and had to backspace a character. Then I typed /ysr and had to backspace three characters. Finally, I used tab completion. You can see that I tried to tab at sn but received a beep; I then tried to tab at sno and had my input completed to snort.

Granted, if I had first used the file utility on my script file, I would have received a warning about this behavior:

```
% file configure.firewall.nov.11.2003
configure.firewall.nov.11.2003: ASCII English text, with CRLF, CR, LF line
terminators, with escape sequences
```

All is not lost, though. This command will get rid of most of the garbage characters:

```
% more configure.firewall.nov.11.2003 | \
   col -b > configure.firewall.nov.11.2003.clean
```

col is an interesting little utility. It silently filters out what it doesn't understand. Here's an example where this actually works to our advantage. col doesn't understand control characters and escape sequences, which is exactly what we wish to get rid of. Including -b also asks col to remove backspaces.

The result is much more readable:

```
1mdlavigne6@~m: cd /usr/ports/security/snort
```

```
% file configure.firewall.nov.11.2003.clean
configure.firewall.nov.11.2003.clean: ASCII English text
```

I've found that using an editor during a script session also produces very messy output into my script file. The preceding col -b command will clean up most of the mess, but I still won't have a very good idea of exactly what I typed while I was in that editor. For this reason, I use the echo command to send little comments to myself:

```
% echo # once you open up /etc/rc.conf
% echo # change this line: linux_enable="NO"
% echo # to this: linux_enable="YES"
% echo # and add this line: sshd_enable="YES"
```

If you really want to get fancy, map one key to "start echo" and another to "end echo" as in "Use Terminal and X Bindings" [Hack #4].

## Recording an Interactive Shell Session

Let's look at an alternate way of recording a session. This time I'll use the -i (or interactive) switch of my shell:

```
% csh -i | & tee test_session.nov.12.2003
```

tcsh is linked to csh in FreeBSD. It doesn't matter which one I type; I'll still end up with the tcsh shell.

In that command, I used -i to start an interactive tcsh shell. I then piped (|) both stdout and stderr (&) to the tee command. If you've ever looked at physical pipe plumbing, you'll recognize the job of a "tee" in a pipe: whatever is flowing will start going in both directions when it hits the "tee." In my case, all stdout and stderr generated by my shell will flow to both my monitor and to the *test_session.nov.12.2003* file. When I'm finished recording my session, I can type Ctrl-c, Ctrl-d, or exit to quit.

Like the previous script command, an interactive csh shell will present me with a new shell. However, this method does not record escape characters, meaning I won't need to use the col -b command to clean up the resulting file.

But if I try to use vi during my session, the shell will refuse to open the editor and will instead present me with this interesting error message:

```
ex/vi: Vi's standard input and output must be a terminal.
```

If I try to use ee, it will open, but none of the commands will work. pico works nicely but still throws garbage into the session file. So, if I need to use an editor during my session, I'll still echo some comments to myself so I can remember what I did while I was in there.

Appending works almost exactly like it does for script, again with the -a (append) switch:

```
% csh -i | & tee -a test_session.nov.12.2003
```

## Letting Other People Watch Your Live Shell Sessions

Regardless of which method you choose to record a session, another user can watch your session as it occurs. In order for this to work, that user must:

- Be logged into the same system
- Know the name and location of your script file

For example, I've created a test account on my system and configured sshd. I'll now see if I can ssh into my system as the user test and watch the results of dru's *test_session.nov.12.2003*.

```
% ssh -l test 192.168.248.4
Password:
%
```

Once I successfully log in, my customized prompt indicates I'm the test user. I can now use the tail command to watch what is happening in dru's session:

```
% tail -f ~dru/test_session.nov.12.2003
```

My prompt will appear to change to indicate I am the user dru. However, I'm not. I'm simply viewing dru's session. In fact, I can see everything that the user dru is seeing on her terminal. This includes all of her input, output, and any error messages she is receiving.

While tail is running, I won't be able to use my prompt. If I try typing anything, nothing will happen. I also can't interact with the user or change what is happening on her terminal. However, I do have a bird's eye view of what that user is experiencing on her terminal. When I'm ready to return to my own prompt, which will also end my view of the session, I simply need to press Ctrl-c.

## See Also

- man script
- man file
- man col
- man tee
- man tail

## Use Multiple Screens on One Terminal

**HACK #12** Who says you can't run multiple sessions from one terminal?

Running a graphical environment is great. You can have numerous applications and utilities running, and you can interact with all of them at the same time. Many people who have grown up with a GUI environment look down upon those poor souls who continue to work in a terminal console environment. "After all," they say, "you can only do one thing at a time and don't get the same information and control that you have in a desktop environment."

It's true; they do say those things. (I am curious to know who *they* are, however.)

It's also true that the utility of a graphical environment diminishes when you need to administer machines remotely. Do you really want to squander network bandwidth just to maintain a GUI session?

Here are some more questions to ask yourself regarding remote administration:

- Are you worried about making your services vulnerable just so you can administer them across the Internet?
- Do you want a secure connection?
- Do you want to run multiple terminal sessions from a single login?
- Do you want to be able to password protect your session to prevent unauthorized access?
- Do you want multiple windows with labels and of different sizes?
- Do you want to copy and paste between the windows?
- Are you prepared to lose a connection to your remote machine in the middle of a critical operation?
- Would you like to be able keep the session active even after you've lost it or you've logged off the remote server?
- Do you want to take over a session that you launched from another machine?
- Would you like to keep a hardcopy log of your sessions?

You are indeed a poor soul if you've reconciled yourself to the standard ssh login without any hope of resolving these questions. But all is not lost—the solution is screen.

### What Is screen?

screen is a terminal screen window manager. That means you can use a console and run multiple terminals at the same time. The fancy term for this ability is *multiplexing*.

Getting and installing screen is straightforward using the ports facility:

```
# cd /usr/ports/misc/screen
# make install clean
```

I'm working with Version 4.00.01 (FAU) 18-Sep-03.

## Getting Started

screen has many options, settings, and commands. Although we'll attempt to address the major features, the definitive reference is, of course, the manpage.

There are three methods of command-line invocation:

screen [ -options ] [ cmd [ args ] ]
> For invoking screen for the first time and running specific options and commands

screen -r [[pid.]tty[.host]]
> For attaching to and detaching from running sessions

screen -r sessionowner/[[pid.]tty[.host]]
> For attaching to and detaching from existing sessions being run by other users

## Multitasking with screen

The best way to understand screen's power is to give you an example of how you can take advantage of it.

Suppose you are sitting at workstation alpha. You want to access your machine, bravo, to download and compile the latest PostgreSQL source code. Log into host bravo as user charlie using SSH:

```
% ssh -l charlie bravo
```

Invoke screen. If you give it a session name, with the -s flag, you can address this session by name. This will pay off shortly.

```
% screen -s A
```

Go ahead and download the source code now:

```
% ftp ftp://ftp3.ca.postgresql.org/pub/source/v7.4/postgresql-7.4.tar.gz
```

**Using windows with screen.** So far, this has no advantage over a normal SSH login. Yet suppose you need to send some email while you're downloading. Instead of putting the download into the background, create another screen window with the key sequence C-a c. This symbolizes that the Ctrl key is pressed with the lowercase letter a and then, after releasing them, you press a second key, in this case c.

At this point the console will go blank. You'll be presented with a second window. Use your favorite email client to compose your message.

**Switching between windows.** You'll probably want to switch between the download and mailer windows. Cycle forward in the window list with C-a n. Cycle backward with C-a p, although you'll likely see no difference with two windows.

**Splitting windows.** Being the efficient person that you are, you'd like to compile the source code as soon as it has downloaded. Even though you haven't completed your email, go back to the original window and extract the tarball:

```
% tar -xzpvf postgresql-7.4.tar.gz
```

Wise administrators read the *INSTALL* file to make sure all the correct options are invoked. It'd be very handy to be able to read the instructions as you compose the configure command in the same console. screen comes to the rescue here, too: split the window horizontally, running configure in the top half and reading the documentation in the bottom half.

Type C-a S to split the screen, where the S is uppercase. You should see a wide horizontal bar in the middle of the screen. The top window will show whatever existed when you split the window. You'll also see the window's ID on the left side of the middle bar, along with the name of the shell.

The bottom window doesn't yet have a shell running. Set the focus to the other window with C-a Tab. Create a new window with C-a c, as usual. Notice that the window has the ID of 2 (shown in the bottom lefthand corner); that's because the email window that you created after starting the download has the ID of *1*.

**Better window switching.** To list all windows associated with this session, use the command C-a ".

If cycling through windows is onerous, you can also switch between windows by ID. For example, C-a ' 1 will go to window *1*.

Be prepared for a little confusion because the screen remains split and now shows the window of your choice in the currently focused window. You can quite easily show the same window in both the top and bottom halves.

Enter window 0 with C-a ' 0, and extract the tarball into its own directory. Enter window 2 with C-a ' 2, and navigate to the uppermost directory of the source code to read the *INSTALL* file.

**Naming windows.** ID numbers identify windows pretty well, but I prefer to use names of my own choosing. Change a window's name with the command C-a A. For example, C-a A email, C-a A source, and C-a A doc seem like a big improvement for the currently active windows.

Now, listing the active windows with C-a " will show the following:

```
NUM NAME
0   source
1   email
2   doc
```

At this point, you have one screen session with three windows. Your terminal is split such that it shows two windows at the same time.

## Attaching and Deattaching

Suppose you are called away from the workstation in the middle of a sensitive operation (that is, you haven't yet sent your email). Type C-a x to protect your session. Depending on your configuration, you will either input a password for the screen or use the default account password.

Now suppose you don't return to your workstation. What do you do? You can ssh into bravo from a new location and attach to your existing screen session with screen -dr A. Remember, A was the name of the screen session.

After finishing and sending your email, kill off that screen. Type the command C-a k in the email window.

With that business finished, scroll back through the *INSTALL* text file to find interesting configuration switches. You *could* retype them, but screen has a perfectly capable copy mode. Type C-a ESC.

Use the cursor keys to navigate to the portions of the document you want to copy. Hit the space bar to mark the beginning of the text to copy. Scroll around to the end of the text with the cursor keys. The current selection will display in reverse video. When you're satisfied, hit the space bar to copy the current selection into the buffer.

Switch to the source window and use C-a ] to paste the copied text.

You don't need the doc window anymore, so switch into it and either exit the shell or use the key sequence C-a k to kill it. You could also merge the split screens together with the key sequence C-a X.

Once you've started compiling, you can close the terminal but leave the session active by detaching it; just type C-a d. One of the nice features about detaching the screen is that it is done automatically if you lose connection with the server, so you won't lose your session. You can reattach to the session later from the same location or from another workstation altogether.

## Additional Features

These are only the basics of what screen can do. Here's a quick listing of other features you might enjoy:

- Since the key bindings are not cast in stone, you change them as you see fit in the *.screenrc* resource file.
- It's possible to authorize other users access to your screen session via an access control list.
- More than one user can access the same screen session.
- You can create any number of windows in a given screen session.
- It's possible to hardcopy all activity in a screen session to a buffer and even a file.
- An extensive system of copy and paste features exist within the screen session.

You can control all of these features with the *.screenrc* resource file. See man screen for details.

## See Also

- man screen
- The GNU Screen home page (*http://www.gnu.org/software/screen*)

# CHAPTER TWO

# Dealing with Files and Filesystems
## Hacks 13-23

Now that you're a bit more comfortable with the Unix environment, it's time to tackle some commands. It's funny how some of the most useful commands on a Unix system have gained themselves a reputation for being user-unfriendly. Do find, grep, sed, tr, or mount make you shudder? If not, remember that you still have novice users who are intimidated by—and therefore aren't gaining the full potential of—these commands.

This chapter also addresses some useful filesystem manipulations. Have you ever inadvertently blown away a portion of your directory structure? Would you like to manipulate /tmp or your swap partition? Do your Unix systems need to play nicely with Microsoft systems? Might you consider ghosting your BSD system? If so, this chapter is for you.

### H A C K  #13  Find Things

Finding files in Unix can be an exercise in frustration for a novice user. Here's how to soften the learning curve.

Remember the first time you installed a Unix system? Once you successfully booted to a command prompt, I bet your first thought was, "Now what?" or possibly, "Okay, where is everything?" I'm also pretty sure your first foray into man find wasn't all that enlightening.

How can you as an administrator make it easier for your users to find things? First, introduce them to the built-in commands. Then, add a few tricks of your own to soften the learning curve.

### Finding Program Paths

Every user should become aware of the three w's: which, whereis, and whatis. (Personally, I'd like to see some why and when commands, but that's another story.)

Use which to find the path to a program. Suppose you've just installed xmms and wonder where it went:

```
% which xmms
/usr/X11R6/bin/xmms
```

Better yet, if you were finding out the pathname because you wanted to use it in a file, save yourself a step:

```
% echo `which xmms` >> somefile
```

Remember to use the backticks (`), often found on the far left of the keyboard on the same key as the tilde (~). If you instead use the single quote (') character, usually located on the right side of the keyboard on the same key as the double quote ("), your file will contain the echoed string which  xmms instead of the desired path.

The user's current shell will affect how which's switches work. Here is an example from the C shell:

```
% which -a xmms
-a: Command not found.
/usr/X11R6/bin/xmms

% which which
which: shell built-in command.
```

This is a matter of which which the user is using. Here, the user used the which which is built into the C shell and doesn't support the options used by the which utility. Where then is that which? Try the whereis command:

```
% whereis -b which
which: /usr/bin/which
```

Here, I used -b to search only for the binary. Without any switches, whereis will display the binary, the manpage path, and the path to the original sources.

If your users prefer to use the real which command instead of the shell version and if they are only interested in seeing binary paths, consider adding these lines to /usr/share/skel/dot.cshrc [Hack #9]:

```
alias which     /usr/bin/which -a
alias whereis   whereis -b
```

The -a switch will list all binaries with that name, not just the first binary found.

## Finding Commands

How do you proceed when you know what it is that you want to do, but have no clue which commands are available to do it? I know I clung to the whatis command like a life preserver when I was first introduced to Unix. For example, when I needed to know how to set up PPP:

```
% whatis ppp
i4bisppp(4)              - isdn4bsd synchronous PPP over ISDN B-channel
network driver
ng_ppp(4)               - PPP protocol netgraph node type
ppp(4)                  - point to point protocol network interface
ppp(8)                  - Point to Point Protocol (a.k.a. user-ppp)
pppctl(8)               - PPP control program
pppoed(8)               - handle incoming PPP over Ethernet connections
pppstats(8)             - print PPP statistics
```

On the days I had time to satisfy my curiosity, I tried this variation:

```
% whatis "(1)"
```

That will show all of the commands that have a manpage in section 1. If you're rusty on your manpage sections, whatis intro should refresh your memory.

## Finding Words

The previous commands are great for finding binaries and manpages, but what if you want to find a particular word in one of your own text files? That requires the notoriously user-unfriendly find command. Let's be realistic. Even with all of your Unix experience, you still have to dig into either the manpage or a good book whenever you need to find something. Can you really expect novice users to figure it out?

To start with, the regular old invocation of find will find filenames, but not the words within those files. We need a judicious use of grep to accomplish that. Fortunately, find's -exec switch allows it to use other utilities, such as grep, without forking another process.

Start off with a find command that looks like this:

```
% find . -type f -exec grep "word" {} \;
```

This invocation says to start in the current directory (.), look through files, not directories (-type f), while running the grep command (-exec grep) in order to search for the word word. Note that the syntax of the -exec switch always resembles:

```
-exec command with_its_parameters {} \;
```

What happens if I search the files in my home directory for the word alias?

```
% find . -type f -exec grep "alias" {} \;
alias h                 history 25
alias j                 jobs -l
Antialiasing=true
```

```
Antialiasing arguments=-sDEVICE=x11 -dTextAlphaBits=4 -dGraphicsAlphaBits=2
-dMaxBitmap=10000000
(proc-arg 0 "antialiasing" "Apply antialiasing (TRUE/FALSE)")
(proc-arg 0 "antialiasing" "Apply antialiasing (TRUE/FALSE)")
```

While it's nice to see that find successfully found the word alias in my home directory, there's one slight problem. I have no idea *which* file or files contained my search expression! However, adding */dev/null* to that command will fix that:

```
# find . -type f -exec grep "alias" /dev/null { } \;
./.cshrc:alias h              history 25
./.cshrc:alias j              jobs -l
./.kde/share/config/kghostviewrc:Antialiasing=true
./.kde/share/config/kghostviewrc:Antialiasing arguments=-sDEVICE=x11
-dTextAlphaBits=4 -dGraphicsAlphaBits=2 -dMaxBitmap=10000000
./.gimp-1.3/pluginrc:        (proc-arg 0 "antialiasing" "Apply antialiasing
(TRUE/FALSE)")
./.gimp-1.3/pluginrc:        (proc-arg 0 "antialiasing" "Apply antialiasing
(TRUE/FALSE)")
```

Why did adding nothing, */dev/null*, automagically cause the name of the file to appear next to the line that contains the search expression? Is it because Unix is truly amazing? After all, it does allow even the state of nothingness to be expressed as a filename.

Actually, it works because grep will list the filename whenever it searches multiple files. When you just use { }, find will pass each filename it finds one at a time to grep. Since grep is searching only one filename, it assumes you already know the name of that file. When you use /dev/null { }, find actually passes grep two files, */dev/null* along with whichever file find happens to be working on. Since grep is now comparing two files, it's nice enough to tell you which of the files contained the search string. We already know */dev/null* won't contain anything, so we just convinced grep to give us the name of the other file.

That's pretty handy. Now let's make it friendly. Here's a very simple script called fstring:

```
% more ~/bin/fstring
#!/bin/sh
# script to find a string
# replaces $1 with user's search string
find . -type f -exec grep "$1" /dev/null { } \;
```

That $1 is a positional parameter. This script expects the user to give one parameter: the word the user is searching for. When the script executes, the shell will replace "$1" with the user's search string. So, the script is meant to be run like this:

```
% fstring word_to_search
```

If you're planning on using this script yourself, you'll probably remember to include a search string. If you want other users to benefit from the script, you may want to include an if statement to generate an error message if the user forgets the search string:

```
#!/bin/sh
# script to find a string
# replaces $1 with user's search string
# or gives error message if user forgets to include search string
if test $1
then
    find . -type f -exec grep "$1" /dev/null {} \;
else
    echo "Don't forget to include the word you would like to search for"
    exit 1
fi
```

Don't forget to make your script executable with chmod +x and to place it in the user's path. */usr/local/bin* is a good location for other users to benefit.

### See Also

- man which
- man whereis
- man whatis
- man find
- man grep

## Get the Most Out of grep

### HACK #14

You may not know where its odd name originated, but you can't argue the usefulness of grep.

Have you ever needed to find a particular file and thought, "I don't recall the filename, but I remember some of its contents"? The oddly named grep command does just that, searching inside files and reporting on those that contain a given piece of text.

### Finding Text

Suppose you wish to search your shell scripts for the text $USER. Try this:

```
% grep -s '$USER' *
add-user:if [ "$USER" != "root" ]; then
bu-user:  echo "  [-u user] - override $USER as the user to backup"
bu-user:if [ "$user" = "" ]; then user="$USER"; fi
del-user:if [ "$USER" != "root" ]; then
mount-host:mounted=$(df | grep "$ALM_AFP_MOUNT/$USER")
.....
```

```
mount-user:  echo "  [-u user] - override $USER as the user to backup"
mount-user:if [ "$user" = "" ]; then user="$USER"; fi
```

In this example, grep has searched through all files in the current directory, displaying each line that contained the text $USER. Use single quotes around the text to prevent the shell from interpreting special characters. The -s option suppresses error messages when grep encounters a directory.

Perhaps you only want to know the name of each file containing the text $USER. Use the -l option to create that list for you:

```
% grep -ls '$USER' *
add-user
bu-user
del-user
mount-host
mount-user
```

## Searching by Relevance

What if you're more concerned about how many times a particular string occurs within a file? That's known as a *relevance search*. Use a command similar to:

```
% grep -sc '$USER' * | grep -v ':0' | sort  -k 2 -t : -r
mount-host:6
mount-user:2
bu-user:2
del-user:1
add-user:1
```

How does this magic work? The -c flag lists each file with a count of matching lines, but it unfortunately includes files with zero matches. To counter this, I piped the output from grep into a second grep, this time searching for ':0' and using a second option, -v, to reverse the sense of the search by displaying lines that *don't* match. The second grep reads from the pipe instead of a file, searching the output of the first grep.

For a little extra flair, I sorted the subsequent output by the second field of each line with sort  -k  2, assuming a field separator of colon (-t  :) and using -r to reverse the sort into descending order.

## Document Extracts

Suppose you wish to search a set of documents and extract a few lines of text centered on each occurrence of a keyword. This time we are interested in the matching lines and their surrounding context, but not in the filenames. Use a command something like this:

```
% grep -rhiw -A4 -B4 'preferences' *.txt > research.txt
% more research.txt
```

This grep command searches all files with the .txt extension for the word preferences. It performs a recursive search (-r) to include all subdirectories, hides (-h) the filename in the output, matches in a case-insensitive (-i) manner, and matches preferences as a complete word but not as part of another word (-w). The -A4 and -B4 options display the four lines immediately after and before the matched line, to give the desired context. Finally, I've redirected the output to the file *research.txt*.

You could also send the output straight to the vim text editor with:

```
% grep -rhiw -A4 -B4 'preferences' *.txt | vim -
Vim: Reading from stdin...
```

vim can be installed from */usr/ports/editors/vim*.

Specifying vim - tells vim to read stdin (in this case the piped output from grep) instead of a file. Type :q! to exit vim.

To search files for several alternatives, use the -e option to introduce extra search patterns:

```
% grep -e 'text1' -e 'text2' *
```

Q. How did grep get its odd name?

A. grep was written as a standalone program to simulate a commonly performed command available in the ancient Unix editor ex. The command in question searched an entire file for lines containing a regular expression and displayed those lines. The command was g/re/p: globally search for a regular expression and print the line.

## Using Regular Expressions

To search for text that is more vaguely specified, use a regular expression. grep understands both basic and extended regular expressions, though it must be invoked as either egrep or grep -E when given an extended regular expression. The text or regular expression to be matched is usually called the pattern.

Suppose you need to search for lines that end in a space or tab character. Try this command (to insert a tab, press Ctrl-V and then Ctrl-I, shown as <tab> in the example):

```
% grep -n '[ <tab>]$' test-file
2:ends in space
3:ends in tab
```

I used the [...] construct to form a regular expression listing the characters to match: space and tab. The expression matches exactly one space *or* one tab character. $ anchors the match to the end of a line. The -n flag tells grep to include the line number in its output.

Alternatively, use:

```
% grep -n '[[:blank:]]$' test-file
2:ends is space
3:ends in tab
```

Regular expressions provide many preformed character groups of the form [[:*description*:]]. Example groups include all control characters, all digits, or all alphanumeric characters. See man re_format for details.

We can modify a previous example to search for either "preferences" or "preference" as a complete word, using an extended regular expression such as this:

```
% egrep -rhiw -A4 -B4 'preferences?' *.txt > research.txt
```

The ? symbol specifies zero or one of the preceding character, making the s of preferences optional. Note that I use egrep because ? is available only in extended regular expressions. If you wish to search for the ? character itself, escape it with a backslash, as in \?.

An alternative method uses an expression of the form (*string1*|*string2*), which matches either one string or the other:

```
% egrep -rhiw -A4 -B4 'preference(s|)' *.txt > research.txt
```

As a final example, use this to seek out all bash, tcsh, or sh shell scripts:

```
% egrep '^#\!/bin/(ba|tc|)sh[[:blank:]]*$' *
```

The caret (^) character at the start of a regular expression anchors it to the start of the line (much as $ at the end anchors it to the end). (ba|tc|) matches ba, tc, or nothing. The * character specifies zero or more of [[:blank:]], allowing trailing whitespace but nothing else. Note that the ! character must be escaped as \! to avoid shell interpretation in tcsh (but not in bash).

> Here's a handy tip for debugging regular expressions: if you don't pass a filename to grep, it will read standard input, allowing you to enter lines of text to see which match. grep will echo back only matching lines.

## Combining grep with Other Commands

grep works well with other commands. For example, to display all tcsh processes:

```
% ps axww | grep -w 'tcsh'
saruman 10329  0.0  0.2    6416  1196  p1  Ss  Sat01PM  0:00.68 -tcsh (tcsh)
```

```
saruman 11351  0.0  0.2    6416  1300 std  Ss  Sat07PM  0:02.54 -tcsh (tcsh)
saruman 13360  0.0  0.0    1116     4 std  R+  10:57PM  0:00.00 grep -w tcsh
%
```

Notice that the grep command itself appears in the output. To prevent this, use:

```
% ps axww | grep -w '[t]csh'
saruman 10329  0.0  0.2    6416  1196 p1   Ss  Sat01PM  0:00.68 -tcsh (tcsh)
saruman 11351  0.0  0.2    6416  1300 std  Ss  Sat07PM  0:02.54 -tcsh (tcsh)
%
```

I'll let you figure out how this works.

### See Also

- man grep
- man re_format (regular expressions)

## Manipulate Files with sed

**HACK #15**

If you've ever had to change the formatting of a file, you know that it can be a time-consuming process.

Why waste your time making manual changes to files when Unix systems come with many tools that can very quickly make the changes for you?

### Removing Blank Lines

Suppose you need to remove the blank lines from a file. This invocation of grep will do the job:

```
% grep -v '^$' letter1.txt > tmp ; mv tmp letter1.txt
```

The pattern ^$ anchors to both the start and the end of a line with no intervening characters—the regexp definition of a blank line. The -v option reverses the search, printing all nonblank lines, which are then written to a temporary file, and the temporary file is moved back to the original.

> grep must never output to the same file it is reading, or the file will end up empty.

You can rewrite the preceding example in sed as:

```
% sed '/^$/d' letter1.txt > tmp ; mv tmp letter1.txt
```

'/^$/d' is actually a sed script. sed's normal mode of operation is to read each line of input, process it according to the script, and then write the processed line to standard output. In this example, the expression '/^$/ is a

regular expression matching a blank line, and the trailing d' is a sed function that deletes the line. Blank lines are deleted and all other lines are
printed. Again, the results are redirected to a temporary file, which is then
copied back to the original file.

## Searching with sed

sed can also do the work of grep:

```
% sed -n '/$USER/p' *
```

This command will yield the same results as:

```
% grep '$USER' *
```

The -n (no-print, perhaps) option prevents sed from outputting each line.
The pattern /$USER/ matches lines containing $USER, and the p function
prints matched lines to standard output, overriding -n.

## Replacing Existing Text

One of the most common uses for sed is to perform a search and replace on
a given string. For example, to change all occurrences of 2003 into 2004 in a
file called *date*, include the two search strings in the format 's/*oldstring*/
*newstring*/', like so:

```
% sed 's/2003/2004/' date
Copyright 2004
...
This was written in 2004, but it is no longer 2003.
...
```

Almost! Noticed that that last 2003 remains unchanged. This is because
without the g (global) flag, sed will change only the *first* occurrence on each
line. This command will give the desired result:

```
% sed 's/2003/2004/g' date
```

Search and replace takes other flags too. To output only changed lines, use:

```
% sed -n 's/2003/2004/gp' date
```

Note the use of the -n flag to suppress normal output and the p flag to print
changed lines.

## Multiple Transformations

Perhaps you need to perform two or more transformations on a file. You can
do this in a single run by specifying a script with multiple commands:

```
% sed 's/2003/2004/g;/^$/d' date
```

This performs both substitution and blank line deletion. Use a semicolon to separate the two commands.

Here is a more complex example that translates HTML tags of the form `<font>` into PHP bulletin board tags of the form [font]:

```
% cat index.html
<title>hello
</title>

% sed 's/<\(.*\)>/[\1]/g' index.html
[title]hello
[/title]
```

How did this work? The script searched for an HTML tag using the pattern '`<.*>`'. Angle brackets match literally. In a regular expression, a dot (.) represents any character and an asterisk (*) means zero or more of the previous item. Escaped parentheses, \( and \), capture the matched pattern laying between them and place it in a numbered buffer. In the replace string, \1 refers to the contents of the first buffer. Thus the text between the angle brackets in the search string is captured into the first buffer and written back inside square brackets in the replace string. sed takes full advantage of the power of regular expressions to copy text from the pattern to its replacement.

```
% cat index1.html
<title>hello</title>

% sed 's/<\(.*\)>/[\1]/g' index1.html
[title>hello</title]
```

This time the same command fails because the pattern .* is greedy and grabs as much as it can, matching up to the second >. To prevent this behavior, we need to match zero or more of any character except <. Recall that [...] is a regular expression that lists characters to match, but if the first character is the caret (^), the match is reversed. Thus the regular expression [^<] matches any single character other than <. I can modify the previous example as follows:

```
% sed 's/<\([^<]*\)>/[\1]/g' index1.html
[title]hello[/title]
```

Remember, grep will perform a case-insensitive search if you provide the -i flag. sed, unfortunately, does not have such an option. To search for title in a case-insensitive manner, form regular expressions using [...], each listing a character of the word in both upper- and lowercase forms:

```
% sed 's/[Tt][Ii][Tt][Ll][Ee]/title/g' title.html
```

## See Also

- `man grep`
- `man sed`
- `man re_format` (regular expressions)
- "sed & Regular Expressions" at *http://main.rtfiber.com.tw/~changyj/sed/*
- Cool sed tricks at *http://www.wagoneers.com/UNIX/SED/sed.html*
- The sed FAQ (*http://doc.ddart.net/shell/sedfaq.htm*)
- The sed Script Archive (*http://sed.sourceforge.net/grabbag/scripts/*)

# Format Text at the Command Line

Combine basic Unix tools to become a formatting expert.

Don't let the syntax of the sed command scare you off. sed is a powerful utility capable of handling most of your formatting needs. For example, have you ever needed to add or remove comments from a source file? Perhaps you need to shuffle some text from one section to another.

In this hack, I'll demonstrate how to do that. I'll also show some handy formatting tricks using two other built-in Unix commands, tr and col.

## Adding Comments to Source Code

sed allows you to specify an address range using a pattern, so let's put this to use. Suppose we want to comment out a block of text in a source file by adding // to the start of each line we wish to comment out. We might use a text editor to mark the block with bc-start and bc-end:

```
% cat source.c
  if (tTd(27, 1))
    sm_dprintf("%s (%s, %s) aliased to %s\n",
        a->q_paddr, a->q_host, a->q_user, p);
  bc-start
    if (bitset(EF_VRFYONLY, e->e_flags))
    {
      a->q_state = QS_VERIFIED;
      return;
    }
  bc-end
    message("aliased to %s", shortenstring(p, MAXSHORTSTR));
```

and then apply a sed script such as:

```
% sed '/bc-start/,/bc-end/s/^/\/\///' source.c
```

to get:

```
  if (tTd(27, 1))
      sm_dprintf("%s (%s, %s) aliased to %s\n",
          a->q_paddr, a->q_host, a->q_user, p);
```

```
//bc-start
//  if (bitset(EF_VRFYONLY, e->e_flags))
//  {
//      a->q_state = QS_VERIFIED;
//      return;
//  }
//bc-end
message("aliased to %s", shortenstring(p, MAXSHORTSTR));
```

The script used search and replace to add // to the start of all lines (s/^/\/\///) that lie between the two markers (/bc-start/,/bc-end/). This will apply to every block in the file between the marker pairs. Note that in the sed script, the / character has to be escaped as \/ so it is not mistaken for a delimiter.

## Removing Comments

When we need to delete the comments and the two bc- lines (let's assume that the edited contents were copied back to *source.c*), we can use a script such as:

```
% sed '/bc-start/d;/bc-end/d;/bc-start/,/bc-end/s/^\/\///' source.c
```

Oops! My first attempt won't work. The bc- lines must be deleted *after* they have been used as address ranges. Trying again we get:

```
% sed '/bc-start/,/bc-end/s/^\/\///;/bc-start/d;/bc-end/d' source.c
```

If you want to leave the two bc- marker lines in but comment them out, use this piece of trickery:

```
% sed '/bc-start/,/bc-end/{/^\/\/bc-/\!s/\/\///;}' source.c
```

to get:

```
if (tTd(27, 1))
    sm_dprintf("%s (%s, %s) aliased to %s\n",
        a->q_paddr, a->q_host, a->q_user, p);
    //bc-start
if (bitset(EF_VRFYONLY, e->e_flags))
{

    a->q_state = QS_VERIFIED;
    return;

}
    //bc-end
message("aliased to %s", shortenstring(p, MAXSHORTSTR));
```

Note that in the bash shell you must use:

```
% sed '/bc-start/,/bc-end/{/^\/\/bc-/!s/\/\///;}' source.c
```

because the bang character (!) does not need to be escaped as it does in tcsh.

What's with the curly braces? They prevent a common mistake. You may imagine that this example:

```
% sed -n '/$USER/p;p' *
```

prints each line containing $USER twice because of the p;p commands. It doesn't, though, because the second p is not restrained by the /$USER/ line address and therefore applies to *every* line. To print twice just those lines containing $USER, use:

```
% sed -n '/$USER/p;/$USER/p' *
```

or:

```
% sed -n '/$USER/{p;p;}' *
```

The construct {...} introduces a function list that applies to the preceding line address or range.

A line address followed by ! (or \! in the tcsh shell) reverses the address range, and so the function (list) that follows is applied to all lines *not* matching. The net effect is to remove // from all lines that don't start with //bc- but that do lie within the bc- markers.

## Using the Holding Space to Mark Text

sed reads input into the pattern space, but it also provides a buffer (called the *holding space*) and functions to move text from one space to the other. All other functions (such as s and d) operate on the pattern space, not the holding space.

Check out this sed script:

```
% cat case.script
# Sed script for case insensitive search
#
# copy pattern space to hold space to preserve it
h
y/ABCDEFGHIJKLMNOPQRSTUVWXYZ/abcdefghijklmnopqrstuvwxyz/
# use a regular expression address to search for lines containing:
/test/ {
i\
vvvv
a\
^^^^
}
# restore the original pattern space from the hold space
x;p
```

First, I have written the script to a file instead of typing it in on the command line. Lines starting with # are comments and are ignored. Other lines specify a sed command, and commands are separated by either a newline or

; character. sed reads one line of input at a time and applies the whole script file to each line. The following functions are applied to each line as it is read:

h

> Copies the pattern space (the line just read) into the holding space.

y/ABC/abc/

> Operates on the pattern space, translating A to a, B to b, and C to c and so on, ensuring the line is all lowercase.

/test/ {...}

> Matches the line just read if it includes the text test (whatever the original case, because the line is now all lowercase) and then applies the list of functions that follow. This example appends text before (i\) and after (a\) the matched line to highlight it.

x

> Exchanges the pattern and hold space, thus restoring the original contents of the pattern space.

p

> Prints the pattern space.

Here is the test file:

```
% cat case
This contains text          Hello
that we want to             TeSt
search for, but in          test
a case insensitive          XXXX
manner using the sed        TEST
editor.                     Bye bye.
%
```

Here are the results of running our sed script on it:

```
% sed -n -f case.script case
This contains text          Hello
vvvv
that we want to             TeSt
^^^^

vvvv
search for, but in          test
^^^^

a case insensitive          XXXX
vvvv
manner using the sed        TEST
^^^^

editor.                     Bye bye.
```

Notice the vvv ^^^ markers around lines that contain test.

## Translating Case

The tr command can translate one character to another. To change the contents of *case* into all lowercase and write the results to file *lower-case*, we could use:

```
% tr 'ABCDEFGHIJKLMNOPQRSTUVWXYZ' 'abcdefghijklmnopqrstuvwxyz' \
  < case > lower-case
```

tr works with standard input and output only, so to read and write files we must use redirection.

## Translating Characters

To translate carriage return characters into newline characters, we could use:

```
% tr \\r \\n < cr > lf
```

where *cr* is the original file and *lf* is a new file containing line feeds in place of carriage returns. \n represents a line feed character, but we must escape the backslash character in the shell, so we use \\n instead. Similarly, a carriage return is specified as \\r.

## Removing Duplicate Line Feeds

tr can also squeeze multiple consecutive occurrences of a particular character into a single occurrence. For example, to remove duplicate line feeds from the *lines* file:

```
% tr -s \\n < lines > tmp ; mv tmp lines
```

Here we use the *tmp* file trick again because tr, like grep and sed, will trash the input file if it is also the output file.

## Deleting Characters

tr can also delete selected characters. If for instance if you hate vowels, run your documents through this:

```
% tr -d aeiou < file
```

## Translating Tabs to Spaces

To translate tabs into multiple spaces, use the -x flag:

```
% cat tabs
col     col     col

% od -x tabs
0000000    636f    6c09    636f    6c09    636f    6c0a    0a00
```

```
0000015
% col -x < tabs > spaces
% cat spaces
col      col      col

% od -h spaces
0000000    636f    6c20    2020    2020    636f    6c20    2020    2020
0000020    636f    6c0a    0a00
0000025
```

In this example I have used od  -x to octal dump in hexadecimal the contents of the before and after files, which shows more clearly that the translation has worked. (09 is the code for Tab and 20 is the code for Space.)

## See Also

- man sed
- man tr
- man col
- man od

## HACK #17 Delimiter Dilemma

Deal with double quotation marks in delimited files.

Importing data from a delimited text file into an application is usually painless. Even if you need to change the delimiter from one character to another (from a comma to a colon, for example), you can choose from many tools that perform simple character substitution with great ease.

However, one common situation is not solved as easily: many business applications export data into a space- or comma-delimited file, enclosing individual fields in double quotation marks. These fields often contain the delimiter character. Importing such a file into an application that processes only one delimiter (PostgreSQL for example) may result in an incorrect interpretation of the data. This is one of those situations where the user should feel lucky if the process fails.

One solution is to write a script that tracks the use of double quotes to determine whether it is working within a text field. This is doable by creating a variable that acts as a text/nontext switch for the character substitution process. The script should change the delimiter to a more appropriate character, leave the delimiters that were enclosed in double quotes unchanged, and remove the double quotes. Rather than make the changes to the original datafile, it's safer to write the edited data to a new file.

## Attacking the Problem

The following algorithm meets our needs:

1. Create the switch variable and assign it the value of 1, meaning "non-text". We'll declare the variable tswitch and define it as tswitch = 1.

2. Create a variable for the delimiter and define it. We'll use the variable delim with a space as the delimiter, so delim = ' '.

3. Decide on a better delimiter. We'll use the tab character, so new_delim = '\t'.

4. Open the datafile for reading.

5. Open a new file for writing.

Now, for every character in the datafile:

1. Read a character from the datafile.

2. If the character is a double quotation mark, tswitch = tswitch * -1.

3. If the character equals the character in delim and tswitch equals 1, write new_delim to the new file.

4. If the character equals that in delim and tswitch equals -1, write the value of delim to the new file.

5. If the character is anything else, write the character to the new file.

## The Code

The Python script *redelim.py* implements the preceding algorithm. It prompts the user for the original datafile and a name for the new datafile. The delim and new_delim variables are hardcoded, but those are easily changed within the script.

This script copies a space-delimited text file with text values in double quotes to a new, tab-delimited file without the double quotes. The advantage of using this script is that it leaves spaces that were within double quotes unchanged.

There are no command-line arguments for this script. The script will prompt the user for source and destination file information.

You can redefine the variables for the original and new delimiters, delim and new_delim, in the script as needed.

```
#!/usr/local/bin/python
import os

print """ Change text file delimiters.
```

---

```
# Ask user for source and target files.
sourcefile = raw_input('Please enter the path and name of the source file:')
targetfile = raw_input('Please enter the path and name of the target file:')

# Open files for reading and writing.
source = open(sourcefile,'r')
dest   = open(targetfile,'w')

# The variable 'm' acts as a text/non-text switch that reminds python
# whether it is working within a text or non-text data field.
tswitch = 1

# If the source delimiter that you want to change is not a space,
# redefine the variable delim in the next line.
delim = ' '

# If the new delimiter that you want to change is not a tab,
# redefine the variable new_delim in the next line.
new_delim = '\t'

for charn in source.read():
        if tswitch == 1:
                if charn == delim:
                        dest.write(new_delim)
                elif charn == '\"':
                        tswitch = tswitch * -1
                else:
                        dest.write(charn)
        elif tswitch == -1:
                if charn == '\"':
                        tswitch = tswitch * -1
                else:
                        dest.write(charn)


source.close()
dest.close()
```

Use of *redelim.py* assumes that you have installed Python, which is available through the ports collection or as a binary package. The Python module used in this code is installed by default.

## Hacking the Hack

If you prefer working with Perl, DBD::AnyData is another good solution to this problem.

## See Also

• The Python home page (*http://www.python.org/*)

# DOS Floppy Manipulation
### #18
Bring simplicity back to using floppies.

If you're like many Unix users, you originally came from a Windows background. Remember your initial shock the first time you tried to use a floppy on a Unix system? Didn't Windows seem so much simpler? Forever gone seemed the days when you could simply insert a floppy, copy some files over, and remove the disk from the drive. Instead, you were expected to plunge into the intricacies of the mount command, only to discover that you didn't even have the right to use the floppy drive in the first place!

There are several ways to make using floppies much, much easier on your FreeBSD system. Let's start by taking stock of the default mechanisms for managing floppies.

## Mounting a Floppy

Suppose I have formatted a floppy on a Windows system, copied some files over, and now want to transfer those files to my FreeBSD system. In reality, that floppy is a storage media. Since it is storing files, it needs a *filesystem* in order to keep track of the locations of those files. Because that floppy was formatted on a Windows system, it uses a filesystem called FAT12.

In Unix, a filesystem can't be accessed until it has been *mounted*. This means you have to use the mount command before you can access the contents of that floppy. While this may seem strange at first, it actually gives Unix more flexibility. An administrator can mount and unmount filesystems as they are needed. Note that I used the word *administrator*. Regular users don't have this ability, by default. We'll change that shortly.

Unix also has the additional flexibility of being able to mount different filesystems. In Windows, a floppy will always contain the FAT12 filesystem. BSD understands floppies formatted with either FAT12 or UFS, the Unix File System. As you might expect from the name, the UFS filesystem is assumed unless you specify otherwise.

For now, become the superuser and let's pick apart the default invocation of the mount command:

```
% su
Password:
# mount -t msdos /dev/fd0 /mnt
#
```

I used the type (-t) switch to indicate that this floppy was formatted from an msdos-based system. I could have used the mount_msdosfs command instead:

```
# mount_msdosfs /dev/fd0 /mnt
```

Both commands take two arguments. The first indicates the device to be mounted. /dev/fd0 represents the first (0) floppy drive (fd) device (/dev).

The second argument represents the *mount point*. A mount point is simply an empty directory that acts as a pointer to the mounted filesystem. Your FreeBSD system comes with a default mount point called */mnt*. If you prefer, create a different mount point with a more useful name. Just remember to keep that directory empty so it will be available as a mount point, because any files in your mount point will become hidden and inaccessible when you mount a device over it.

> This can be a feature in itself if you have a filesystem that should always be mounted. Place a *README* file in */mnt/ important_directory* containing: "If you can see this file, contact the administrator at this number...."

In this example, I'll create a mount point called */floppy*, which I'll use in the rest of the examples in this hack:

```
# mkdir /floppy
```

## Common Error Messages

This is a good place to explain some common error messages. Trust me, I experienced them all before I became proficient at this whole mount business. At the time, I wished for a listing of error messages so I could figure out what I had done wrong and how to fix it.

Let's take a look at the output of this command:

```
# mount /dev/fd0 /mnt
mount: /dev/fd0 on /mnt: incorrect super block
```

Remember my first mount command? I know it worked, as I just received my prompt back. I know this command didn't work, because mount instead wrote me a message explaining why it did *not* do what I asked.

That error message isn't actually as bad as it sounds. I forgot to include the type switch, meaning mount assumed I was using UFS. Since this is a FAT12 floppy, it simply didn't understand the filesystem.

This error message also looks particularly nasty:

```
fd0: hard error cmd=read fsbn 0 of 0-3 (No status)
msdosfs: /dev/fd0: Input/output error
```

If you get that one, quickly reach down and push in the floppy before anyone else notices. You forgot to insert it into the bay.

Here's another error message:

```
msdosfs: /dev/fd0: Operation not permitted
```

Oops. Looks like I didn't become the superuser before trying that mount command.

How about this one:

```
mount: /floppy: No such file or directory
```

Looks like I forgot to make that mount point first. A mkdir /floppy should fix that one.

The one error message you do not want to see is a system panic followed by a reboot. It took me a while to break myself of the habit of just ejecting a floppy once I had copied over the files I wanted. That's something you just don't do in Unix land.

You must first warn your operating system that you have finished using a filesystem before you physically remove it from the computer. Otherwise, when it goes out looking for a file, it will panic when it realizes that it has just disappeared off of the edge of the universe! (Well, the computer's universe anyway.) Put yourself in your operating system's shoes for a minute. The user entrusted something important to your care. You blinked for just a split second and it was gone, nowhere to be found. You'd panic too!

## Managing the Floppy

How do you warn your operating system that the universe has shrunk? You unmount the floppy before you eject it from the floppy bay. Note that the actual command used is missing the first n and is instead spelled umount:

```
# umount /floppy
```

Also, the only argument is the name of your mount point. In this example, it's /floppy.

How can you tell if a floppy is mounted? The disk free command will tell you:

```
# df
Filesystem  1K-blocks      Used    Avail Capacity  Mounted on
/dev/ad0s1a    257838     69838   167374     29%   /
devfs               1         1        0    100%   /dev
/dev/ad0s1e    257838       616   236596      0%   /tmp
/dev/ad0s1f  13360662   2882504  9409306     23%   /usr
/dev/ad0s1d    257838     28368   208844     12%   /var
/dev/fd0         1424         1     1423      0%   /floppy
```

as will the mount command with no arguments:

```
# mount
/dev/ad0s1a on / (ufs, local)
devfs on /dev (devfs, local)
/dev/ad0s1e on /tmp (ufs, local, soft-updates)
/dev/ad0s1f on /usr (ufs, local, soft-updates)
/dev/ad0s1d on /var (ufs, local, soft-updates)
/dev/fd0 on /floppy  (msdosfs, local)
```

This system currently has a floppy */dev/fd0* mounted on */floppy*, meaning you'll need to issue the umount command before ejecting the floppy.

Several other filesystems are also mounted, yet I only used the mount command on my floppy drive. When did they get mounted and how? The answer is in */etc/fstab*, which controls which filesystems to mount at boot time. Here's my */etc/fstab*; it's pretty similar to the earlier output from df:

```
# more /etc/fstab
# Device     Mountpoint           FStype     Options      Dump   Pass#
/dev/ad0s1b  none                 swap       sw           0      0
/dev/ad0s1a  /                    ufs        rw           1      1
/dev/ad0s1e  /tmp                 ufs        rw           2      2
/dev/ad0s1f  /usr                 ufs        rw           2      2
/dev/ad0s1d  /var                 ufs        rw           2      2
/dev/acd0    /cdrom               cd9660     ro,noauto    0      0
proc         /proc                procfs     rw           0      0
linproc      /compat/linux/proc   linprocfs  rw           0      0
```

Each mountable filesystem has its own line in this file. Each has its own unique mount point and its filesystem type listed. See how the */cdrom* mount point has the options ro,noauto instead of rw? The noauto tells your system not to mount your CD-ROM at bootup. That is a good thing—if there's no CD in the bay at boot time, the kernel will either give an error message or pause for a few seconds, looking for that filesystem.

However, you can mount a data CD-ROM at any time by simply typing:

```
# mount /cdrom
```

That command was shorter than the usual mount command for one reason: there was an entry for */cdrom* in */etc/fstab*. That means you can shorten the command to mount a floppy by creating a similar entry for */floppy*. Simply add this line to */etc/fstab*:

```
/dev/fd0    /floppy    msdos    rw,noauto    0    0
```

Test your change by inserting a floppy and issuing this command:

```
# mount /floppy
```

If you receive an error, check */etc/fstab* for a typo and try again.

## Allowing Regular Users to Mount Floppies

Now that the superuser can quickly mount floppies, let's give regular users this ability. First, we have to change the default setting of the vfs.usermount variable:

```
# sysctl vfs.usermount=1
vfs.usermount: 0 -> 1
```

By changing the default 0 to a 1, we've just enabled users to mount virtual filesystems. However, don't worry about your users running amok with this new freedom—the devices themselves are still owned by root. Check out the permissions on the floppy device:

```
# ls -l /dev/fd0
crw-r----- 1 root  operator   9,  0 Nov 28 08:31 /dev/fd0
```

If you'd like any user to have the right to mount a floppy, change the permissions so everyone has read and write access:

```
# chmod 666 /dev/fd0
```

> Now, if you don't want *every* user to have this right, you could create a group, add the desired users to that group, and assign that group permissions to */dev/fd0*.

You're almost there. The only kicker is that the user has to own the mount point. The best place to put a user's mount point is in his home directory. So, logged in as your usual user account:

```
% mkdir ~/floppy
```

Now, do you think the mount command will recognize that new mount point?

```
% mount ~/floppy
mount: /home/dru/floppy: unknown special file or file system
```

Oh boy. Looks like we're back to square one, doesn't it? Remember, that entry in */etc/fstab* only refers to root's mount point, so I can't use that shortcut to refer to my own mount point. While it's great to have the ability to use the mount command, I'm truly too lazy to have to type out mount -t msdos /dev/fd0 ~/floppy, let alone remember it.

Thank goodness for aliases. Try adding these lines to the alias section of your ~.*cshrc* file:

```
alias mf    mount -t msdos /dev/fd0 ~/floppy
alias uf    umount ~/floppy
```

Now you simply need to type mf whenever you want to mount a floppy and uf when it's time to unmount the floppy. Or perhaps you'll prefer to create a keyboard shortcut [Hack #4].

## Formatting Floppies

Now that you can mount and unmount floppies with the best of them, it's
time to learn how to format them. Again, let's start with the default invocations required to format a floppy, then move on to some ways to simplify
the process.

When you format a floppy on a Windows or DOS system, several events
occur:

1. The floppy is low-level formatted, marking the tracks and sectors onto
   the disk.

2. A filesystem is installed onto the floppy, along with two copies of its
   FAT table.

3. You are given the opportunity to give the floppy a volume label.

The same process also has to occur when you format a floppy on a FreeBSD
system. On a 5.x system, the order goes like this:

```
% fdformat -f 1440 /dev/fd0
Format 1440K floppy `/dev/fd0'? (y/n): y
Processing ----------------------------------------

% bsdlabel -w /dev/fd0 fd1440

% newfs_msdos /dev/fd0
/dev/fd0: 2840 sectors in 355 FAT12 clusters (4096 bytes/cluster)
bps=512 spc=8 res=1 nft=2 rde=512 sec=2880 mid=0xf0 spf=2 spt=18 hds=2 hid=0
```

First, notice that we don't use the mount command. You can't mount a filesystem before you have a filesystem! (You do have to have the floppy in the
drive, though.) Take a look at the three steps:

1. fdformat does the low-level format.

2. bsdlabel creates the volume label.

3. newfs_msdos installs the FAT12 filesystem.

If I see the following error message when I try to mount the floppy, I'll realize
that I forgot that third step:

```
% mf
msdosfs: /dev/fd0: Invalid argument
```

Because my mf mount floppy alias uses the msdos filesystem, it will complain
if the floppy isn't formatted with FAT12.

## Automating the Format Process

Any three-step process is just begging to be put into a shell script. I like to keep these scripts under ~/*bin*. If you don't have this directory yet, create it. Then create a script called ff (for *format floppy*):

```
% cd
% mkdir bin
% cd bin
% vi ff
#!/bin/sh
#this script formats a floppy with FAT12
#that floppy can also be used on a Windows system

# first, remind the user to insert the floppy
echo "Please insert the floppy and press enter"
read pathname

# then, proceed with the three format steps

fdformat -f 1440 /dev/fd0
bsdlabel -w /dev/fd0 fd1440
newfs_msdos /dev/fd0
echo "Format complete."
```

Note that this script is basically those three commands, with comments thrown in so I remember what the script does. The only new part is the read pathname line. I added it to force the user to press Enter before the script proceeds.

Remember to make the script executable:

```
% chmod +x ff
```

I'll then return to my home directory and see how it works. Since I use the C shell, I'll use the rehash command to make the shell aware that there is a new executable in my path:

```
% cd
% rehash
% ff
Please insert the floppy and press enter

Format 1440K floppy `/dev/fd0'? (y/n): y
Processing -------------------------------------
/dev/fd0: 2840 sectors in 355 FAT12 clusters (4096 bytes/cluster)
bps=512 spc=8 res=1 nft=2 rde=512 sec=2880 mid=0xf0 spf=2 spt=18 hds=2 hid=0
Format complete.
```

Not too bad. I can now manipulate floppies with my own custom mf, uf, and ff commands.

## See Also

- man `fstab`
- man `fdformat`
- man `bsdlabel`
- man `newfs`
- The Creating and Using Floppies section of the FreeBSD Handbook (*http://www.freebsd.org/doc/en_US.ISO8859-1/books/handbook/floppies.html*)
- The Mounting and Unmounting File Systems section of the FreeBSD Handbook (*http://www.freebsd.org/doc/en_US.ISO8859-1/books/handbook/mount-unmount.html*)

# Access Windows Shares Without a Server

Share files between Windows and FreeBSD with a minimum of fuss.

You've probably heard of some of the Unix utilities available for accessing files residing on Microsoft systems. For example, FreeBSD provides the `mount_smbfs` and `smbutil` utilities to mount Windows shares and view or access resources on a Microsoft network. However, both of those utilities have a caveat: they require an SMB *server*. The assumption is that somewhere in your network there is at least one NT or 2000 Server.

Not all networks have the budget or the administrative expertise to allow for commercial server operating systems. Sure, you can install and configure Samba, but isn't that overkill for, say, a home or very small office network? Sometimes you just want to share some files between a Windows 9x system and a Unix system. It's a matter of using the right-sized tool for the job. You don't bring in a backhoe to plant flowers in a window box.

## Installing and Configuring Sharity-Light

If your small network contains a mix of Microsoft and Unix clients, consider installing Sharity-Light on the Unix systems. This application allows you to mount a Windows share from a Unix system. FreeBSD provides a port for this purpose (see the Sharity-Light web site for other supported platforms):

```
# cd /usr/ports/net/sharity-light
# make install clean
```

Since Sharity-Light is a command-line utility, you should be familiar with UNC or the Universal Naming Convention. UNC is how you refer to Microsoft shared resources from the command line. A UNC looks like \\*NetBIOSname*\*sharename*. It starts with double backslashes, then contains the NetBIOS name of the computer to access and the name of the share on that computer.

Before using Sharity-Light, you need to know the NetBIOS names of the computers you wish to access. If you have multiple machines running Microsoft operating systems, the quickest way to view each system's name is with nbtstat. From one of the Windows systems, open a command prompt and type:

```
C:> nbtstat -A 192.168.2.10

        NETBIOS Remote Machine Name Table

    Name        Type        Status
---------------------------------------------
LITTLE_WOLF  <00> UNIQUE    Registered
<snip>
```

Repeat for each IP address in your network. Your output will be several lines long, but the entry (usually the first) containing <00> is the one with the name you're interested in. In this example, LITTLE_WOLF is the NetBIOS name associated with 192.168.2.10.

Even though nbtstat ? indicates that -A is used to view a *remote* system, it also works with the IP address of the local system. This allows you to check all of the IP addresses in your network from the same system.

Once you know which IP addresses are associated with which NetBIOS names, you'll need to add that information to */etc/hosts* on your Unix systems:

```
# more /etc/hosts
127.0.0.1       localhost
192.168.2.95    genisis       #this system
192.168.2.10    little_wolf   #98 system sharing cygwin2
```

You'll also need to know the names of the shares you wish to access. Again, from a Microsoft command prompt, repeat this command for each NetBIOS name and make note of your results:

```
C:> net view \\little_wolf
Shared resources at \\LITTLE_WOLF

Sharename    Type      Comment
---------------------------------------
CYGWIN2      Disk
The command was completed successfully.
```

Here the computer known as LITTLE_WOLF has only one share, the *CYGWIN2* directory.

Finally, you'll need a mount point on your Unix system, so you might as well give it a useful name. Since the typical floppy mount point is /floppy and the typical CD mount point is /cdrom, let's use /windows:

```
# mkdir /windows
```

## Accessing Microsoft Shares

Once you know the names of your computers and shares, using Sharity-Light is very easy. As the superuser, mount the desired share:

```
# shlight //little_wolf/cygwin2 /windows
Password:
Using port 49923 for NFS.
```

> Watch your slashes. Microsoft uses the backslash (\) at the command line, whereas Unix and Sharity-Light use the forward slash (/).

Note that I was prompted for a password because Windows 9x and ME users have the option of password protecting their shares. This particular share did not have a password, so I simply pressed Enter.

> Adding -n to the previous command will forego the password prompt. Type shlight -h to see all available options.

However, if the share is on a Windows NT Workstation, 2000 Pro, or XP system, you must provide a username and password valid on that system. The syntax is:

```
# shlight //2000pro/cdrom /windows -U username -P password
```

Once the share is mounted, it works like any other mount point. Depending on the permissions set on the share, you should be able to browse that shared directory, copy over or add files, and modify files. When you're finished using the share, unmount it:

```
$ unshlight /windows
```

## See Also

- The Sharity-Light README and FAQ (/usr/local/share/doc/Sharity-Light/)
- The Sharity-Light web site (http://www.obdev.at/products/sharity-light/index.html)
- The Samba web site (http://www.samba.org/)

## Deal with Disk Hogs

**#20**   Fortunately, you no longer have to be a script guru or a find wizard just to keep up with what is happening on your disks.

Think for a moment. What types of files are you always chasing after so they don't waste resources? Your list probably includes temp files, core files, and old logs that have already been archived. Did you know that your system already contains scripts capable of cleaning out those files? Yes, I'm talking about your periodic scripts.

### Periodic Scripts

You'll find these scripts in the following directory on a FreeBSD system:

```
% ls /etc/periodic/daily | grep clean
100.clean-disks
110.clean-tmps
120.clean-preserve
130.clean-msgs
140.clean-rwho
150.clean-hoststat
```

Are you using these scripts? To find out, look at your */etc/periodic.conf* file. What, you don't have one? That means you've never tweaked your default configurations. If that's the case, copy over the sample file and take a look at what's available:

```
# cp /etc/defaults/periodic.conf /etc/periodic.conf
# more /etc/periodic.conf
```

**daily_clean_disks.** Let's start with daily_clean_disks. This script is ideal for finding and deleting files with certain file extensions. You'll find it about two pages into *periodic.conf*, in the Daily options section, where you may note that it's not enabled by default. Fortunately, configuring it is a heck of a lot easier than using cron to schedule a complex find statement.

> Before you enable any script, test it first, *especially* if it'll delete files based on pattern-matching rules. Back up your system first!
>
> For example, suppose you want to delete old logs with the *.bz2* extension. If you're not careful when you craft your daily_clean_disks_files line, you may end up inadvertently deleting *all* files with that extension. Any user who has just compressed some important data will be very miffed when she finds that her data has mysteriously disappeared.

Let's test this scenario. I'd like to prune all *.core* files and any logs older than *.0.bz2*. I'll edit that section of */etc/periodic.conf* like so:

```
# 100.clean-disks
daily_clean_disks_enable="YES"          # Delete files daily
daily_clean_disks_files="*.[1-9].bz2 *.core"   # delete old logs, cores
daily_clean_disks_days=1                 # on a daily basis
daily_clean_disks_verbose="YES"          # Mention files deleted
```

Notice my pattern-matching expression for the *.bz2* files. My expression matches any filename (*) followed by a dot and a number from one to nine (.[1-9]), followed by another dot and the *.bz2* extension.

Now I'll verify that my system has been backed up, and then manually run that script. As this script is fairly resource-intensive, I'll do this test when the system is under a light load:

```
# /etc/periodic/daily/100.clean-disks

Cleaning disks:
/usr/ports/distfiles/MPlayer-0.92.tar.bz2
/usr/ports/distfiles/gnome2/libxml2-2.6.2.tar.bz2
/usr/ports/distfiles/gnome2/libxslt-1.1.0.tar.bz2
```

Darn. Looks like I inadvertently nuked some of my *distfiles*. I'd better be a bit more explicit in my matching pattern. I'll try this instead:

```
# delete old logs, cores
daily_clean_disks_files="messages.[1-9].bz2 *.core"
```

```
# /etc/periodic/daily/100.clean-disks

Cleaning disks:
/var/log/messages.1.bz2
/var/log/messages.2.bz2
/var/log/messages.3.bz2
/var/log/messages.4.bz2
```

That's a bit better. It didn't delete */var/log/messages* or */var/log/messages.1.bz2*, which I like to keep on disk. Remember, always test your pattern matching *before* scheduling a deletion script. If you keep the verbose line at YES, the script will report the names of files it deletes.

**daily_clean_tmps.** The other cleaning scripts are quite straightforward to configure. Take daily_clean_tmps, for example:

```
# 110.clean-tmps
daily_clean_tmps_enable="NO"             # Delete stuff daily
daily_clean_tmps_dirs="/tmp"             # Delete under here
daily_clean_tmps_days="3"                # If not accessed for
daily_clean_tmps_ignore=".X*-lock quota.user quota.group"  # Don't delete
                                         # these
daily_clean_tmps_verbose="YES"           # Mention files deleted
```

This is a quick way to clean out any temporary directories. Again, you get to choose the locations of those directories. Here is a quick way to find out which directories named *tmp* are on your system:

```
# find / -type d -name tmp
/tmp
/usr/tmp
/var/spool/cups/tmp
/var/tmp
```

That command asks find to start at root (/) and look for any directories (-type d) named *tmp* (-name tmp). If I wanted to clean those daily, I'd configure that section like so:

```
# 110.clean-tmps

# Delete stuff daily
daily_clean_tmps_enable="YES"
daily_clean_tmps_dirs="/tmp /usr/tmp /var/spool/cups/tmp /var/tmp"

# If not accessed for
daily_clean_tmps_days="1"

# Don't delete these
daily_clean_tmps_ignore=".X*-lock quota.user quota.group"

# Mention files deleted
daily_clean_tmps_verbose="YES"
```

Again, I immediately test that script after saving my changes:

```
# /etc/periodic/daily/110.clean-tmps

Removing old temporary files:
   /var/tmp/gconfd-root
```

This script will not delete any locked files or temporary files currently in use. This is an excellent feature and yet another reason to run this script on a daily basis, preferably at a time when few users are on the system.

**daily_clean_preserve.** Moving on, the next script is daily_clean_preserve:

```
# 120.clean-preserve
daily_clean_preserve_enable="YES"          # Delete files daily
daily_clean_preserve_days=7                # If not modified for
daily_clean_preserve_verbose="YES"         # Mention files deleted
```

What exactly is preserve? The answer is in man  hier. Use the manpage search function (the / key) to search for the word preserve:

```
# man hier
/preserve
        preserve/ temporary home of files preserved after an accidental
                  death of an editor; see (ex)1
```

Now that you know what the script does, see if the default settings are suited for your environment. This script is run daily, but keeps preserved files until they are seven days old.

The last three clean scripts deal with cleaning out old files from msgs, rwho and sendmail's hoststat cache. See man periodic.conf for more details.

Incidentally, you don't have to wait until it is time for periodic to do its thing; you can manually run any periodic script at any time. You'll find them all in subdirectories of /etc/periodic/.

## Limiting Files

Instead of waiting for a daily process to clean up any spills, you can tweak several knobs to prevent these files from being created in the first place. For example, the C shell itself provides limits, any of which are excellent candidates for a customized *dot.cshrc* file [Hack #9].

To see the possible limits and their current values:

```
% limit
cputime         unlimited
filesize        unlimited
datasize        524288 kbytes
stacksize       65536 kbytes
coredumpsize    unlimited
memoryuse       unlimited
vmemoryuse      unlimited
descriptors     4557
memorylocked    unlimited
maxproc         2278
sbsize          unlimited
```

You can test a limit by typing it at the command line; it will remain for the duration of your current shell. If you like the limit, make it permanent by adding it to .cshrc. For example:

```
% limit filesize 2k
% limit | grep filesize
filesize     2 kbytes
```

will set the maximum file size that can be created to 2 KB. The limit command supports both k for kilobytes and m for megabytes. Do note that this limit does not affect the total size of the area available to store files, just the size of a newly created file. See the Quotas section of the FreeBSD Handbook if you intend to limit disk space usage.

Having created a file limit, you'll occasionally want to exceed it. For example, consider decompressing a file:

```
% uncompress largefile.Z
Filesize limit exceeded
```

```
% unlimit filesize
% uncompress largefile.Z
%
```

The unlimit command will allow me to override the file-size limit temporarily (for the duration of this shell). If you really do want to force your users
to stick to limits, read man limits.

Now back to shell limits. If you don't know what a core file is, you probably don't need to collect them. Sure, periodic can clean those files out for
you, but why make them in the first place? Core files are large. You can limit
their size with:

```
limit coredumpsize 1m
```

That command will limit a core file to 1 MB, or 1024 KB. To prevent core
files completely, set the size to 0:

```
limit coredumpsize 0
```

If you're interested in the rest of the built-in limits, you'll find them in man
tcsh. Searching for coredumpsize will take you to the right spot.

## The Other BSDs

The preceding discussion is based on FreeBSD. Other BSD systems ship
with similar scripts that do identical tasks, but they are kept in a single file
instead of in a separate directory.

**NetBSD.** For daily, weekly, and monthly tasks, NetBSD uses the */etc/daily*,
*/etc/weekly*, and */etc/monthly* scripts, whose behavior is controlled with the
*/etc/daily.conf*, */etc/weekly.conf*, and */etc/monthly.conf* configuration files.
For more information about them, read man daily.conf, man weekly.conf,
and man monthly.conf.

**OpenBSD.** OpenBSD uses three scripts, */etc/daily*, */etc/weekly*, and */etc/
monthly*. You can learn more about them by reading man daily.

## See Also

- man periodic.conf
- man limits
- man tcsh
- The Quotas section of the FreeBSD Handbook (*http://www.freebsd.org/doc/
  en_US.ISO8859-1/books/handbook/quotas.html*)

## HACK #21 Manage Temporary Files and Swap Space

Add more temporary or swap space without repartitioning.

When you install any operating system, it's important to allocate sufficient disk space to hold temporary and swap files. Ideally, you already know the optimum sizes for your system so you can partition your disk accordingly during the install. However, if your needs change or you wish to optimize your initial choices, your solution doesn't have to be as drastic as a repartition—and reinstall—of the system.

man tuning has some practical advice for guesstimating the appropriate size of swap and your other partitions.

### Clearing /tmp

Unless you specifically chose otherwise when you partitioned your disk, the installer created a */tmp* filesystem for you:

```
% grep tmp /etc/fstab
/dev/ad0s1e    /tmp    ufs    rw    2    2

% df -h /tmp
Filesystem   Size   Used   Avail   Capacity   Mounted on
/dev/ad0s1e  252M   614K   231M    0%         /tmp
```

Here I searched */etc/fstab* for the */tmp* filesystem. This particular filesystem is 256 MB in size. Only a small portion contains temporary files.

The df (disk free) command will always show you a number lower than the actual partition size. This is because eight percent of the filesystem is reserved to prevent users from inadvertently overflowing a filesystem. See man tunefs for details.

It's always a good idea to clean out */tmp* periodically so it doesn't overflow with temporary files. Consider taking advantage of the built-in periodic script */etc/periodic/daily/110.clean-tmps* [Hack #20].

You can also clean out */tmp* when the system reboots by adding this line to */etc/rc.conf*:

```
clear_tmp_enable="YES"
```

## Moving /tmp to RAM

Another option is to move /tmp off of your hard disk and into RAM. This has the built-in advantage of automatically clearing the filesystem when you reboot, since the contents of RAM are volatile. It also offers a performance boost, since RAM access time is much faster than disk access time.

Before moving /tmp, ensure you have enough RAM to support your desired /tmp size. This command will show the amount of installed RAM:

```
% dmesg | grep memory
real memory  = 335462400 (319 MB)
avail memory = 320864256 (306 MB)
```

Also check that your kernel configuration file contains device md (or memory disk). The GENERIC kernel does; if you've customized your kernel, double-check that you still have md support:

```
% grep -w md /usr/src/sys/i386/conf/CUSTOM
device          md      # Memory "disks"
```

Changing the /tmp line in /etc/fstab as follows will mount a 64 MB /tmp in RAM:

```
md /tmp mfs rw,-s64m 2 0
```

Next, unmount /tmp (which is currently mounted on your hard drive) and remount it using the new entry in /etc/fstab:

```
# umount /tmp
# mount /tmp

# df -h /tmp
Filesystem     Size   Used  Avail Capacity  Mounted on
/dev/md0       63M    8.0K   58M    0%      /tmp
```

Notice that the filesystem is now md0, the first memory disk, instead of ad0s1e, a partition on the first IDE hard drive.

## Creating a Swap File on Disk

Swap is different than /tmp. It's not a storage area for temporary files; instead, it is an area where the filesystem *swaps* data between RAM and disk. A sufficient swap size can greatly increase the performance of your filesystem. Also, if your system contains multiple drives, this swapping process will be much more efficient if each drive has its own swap partition.

The initial install created a swap filesystem for you:

```
% grep swap /etc/fstab
/dev/ad0s1b    none    swap    sw    0    0
```

```
% swapinfo
Device         1K-blocks    Used    Avail Capacity  Type
/dev/ad0s1b       639688      68    639620       0%  Interleaved
```

Note that the swapinfo command displays the size of your swap files. If you prefer to see that output in MB, try the swapctl command with the -lh flags (which make the listing more human):

```
% swapctl -lh
Device:        1048576-blocks    Used:
/dev/ad0s1b               624       0
```

To add a swap area, first determine which area of disk space to use. For example, you may want to place a 128 MB swapfile on /usr. You'll first need to use dd to create this as a file full of null (or zero) bytes. Here I'll create a 128 MB swapfile as /usr/swap0:

```
# dd if=/dev/zero of=/usr/swap0 bs=1024k count=128
128+0 records in
128+0 records out
134217728 bytes transferred in 4.405036 secs (30469156 bytes/sec)
```

Next, change the permissions on this file. Remember, you don't want users storing data here; this file is for the filesystem:

```
# chmod 600 /usr/swap0
```

Since this is really a file on an existing filesystem, you can't mount your swapfile in /etc/fstab. However, you can tell the system to find it at boot time by adding this line to /etc/rc.conf:

```
swapfile="/usr/swap0"
```

To start using the swapfile now without having to reboot the system, use mdconfig:

```
# mdconfig -a -t vnode -f /usr/swap0 -u 1 && swapon /dev/md1
```

The -a flag attaches the memory disk. -t vnode marks that the type of swap is a file, not a filesystem. The -f flag sets the name of that file: /usr/swap0.

The unit number -u 1 must match the name of the memory disk /dev/md1. Since this system already has /tmp mounted on /dev/md0, I chose to mount swap on /dev/md1. && swapon tells the system to enable that swap device, but only if the mdconfig command succeeded.

swapctl should now show the new swap partition:

```
% swapctl -lh
Device:        1048576-blocks    Used:
/dev/ad0s1b               624       0
/dev/md1                  128       0
```

## Monitoring Swap Changes

Whenever you make changes to swap or are considering increasing swap, use systat to monitor how your swapfiles are being used in real time:

```
% systat -swap
```

The output will show the names of your swap areas and how much of each is currently in use. It will also include a visual indicating what percentage of swap contains data.

## OpenBSD Differences

You can make this hack work on OpenBSD, as long as you remember that the RAM disk device is rd and its configuration tool is rdconfig. Read the relevant manpages, and you'll be hacking away.

## See Also

- man tuning (practical advice on *tmp* and swap)
- man md
- man mdconfig
- man swapinfo
- man swapctl
- man systat
- The BSD Handbook entry on adding swap (*http://www.freebsd.org/doc/en_US.ISO8859-1/books/handbook/adding-swap-space.html*)

# HACK #22 Recreate a Directory Structure Using mtree

Prevent or recover from rm disasters.

Someday the unthinkable may happen. You're doing some routine maintenance and are distracted by a phone call or perhaps another employee's question. A moment later, you're faced with the awful realization that your fingers typed either a rm * or a rm -R in the wrong place, and now a portion of your system has evaporated into nothingness.

Painful thought, isn't it? Let's pause for a moment to catch our breath and examine a few ways to prevent such a scenario from happening in the first place.

Close your eyes and think back to when you were a fresh-faced newbie and were introduced to the omnipotent rm command. Return to the time when you actually read man rm and first discovered the -i switch. "What a great idea," you thought, "to be prompted for confirmation before irretrievably deleting a file from disk." However, you soon discovered that this switch can be a royal PITA. Face it, it's irritating to deal with the constant question of whether you're sure you want to remove a file when you just issued the command to remove that file.

## Necessary Interaction

Fortunately, there is a way to request confirmation only when you're about to do something as rash as rm *. Simply make a file called -i. Well, actually, it's not quite that simple. Your shell will complain if you try this:

```
% touch -i
touch: illegal option -- i
usage: touch [-acfhm] [-r file] [-t [[CC]Y]MMDDhhmm[.SS]] file ...
```

You see, to your shell, -i looks like the -i switch, which touch doesn't have. That's actually part of the magic. The reason why we want to make a file called -i in the first place is to fool your shell: when you type rm *, the shell will expand * into all of the files in the directory. One of those files will be named -i, and, voila, you've just given the interactive switch to rm.

So, how do we get past the shell to make this file? Use this command instead:

```
% touch ./-i
```

The ./ acts as a sort of separator instruction to the shell. To the left of the ./ go any options to the command touch; in this case, there are none. To the right of the ./ is the name of the file to touch in "this directory."

In order for this to be effective, you need to create a file called -i in every directory that you would like to protect from an inadvertent rm *.

An alternative method is to take advantage of the rmstar shell variable found in the tcsh shell. This method will always prompt for confirmation of a rm *, regardless of your current directory, as long as you always use tcsh. Since the default shell for the superuser is tcsh, add this line to */root/.cshrc*:

```
set rmstar
```

 This is also a good line to add to */usr/share/skel/dot.cshrc* [Hack #9].

If you want to take advantage of the protection immediately, force the shell to reread its configuration file:

```
# source /root/.cshrc
```

## Using mtree

Now you know how to protect yourself from rm *. Unfortunately, neither method will save you from a rm -R. If you do manage to blow away a portion of your directory structure, how do you fix the mess with a minimum of fuss, fanfare, and years of teasing from your coworkers? Sure, you can always restore from backup, but that means filling in a form in triplicate, carrying it with you as you walk to the other side of the building where backups are stored, and sheepishly handing it over to the clerk in charge of tape storage.

Fortunately for a hacker, there is always more than one way to skin a cat, or in this case, to save your skin. That directory structure had to be created in the first place, which means it can be recreated.

When you installed FreeBSD, it created a directory structure for you. The utility responsible for this feat is called mtree.

To see which directory structures were created with mtree:

```
% ls /etc/mtree/
./                  BSD.root.dist          BSD.x11-4.dist
../                 BSD.sendmail.dist      BSD.x11.dist
BSD.include.dist    BSD.usr.dist
BSD.local.dist      BSD.var.dist
```

Each of these files is in ASCII text, meaning you can read, and more interestingly, edit their contents. If you're a hacker, I know what you're thinking. Yes, you can edit a file to remove the directories you don't want and to add other directories that you do.

Let's start with a simpler example. Say you've managed to blow away */var*. To recreate it:

```
# mtree -deU -f /etc/mtree/BSD.var.dist -p /var
```

where:

-d

> Ignores everything except directory files.

-e

> Doesn't complain if there are extra files.

-U

> Recreates the original ownerships and permissions.

-f /etc/mtree/BSD.var.dist

> Specifies how to create the directory structure; this is an ASCII text file if you want to read up ahead of time on what exactly is going to happen.

```
-p /var
```
> Specifies where to create the directory structure; if you don't specify, it will be placed in the current directory.

When you run this command, the recreated files will be echoed to standard output so you can watch as they are created for you. A few seconds later, you can:

```
% ls /var
./              crash/          heimdal/        preserve/       yp/
../             cron/           lib/            run/
account/        db/             log/            rwho/
at/             empty/          mail/           spool/
backups/        games/          msgs/
```

That looks a lot better, but don't breathe that sigh of relief quite yet. You still have to recreate all of your log files. Yes, */var/log* is still glaringly empty. Remember, mtree creates a directory structure, not all of the files within that directory structure. If you have a directory structure containing thousands of files, you're better off grabbing your backup tape.

There is hope for */var/log*, though. Rather than racking your brain for the names of all of the missing log files, do this instead:

```
% more /etc/newsyslog.conf
# configuration file for newsyslog
# $FreeBSD: src/etc/newsyslog.conf,v 1.42 2002/09/21 12:07:35 markm Exp $
#
# Note: some sites will want to select more restrictive protections than the
# defaults.  In particular, it may be desirable to switch many of the 644
# entries to 640 or 600.  For example, some sites will consider the
# contents of maillog, messages, and lpd-errs to be confidential.  In the
# future, these defaults may change to more conservative ones.
#
# logfilename            [owner:group]    mode count size when   [ZJB]
[/pid_file] [sig_num]
/var/log/cron                             600  3     100  *      J
/var/log/amd.log                          644  7     100  *      J
/var/log/auth.log                         600  7     100  *      J
/var/log/kerberos.log                     600  7     100  *      J
/var/log/lpd-errs                         644  7     100  *      J
/var/log/xferlog                          600  7     100  *      J
/var/log/maillog                          640  7     *    @T00   J
/var/log/sendmail.st                      640  10    *    168    B
/var/log/messages                         644  5     100  *      J
/var/log/all.log                          600  7     *    @T00   J
/var/log/slip.log        root:network     640  3     100  *      J
/var/log/ppp.log         root:network     640  3     100  *      J
/var/log/security                         600  10    100  *      J
/var/log/wtmp                             644  3     *    @01T05  B
/var/log/daily.log                        640  7     *    @T00   J
```

```
/var/log/weekly.log              640   5     1     $W6D0  J
/var/log/monthly.log             640   12    *     $M1D0  J
/var/log/console.log             600   5     100   *      J
```

There you go, all of the default log names and their permissions. Simply touch the required files and adjust their permissions accordingly with chmod.

## Customizing mtree

Let's get a little fancier and hack the mtree hack. If you want to be able to create a homegrown directory structure, start by perusing the instructions in */usr/src/etc/mtree/README*.

The one rule to keep in mind is *don't use tabs*. Instead, use four spaces for indentation. Here is a simple example:

```
% more MY.test.dist
#home grown test directory structure
/set type=dir uname=test gname=test mode=0755
    .
    test1
    ..
      test2
          subdir2a
          ..
          subdir2b
              ..
              subsubdir2c    mode=01777
              ..
              ..
    ..
```

Note that you can specify different permissions on different parts of the directory structure.

Next, I'll apply this file to my current directory:

```
# mtree -deU -f MY.test.dist
```

and check out the results:

```
# ls -F
test1/
test2/
# ls -F test1
#
# ls -F test2
subdir2a/
subdir2b/
# ls -F test2/subdir2b
subsubdir2c/
```

As you can see, mtree can be a real timesaver if you need to create custom directory structures when you do installations. Simply take a few moments to create a file containing the directory structure and its permissions. You'll gain the added bonus of having a record of the required directory structure.

### See Also

- `man mtree`
- The Linux `mtree` port (*http://www.wie-auch-immer.de/mtree/*)

## Ghosting Systems
### #23
Use an open source alternative to commercial ghosting software.

Do you find yourself installing multiple systems, all containing the same operating system and applications? As an IT instructor, I'm constantly installing systems for my next class or trying to fix the ramifications of a mis-configuration from a previous class.

As any system administrator can attest to, *ghosting* or hard drive–cloning software can be a real godsend. Backups are one thing; they retain your data. However, an image is a true timesaver—it's a copy of the operating system itself, along with any installed software and all of your configurations and customizations.

I haven't always had the luxury of a commercial ghosting utility at hand. As you can well imagine, I've tried every homegrown and open source ghosting solution available. I started with various invocations of `dd`, `gzip`, `ssh`, and `dump`, but kept running across the same fundamental problem: it was easy enough to create an image, but inconvenient to deploy that image to a fresh hard drive. It was doable in the labs that used removable drives, but, other-wise, I had to open up a system, cable in the drive to be deployed, copy the image, and recable the drive into its own system.

Forget the wear and tear on the equipment; that solution wasn't working out to be much of a timesaver! What I really needed was a floppy that con-tained enough intelligence to go out on the network and retrieve and restore an image. I tried several open source applications and found that Ghost For Unix, g4u, best fit the bill.

### Creating the Ghost Disk

You're about two minutes away from creating a bootable g4u floppy. Simply download *g4u-1.12fs* from *http://theatomicmoose.ca/g4u/* and copy it to a floppy:

```
# cat g4u-1.12fs > /dev/fd0
```

Your only other requirement is a system with a drive capable of holding your images. It can be any operating system, as long as it has an installed FTP server. If it's a FreeBSD system, you can configure an FTP server through /stand/sysinstall. Choose Configure from the menu, then Networking. Use your spacebar to choose Anon FTP.

Choose Yes to the configuration message and accept the defaults by tabbing to OK. The welcome message is optional. Exit sysinstall once you're finished.

You'll then need to remove the remark (#) in front of the FTP line in /etc/ inetd.conf, so it looks like this:

```
ftp    stream    tcp    nowait    root    /usr/libexec/ftpd    ftpd -l
```

If inetd is already running, inform it of the configuration change using killall -1 inetd. Otherwise, start inetd by simply typing inetd. To ensure the service is running:

```
# sockstat | grep 21
root    inetd    22433    4    tcp4    *:21        *:*
```

In this listing, the local system is listening for requests on port 21, and there aren't any current connections listed in the remote address section (*:*).

g4u requires a username and a password before it will create or retrieve an image. The default account is install, but you can specify another user account when you use g4u. To create the install account on a FreeBSD FTP server:

```
# pw useradd install -m -s /bin/csh
```

> Make sure that the shell you give this user is listed in /etc/ shells or FTP authentication will fail.

Then, use passwd install to give this account a password you will remember.

## Creating an Image

Before you create an image, fully configure a test system. For example, in my security lab, I usually install the latest release of FreeBSD, add my customized /etc/motd and shell prompt, configure X, and install and configure the applications students will use during their labs.

It's a good idea to know ahead of time how large the hard drive is on the test system and how it has been partitioned. There are several ways to find out on a FreeBSD system, depending upon how good you are at math. One way is to go back into /stand/sysinstall and choose Configure then Fdisk. The first long line will give the size of the entire hard drive:

```
Disk name:      ad0
DISK Geometry:  19885 cyls/16 heads/63 sectors = 20044080 sectors (9787MB)
```

Press q to exit this screen. If you then type fdisk at the command line, you'll see the size of your partitions:

```
# fdisk
<snip>
The data for partition 1 is:
sysid 165 (0xa5), (FreeBSD/NetBSD/386BSD)
    start 63, size 4095441 (1999 Meg), flag 80 (active)
<snip>
The data for partition 2 is:
<UNUSED>
The data for partition 3 is:
<UNUSED>
The data for partition 4 is:
<UNUSED>
```

This particular system has a 9787 MB hard drive that has one 1999 MB partition containing FreeBSD.

> Whenever you're using any ghosting utility, create an image using the smallest hard drive size that you have available, but which is also large enough to hold your desired data. This will reduce the size of the image and prevent the problems associated with trying to restore an image to a smaller hard drive.

Once you're satisfied with your system, insert the floppy and reboot.

g4u will probe for hardware and configure the NIC using DHCP. Once it's finished, you'll be presented with this screen:

```
Welcome to g4u Harddisk Image Cloning V1.12!

* To upload disk-image to FTP, type:    uploaddisk serverIP [image] [disk]
* To upload partition to FTP, type:     uploadpart serverIP [image]
[disk+part]
* To install harddisk from FTP, type:   slurpdisk  serverIP [image] [disk]
* To install partition from FTP, type:  slurppart  serverIP [image]
[disk+part]
* To copy disks locally, type:          copydisk disk0 disk1

[disk] defaults to wd0 for first IDE disk, [disk+part] defaults to wd0d
for the whole first IDE disk. Use wd1 for second IDE disk, sd0 for first
SCSI disk, etc. Default image for slurpdisk is 'rwd0d.gz'. Run 'dmesg' to
see boot messages, 'disks' for recognized disks, 'parts <disk>' for list
of (BSD-type!) partitions on disk '<disk>" (wd0, ...), run any other
commands without args to see usage message.
```

Creating the image is as simple as invoking uploaddisk with the IP address of the FTP server. If you wish, include a useful name for the image; in this example, I'll call the image *securitylab.gz*:

```
# uploaddisk 192.168.2.95 securitylab.gz

( cat $tmpfile ; dd progress=1 if=/dev/rwd0d bs=1m | gzip -9 ) | ftp -n
tmpfile:
open 192.168.2.95
user install
bin
put - securitylab.gz
bye
5
4
3
2
1
working...
Connected to 192.168.2.95.
220 genisis FTP server (Version 6.00LS) ready.
331 Password required for install.
Password: type_password_here
230 User install logged in.
Remote system type is UNIX.
Using binary mode to transfer files.
200 Type set to I.
remote: securitylab.gz
227 Entering Passive Mode (192,168,2,95,192,1)
150 Opening BINARY mode data connection for 'securitylab.gz'.
..................
```

This will take a while. How long depends upon the size of the drive and the speed of your network. When it is finished, you'll see a summary:

```
9787+1 records in
9787+1 records out
10262568960 bytes transferred in 6033.533 secs (1700921 bytes/sec)
226 Transfer complete.
3936397936 bytes sent in 1:40:29 (637.58 KB/s)
221 Goodbye.
#
```

You can also check out the size of the image on the FTP server:

```
% du -h ~install/securitylab.gz
3.7G /home/install/securitylab.gz
```

That's not too bad. It took just over an hour and a half to compress that 9 GB drive to a 3.7 GB image. The g4u web site also has some hints for further reducing the size of the image or increasing the speed of the transfer.

If you use images on a regular basis, consider upgrading hubs or older switches to 100 MB switches. This can speed up your transfer rates significantly.

It's also possible to create an image of each particular filesystem, but I find it easier just to image a fairly small drive. This is because an image of the entire drive includes the master boot record (MBR) or the desired partitioning scheme.

## Deploying the Image

When you wish to install the image, use the floppy to boot the system to receive the image. Once you receive the prompt, specify the name of the image and the IP address of the FTP server:

```
# slurpdisk 192.168.2.95 securitylab.gz
```

It doesn't matter what was previously on that drive. Since the MBR is recreated, the new drive will just contain the imaged data. Once the deployment is finished, simply reboot the system without the floppy.

If the new drive is bigger than the image, you'll have free space left over on the drive that you can partition with a partitioning utility. Remember, don't try to deploy an image to a smaller drive!

## See Also

• The Ghost For Unix web site (*http://www.feyrer.de/g4u/*)

# CHAPTER THREE

# The Boot and Login Environments

## Hacks 24-34

When it comes to configuring systems, many users are reluctant to change the default boot process. Visions of unbootable systems, inaccessible data, and reinstalls dance in their heads. Yes, it is good to be mindful of such things as they instill the necessary attention to detail you'll need to use when making changes. However, once you've taken the necessary precautions, do take advantage of the hacks found in this chapter. Many of them will increase the security of your system.

This chapter also includes several password hacks. You'll learn how to create an effective password policy and monitor compliance to that policy. You'll find tools designed to assist you and your users in making good password choices. You'll also learn how to configure OTP, an excellent choice for when you're on the road and wish to access your network's resources securely.

## HACK #24  Customize the Default Boot Menu

Configure a splash screen.

You're not quite sure what you did to give the impression that you don't already have enough to do. Somehow, though, you were elected at the latest staff meeting to create a jazzy logo that will appear on every user's computer when they boot up in the morning.

While you may not be able to tell from first glance, the FreeBSD boot menu supports a surprising amount of customization. Let's start by examining your current menu to see which tools you have to work with.

### The Default Boot Menu

Your default boot menu will vary slightly depending upon your version of FreeBSD and whether you chose to install the boot menu when you installed the system. Let's start with the most vanilla boot prompt and work our way up from there. In this scenario, you'll see this message as your system boots:

```
Hit [Enter] to boot immediately, or any other key for command prompt.
Booting [/boot/kernel/kernel] in 10 seconds...
```

FreeBSD 5.1 introduced a quasi-graphical boot menu that includes a picture of Beastie and the following options:

```
Welcome to FreeBSD!

    1. Boot FreeBSD [default]
    2. Boot FreeBSD with ACPI disabled
    3. Boot FreeBSD in Safe Mode
    4. Boot FreeBSD in single user mode
    5. Boot FreeBSD with verbose logging
    6. Escape to loader prompt
    7. Reboot

        Select option, [Enter] for default
        or [Space] to pause timer   10
```

It is possible to get this menu without doing a full install of FreeBSD 5.1. If you're like me and use cvsup **[Hack #80]** and buildworld to keep up-to-date, you already have the necessary files but need to do a bit of editing to enable this boot menu. Even if you already have the boot menu, follow along because we're about to discover some of the logic behind the FreeBSD boot process. This will be excellent preparation for learning how to hack in your own customizations.

Let's start by taking a look at the directory that contains all of the boot information. Not surprisingly, it's called /boot:

```
# ls /boot -F
beastie.4th    cdboot*        kernel.old/    loader.rc      support.4th
boot           defaults/      loader*        mbr
boot0          device.hints   loader.4th     modules/
boot1          frames.4th     loader.conf    pxeboot
boot2          kernel/        loader.help    screen.4th
```

The actual file containing the new menu is *beastie.4th*. If your sources are out-of-date and you don't have this file, you can download it from *http://www.freebsd.org/cgi/cvsweb.cgi/src/sys/boot/forth/*. Be sure to download also the latest versions of *frames.4th* and *screen.4th*.

The /boot directory also contains the loader executable. This application is responsible for finishing the boot process. To do so, it depends on two configuration files, *loader.rc* and *loader.conf*. Let's take a peek at *loader.rc*:

```
# more loader.rc
\ Loader.rc
\ $FreeBSD: src/sys/boot/forth/loader.rc,v 1.2 1999/11/24 17:59:37 dcs Exp $
\
```

```
\ Includes additional commands
include /boot/loader.4th

\ Reads and processes loader.rc
start

\ Tests for password -- executes autoboot first if a password was defined
check-password

\ Unless set otherwise, autoboot is automatic at this point
```

We're aiming to be hackers here, not destroyers of systems.
A system that refuses to boot completely is not a very fun
system to work on. So, before mucking about with any of the
files in /boot, make sure you have your Emergency Repair Kit
ready (see "Create an Emergency Repair Kit" [Hack #71] and
"Use the FreeBSD Recovery Process" [Hack #72] for more
information). Also, take extra care in your editing and be
especially alert for typos before saving your changes.

Lines that begin with a backslash (\) are comments. Additionally, you can
add your own comments to lines containing a command by preceding your
comment with a # like this:

```
include /boot/loader.4th    # do NOT remove this line!
start                       # do NOT remove this line!
```

Those are good comments to add, as you want to make sure you *never*
remove those two lines—they are necessary to the workings of your boot
loader.

Before editing this file, make a backup copy first:

```
# cp loader.rc loader.rc.orig
```

Then, to tell your system to use *beastie.4th*, *carefully* add the following lines
to the bottom of */boot/loader.rc*.

```
\ Load in the boot menu
include /boot/beastie.4th

\ Do the normal initialization and startup
initialize drop

\ Start the boot menu
beastie-start
```

Triple-check for typos. When you're ready, make sure that you've saved all
of your work and check that no one else is connected to the system. In order
to test out the change, you're going to have to reboot:

```
# reboot
```

If all went well, you now have a Beastie menu to assist you in your bootup selection. If your boss had something else in mind other than the ultracool Beastie menu, let him know that have you not yet begun to customize!

## Configuring the Splash Screen

Remember the other file I mentioned, *loader.conf*? Well, you should actually have two files with that name. */boot/defaults/loader.conf* is the system default, and you should never edit *this* file. Instead, copy it over to */boot/loader.conf* and make your changes there. That way, not only do you have a chance to see what is available for customization, you also reduce your risk of typos. Each line in this file is commented and additional information can be gleaned from man loader.conf.

Locate the Splash screen configuration section so you can configure that company logo your boss keeps insisting on. This is what it looks like by default:

```
splash_bmp_load="NO"      # Set this to YES for bmp splash screen!
splash_pcx_load="NO"      # Set this to YES for pcx splash screen!
vesa_load="NO"            # Set this to YES to load the vesa module
bitmap_load="NO"          # Set this to YES if you want splash screen!
bitmap_name="splash.bmp"  # Set this to the name of the bmp or pcx file
bitmap_type="splash_image_data" # and place it on the module_path
```

Obviously, we'll have to change the NO in one of those splash lines to a YES. Which one depends upon your picture format. The two types of images that can be loaded are bmp or pcx. Depending upon the image you have to work with, change the appropriate NO to a YES.

If the image also happens to have eight or more bits of color, set vesa_load to YES. If you have no idea what type or size of picture you're dealing with, use the file command:

```
# file logo.bmp
logo.bmp:  PC bitmap data, Windows 3.x format, 408 x 167 x 8
```

This particular logo is a bitmap that is 408 × 167 pixels at 8 bits of color.

Don't forget to set the path of your bitmap file, and make sure you remember to copy that bitmap to the specified location:

```
bitmap_name="/boot/logo.bmp"
```

Leave this line as is:

```
bitmap_type="splash_image_data"    # and place it on the module_path
```

Finally, enable bitmap loading:

```
bitmap_load="YES"
```

When you're editing */boot/loader.conf*, keep in mind that you are asking the loader program to load various portions of the kernel. If you have changed your kernel configuration file [Hack #54], double-check that you haven't stripped your kernel of a function you're now asking loader to load. For example, before rebooting I should double-check that splash functionality is still in my kernel. Here, my new kernel configuration file is named *NEW*:

```
# grep splash /usr/src/sys/i386/conf/NEW
device          splash          # Splash screen and screen saver support
```

splash also requires device sc, so ensure that is your console type:

```
# grep -w sc /usr/src/sys/i386/conf/NEW
device    sc
```

The -w flag tells grep to treat sc as a word rather than attempt to match any word containing the letters sc.

Once you're happy with your changes, make sure no one is working on the system and then reboot. Your bitmap image should appear right after you make your choice at the Beastie menu. It will remain on the screen until you press a key. This behavior has the advantage of displaying your company logo instead of the usual startup messages. However, if you ever need to see those messages, simply press a key and your bitmap will disappear.

## The Terminal Screensaver

As it is set up now, the bitmap will also act as a terminal screensaver that will kick in after five minutes. To change the screensaver's timeout value, add this line to */etc/rc.conf*:

```
blanktime="60"
```

The number you choose represents the number of seconds. If you decide you don't like the screensaver functionality, add this line to */etc/rc.conf*:

```
saver="NO"
```

Those changes to */etc/rc.conf* won't take effect until you reboot the system. To enforce those settings immediately, at least until the next reboot, use the vidcontrol command:

```
# vidcontrol -t 60
```

```
# vidcontrol -t off
```

Regardless of your timeout setting, you can still launch the screensaver at will—say, when you leave your terminal—by pressing the Shift and Pause keys simultaneously. You may just want to do that before you go grab your boss to show him that jazzy company logo.

## See Also

- man `loader`
- man `splash`
- */usr/share/examples/bootforth/* (bootloader examples for the experienced hacker who understands Forth)
- The Boot section of the FreeBSD Handbook (*http://www.freebsd.org/doc/en_US.ISO8859-1/books/handbook/boot.html*)
- *http://www.baldwin.cx/splash* (splash images to get you started)

 **Protect the Boot Process**

**#25** Thwart unauthorized physical access to a system.

Creating a snazzy boot environment for users is one thing. However, when it comes to booting up servers, your mind automatically shifts gears to security mode. Your goal is to ensure that only a very precious few on very rare occasions ever see the boot process on a server. After all, the golden rule in security land is "physical access equals complete access."

Here's a prime example—consider recovering from an unknown or forgotten root password. Go into the server closet, reboot that system, and press a key to interrupt the boot process to change the password. A few moments later, the system continues to boot as normal. This can be a real lifesaver if an admin leaves without divulging the root password. However, consider the security implications of an unauthorized user gaining physical access to that server: instant root access!

### Limiting Unauthorized Reboots

Let's start by ensuring that regular users can't reboot the system either inadvertently or maliciously. By default, if a user presses Ctrl-Alt-Delete, the system will clean up and reboot. Typically this isn't an issue for servers, as most administration is done remotely and the server is safely locked away in a server closet. However, it can wreak havoc on workstations, especially if the user is used to working in a Windows environment and has become accustomed to pressing Ctrl-Alt-Delete. It's also worthwhile disabling on a server, as it ensures that a person has to first become the superuser in order to issue the reboot command.

 If you're logged into a remote machine over SSH and try Ctrl-Alt-Delete, it will affect your own machine, not the remote machine. reboot works well over the network, though.

Disabling this feature requires a kernel rebuild. (See "Strip the Kernel" [Hack #54] for detailed instructions.) Add one of these lines to your kernel configuration file, then rebuild and reinstall the kernel:

```
options SC_DISABLE_REBOOT  # if using syscons console driver

# or

options PCVT_CTRL_ALT_DEL  # if using pcvt console driver
```

You're probably thinking, "If I wanted to reboot a system and didn't know the superuser password, I'd simply hit the power button." Yup! That kernel option certainly won't prevent that, but a carefully thought out CMOS* configuration will decide if and how that system will reboot.

At a minimum, the CMOS configuration should allow only one boot device. This is to prevent an intruder from trying to boot an alternate kernel from a floppy, CD-ROM drive, or other supported boot device. Additionally, you should set a password for CMOS and record it in a safe place. This will prevent an intruder from simply changing the CMOS configuration. Keep in mind that this is not fail-proof; you are merely adding layers of inconvenience. A determined intruder can simply pop open the case and drain the CMOS battery, but that takes time and additional effort.

## Password Protecting Single-User Mode

All the magic happens when you interrupt the boot process. This is where you can change the superuser password without having to first know the superuser password. This is where you can unload the currently loaded kernel and replace it with another. This is where you can change any configuration file or binary without worrying about securelevels or system flags [Hack #56]. This is the reason why you lock up your servers, monitor access to the server room, and run them headless [Hack #26].

Fortunately, interrupting the boot process requires keyboard input, meaning the user needs physical access to the system. What happens when a malicious user does bypass your physical security measures, gaining physical access to the system? All she has to do is interrupt that boot process, and the system is hers to do as she wishes.

On a system without the graphical boot menu [Hack #24], pressing any key at the timer will pause the boot process. If the system has the graphical boot

---

* CMOS is battery-powered memory that holds system settings such as the time, date, and system configuration.

menu, pressing 6 to Escape to loader prompt will show the same timer. The timer option looks like this:

```
Hit [Enter] to boot immediately, or any other key for command prompt.
Booting [/boot/kernel/kernel] in 10 seconds...
```

If you press any key other than Enter, you'll receive this:

```
Type '?' for a list of commands, 'help' for more detailed help.
OK boot -s
```

Type boot -s to enter single-user mode. The kernel will appear to load normally, but, instead of processing the rc scripts, this prompt will appear:

```
Enter full pathname of shell or RETURN for /bin/sh:
#
```

Once you've finished making your desired changes, simply type exit. The system will continue to boot into multiuser mode.

Now, how do you prevent a user from doing that? Password protect single-user mode by editing /etc/ttys. Find this line:

```
# If console is marked "insecure", then init will ask for the root password
# when going to single-user mode.
console none            unknown off secure
```

Follow the comments and change the word secure to insecure. While that may seem nonintuitive, you're saying the system is considered to be insecure, thus you want a password. The next time a user attempts single-user mode, the kernel will load, but the user will receive this prompt instead:

```
Enter root password, or ^D to go multi-user
Password:
```

 You must not forget the root password if you password protect single-user mode!

## Password Protecting loader

Let's return to the timer section of the boot process. A user can type more than boot -s after interrupting the boot process. In fact, if you press ? at that OK prompt, you'll see that you can unload the current kernel, load another kernel, load and unload kernel modules, and view and change variables. You can muck about with just about every part of the boot process that would normally be controlled by the loader command.

Fortunately, you can also require a user to input a password before receiving that OK prompt. Set the password by adding this line to /boot/loader.conf:

```
password=12345
```

Of course, your password should be harder to guess than 12345. Now the boot process will prompt the user for a password. Without that password, you cannot enter single-user mode or load or unload kernel modules. You can still boot; you just cannot interrupt the boot process.

Also, if your CMOS supports it, you can require a password to boot the machine. However, this is often considered to be a bad thing, especially on a co-located web or mail server.

 The password in */boot/loader.conf* is in clear text. Although you can't encrypt this password, you can tighten up its permissions so only the superuser can read it:

```
# chmod 600 /boot/loader.conf
```

## See Also

* `man boot`
* `man loader`
* The Boot Process section of the FreeBSD Handbook (*http://www.freebsd. org/doc/en_US.ISO8859-1/books/handbook/boot-blocks.html*)
* Resetting the Root Password in the FreeBSD FAQ (*http://www.freebsd.org/ doc/en_US.ISO8859-1/books/faq/admin.html#FORGOT-ROOT-PW*)

## HACK #26 Run a Headless System

For those times when you want to run a system "headless."

Sometimes it is a simple matter of economy. Perhaps you've managed to scrounge up another system, but you don't have enough monitors, keyboards, or mice to go around. You also don't have the budget to purchase either those or a KVM switch. Sometimes it is a matter of security. Perhaps you're introducing a PC to a server closet and your physical security policy prevents server closet devices from being attached to monitors, keyboards, and mice.

Before you can run a system "headless," you need to have an alternative for accessing that system. Once you've removed input and output peripherals, your entry point into the system is now either through the network card or a serial port.

Going in through the network card is the easiest and is quite secure if you're using SSH. However, you should also consider a plan B. What if for some reason the system becomes inaccessible over the network? How do you get into the system then? Do you really want to gather up a spare monitor, keyboard, and mouse and carry them into the server closet?

A more attractive plan B may be to purchase a *null modem cable* as insurance. This is a crossed serial cable that is designed to go from one computer's serial port to another computer's serial port. This type of cable allows you to access a system without going through the network, which is a real lifesaver when the system isn't responding to the network. You can purchase this type of cable at any store that sells networking cables.

Your last consideration is whether the system BIOS will cooperate with your plan. Most newer BIOSes will. Many have a CMOS option that can be configured to disable "halt on errors." It's always a good idea to check out your available CMOS options before you start unplugging your peripherals.

## Preparing the System

I've just installed a new FreeBSD 5.1 system. Since I didn't have a null modem cable handy, I installed the old-fashioned way with the monitor and keyboard attached. If you do have a null modem cable and want to experiment with a headless install, follow the directions in the Handbook section referenced at the end of this hack.

Since I want to access the server over the network, I'll double-check that the NIC is properly configured and that sshd is running:

```
% ifconfig ed0
ed0: flags=8843<UP,BROADCAST,RUNNING,SIMPLEX,MULTICAST> mtu 1500
        inet 192.168.2.94 netmask 0xffffff00 broadcast 192.168.2.255
        ether 00:80:ad:79:4e:fd

% sockstat | grep sshd
root     sshd      389   4  tcp4   *:22                  *:*
```

The ifconfig command is used to verify an interface's configuration; in this example, the interface is ed0. The flags indicate that this interface is UP and RUNNING. The interface also has an IP address of 192.168.2.94.

The sockstat command is similar to the netstat command, but I find it provides a more intuitive output. For each open port it will display the owner of the service (root), the name of the service (sshd), the PID (389), the socket file descriptor (4), the transport (tcp4), the local address (*:22), and the foreign address (*.*).

The PID is useful if you need to send a signal to the process. The local address indicates which interfaces on this system (in this case, all, or *) are listening on which port number (22). There aren't any current sessions, as the foreign address section is *.*. If there were a current session, it would show the address of the other system followed by the socket number being used for the connection.

If for some reason sshd isn't running on your system, add the following line to */etc/rc.conf*:

```
sshd_enable="YES"
```

and double-check that it'll be available at bootup, like so:

```
# /etc/rc.d/sshd rcvar
#sshd
$sshd_enable=YES
```

Finally, typing sshd as the superuser should start the daemon. You can prove this by checking that it's listening with sockstat | grep sshd.

One last test—I'll make sure I can log into the system over the network:

```
% ssh 192.168.2.94
Password:
%
```

Now that I knew the system was accessible over the network, it was time for the moment of truth. After halting the system, I entered its CMOS configuration. I was a little bit worried because there weren't any options dealing with "halt errors." Undaunted, I left CMOS and powered off and unplugged the monitor, keyboard, and mouse. I then opened the case and physically removed the video card.

When I powered up, the system responded with a longer than ordinary beep. But after a few seconds, my hard drive light flashed and I could hear the operating system probing my devices and loading the drivers. After a moment or so, I tried to ssh into the system and was greeted with my password prompt! Assuming your BIOS is willing to cooperate, FreeBSD has no problem loading headless.

## If the Headless System Becomes Inaccessible

Should your system ever stop responding over the network, you'll be glad you purchased that null modem serial cable. Connect one end to the COM port of the headless system, and the other end to the COM port of another system that you can access either directly or over the network.

If that other system is running a Windows operating system, go to Start → Programs → Accessories → Communications → HyperTerminal (or open *hypertrm.exe*). You'll need to create a new connection, so choose a name and icon for it. Under Connect using:, choose the COM port to which the serial cable is attached.

You'll also have to configure the port properties for that COM port. Change the default 2400 bits per second to 9600. Finally, change hardware flow control to *none*. Press Enter, and you should be connected to the headless system. If you're not, double-check that you chose the correct COM port.

If you're attaching from a system running any variant of Unix, you can use either the cu or tip commands to connect via the serial cable.

To use cu, simply specify your COM port using the line switch -l and a speed of 9600 baud using the speed switch -s. For example, this syntax allows you to connect to COM2 or cuaa1:

```
# cu -l /dev/cuaa1 -s 9600
Connected.
```

You should now be able to see what is happening on your headless system. One of the advantages of connecting through a serial cable is that you can watch the boot process of the system. You can't do this over a network connection, because initializing the network occurs toward the end of a successful boot.

Before the network can be initialized, the kernel must successfully load into memory and the necessary hardware must be probed. If you're having problems booting a system, it is usually due to a missing or corrupt kernel or a hardware problem.

To disconnect from the cu session, type ~., then press the Enter key. You should receive a Disconnected. message and receive the prompt of the system you started from.

The tip utility doesn't use line or speed switches. It instead expects you to use one of the finger friendly shortcuts found at the end of the */etc/remote* file. Let's take a look at that section:

```
# tail /etc/remote
# Hardwired line
cuaa0b|cua0b:dv=/dev/cuaa0:br#2400:pa=none:
cuaa0c|cua0c:dv=/dev/cuaa0:br#9600:pa=none:

# Finger friendly shortcuts
com1:dv=/dev/cuaa0:br#9600:pa=none:
com2:dv=/dev/cuaa1:br#9600:pa=none:
com3:dv=/dev/cuaa2:br#9600:pa=none:
com4:dv=/dev/cuaa3:br#9600:pa=none:
```

Notice that there is an entry for each COM port. This means that to connect to COM2, you simply have to type:

```
# tip com2
connected
```

You need a little bit more coordination to disconnect, though. Hold down Shift while you press the ~ key. Keep your finger on Shift as you press the Ctrl key, then the letter D:

```
# ~^D
[EOT]
```

## See Also

- man tip
- man cu
- The Advanced Installation Guide in the FreeBSD Handbook (*http://www. freebsd.org/doc/en_US.ISO8859-1/books/handbook/install-advanced.html*)

**HACK**
**#27**
## Log a Headless Server Remotely

More on headless systems, but this time from the NetBSD perspective.

We've already seen in "Run a Headless System" **[Hack #26]** that it's important to have an alternative method for connecting to a headless server. It's also important to be able to receive a headless system's console messages. This hack will show how to configure both on a NetBSD system.

### Enabling a Serial Console

If you have another machine close to your headless server, it may be convenient to enable the serial console so that you can connect to it using a serial communication program. tip, included in the base system, and minicom, available through the packages collection, allow you to handle the server as if you were working on a real physical console.

To enable the serial console under NetBSD, simply tell the bootblocks to use the serial port as the console; they will configure the kernel on the fly to use it instead of the physical screen. You also need kernel support for the serial port device, which is included in the default GENERIC kernel.

However, changing the bootblocks configuration is a bit tricky because you need write permissions to the raw root device. As we are talking about a server, I assume the securelevel functionality is enabled; you *must* temporarily disable it by adding the options INSECURE line to your kernel. While in the kernel configuration file, double-check that it includes serial port support. Then, recompile your kernel.

Once you have access to the raw partition, update the bootblocks using the installboot utility. The process depends on the NetBSD version you are using.

If you are running 2.0 or higher, use the command shown next. Replace the *bootxx_ffsv1* file with the one that matches your root filesystem type; failure to do so will render your system unbootable.

```
# /usr/sbin/installboot -o console=com0 /dev/rwd0a /usr/mdec/bootxx_ffsv1
```

If you are running 1.6, use the following command instead:

```
# /usr/mdec/installboot /usr/mdec/biosboot_com0.sym /dev/rwd0a
```

When done, rebuild your kernel without the `options INSECURE` line to reenable securelevel. You can also remove the console drivers `wscons` and `pccons` to reduce the kernel size, though you must keep the serial port driver.

 As an alternative to building an insecure kernel, you can boot from a floppy disk to get direct access to the partition and update the bootblocks as described earlier. The floppies you used to install the system are fine.

## Setting Up the Logging Server

Even if you have configured a serial console, you won't always be connected to it. Therefore, it is very convenient to redirect important console messages to another machine that has a physical screen connected to it. `syslogd` lets you do this.

Start by allowing incoming `syslogd` connections on the machine that will be receiving log messages. (I call mine `logger.local`.) To do this, add the following lines to */etc/rc.conf*:

```
syslogd=YES
syslogd_flags=
```

The first option is not really needed, as `syslogd` is enabled by default. The second option overrides the secure (s) flag that otherwise would be passed to the daemon through */etc/defaults/rc.conf*. This flag tells `syslogd` not to listen on a UDP socket, and in this scenario we want to receive log messages over the network.

Then, restart the daemon:

```
# /etc/rc.d/syslogd restart
```

`logger.local` can now receive incoming `syslogd` connections from any host. If required, you can restrict this by using the built-in firewall, `ipf`.

## Setting Up the Headless System

You are ready to configure your headless server to send messages to the logger machine. As an example, we are going to redirect all messages that are actually sent to the serial console to `logger.local`.

Open *letc/syslog.conf* in your favorite editor. You will notice that the first uncommented line directs messages to */dev/console*. Append the @logger.local string to it, separated by a comma. After the changes, you should end up with something like:

```
*.err;kern.*;auth.notice;authpriv.none;mail.crit   /dev/console,@logger.local
```

Repeat for any other categories you want to redirect. When done, restart syslogd as shown earlier.

## Shutting Down the Server Using wsmoused

The next two sections of this hack require NetBSD 2.0 and above.

If you are running a headless system at home, you may want to shut it down at night. You could do this by sshing into the server and executing shutdown manually, but this requires a second system. However, since you have physical access to the headless system, you can simply use wsmoused, which will let you execute two or three commands from a mouse—one for each mouse button.

wsmoused's "action mode" lets you assign commands to mouse buttons. Here's a sample configuration file to shut down and reboot the machine, which you can copy to */etc/wsmoused.conf*:

```
device = /dev/wsmoused;
modes = action;

mode action {
        button_0_down = "shutdown -p now";
        button_2_down = "shutdown -r now";
}
```

Here I've mapped the left mouse button, 0, to the command that will halt the system and the right mouse button, 2, to the command that will reboot the system. (The middle mouse button is 1.) Since I don't plan on using this mouse for its usual input functions, such as copy and paste, this is a really convenient way to power off the system quickly and safely.

Enable the startup of wsmoused at boot time:

```
# echo "wsmoused=YES" >> /etc/rc.conf
```

If you have a dial-up connection, you could use a similar configuration to connect and disconnect the link.

## Beep on Halt

Some headless servers don't support APM or ACP, so the kernel can't power them down automatically. The i386 architecture has another option: beep on halt. It beeps the speaker multiple times when it is safe to power off the machine after a successful halt.

To enable this feature, add the following line to your kernel configuration file and rebuild it:

```
options BEEP_ONHALT
```

In case you do not like the default tone, you have several other options. Here they're shown with their default values:

```
options BEEP_ONHALT_COUNT=3   # Times to beep
options BEEP_ONHALT_PITCH=1500 # Default frequency (in Hz)
options BEEP_ONHALT_PERIOD=250 # Default duration (in msecs)
```

## See Also

- man 8 installboot
- man syslogd
- man wsmoused
- man shutdown

## Remove the Terminal Login Banner

### HACK #28

Give users the information you want them to receive when they log in.

The default login process on a FreeBSD system produces a fair bit of information. The terminal message before the login prompt clearly indicates that the machine is a FreeBSD system. After logging in, a user will receive a copyright message and a Message of the Day (or motd), both of which contain many references to FreeBSD.

This may or may not be a good thing, depending upon the security requirements of your network. Your organization may also require you to provide legal information regarding network access or perhaps a banner touting the benefits of your corporation. Fortunately, a few simple hacks are all that stand between the defaults and your network's particular requirements.

### Changing the Copyright Display

Let's start with the copyright information. That's this part of the default login process:

```
Copyright (c) 1992-2003 The FreeBSD Project.
Copyright (c) 1979, 1980, 1983, 1986, 1988, 1989, 1991, 1992, 1993, 1994
The Regents of the University of California. All rights reserved.
```

To prevent users from seeing this information, simply:

```
# touch /etc/COPYRIGHT
```

## Changing the Message of the Day

Technically, you could add your own information to */etc/COPYRIGHT* instead of leaving it as an empty file. However, it is common practice to put your information in */etc/motd* instead. The default */etc/motd* contains very useful information to the new user, but it does get rather old after a few hundred logins.

You can edit */etc/motd* to say whatever suits your purposes—anything from your favorite sci-fi excerpt to all the nasty things that will happen to someone if they continue to try to log into your system. Here's a very simple example:

```
# more /etc/motd
*********************************************************
*****            Authorized users only!!          *****
*********************************************************
```

You'll note that after you customize your motd, users will still see this text prepended to it:

```
FreeBSD 5.1-RELEASE (GENERIC) #0: Thu Jun 5 02:55:42 GMT 2003
```

If you don't want to advertise your operating system version and kernel information, you'll need one more hack. Add this line to */etc/rc.conf*:

```
update_motd="NO"
```

If you're using FreeBSD 5.x, you no longer have to reboot or go into single-user mode to initialize a change to */etc/rc.conf*. Instead, you can use one of the many scripts available in */etc/rc.d*. Let's see if there's a script that deals with motd:

```
# ls -F /etc/rc.d | grep motd
motd*
```

Excellent. Let's see what syntax that command expects:

```
# /etc/rc.d/motd
Usage: /etc/rc.d/motd [fast|force](start|stop|restart|rcvar)
```

Parameters in square brackets are optional, whereas parameters in parentheses are mandatory. Notice each option is separated by the *or* symbol (|), meaning you just pick one out of the list. In our case, we want to use the rcvar parameter. This will tell the motd script to reread its setting in */etc/rc.conf*:

```
# /etc/rc.d/motd rcvar
# motd
$update_motd=NO
```

OpenBSD users, read man motd and /etc/rc (search for motd) to understand how the system constructs the banner. Otherwise, it'll update when you least expect it!

## Changing the Login Prompt

Finally, let's change the text that first appears at the login prompt. This requires an edit to /etc/gettytab. This is a fairly important file as it controls access to your terminals, which is how users access the system. Before editing this file, always make a backup copy first:

```
# cp /etc/gettytab /etc/gettytab.orig
```

Next, open up /etc/gettytab in your favorite text editor and look for this line:

```
default:\
    :cb:ce:ck:lc:fd#1000:im=\r\n %s/%m (%h) (%t) \r\n\r\n:sp#1200:\
```

See the part in bold? That's the part you can replace with what you'd like the world to see when they receive their login prompt. Right now, they see this:

```
FreeBSD/i386 (host.domain.com) (ttyv1)
```

That's because that default string contains the variables in Table 3-1.

*Table 3-1. Login prompt variables*

| Variable | Meaning |
| --- | --- |
| %s | Operating system |
| %m | Architecture |
| %h | Hostname |
| %t | tty name |

You can very carefully change those characters to something else. For example, mine looks like this:

```
    :cb:ce:ck:lc:fd#1000:im=\r\n I'm a node in Cyberspace. Who are you? \
\r\n\r\n:sp#1200:\
```

Again, I've put my changes in bold for emphasis. Carefully double-check that you didn't lose any carriage return (\r) or newline (\n) characters along the way, then save your change.

## Testing Your Changes

It's important to test your change immediately *at a different terminal* to ensure you can still log into your system. This way, if you did make a typo that prevents logins, you can return to your previous terminal and fix it.

I'll press Alt-F4 to go to a terminal with a login prompt. I'll probably still see the old terminal message, so I'll log in, log out, then log in again:

```
login:
Password:
% exit
logout
I'm a node in cyberspace. Who are you?

login:
```

## See Also

- man motd
- man gettytab
- The /etc/rc.d section of the FreeBSD Handbook (http://www.freebsd.org/doc/en_US.ISO8859-1/books/handbook/configtuning-rcng.html)

### HACK #29  Protecting Passwords With Blowfish Hashes

Take these simple steps to thwart password crackers.

All good administrators know that passwords can be a weak link in the security chain. A malicious and determined user armed with a password cracker could conceivably guess enough of your network's passwords to access unauthorized resources.

### Protecting System Passwords in General

Fortunately, you can make a password cracker's life very difficult in several ways. First, educate your users to choose complex, hard-to-guess passwords that are meaningful enough for them to remember. This will thwart dictionary password crackers [Hack #30], which use lists of dictionary and easy-to-guess words.

Second, be aware of who has superuser privileges and who has the right to backup /etc. This directory contains the two password databases that are required to run a brute-force password cracker. As the name implies, this type of cracker will eventually guess every password in your password databases as it systematically tries every possible keyboard combination. Your best protection from this type of cracker is to prevent access to those password databases. This includes locking up your backup tapes and monitoring their access.

It is also a good idea to increase the amount of time it would take a brute-force cracker to crack a password database. FreeBSD, like most Unix systems, adds a magic bit of randomness—known as a *salt*—to the password when it is stored in the password database. The upshot is that a password cracker may have to try up to 4,096 different combinations for each and every password it tries to guess.

Using a strong algorithm to protect your passwords can also slow down a brute-force cracker. FreeBSD supports a hard-to-crack algorithm known as Blowfish. One of the first things I do after a FreeBSD install is to configure the password database to use Blowfish. While it is easier to do this before you create your users, it is still worth your while to implement it after you've created your user accounts.

## Protecting System Passwords with Blowfish

To use Blowfish, start by opening up */etc/login.conf* in your favorite editor. Look for this line:

```
:passwd_format=md5:\
```

Carefully edit it so it looks like this:

```
:passwd_format=blf:\
```

Check for typos before saving your change.

You may have noticed this comment when you modified */etc/login.conf*:

```
# Remember to rebuild the database after each change to this file:
#
#        cap_mkdb /etc/login.conf
#
```

Let's take a closer look at what we're being asked to do. According to that comment, *login.conf* is more than a configuration file, it is a database. Not only that, it is a *capability database*, a database that supports different capabilities. That is the reason behind the weird syntax within *login.conf*. Whenever you edit a capability database, you have to use the cap_mkdb command to integrate your changes within the database.

So, follow the directions:

```
# cap_mkdb /etc/login.conf
```

**Converting existing passwords.** If you have any existing users, you need to convert their passwords from MD5 to Blowfish. This is why it's a good idea to make the change before you create your users.

If you've already created users, it's back to the password database to find all of the active accounts. Inactive accounts—accounts that don't allow logins—have the * character instead of an encrypted password. Since we want to find all of the lines in the password database that *do not* contain an aster-isk, we need an inverted grep:

```
# grep -v '*' /etc/master.passwd
root:$1$ywXbyPT/$GC8tXN91c.lsKRpLZori61:0:0::0:0:Charlie &:/root:/bin/csh
dru:$1$GFm1nh6I$jh3v4I.QNf450ARgltZU5.:1008:0::0:0:User &:/home/dru:/bin/csh
```

Well, that worked, but we could make the output look much prettier:

```
# grep -v '*' /etc/master.passwd | cut -d ':' -f 1
root
dru
```

Let's pick apart that command syntax. grep -v creates a reverse filter. In effect, it says, "Show me the lines in */etc/master.passwd* that do *not* contain an *." Since those lines are long and contain much more than just the user-name, I piped the output to the cut utility to literally cut out the portions I don't need to see. Notice that the usernames are the very first thing in each line, and they are always followed by the : field separator. -d tells cut to consider the colon character, not the tab character, as the separator. -f 1 tells cut that I'm interested in the very first field of that line.

It looks like my particular system has two active accounts: root and dru. Notice in the original output the long sequence of characters that starts with $1 and ends with :. No, my users' passwords aren't quite that complex. Rather, you're seeing the password after it's been encrypted by the MD5 algorithm. That $1 means MD5. It'll be $2 after we switch to Blowfish encryption. (Be aware that you can't edit the file directly; the entire pass-word must be changed.)

I'll now change those two passwords:

```
# passwd dru
Changing local password for dru
New Password:
Retype New Password:

# passwd
Changing local password for root
New Password:
Retype New Password:
```

Note that the superuser can change any user's password by specifying the appropriate username. If you don't specify a name, you will instead change the root password.

When you're finished, repeat the original grep -v command and double-check that all of the encrypted passwords now start with $2.

Don't forget to tell your users that you have changed their passwords! Also caution them to use passwd to reset their password to a value known only to themselves.

**Forcing new passwords to use Blowfish.** Finally, configure the adduser utility to use Blowfish whenever you create a new user by editing */etc/auth.conf*. Look for this line:

```
# crypt_default = md5 des
```

and carefully change it to:

```
crypt_default = blf
```

Once you've saved your change, test it by creating a new user. The easiest way to do this is to type adduser and follow the prompts.

### See Also

- man passwd
- man adduser
- Blowfish information by Bruce Schneier, the creator of the algorithm, at *http://www.schneier.com/blowfish.html*

## Monitor Password Policy Compliance

HACK
#30

When to use a password cracker utility.

Now that you've tightened up your password policy to thwart password crackers, it's time to learn how to use a password cracker to monitor the effectiveness of that password policy.

You're probably thinking, "Hey, wait a minute! Isn't that some sort of oxymoron? An administrator cracking passwords?" Well, it depends upon the type of password cracker you plan on using.

A brute-force password cracker such as John the ripper or slurpie will systematically try every possible keyboard combination until it has cracked every password in the password database. Does an administrator need to know every password in his network? Definitely not.

However, an administrator does need to know if her users are choosing easy-to-guess passwords, especially if she's responsible for enforcing compliance to the network's password policy. A properly tweaked dictionary password cracker such as crack is an effective way to monitor that compliance.

It is important that a network's security policy indicates in writing who runs the dictionary cracker, when it is run, and how the results are handled. For example, if the password policy forces users to change their passwords every 30 days, the following day is an excellent time for the delegated administrator to run the cracker. Ideally, the cracker will return no results. This means all users chose a strong password. Should the cracker find some weak passwords, the security policy should clearly outline the procedure used to ensure that noncompliant users change their passwords to ones that are harder to guess.

## Installing and Using crack

Let's take a look at the most commonly used dictionary password cracker used on Unix systems, crack. You'll have to be the superuser for this entire hack because, fortunately, only the superuser has permission to crack the passwd database. crack should build on any Unix system; I'll demonstrate on FreeBSD:

```
# cd /usr/ports/security/crack
# make install clean
```

On my system, this creates the */usr/local/crack* directory which only the superuser can access. I need to cd into that directory in order to crack passwords. I'll start with a simple crack, then show you how to tweak this utility to serve your particular network.

```
# cd /usr/local/crack
# ./Crack -fmt bsd /etc/master.passwd
```

Crack is a Bourne shell script contained within this directory, so you'll have to run it with the command ./Crack. Use the -fmt switch to indicate the type of system; in my case, it is bsd. Finally, pass the path of the database containing the actual password hashes. On my system, this is the BSD shadow password database at */etc/master.passwd*. The command and output on my test system is:

```
# ./Crack -fmt bsd /etc/master.passwd
Crack 5.0a: The Password Cracker.
(c) Alec Muffett, 1991, 1992, 1993, 1994, 1995, 1996
System: FreeBSD genisis 5.1-RELEASE FreeBSD 5.1-RELEASE #7: \
     Tue Jul 29 09:54:11 EDT 2003 dru@genisis:/usr/obj/usr/src/sys/NEW i386
Home: /usr/local/crack
Invoked: ./Crack -fmt bsd /etc/master.passwd
Stamp: freebsd-5-i386_

Crack: making utilities in run/bin/freebsd-5-i386_
find . -name "*~" -print | xargs -n50 rm -f
( cd src; for dir in * ; do ( cd $dir ; make clean ) ; done )
rm -f dawglib.o debug.o rules.o stringlib.o *~
/bin/rm -f *.o tags core rpw destest des speed libdes.a .nfs* *.old \
    *.bak destest rpw des speed
```

```
rm -f *.o *~
`../../run/bin/freebsd-5-i386_/libc5.a' is up to date.
all made in util
Crack: The dictionaries seem up to date...
Crack: Sorting out and merging feedback, please be patient...
Crack: Merging password files...
Crack: Creating gecos-derived dictionaries
mkgecosd: making non-permuted words dictionary
mkgecosd: making permuted words dictionary
Crack: launching: cracker -kill run/Kgenisis.27478
Done
```

Note that the word Done is a bit of a misnomer. The gecos test is finished, but the actual dictionary attack has just begun and is quietly perking along in the background:

```
# ps -acux | grep cracker
root     14013 97.0  2.8  9448 8916  v5  R    10:32AM   4:17.68 cracker
```

**Monitoring the results.** Let's take a look at my current results, then analyze what is happening here:

```
# ./Reporter -quiet
---- passwords cracked as of Mon Nov 17 10:33:18 EST 2003 ----

1069099872:Guessed test [test]  User & [/etc/master.passwd /bin/csh]

---- done ----
```

The Reporter script, which is also found in the */usr/local/crack/* directory, sends the current results of the dictionary crack to standard output. I ran Reporter shortly after Crack had returned my prompt. Notice that it found that the password for the test account was test.

The reason why it found this password so quickly is because of the gecos field in */etc/master.passwd*. If you're familiar with man master.passwd, you know that the gecos field contains the user's full name, possibly followed by her extension, office phone number, and home phone number. This means that if a user uses any of those values for a password, her password can be cracked within a second or two.

The actual dictionary attack will take a while to run. How long will depend upon the speed of your CPU. However, you should expect crack to run for a good portion of a business day.

Why so long? If you've ever had the opportunity to run a dictionary cracker on a non-Unix system, you may have had your results back in well under an hour. The answer is that BSD password hashes are protected by a salt. In simple terms, the salt adds random characters to a user's password before the encryption algorithm creates the hash. Those are encrypted hashes, not the actual passwords, stored in */etc/master.passwd*. In order for the password cracker to bypass the salt, it has to try many variations of the same word before it can determine if that word is indeed the user's password.

You may want to write a script that will tell you when Crack is finished. Here is a simple example:

```
#!/bin/sh
#script to see if Crack is still running
#and to display current report

while ps -acux | grep -l "cracker" > /dev/null
do sleep 600
    echo "Still running. Here's the latest report:"
    cd /usr/local/crack && ./Reporter -quiet
done

echo "Execution is complete."
```

This script uses a simple while loop that runs every ten minutes (600 seconds). If cracker still shows up as a running process in the ps output, the ./Reporter -quiet script will run. Otherwise, the script ends, printing Execution is complete.

 If you'd like to receive a pop-up message showing the results of the script, see "Fun with X" [Hack #100].

**Cleanup.** Your security policy should also provide guidelines on how to clean up after crack finishes. The program stores several working files in the run subdirectory. They will all have a numeric extension:

```
# ls run
D.boot.69783     Egenisis.69783    bin/
Dgenisis.69783   Kgenisis.69783    dict/
```

When you remove those files, ensure you leave the subdirectories intact:

```
# cd run
# rm *.69783

# ls
bin/    dict/
```

## Customizing Password Dictionaries

Once you implement regular dictionary cracks, you'll find that after a few months, your users will start to consistently choose strong passwords. However, bear in mind that a dictionary cracker is only as good as its dictionaries.

The dictionaries that come with crack are a good start if your users speak English.

Let's start by seeing what dictionaries crack included:

```
# ls dict/1/
abbr.dwg                        list.dwg
assurnames.dwg                  male-names.dwg
asteroids.dwg                   movies.dwg
bad_pws.dat.dwg                 myths-legends.dwg
biology.dwg                     names.french.dwg
cartoon.dwg                     numbers.dwg
chars.dwg                       other-names.dwg
common-passwords.txt.dwg        paradise.lost.dwg
crl.words.dwg                   phrases.dwg
dosref.dwg                      places.dwg
family-names.dwg                python.dwg
famous.dwg                      roget.words.dwg
fast-names.dwg                  sf.dwg
female-names.dwg                sports.dwg
given-names.dwg                 trek.dwg
jargon.dwg                      unix.dict.dwg
junk.dwg                        yiddish.dwg
lcarrol.dwg
```

Notice that each built-in dictionary ends with a *dwg* extension. However, crack understands any dictionary or word list, even if it is compressed (i.e., its filename ends in either *.Z* or *.gz*).

If you use the file command on the *dwg* files, you'll find that each file is ASCII text. Mind you, the contents don't look like the average dictionary file:

```
# head abbr.dwg
#!xdawg
02bon2b
04sa7ya
0bbroyg
6bvgw
0egbdf
0fsasya
0gok
0oottfogvh
0roygbiv
```

Don't worry, those aren't the actual words. Instead, the numbers sort the words by likelihood. That is, the words don't appear in alphabetical order, but rather in the order they're likely to appear as a password. For example, the word password is much more likely to be used as a password than pasul.

If your users speak other languages, consider downloading additional dictionaries. Start at the Cerias site mentioned at the end of this hack. It's well worth your while to browse through the site's *dictionaries*, *local*, and *wordlists* subdirectories looking for dictionaries that suit your particular needs.

Let's go there now and check out the possible word lists:

```
# ftp ftp.cerias.purdue.edu
Connected to ftp.cerias.purdue.edu.
<snip long banner>
Name (ftp.cerias.purdue.edu:dru): anonymous
331 Guest login ok, send your complete e-mail address as password.
230 Logged in anonymously.
Remote system type is UNIX.
Using binary mode to transfer files.
ftp> cd pub/dict/wordlists
250 "/pub/dict/wordlists" is new cwd.
ftp> ls
227 Entering Passive Mode (128,10,252,10,169,45)
150 Data connection accepted from 1.2.3.4:49460; transfer starting.

-rw-rw-r--   1 ftpuser  ftpusers      1971 Jun 14  2000 README.gz
drwxrwxr-x   2 ftpuser  ftpusers      4096 Jun 14  2000 aussie
drwxrwxr-x   2 ftpuser  ftpusers      4096 Jun 14  2000 chinese
drwxrwxr-x   2 ftpuser  ftpusers      4096 Jun 14  2000 computer
drwxrwxr-x   2 ftpuser  ftpusers      4096 Jun 14  2000 danish
drwxrwxr-x   2 ftpuser  ftpusers      4096 Jun 14  2000 dictionaries
drwxrwxr-x   2 ftpuser  ftpusers      4096 Jun 14  2000 dutch
drwxrwxr-x   2 ftpuser  ftpusers      4096 Jun 14  2000 french
drwxrwxr-x   2 ftpuser  ftpusers      4096 Jun 14  2000 german
drwxrwxr-x   2 ftpuser  ftpusers      4096 Jun 14  2000 italian
drwxrwxr-x   2 ftpuser  ftpusers      4096 Jun 14  2000 japanese
drwxrwxr-x   2 ftpuser  ftpusers      4096 Jun 14  2000 literature
drwxrwxr-x   2 ftpuser  ftpusers      4096 Jun 14  2000 movieTV
drwxrwxr-x   2 ftpuser  ftpusers      4096 Jun 14  2000 names
drwxrwxr-x   2 ftpuser  ftpusers      4096 Jun 14  2000 norwegian
drwxrwxr-x   2 ftpuser  ftpusers      4096 Jun 14  2000 places
drwxrwxr-x   2 ftpuser  ftpusers      4096 Jun 14  2000 random
drwxrwxr-x   2 ftpuser  ftpusers      4096 Jun 14  2000 religion
drwxrwxr-x   2 ftpuser  ftpusers      4096 Jun 14  2000 science
drwxrwxr-x   2 ftpuser  ftpusers      4096 Jun 14  2000 spanish
drwxrwxr-x   2 ftpuser  ftpusers      4096 Jun 14  2000 swedish
drwxrwxr-x   2 ftpuser  ftpusers      4096 Jun 14  2000 yiddish
226 Listing completed.
```

My network includes several French-speaking users, so I'll take a look at the French word list:

```
ftp> cd french
250 "/pub/dict/wordlists/french" is new cwd.
ftp> ls
227 Entering Passive Mode (128,10,252,10,175,158)
150 Data connection accepted from 1.2.3.4:49530; transfer starting.
-rw-rw-r--   1 ftpuser  ftpusers    332537 Jun 14  2000 dico.gz
226 Listing completed.
```

Before downloading the word list, I'll use the local change directory command to ensure I'm downloading the file to the correct directory on my system:

```
ftp> lcd /usr/local/crack/dict/1
Local directory now /usr/local/crack/dict/1
ftp> get dico.gz
local: dico.gz remote: dico.gz
227 Entering Passive Mode (128,10,252,10,175,160)
150 Data connection accepted from 1.2.3.4:49531;
    transfer starting for dico.gz (332537 bytes).
226 Transfer completed.
332537 bytes received in 00:02 (142.24 KB/s)
ftp> bye
221 Goodbye.
```

Now that I have a new word list in */usr/local/crack/dict/1/*, I'll run the following command:

```
# cd /usr/local/crack
# make rmdict
# rm -rf run/dict
```

That's it. The next time I run ./Crack, I'll see the following message appended to the usual Crack message:

```
Crack: making dictionary groups, please be patient...
doing group 1...
doing group 2...
doing group 3...
mkdictgrps: uniq'ing dictionary groups...
group 1 and 2...
group 1 and 3...
group 2 and 3...
mkdictgrps: compressing dictionary groups...
Crack: Created new dictionaries...
Crack: Sorting out and merging feedback, please be patient...
Crack: Merging password files...
Crack: Creating gecos-derived dictionaries
mkgecosd: making non-permuted words dictionary
mkgecosd: making permuted words dictionary
Crack: launching: cracker -kill run/Kgenisis.55941
Done
```

This indicates that crack has found the new dictionary and is merging it into its logic.

## See Also

- The crack web site (*http://www.crypticide.org/users/alecm*)
- The Cerias FTP site containing cracker dictionaries (*ftp://ftp.cerias.purdue.edu/pub/dict/*)

## HACK #31    Create an Effective, Reusable Password Policy

Traditionally, it has been difficult for a Unix administrator to create and enforce a reusable password policy. Fortunately, PAM addresses this.

If you're using FreeBSD 5.0 or higher, your system has a PAM (Pluggable Authentication Modules) module specifically designed to assist in the creation and enforcement of a reusable password policy. If you're running a different version of BSD, see the end of this hack for other sources for this module.

### Introducing pam_passwdqc

Before using this module, spend some time reading man pam_passwdqc, as it thoroughly covers each option and its possible values. Any values contained within parentheses are defaults. As you read through this manpage, compare those defaults with your own network's security policy and make note of any values that will require a change.

This PAM module is fairly comprehensive, allowing you to enable many of the features expected in a password policy. Here's an overview of the configurable features:

- Minimum and maximum password lengths
- Force a mix of digits, lowercase, uppercase, symbols, and non-ASCII characters
- Minimum number of words in a passphrase
- Minimum number of characters to consider as a string (dictionary word)
- Ability to search for strings that are words written backwards, or are words written in a mix of upper- and lowercase
- Check new password for similar string contained within old password
- Suggest a randomly generated password
- Setting to either warn about weak passwords or enforce strong passwords
- How many times a user is allowed to retry setting a password if he fails to choose a strong password

### Enabling pam_passwdqc

Once you've finished perusing the manpage, you should have a list of values that you'll want to modify to reflect your network's security policy. Enabling pam_passwdqc is simply a matter of adding or editing a line so that it contains your customized options.

On FreeBSD 4.x, add that line to the password section of *letc/pam.conf*. On 5.x, edit instead the password section of *letc/pam.d/passwd*. Let's look at that file on a FreeBSD 5.1 system:

```
# more /etc/pam.d/passwd
# $FreeBSD: src/etc/pam.d/passwd,v 1.1 2002/04/15 03:01:31 des Exp $
# PAM configuration for the "passwd" service
# passwd(1) does not use the auth, account or session services.
# password
#password        requisite       pam_passwdqc.so          enforce=users
password         required        pam_unix.so       no_warn try_first_pass
```

Obviously, you'll need to uncomment the pam_passwdqc.so line to enable the module. Note the one included option, enforce=users, overrides the default setting of enforce=everyone.

Let's see what happens when I remove that remark and then try to use passwd as a regular user named test. Even though passwords aren't echoed to the terminal, I've shown in this output the passwords that I typed in:

```
% passwd
Changing local password for test
Old Password: test
You can now choose the new password or passphrase.
A valid password should be a mix of upper and lower case letters,
digits and other characters.  You can use an 8 character long
password with characters from at least 3 of these 4 classes, or
a 7 character long password containing characters from all the
classes.  Characters that form a common pattern are discarded by
the check.
A passphrase should be of at least 3 words, 12 to 40 characters
long and contain enough different characters.
Alternatively, if noone else can see your terminal now, you can
pick this as your password: "inward!smell:Milan".
```

As you can see, the password policy is provided, along with an example of a strong password that meets the policy requirements. Except for that one option, this particular policy includes the default settings mentioned in man pam_passwdqc.

```
Enter new password: test
Weak password: is the same as the old one.
Try again.
```

Here I tried to use the same password. Even worse, it doesn't meet any of the password policy's requirements. However, pam_passwdqc rejected the password, gave me another try, and patiently repeated the password policy along with another password suggestion:

```
You can now choose the new password or passphrase.
A valid password should be a mix of upper and lower case letters,
digits and other characters.  You can use an 8 character long
```

```
password with characters from at least 3 of these 4 classes, or
a 7 character long password containing characters from all the
classes.  Characters that form a common pattern are discarded by
the check.
A passphrase should be of at least 3 words, 12 to 40 characters
long and contain enough different characters.
Alternatively, if noone else can see your terminal now, you can
pick this as your password: "Sony,seed,cereal".
Enter new password: test1
Weak password: too short.
Try again.
```

Well, I tried another variation of my old password, but it is still too short. Here we go again:

```
You can now choose the new password or passphrase.
A valid password should be a mix of upper and lower case letters,
digits and other characters.  You can use an 8 character long
password with characters from at least 3 of these 4 classes, or
a 7 character long password containing characters from all the
classes.  Characters that form a common pattern are discarded by
the check.
A passphrase should be of at least 3 words, 12 to 40 characters
long and contain enough different characters.
Alternatively, if noone else can see your terminal now, you can
pick this as your password: "torso&lotus_burly".
Enter new password: test1234
Weak password: not enough different characters or classes for this length.
passwd: pam_chauthtok(): authentication token failure
%
```

Looks like the default retry count is three, as I was booted out after three tries. This time the password was long enough at eight characters, but only contained numbers and lowercase characters. The instructions clearly state that an eight-character password needs a mix of three different types of characters.

It's important to note that if the superuser changes a user's password, she will receive the same error messages if the password does not comply with the policy. However, after the error message, the superuser will be asked to retype that poor password and it will be accepted. Why? Because of that enforce=users option. If you remove that option, it will default back to enforce=everyone, which requires even the superuser to choose good passwords. The method you choose will depend upon the security requirements of your password policy.

## Adding Your Own Options

It's easy to change the default settings. Simply add your option to the end of the *pam_passwdqc.so* line. Then, test your change as a regular user to see what effect it has. You may want to create a test account for just this purpose.

For example, to force users to choose a password that is 10 characters long and a mix of uppercase letters, lowercase letters, numbers, and symbols, set N4 to 10 and disable the other options. Don't know what N4 is? Better reread that section of the manpage before changing this parameter.

```
password  requisite  pam_passwdqc.so \
min=disabled,disabled,disabled,disabled,10
```

Or, to force users to use the randomly picked password:

```
password          requisite          pam_passwdqc.so          random=42,only
```

Here I've used the default random value of 42. You can experiment by increasing that number until the randomly generated passwords meet your strength requirements. Settings much higher than 70 may produce error messages; this is what the end user will see:

```
System configuration error. Please contact your administrator.
passwd: pam_chauthtok(1): authentication token failure
```

The superuser will see:

```
This system is configured to use randomly generated passwords
only, but the attempt to generate a password has failed. This
could happen for a number of reasons: you could have requested
an impossible password length, or the access to kernel random
number pool could have failed.
passwd: pam_chauthtok(1): authentication token failure
```

That's your hint to choose a lower random number.

Once you've settled on a reasonable number, this is what users will see when they change their passwords:

```
% passwd
Changing local password for test
Old Password:

You can now choose the new password.
This system is configured to permit randomly generated passwords
only.  If noone else can see your terminal now, you can pick this
as your password: "lounge-mummy:cellar-dozen".  Otherwise, come back later.
Enter new password:
```

A user who hates that password can retry a few times to see other possibilities. Pressing Enter will generate another random password. Typing in anything other than the randomly generated password will cause the password change to fail.

## Additional Configuration

You may have noticed that pam_passwdqc does not control how often a user is forced to change his password. Set this instead in /etc/login.conf. Besides the actual expiry period, you can also change the amount of advance warning users will receive about an impending password change.

If you make any changes to /etc/login.conf, test your changes by immediately logging in at *another* terminal. A typo in this file can prevent logins to a system!

For example, adding these lines to the default:\ section will set a password expiry of 30 days, giving 5 days warning:

```
:warnpassword=5d:\
:passwordtime=30d:\
```

> If one of those entries happens to be the final entry in the default:\ section, don't include the trailing \ in that last entry.

Don't forget to rebuild the database once you've saved your changes:

```
# cap_mkdb /etc/login.conf
```

## See Also

- man pam_passwdqc
- man login.conf
- The Pluggable Password Checking web site (*http://www.openwall.com/passwdqc/README.shtml*)
- The PAM Essentials section of the FreeBSD Handbook (*http://www.freebsd.org/doc/en_US.ISO8859-1/articles/pam/index.html*)

# Automate Memorable Password Generation
#### #32    Make it easier for your users to choose good passwords.

It doesn't matter whether you're an administrator responsible for enforcing a password policy or an end user trying to comply with said policy. You're struggling against human nature when you ask users to choose—and remember—hard-to-guess passwords. Passwords that aren't random are easy to guess, and passwords that are too random tend to manifest themselves on sticky notes under users' keyboards or in their top drawers.

Wouldn't it be great if you could somehow offer users random but memorable password choices? There's a standard designed for just this purpose: APG, the Automated Password Generator.

## Installing and Using apg

If you're running FreeBSD, you can install apg from the ports collection:

```
# cd /usr/ports/security/apg
# make install clean
```

Once the port is installed, any user can run apg to generate a list of random, but pronounceable and memorable, passwords:

```
% apg -q -m 10 -x 10 -M NC -n 10
plerOcGot5 (pler-Oc-Got-FIVE)
fobEbpigh6 (fob-Eb-pigh-SIX)
Ekjigyerj7 (Ek-jig-yerj-SEVEN)
CaujIvOwk8 (Cauj-Iv-Owk-EIGHT)
yenViapag0 (yen-Viap-ag-ZERO)
Fiwioshev3 (Fi-wi-osh-ev-THREE)
Twomitvac4 (Twom-it-vac-FOUR)
varbidCyd2 (varb-id-Cyd-TWO)
KlepezHap0 (Klep-ez-Hap-ZERO)
Naccudhav8 (Nac-cud-hav-EIGHT)
```

Notice that each password comes with a pronunciation guide, since it's easier to remember something you can pronounce.

Also, note that syntax. We're definitely going to have to do something about all of those switches! But first, let's take a look at Table 3-2 and make sure we understand them.

*Table 3-2. apg switches*

| Option | Explanation |
| --- | --- |
| -q | Suppresses warnings (think quiet), which will be useful when we write a script |
| -m 10 | Sets the minimum password length to 10 characters |
| -x 10 | Sets the maximum password length to 10 characters |
| -M NC | Requires numerals and capitals |
| -n 10 | Generates 10 password choices |

While this utility is very handy, we can definitely hack in our own improvements. For starters, users aren't going to use a utility that requires a line's worth of switches. Second, we don't want to install this utility on every system in our network. Instead, let's work out a CGI script. That way users can access the script from their web browsers.

## Improving apg

First, let's sort out all of the switches we'll use in the script. We need something to add a punctuation character in the middle, or we won't meet Air Force password regulations. The simplest fix is to run apg twice with smaller password requirements, concatenating the results. The first run, without punctuation characters, looks like this:

```
% apg -q -m 4 -x 4 -M NC -E Ol -n 10
Dij6 (Dij-SIX)
Voj6 (Voj-SIX)
PamO (Pam-ZERO)
Dev9 (Dev-NINE)
Non6 (Non-SIX)
Eyd7 (Eyd-SEVEN)
Vig9 (Vig-NINE)
Not8 (Not-EIGHT)
Nog2 (Nog-TWO)
Von9 (Von-NINE)
```

Here I've reduced the minimum and maximum password length to four characters. I've also added the option -E Ol to exclude capital "oh" and small "ell" from passwords, because they're easily confused with the digits zero and one.

The second run includes the -S option, which makes the password generator use special characters:

```
% apg -q -m 4 -x 4 -M S -E Ol -n 10
orc) (orc-RIGHT_PARENTHESIS)
tof| (tof-VERTICAL_BAR)
fed^ (fed-CIRCUMFLEX)
gos@ (gos-AT_SIGN)
sig& (sig-AMPERSAND)
eif) (eif-RIGHT_PARENTHESIS)
eds{ (eds-LEFT_BRACE)
lek> (lek-GREATER_THAN)
tij: (tij-COLON)
rot] (rot-RIGHT_BRACKET)
```

Now for a CGI script to paste the results together. I've numbered each line of the script for explanation purposes. Don't include line numbers when you create your own script.

This script is written in the Korn shell, but can be modified for any shell. To run as is, install the Korn shell from */usr/ports/shells/ksh93*.

```
1  #!/bin/ksh
2  # run apg twice, concatenate results.
3  # exclude most special characters requiring shift key,
4  # capital "oh" (looks like zero),
5  # lowercase "ell" (looks like digit "one")

6  PATH=/bin:/usr/bin:/usr/local/bin; export PATH
7  umask 077
```

```
 8   a=/tmp/apg.$RANDOM
 9   b=/tmp/apg.$RANDOM

10   cat << EOF
11   Content-type: text/html

12   <!DOCTYPE html PUBLIC "-//IETF//DTD HTML 2.0//EN">
13   <html>
14     <head>
15       <title>Help generating a new password</title>
16     </head>

17     <body>
18       <h3>Help generating a new password</h3>

19       <blockquote>
20         These passwords should be reasonably safe.
21         Feel free to use one, or reload the page
22         for a new batch.</p>
23         <blockquote> <pre> <font size="+1">
24   EOF

25   apg -q -m 4 -x 4 -M NC -E '!@#$%^&*()\\' -n 10 > $a
26   apg -q -m 4 -x 4 -M S  -E '!@#$%^&*()\\' -n 10 > $b

27   # tr command is for bug workaround; apg is not supposed to
28   # include characters specified after -E option.

29   paste $a $b |
30       tr 'l' 'L' |
31       awk '
32         BEGIN {
33           printf "Password\tRough guess at pronunciation\n<hr />"
34         }
35         {
36           printf "%s%s\t%s %s\n", $1, $3, $2, $4
37         }'

38   cat << EOF
39         </font>
40         </pre>
41         </blockquote>
42       </blockquote>
43       <hr />
44     </body>
45   </html>
46   EOF

47   rm $a $b
48   exit 0
```

## Script Walkthrough

Line 6 sets the PATH to a known safe value. This lessens the possibility that an attacker can cause this program to execute a hazardous binary. Make sure apg is in this path.

Line 7 sets the umask so that only this user can read the temporary files to be generated later.

Lines 8 and 9 work because Korn shell scripts generate random numbers automatically. If /bin/ksh is not on your system, use mktemp to generate temporary files safely.

Lines 10–24 print the page header. I usually make a sample page and then run it through /usr/ports/www/tidy to get a decent DOCTYPE header and indentation.

Lines 25 and 26 issue apg commands to generate two separate files containing four-character passwords.

Lines 31–37 use an awk script to print the password plus its pronunciation. The BEGIN section prints only once, before any lines are read. The printf section expects lines with four fields: two pairs of password and pronunciation strings from the temporary files. The first and third fields are printed together to form the password, and the second and fourth fields are printed together to form the pronunciation guess.

Lines 38–46 finish the page.

Lines 47 and 48 clean up the temporary files.

## See Also

- man apg
- man mktemp
- The APG web site (*http://www.adel.nursat.kz/apg/*)
- FIPS 181, the APG Standard (*http://www.itl.nist.gov/fipspubs/fip181.htm*)

## Use One Time Passwords

**HACK #33**

Sometimes even a complex password may not meet your security needs.

If you are on the road and need to access the corporate network from a non-secure computer in a public place, the risk of password leakage increases. Could the person next to you be shoulder surfing, watching as you log into the network? Does the computer you're using have some sort of installed spyware or keystroke logger? Is there a packet sniffer running somewhere on the network? In such a situation, a One Time Password can be a real lifesaver.

## Configuring OPIE

FreeBSD comes with OPIE, or One-time Passwords In Everything, a type of software OTP system. It is easy to configure and doesn't require any additional hardware or proprietary software running on a server. Ideally, you should configure OPIE before leaving your secure network. For example, if you plan on traveling with your laptop, configure OPIE while connected to the office network. Make sure you are logged in as your regular user account to the particular system you'll need to access while on the road.

Start by adding yourself to the OPIE database, or /etc/opiekeys, using opiepasswd. If you intend to access your workstation while on the road, run this command while physically sitting at your workstation. Include the console switch (-c) to indicate you are at that station's console, so it is safe to enter a passphrase:

```
% opiepasswd -c
Adding dru:
Only use this method from the console; NEVER from remote. If you are using
telnet, xterm, or a dial-in, type ^C now or exit with no password.
Then run opiepasswd without the -c parameter.
Using MD5 to compute responses.
Enter new secret pass phrase:
Secret pass phrases must be between 10 and 127 characters long.
Enter new secret pass phrase:
Again new secret pass phrase:

ID dru OTP key is 499 dh0391
CHUG ROSA HIRE MALT DEBT EBEN
```

See that warning at the beginning? If you don't have physical access to the system's keyboard—say, you're logging into a server—make sure you use ssh to log into that system before running the opiepasswd -c command. Your only protection from another user using your one-time password is your passphrase, which is basically a long password that can include spaces. If that passphrase is transmitted over the network in clear text, you've defeated the whole purpose of this exercise.

Note that the passphrase isn't used as a password per se; instead, it is used to prove who added the account to the database and is therefore the rightful owner of the resulting response or one-time password. You'll need to issue that passphrase whenever you need to view your responses. Responses are always comprised of six uppercase nonsense words.

Next, verify that you are indeed in the OPIE database:

```
% opieinfo
498 dh0391
```

The opieinfo command displays the count (498) that will be used at the next login. It will also display the seed associated with that count (dh0391). In this example, it is expecting the response associated with 498, but I only know the response for 499. I'll need to use an OTP password calculator to figure out the correct response; that calculator is really just the opiekey command.

You could use the calculator from a separate terminal every time you login, but it is usually more convenient to print a list of responses and regenerate a new list whenever you run out of responses.

## Generating Responses

In order to use the calculator, you need to know three things:

- Your current counter
- Your seed
- Your secret passphrase

The challenge at the login prompt will display the current counter and seed. However, it is important that only you know your secret passphrase. Otherwise, anyone could calculate the response and log into your account.

To generate a list of responses, use the number switch (-n), followed by the number of desired responses and your current count and seed:

```
% opiekey -n 5 498 dh0391
Using the MD5 algorithm to compute response.
Reminder: Don't use opiekey from telnet or dial-in sessions.
Enter secret pass phrase:
494: MEAN ADD NEON CAIN LION LAUD
495: LYLE HOLD HIGH HOME ITEM MEL
496: WICK BALI MAY EGO INK TOOK
497: RENT ARM WARN ARC LICE DOME
498: LEAD JAG MUCH MADE NONE WRIT
```

You can either direct that output to a printer or record those responses by hand. Either way, store those responses in a safe place such as your wallet, as these are your next five one-time passwords. The next time you log in, use the response that matches the count at your login prompt:

```
login: dru
otp-md5 498 dh0391 ext
Password: (here I pressed Enter)
otp-md5 498 dh0391 ext
Password [echo on]: LEAD JAG MUCH MADE NONE WRIT
```

Once you configure OPIE on a 5.1 FreeBSD system, you will be required to respond to the OTP challenge whenever you log into that system. If you press Enter, you'll turn on echo so you can see the response as you type it.

Echo is usually a bad thing when logging in because anyone can see your password. However, with a one-time password, it doesn't matter if anyone sees that password, as it can't be reused. Also, unlike a reusable password, the response is not case-sensitive, so it doesn't matter if you type it in upper- or lowercase. Do take care, though, that no one sees your list of responses or your passphrase.

If your counter gets low—say, 10 or less—reset it before it hits 0. Use opiepasswd again, but this time specify a new count and a new seed. Here I'll use a count of 499 and a new seed of dh1357:

```
% opiepasswd -n 499 -s dh1357
Updating dru:
You need the response from an OTP generator.
Old secret pass phrase:
        otp-md5 8 dh0391 ext
        Response: loot omit safe eric jolt dark
New secret pass phrase:
        otp-md5 499 dh1357
        Response: hewn as dot mel mali mann
```

How long it will take you to cycle through your OTP passwords will depend upon how often you need to log in. You may find it convenient to generate a week's worth of responses at the beginning of each week.

It's also a good idea to consider how often to change your passphrase. You'll be prompted to when you reset your counter. For example, if you plan on changing your passphrase every 100 responses, specify -n 100 when you run opiepasswd. The passphrase itself needs to be memorable. Fortunately, it can contain spaces, so you can input, say, a line from a song or a poem.

## Choosing When to Use OTP

Starting with FreeBSD 5.1-RELEASE, users are forced to use OTP once they've added themselves to the OPIE database. It doesn't matter if the user logs into that system using a local keyboard or over the network using ssh. This behavior is controlled by PAM, or, to be more specific, the auth section of /etc/pam.d/login:

```
% more /etc/pam.d/login
#
# $FreeBSD: src/etc/pam.d/login,v 1.11 2002/05/08 00:33:02 des Exp $
#
# PAM configuration for the "login" service
#

# auth
auth    required    pam_nologin.so    no_warn
auth    sufficient  pam_self.so       no_warn
auth    sufficient  pam_opie.so       no_warn no_fake_prompts
```

```
auth     requisite     pam_opieaccess.so     no_warn
#auth    sufficient    pam_kerberosIV.so     no_warn try_first_pass
#auth    sufficient    pam_krb5.so           no_warn try_first_pass
#auth    sufficient    pam_ssh.so            no_warn try_first_pass
auth     required      pam_unix.so           no_warn try_first_pass nullok
snip
```

Perhaps you'd like users to have the option of using their regular password when logging in locally, but force them to use OTP when logging in over the network. To achieve that, add the allow_local option to the opieaccess line so it looks like this:

```
auth     requisite     pam_opieaccess.so     allow_local no_warn
```

This option lets the user type either her regular password or her OTP response *if* she's logging in locally. However, if she's logging in over the network, the login attempt will fail unless she gives the correct OTP response.

### See Also

- man opiepasswd
- man opieinfo
- man opiekey
- man pam_opie
- */usr/share/doc/en_US.ISO8859-1/articles/pam/article.html* (FreeBSD PAM documentation)

### HACK #34  Restrict Logins

Go beyond who can log in by configuring when and from where.

In this chapter, we've covered many methods of securing the boot and login environments. It's probably no surprise that you can further control who can log into your system and when: Unix systems contain many built-in mechanisms, allowing you to choose the most appropriate means and policy for your network.

Furthermore, the defaults may not always suit your needs. Do you really want users to be logged into multiple terminals when they can effectively do their work from one? For that matter, do you want any user, including non-employees, to try his hand at logging into your systems at any hour of the night and day? Here's how to tighten up some defaults.

### /etc/ttys

Since users log into terminals, a logical file to secure is the terminal configuration file, */etc/ttys*. We briefly saw this file in "Customize the Default Boot Menu" [Hack #24] when we password protected single-user mode.

This file is divided into three sections, one for each of the three types of terminals. Let's concern ourselves with the virtual terminals, ttyv, which are the terminals available for users physically seated at the system's keyboard.

```
# grep ttyv /etc/ttys
ttyv0    "/usr/libexec/getty Pc"        cons25    on  secure
ttyv1    "/usr/libexec/getty Pc"        cons25    on  secure
ttyv2    "/usr/libexec/getty Pc"        cons25    on  secure
ttyv3    "/usr/libexec/getty Pc"        cons25    on  secure
ttyv4    "/usr/libexec/getty Pc"        cons25    on  secure
ttyv5    "/usr/libexec/getty Pc"        cons25    on  secure
ttyv6    "/usr/libexec/getty Pc"        cons25    on  secure
ttyv7    "/usr/libexec/getty Pc"        cons25    on  secure
ttyv8    "/usr/X11R6/bin/xdm -nodaemon" xterm     off secure
```

The word on indicates that that terminal is available for logins. By default, the first eight terminals, ttyv0 through ttyv7, will accept logins. You've probably discovered this yourself by pressing Alt-F$x$, where $x$ is a number between 1 and 8. On a server system, you may need only one virtual terminal. Disable the other terminals by changing the word on to off.

If the system is running headless [Hack #26], disable all of the virtual terminals only *after* you've ensured that you have an alternate way to access the system.

The word secure means that the system is physically secure, implying that it's okay for a user to walk up to the keyboard and log in as root. Since it's *never* okay for a user to log in as root, you should disable that default. For whatever virtual terminals you've left on, either change the word secure to insecure or simply remove the word secure.

Be careful when editing /etc/ttys. A typo could prevent logins to your system. Always log in from another terminal before making changes, and test your changes immediately before logging out.

## /etc/login.access

Now let's see what can be done with /etc/login.access. At its most stringent, you can use this file to prevent all remote logins, meaning you can log in only if you are physically sitting at that system:

```
-:ALL:ALL EXCEPT LOCAL
```

Note the syntax that is used for each line in this file. The - means access denied. Its alter ego is +, which means access granted. The first ALL is a wildcard for all users. The second ALL is a wildcard for all locations. The EXCEPT LOCAL is the exception that allows just the local location.

You could modify that rule slightly to disallow remote and local root logins:

```
-:root:ALL
```

Take some care when modifying this file. Its syntax supports both user and group names, allowing you to specify exactly who is allowed to log into a system. This can be extremely useful in limiting access to a server system.

The syntax also supports IP addresses. This can also be useful in ensuring that only hosts in your network or a particular subnet can access certain systems. But, as in any security mechanism that relies on IP addresses, do keep in mind that IP addresses can be spoofed.

Finally, if you make changes to this file, *test your changes immediately*. If you restrict access to certain users, ensure those users can still log in. Further, try to log in as other users to ensure that they are actually being denied access.

## /etc/ssh/sshd_config

Think for a moment. Other than logins to virtual terminals, how else do your users log into systems? Most likely (and, hopefully) through ssh. You can control exactly who can ssh into a system by adding a line to the */etc/ssh/sshd_config* file of the system running the SSH daemon.

There are two ways you can control this. One is through AllowGroups. By default, all groups—meaning all users—can ssh into a system. The other way is through AllowUsers, where again, all users are allowed by default.

Suppose I want to allow only the users genisis, biko, and dru to ssh into a particular system. I could create a group called remote that contains those users:

```
# grep 100 /etc/group
#
# pw groupadd remote -g 100 -M genisis biko dru
```

In this example, I first double-checked that the group ID of 100 was not currently in use. I then created, with pw groupadd, the remote group with a GID of 100 (-g 100) and with those three members (-M genisis biko dru).

Now I can limit ssh access to just the members of that group:

```
# echo 'AllowGroups remote' >> /etc/ssh/sshd_config
```

Alternatively, I could have just added those three users directly:

```
# echo 'AllowUsers genisis biko dru' >> /etc/ssh/sshd_config
```

Any user who does not match either AllowGroups or AllowUsers will still receive a password prompt when attempting to connect to the SSH daemon. However, the connection attempt will fail with a permission denied message, even if the user provides a correct username and password. The SSH daemon will print a message regarding the failed attempt to its console, sending a copy to */var/log/messages* and emailing to root as part of the daily security run output.

To be even pickier, *if your users always log in from the same system*, you can do this:

```
AllowUsers genisis@10.0.0.2 biko@10.0.0.3 dru@10.0.0.4
```

However, don't be that picky if your users don't have static IPs!

Remember, if you make any changes to the SSH daemon's configuration file, you'll need to send a "signal one" to sshd to notify it of the changes:

```
# killall -1 sshd
```

After informing sshd of the changes, *immediately* use a ssh client to test your changes. For example, if I instead add the line Allowusers genisis biko dru, I'll find that user nastygirl is still able to connect. Why? The parameters in */etc/ssh/sshd_config* are *case-sensitive*. You don't want to find out six months later that anyone was allowed to connect when you thought you had restricted connections to certain users.

## /etc/login.conf

We've restricted who can log in and from where for both local and remote ssh logins, but we still haven't restricted *when* those users can log in. To do that, let's look at some other options that are available in our old friend */etc/login.conf* [Hack #30].

This file supports the options times.allow and times.deny. For example, to allow all users to log in between 9:00 AM and 5:00 PM every Monday through Friday, add this line to the default:\ section:

```
:times.allow=Mo-Fr0900-1700:\
```

Once you introduce the times.allow option, access will automatically be denied for the time period *not* listed.

The converse also works. That is, you can specify the denied times in times.deny, and all other times will be allowed.

Remember, whenever you make a change to */etc/login.conf*, rebuild the database with cap_mkdb /etc/login.conf and test your changes.

## See Also

- man ttys
- man login.access
- man sshd_config
- man login.conf

CHAPTER  FOUR
_____

# Backing Up
## Hacks 35-41




When I began gathering contributions for this book, it soon become obvious that there would be an entire chapter on backups. Not only do BSD users follow the mantra "backup, backup, backup," but every admin seems to have hacked his own solution to take advantage of the tools at hand and the environment that needs to be backed up.

If you're looking for tutorials on how to use dump and tar, you won't find them here. However, you will find nonobvious uses for their less well-known counterparts pax and cpio. I've also included a hack on backing up over ssh, to introduce the novice user to the art of combining tools over a secure network connection.

You'll also find scripts that fellow users have created to get the most out of their favorite backup utility. Finally, there are hacks that introduce some very useful open source third-party utilities.

### Back Up FreeBSD with SMBFS

A good backup can save the day when things go wrong. A bad—or missing—backup can ruin the whole week.

Regular backups are vital to good administration. You can perform backups with hardware as basic as a SCSI tape drive using 8mm tape cartridges or as advanced as an AIT tape library system using cartridges that can store up to 50 GB of compressed data. But what if you don't have the luxury of dedicated hardware for *each* server?

Since most networks are comprised of multiple systems, you can archive data from one server across the network to another. We'll back up a FreeBSD system using the tar and gzip archiving utilities and the smbutil and mount_smbfs commands to transport that data to network shares. These procedures were tested on FreeBSD 4.6-STABLE and 5.1-RELEASE.

_____

## Adding NETSMB Kernel Support

Since SMB is a network-aware filesystem, we need to build SMB support into the kernel. This means adding the proper options lines to the custom kernel configuration file. For information on building a custom kernel, see "Strip the Kernel" [Hack #54], the Building and Installing a Custom Kernel section (9.3) of the FreeBSD Handbook, and relevant information contained in */usr/src/sys/i386/conf*.

Add the following options under the makeoptions section:

```
options     NETSMB          # SMB/CIFS requester
options     NETSMBCRYPTO    # encrypted password support for SMB
options     LIBMCHAIN       # mbuf management library
options     LIBICONV
options     SMBFS
```

Once you've saved your changes, use the make buildkernel and make installkernel commands to build and install the new kernel.

## Establishing an SMB Connection with a Host System

The next step is to decide which system on the network to connect to. Obviously, the destination server needs to have an active share on the network, as well as enough disk space available to hold your archives. It will also need a valid user account with which you can log in. You'll probably also want to choose a system that's backed up regularly to removable media. I'll use a machine named smbserver1.

> The smbutil and mount_smbfs commands both come standard with the base install of FreeBSD. Their only requirements are the five kernel options listed in the preceding section.

Once you have chosen the proper host, make an SMB connection manually with the smbutil login command. This connection will remain active, allowing you to interact with the SMB server, until you issue the smbutil logout command. So, to log in:

```
# smbutil login //jwarner@smbserver1
Password:
Connected to smbserver1
```

And to log out:

```
# smbutil logout //jwarner@smbserver1
Password:
Connection unmarked as permanent and will
be closed when possible
```

## Mounting a Share

Once you're sure you can manually initiate a connection with the host system, create a mount point where you can mount the remote share. I'll create a mount point directory called /backup:

```
# mkdir /backup
```

Next, reestablish a connection with the host system and mount its share:

```
# smbutil login //jwarner@smbserver1
Password:
Connected to smbserver1

# mount_smbfs -N //jwarner@smbserver1/sharename /backup
```

Note that I used the -N switch to mount_smbfs to avoid having to supply a password a second time. If you prefer to be prompted for a password when mounting the share, simply omit the -N switch.

## Archiving and Compressing Data with tar and gzip

After connecting to the host server and mounting its network share, the next step is to back up and copy the necessary files. You can get as complicated as you like, but I'll create a simple shell script, *bkup*, inside the mounted share that compresses important files and directories.

This script will make compressed archives of the /boot, /etc, /home, and /usr/local/etc directories. Add to or edit this list as you see fit. At a minimum, I recommend including the /etc and /usr/local/etc directories, as they contain important configuration files. See man hier for a complete description of the FreeBSD directory structure.

```
#!/bin/sh
# script that backs up the following four directories:
tar cvvpzf boot.tar.gz /boot
tar cvvpzf etc.tar.gz  /etc
tar cvvpzf home.tar.gz /home
tar cvvpzf usr_local_etc.tar.gz /usr/local/etc
```

> This script is an example to get you started. There are many ways to use tar. Read man 1 tar carefully, and tailor the script to suit your needs.

Be sure to make this file executable:

```
# chmod 755 bkup
```

Run the script to create the archives:

```
# ./bkup
tar: Removing leading / from absolute path names in the archive.
drwxr-xr-x root/wheel        0 Jun 23 18:19 2002 boot/
drwxr-xr-x root/wheel        0 May 11 19:46 2002 boot/defaults/
-r--r--r-- root/wheel    10957 May 11 19:46 2002 boot/defaults/loader.conf
-r--r--r-- root/wheel      512 Jun 23 18:19 2002 boot/mbr
(snip)
```

After the script finishes running, you'll have *\*.tar.gz* files of the directories you chose to archive:

```
# ls | more
bkup
boot.tar.gz
etc.tar.gz
home.tar.gz
usr_local_etc.tar.gz
```

Once you've tested your shell script manually and are happy with your results, add it to the cron scheduler to run on scheduled days and times.

Remember, how you choose to implement your backups isn't important—backing up regularly is. Facing the problem of deleted or corrupted data isn't a matter of "if" but rather a matter of "when." This is why good backups are essential.

## Hacking the Hack

Things to consider when modifying the script to suit your own purposes:

- Add entries to automatically mount and unmount the share (see "Scan a Network of Windows Computers for Viruses" **[Hack #68]** for an example).
- Use your backup utility of choice. You're not limited to just tar!

## See Also

- man 1 smbutil
- man 8 mount_smbfs
- man 7 hier
- man 1 tar
- man 1 gzip
- The Building and Installing a Custom Kernel section of the FreeBSD Handbook (*http://www.freebsd.org/doc/en_US.ISO8859-1/books/handbook/kernelconfig-building.html*)

## Create Portable POSIX Archives

HACK #36

Create portable tar archives with pax.

Some POSIX operating systems ship with GNU tar as the default tar utility (NetBSD and QNX6, for example). This is problematic because the GNU tar format is not compatible with other vendors' tar implementations. GNU is an acronym for "GNU's not UNIX"—in this case, GNU's not POSIX either.

### GNU Versus POSIX tar

For filenames or paths longer than 100 characters, GNU uses its own @LongName tar format extension. Some vendors' tar utilities will choke on the GNU extensions. Here is what Solaris's archivers say about such an archive:

```
% pax -r < gnu-archive.tar
pax: ././@LongLink : Unknown filetype
% tar xf gnu-archive.tar
tar: directory checksum error
```

There definitely appears to be a disadvantage with the distribution of non-POSIX archives. A solution is to use pax to create your tar archives in the POSIX format. I'll also provide some tips about using pax's features to compensate for the loss of some parts of GNU tar's extended feature set.

### Replacing tar with pax

The NetBSD and QNX6 pax utility supports a tar interface and can also read the @LongName GNU tar format extension. You can use pax as your tar replacement, since it can read your existing GNU-format archives and can create POSIX archives for future backups. Here's how to make the quick conversion.

First, replace /usr/bin/tar. That is, rename GNU tar and save it in another directory, in case you ever need to restore GNU tar to its previous location:

```
# mv /usr/bin/tar /usr/local/bin/gtar
```

Next, create a symlink from pax to tar. This will allow the pax utility to emulate the tar interface if invoked with the tar name:

```
# ln -s /bin/pax /usr/bin/tar
```

Now when you use the tar utility, your archives will really be created by pax.

## Compress Archives Without Using Intermediate Files

Let's say you're on a system that doesn't have issues with tar. Why else would you consider using pax as your backup solution?

For one, you can use pax and pipelines to create compressed archives, *without* using intermediate files. Here's an example pipeline:

```
% find /home/kirk -name '*.[ch]' | pax -w | pgp -c
```

The pipeline's first stage uses find to generate the exact list of files to archive. When using tar, you will often create the file list using a subshell. Unfortunately, the subshell approach can be unreliable. For example, this user has so much source code that the complete file list does not fit on the command line:

```
% tar cf kirksrc.tar $(find /home/kirk -name '*.[ch]')
/bin/ksh: tar: Argument list too long
```

However, in more cases, the pipeline approach will work as expected.

During the second stage, pax reads the list of files from stdin and writes the archive to stdout. The pax found on all of the BSDs has built-in gzip support, so you can also compress the archive during this stage by adding the -z argument.

When creating archives, invoke pax without the -v (verbose) argument. This way, if there are any pax error messages, they won't get lost in the extra output.

The third stage compresses and/or encrypts the archive. An intermediate tar archive isn't required as the utility reads its data from the pipeline. This example uses pgp, the Pretty Good Privacy encryption system, which can be found in the ports collection.

## Attribute-Preserving Copies

POSIX provides two utilities for copying file hierarchies: cp -R and pax -rw. For regular users, cp -R is the common method. But for administrative use, pax -rw preserves more of the original file attributes, including hard-link counts and file access times. pax -rw also gives you a better copy of the original file hierarchy.

For an example, let's back up three executables. Note that egrep, fgrep, and grep are all hard links to the same executable.The link count is three, and all have the same inode number. ls -li displays the inode number in column 1 and the link count in column 3:

```
# ls -il /usr/bin/egrep /usr/bin/fgrep /usr/bin/grep
31888 -r-xr-xr-x  3 root  wheel  73784 Sep  8  2002 /usr/bin/egrep
```

```
31888 -r-xr-xr-x  3 root  wheel  73784 Sep  8  2002 /usr/bin/fgrep
31888 -r-xr-xr-x  3 root  wheel  73784 Sep  8  2002 /usr/bin/grep
```

With pax -rw, we will create one executable with the same date as the original:

```
# pax -rw /usr/bin/egrep /usr/bin/fgrep /usr/bin/grep /tmp/
# ls -il /tmp/usr/bin/
47 -r-xr-xr-x  3 root  wheel  73784 Sep  8  2002 egrep
47 -r-xr-xr-x  3 root  wheel  73784 Sep  8  2002 fgrep
47 -r-xr-xr-x  3 root  wheel  73784 Sep  8  2002 grep
```

Can we do the same thing using cp -R? Nope. Instead, we create three new files, each with a unique inode number, a link count of one, and a new date:

```
# rm /tmp/usr/bin/*
# cp -R /usr/bin/egrep /usr/bin/fgrep /usr/bin/grep /tmp/usr/bin/
# ls -il /tmp/usr/bin/
49 -r-xr-xr-x  1 root  wheel  73784 Dec 19 11:26 egrep
48 -r-xr-xr-x  1 root  wheel  73784 Dec 19 11:26 fgrep
47 -r-xr-xr-x  1 root  wheel  73784 Dec 19 11:26 grep
```

## Rooted Archives and the Substitution Argument

If you have ever used GNU tar and received this message:

```
tar: Removing leading `/' from absolute path names in the archive
```

then you were using a tar archive that was rooted, where the files all had absolute paths starting with the forward slash (/). It is not a good idea to clobber existing files unintentionally with foreign binaries, which is why the GNU tar utility automatically strips the leading / for you.

To be safe, you want your unarchiver to create files relative to your current working directory. Rooted archives try to violate this rule by creating files relative to the root of the filesystem, ignoring the current working directory. If that archive contained */etc/passwd*, unarchiving it could replace your current password file with a foreign copy. You may be surprised when you cannot log into your system anymore!

You can use the pax substitution argument to remove the leading /. This will ensure that the unarchived files will be created relative to your current working directory, instead of at the root of your filesystem:

```
# pax -A -r -s '-^/--' < rootedarchive.tar
```

Here, the -A argument requests that pax not strip the leading / automatically, as we want to do this ourselves. This argument is required only to avoid a bug in the NetBSD pax implementation that interferes with the -s argument. We also want pax to unarchive the file, so we pass the -r argument.

The -s argument specifies an ed-style substitution expression to be performed on the destination pathname. In this example, the leading / will be stripped from the destination paths. See man ed for more information.

If we used the traditional / delimiter, the substitution expression would be /^\///. (The second / isn't a delimiter, so it has to be escaped with a \.) You will find that / is the worst delimiter, because you have to escape all the slashes found in the paths. Fortunately, you can choose another delimiter. Pick one that isn't present in the paths, to minimize the number of escape characters you have to add. In the example, we used the - character as the delimiter, and therefore no escapes were required.

The substitution argument can be used to rename files for a beta software release, for example. Say you develop X11R6 software and have multiple development versions on your box:

```
/usr/X11R6.saturday
/usr/X11R6.working
/usr/X11R6.notworking
/usr/X11R6.released
```

and you want to install the /usr/X11R6.working directory as usr/X11R6 on the beta system:

```
# pax -A -w -s '-^/usr/X11R6.working-usr/X11R6-' /usr/X11R6.working \
  > /tmp/beta.tar
```

This time, the -s argument specifies a substitution expression that will replace the beginning of the path /usr/X11R6.working with usr/X11R6 in the archive.

## Useful Resources for Multiple Volume Archives

POSIX does not specify the format of multivolume archive headers, meaning that every archiver may use a different intervolume header format. If you have a lot of multivolume tar archives and plan to switch to a different tar implementation, you should test whether you can still recover your old multivolume archives.

This practice may have been more common when Minix/QNX4 users archived their 20 MB hard disks to a stack of floppy disks. Minix/QNX4 users had the vol utility to handle multiple volumes; instead of adding the multivolume functionality to the archiver itself, it was handled by a separate utility. You should be able to switch archiver implementations transparently because vol did the splitting, not the archiver.

The vol utility performs the following operations:

- At the end-of-media, prompts for the next volume
- Verifies the ordering of the volumes
- Concatenates the multiple volumes

Unfortunately, the vol utility isn't part of the NetBSD package collection. If you create a lot of multivolume archives, you may want to look into porting one of the following utilities:

vol

> Creates volume headers for tar; developed by Brian Yost and available at *http://groups.google.com/groups?selm=80%40mirror.UUCP&output=gplain*

multivol

> Provides multiple volume support; created by Marc Schaefer and available at *http://www.ibiblio.org/pub/Linux/system/backup/multivol-2.1.tar.bz2*

## See Also

- man pax
- NetBSD's PGP package (*ftp://ftp.NetBSD.org/pub/NetBSD/packages/pkgsrc/security/pgp2/README.html*)
- The GNU tar manpage on GNU tar and POSIX tar (*http://www.gnu.org/software/tar/manual/html_node/tar_117.html*)
- The pax -A bug report and fix (*http://www.NetBSD.org/cgi-bin/query-pr-single.pl?number=23776*)

## HACK #37 Interactive Copy

When cp alone doesn't quite meet your copy needs.

The cp command is easy to use, but it does have its limitations. For example, have you ever needed to copy a batch of files with the same name? If you're not careful, they'll happily overwrite each other.

### Finding Your Source Files

I recently had the urge to find all of the scripts on my system that created a menu. I knew that several ports used scripts named configure and that some of those scripts used dialog to provide a menu selection.

It was easy enough to find those scripts using find:

```
% find /usr/ports -name configure -exec grep -l "dialog" /dev/null { } \;
/usr/ports/audio/mbrolavox/scripts/configure
/usr/ports/devel/kdesdk3/work/kdesdk-3.2.0/configure
/usr/ports/emulators/vmware2/scripts/configure
(snip)
```

This command asks find to start in */usr/ports*, looking for files -named configure. For each found file, it should search for the word dialog using -exec grep. The -l flag tells grep to list only the names of the matching files, without including the lines that match the expression. You may recognize the /dev/null { } \; from "Find Things" [Hack #13].

Normally, I could tell cp to use those found files as the source and to copy them to the specified destination. This is done by enclosing the find command within a set of backticks (`), located at the far top left of your keyboard. Note what happens, though:

```
% mkdir ~/scripts
% cd ~/scripts
% cp `find /usr/ports -name configure -exec grep -l "dialog" \
    /dev/null {} \;` .
% ls ~/scripts
configure
```

Although each file that I copied had a different pathname, the filename itself was configure. Since each copied file overwrote the previous one, I ended up with one remaining file.

## Renaming a Batch of Source Files

What's needed is to rename those source files as they are copied to the destination. One approach is to replace the slash (/) in the original file's pathname with a different character, resulting in a unique filename that still reflects the source of that file.

As we saw in "Manipulate Files with sed" [Hack #15], sed is designed to do such replacements. Here's an approach:

```
% pwd
/usr/home/dru/scripts
% find /usr/ports -name configure -exec grep -l "dialog" /dev/null {} \; \
    -exec sh -c 'cp {} `echo {} | sed s:/:=:g`' \;

% ls
=usr=ports=audio=mbrolavox=scripts=configure
=usr=ports=devel=kdesdk3=work=kdesdk-3.2.0=configure
=usr=ports=emulators=vmware2=scripts=configure
(snip)
```

This invocation of find starts off the same as my original search. It then adds a second -exec, which passes an argument -c as input to the sh shell. The shell will cp the source files (specified by { }), but only after sed has replaced each slash in the pathname with an equals sign (=). Note that I changed the sed delimiter from the default slash to the colon (:) so I didn't have to escape my / string. You don't have to use = as the new character; choose whatever suits your purposes.

awk can also perform this renaming feat. The following command is more or less equivalent to the previous command:

```
% find /usr/ports -name configure -exec grep -l "dialog" /dev/null {} \; \
    | awk '{dst=$0;gsub("/","=",dst); print "cp",$0,dst}' | sh
```

## Renaming Files Interactively

Depending upon how many files you plan on copying over and how picky you are about their destination names, you may prefer to do an interactive copy.

Despite its name, cp's interactive switch (-i) will fail miserably in my scenario:

```
% cp -i `find /usr/ports -name configure -exec grep -l "dialog" \
    /dev/null {} \;` .
overwrite ./configure? (y/n [n]) n
not overwritten
overwrite ./configure? (y/n [n])
(snip)
```

Since each file is still named configure, my only choices are either to overwrite the previous file or to not copy over the new file. However, both cpio and pax are capable of interactive copies. Let's start with cpio:

```
% find /usr/ports -name configure -exec grep -l "dialog" /dev/null {} \; \
    | cpio -o > ~/scripts/test.cpio && cpio -ir < ~/scripts/test.cpio
```

Here I've piped my find command to cpio. Normally, I would invoke cpio once in copy-pass mode. Unfortunately, that mode doesn't support -r, the interactive rename switch. So, I directed cpio to send its output (-o >) to an archive named ~/scripts/test.cpio. Instead of piping that archive, I used && to delay the next cpio operation until the previous one finishes. I then used -ir to perform an interactive copy in that archive so I could type in the name of each destination file.

Here are the results:

```
cpio: /usr/ports/audio/mbrolavox/scripts/configure: truncating inode number
cpio: /usr/ports/devel/kdesdk3/work/kdesdk-3.2.0/configure: truncating
inode number
cpio: /usr/ports/emulators/vmware2/scripts/configure: truncating inode
number
(snip other archive messages)
5136 blocks
rename /usr/ports/audio/mbrolavox/scripts/configure -> mbrolavox.configure
rename /usr/ports/devel/kdesdk3/work/kdesdk-3.2.0/configure ->
kdesdk3.configure
rename /usr/ports/emulators/vmware2/scripts/configure -> vmware2.configure
(snip remaining rename operations)
5136 blocks
```

After creating the archive, cpio showed me the source name so I could rename the destination file. While requiring interaction on my part, it does let me fine-tune exactly what I'd like to call each script. I must admit that my names are much nicer than those containing all of the equals signs.

pax is even more efficient. In the preceding command, the first cpio has to wait until find completes, and the second cpio has to wait until the first cpio finishes. Compare that to this command:

```
% find /usr/ports -name configure -exec grep -l "dialog" /dev/null {} \; \
  | pax -rwi .
```

Here, I can pipe the results of find directly to pax, and pax has very user-friendly switches. In this command, I asked to read and write interactively to the current directory. There's no temporary archive required, and everything happens at once. Even better, pax starts working on the interaction before find finishes. Here's what it looks like:

```
ATTENTION: pax interactive file rename operation.
-rwxr-xr-x Nov 11 07:53 /usr/ports/audio/mbrolavox/scripts/configure
Input new name, or a "." to keep the old name, or a "return" to skip
this file.
Input > mbrovalox.configure
Processing continues, name changed to: mbrovalox.configure
```

This repeats for each and every file that matched the find results.

### See Also

- man cp
- man cpio
- man pax

## Secure Backups Over a Network

**Why bother with installing and configuring a new network service for backups if you only need directory snapshots for now? If you already have ssh running on your network, you're most of the way there.**

When it comes to backups, Unix systems are extremely flexible. For starters, they come with built-in utilities that are just waiting for an administrator's imagination to combine their talents into a customized backup solution. Add that to one of Unix's greatest strengths: its ability to see everything as a file. This means you don't even need backup hardware. You have the ability to send your backup to a file, to a media, to another server, or to whatever is available.

As with any customized solution, your success depends upon a little forethought. In this scenario, I don't have any backup hardware, but I do have a network with a 100 Mbps switch and a system with a large hard drive capable of holding backups.

## Initial Preparation

On the system with that large hard drive, I have sshd running. (An alternative to consider is the scponly shell; see "Restrict an SSH server" [Hack #63]). I've also created a user and a group called rembackup:

```
# pw groupadd rembackup
# pw useradd rembackup -g rembackup -m -s /bin/csh
# passwd rembackup
Changing local password for rembackup
New Password:
Retype New Password:
#
```

If you're new to the pw command, the -g switch puts the user in the specified group (which must already exist), the -m switch creates the user's home directory, and the -s switch sets the default shell. (There's really no good mnemonic; perhaps no one remembers what, if anything, pw stands for.)

Next, from the system I plan on backing up, I'll ensure that I can ssh in as the user rembackup. In this scenario, the system with the large hard drive has an IP address of 10.0.0.1:

```
% sshd -l rembackup 10.0.0.1
The authenticity of host '10.0.0.1 (10.0.0.1)' can't be established.
DSA key fingerprint is e2:75:a7:85:46:04:71:51:db:a8:9e:83:b1:5c:7a:2c.
Are you sure you want to continue connecting (yes/no)? yes
Warning: Permanently added '192.168.2.93' (DSA) to the list of known hosts.
Password:
%
% exit
logout
Connection to 10.0.0.1 closed.
```

Excellent. Since I can log in as rembackup, it looks like both systems are ready for a test backup.

## The Backup

I'll start by testing my command at a command line. Once I'm happy with the results, I'll create a backup script to automate the process.

```
# tar czvf - /usr/home | ssh rembackup@10.0.0.1 "cat > genisis_usr_home.tgz"
usr/home/
usr/home/dru/
usr/home/dru/.cshrc
usr/home/dru/mail/
usr/home/mail/sent-mail
Password:
```

This tar command creates (c) a compressed (z) backup to a file (f) while showing the results verbosely (v). The minus character (-) represents the specified file, which in this case is stdout. This allows me to pipe stdout to the ssh command. I've provided */usr/home*, which contains all of my users' home directories, as the hierarchy to back up.

The results of that backup are then piped (|) to ssh, which will send that output (via cat) to a compressed file called *genisis_usr_home.tgz* in the rembackup user's home directory. Since that directory holds the backups for my network, I chose a filename that indicates the name of the host, genisis, and the contents of the backup itself.

**Automating the backup.** Now that I can securely back up my users' home directories, I can create a script. It can start out as simple as this:

```
# more /root/bin/backup
#!/bin/sh
# script to backup /usr/home to backup server
tar czvf - /usr/home | ssh rembackup@10.0.0.1 "cat > genisis_usr_home.tgz"
```

However, whenever I run that script, I'll overwrite the previous backup. If that's not my intention, I can include the date as part of the backup name:

```
tar czvf - /usr/home | ssh rembackup@10.0.0.1 "cat > \
    genisis_usr_home.`date +%d.%m.%y`.tgz"
```

Notice I inserted the date command into the filename using backticks. Now the backup file will include the day, month, and year separated by dots, resulting in a filename like *genisis_usr_home.21.12.03.tgz*.

Once you're happy with your results, your script is an excellent candidate for a cron job.

### See Also

* man tar
* man ssh
* man pw

## HACK #39 Automate Remote Backups
Make remote backups automatic and effortless.

One day, the IDE controller on my web server died, leaving the files on my hard disk hopelessly corrupted. I faced what I had known in the back of my mind all along: I had not been making regular remote backups of my server, and the local backups were of no use to me now that the drive was corrupted.

The reason for this, of course, is that doing remote backups wasn't automatic and effortless. Admittedly, this was no one's fault but my own, but my frustration was sufficient enough that I decided to write a tool that would make automated remote snapshots so easy that I wouldn't ever have to worry about it again. Enter `rsnapshot`.

## Installing and Configuring rsnapshot

Installation on FreeBSD is a simple matter of:

```
# cd /usr/ports/sysutils/rsnapshot
# make install
```

I didn't include the `clean` target here, as I'd like to keep the work subdirectory, which includes some useful scripts.

> If you're not using FreeBSD, see the original HOWTO at the project web site for detailed instructions on installing from source.

The install process neither creates nor installs the config file. This means that there is absolutely no possibility of accidentally overwriting a previously existing config file during an upgrade. Instead, copy the example configuration file and make changes to the copy:

```
# cp /usr/local/etc/rsnapshot.conf.default /usr/local/etc/rsnapshot.conf
```

The *rsnapshot.conf* config file is well commented, and much of it should be fairly self-explanatory. For a full reference of all the various options, please consult `man rsnapshot`.

rsnapshot uses the */.snapshots/* directory to hold the filesystem snapshots. This is referred to as the *snapshot root*. This must point to a filesystem where you have lots of free disk space.

> Note that fields are separated by tabs, not spaces. This makes it easier to specify file paths with spaces in them.

**Specifying backup intervals.** rsnapshot has no idea how often you want to take snapshots. In order to specify how much data to save, you need to tell rsnapshot which intervals to keep, and how many of each.

By default, a snapshot will occur every four hours, or six times a day (these are the hourly intervals). It will also keep a second set of snapshots, taken once a day and stored for a week (or seven days):

```
interval    hourly  6
interval    daily   7
```

Note that the hourly interval is specified first. This is very important, as the first interval line is assumed to be the smallest unit of time, with each additional line getting successively bigger. Thus, if you add a yearly interval, it should go at the bottom, and if you add a minutes interval, it should go before the hourly interval. It's also worth noting that the snapshots are pulled up from the smallest interval to the largest. In this example, the daily snapshots are pulled from the oldest hourly snapshot, not directly from the main filesystem.

The backup section tells `rsnapshot` which files you actually want to back up:

```
backup      /etc/      localhost/etc/
```

In this example, backup is the backup point, */etc/* is the full path to the directory we want to take snapshots of, and *localhost/etc/* is a subdirectory *inside the snapshot root* where the snapshots are stored. If you are taking snapshots of several machines on one dedicated backup server, it's a good idea to use hostnames as directories to keep track of which files came from which server.

In addition to full paths on the local filesystem, you can also back up remote systems using `rsync` over `ssh`. If you have `ssh` enabled (via the `cmd_ssh` parameter), specify a path similar to this:

```
backup      backup@example.com:/etc/      example.com/etc/
```

This behaves fundamentally the same way as specifying local pathnames, but you must take a few extra things into account:

- The `ssh` daemon must be running on *example.com*.
- You must have access to the specified account on the remote machine (in this case, the backup user on *example.com*). See "Secure Backups Over a Network" **[Hack #38]** for instructions on setting this up.
- You must have key-based logins enabled for the specified user at *example.com*, without passphrases.
- This backup occurs over the network, so it may be slower. Since this uses `rsync`, this is most noticeable during the first backup. Depending on how much your data changes, subsequent backups should go much faster.

 One thing you can do to mitigate the potential damage from a backup server breach is to create alternate users on the client machines with their UIDs and GIDs set to 0, but with a more restrictive shell, such as `scponly` **[Hack #63]**.

**Preparing for script automation.** With the `backup_script` parameter, the second column is the full path to an executable backup script, and the third column is the local path in which you want to store it. For example:

```
backup_script      /usr/local/bin/backup_pgsql.sh     localhost/postgres/
```

> You can find the *backup_pgsql.sh* example script in the *utils/* directory of the source distribution. Alternatively, if you didn't include the `clean` target when you installed the FreeBSD port, the file will be located in */usr/ports/sysutils/ rsnapshot/work/rsnapshot-1.0.9/utils*.

Your backup script only needs to dump its output into its current working directory. It can create as many files and directories as necessary, but it should not put its files in any predetermined path. This is because `rsnapshot` creates a temp directory, changes to that directory, runs the backup script, and then syncs the contents of the temp directory to the local path you specified in the third column. A typical backup script might look like this:

```
#!/bin/sh

/usr/bin/mysqldump -uroot mydatabase > mydatabase.sql
/bin/chown 644 mydatabase.sql
```

There are a couple of example scripts in the *utils/* directory of the `rsnapshot` source distribution to give you more ideas.

> Remember that backup scripts will be invoked as the user running `rsnapshot`. Make sure your backup scripts are not writable by anyone else.

**Testing your config file.** After making your changes, verify that the config file is syntactically valid and that all the supporting programs are where you think they are:

```
# rsnapshot configtest
```

If all is well, the output should say `Syntax OK`. If there's a problem, it should tell you exactly what it is.

The final step to test your configuration is to run `rsnapshot` with the `-t` flag, for test mode. This will print out a verbose list of the things it will do, without actually doing them. For example, to simulate an hourly backup:

```
# rsnapshot -t hourly
```

**Scheduling rsnapshot.** Now that you have your config file set up, it's time to schedule rsnapshot to run from cron. Add the following lines to root's crontab:

```
0 */4 * * *     /usr/local/bin/rsnapshot hourly
30 23 * * *     /usr/local/bin/rsnapshot daily
```

## The Snapshot Storage Scheme

All backups are stored within a configurable snapshot root directory. In the beginning it will be empty. rsnapshot creates subdirectories for the various defined intervals. After a week, the directory should look something like this:

```
# ls -l /.snapshots/
drwxr-xr-x   7 root     root        4096 Dec 28 00:00 daily.0
drwxr-xr-x   7 root     root        4096 Dec 27 00:00 daily.1
drwxr-xr-x   7 root     root        4096 Dec 26 00:00 daily.2
drwxr-xr-x   7 root     root        4096 Dec 25 00:00 daily.3
drwxr-xr-x   7 root     root        4096 Dec 24 00:00 daily.4
drwxr-xr-x   7 root     root        4096 Dec 23 00:00 daily.5
drwxr-xr-x   7 root     root        4096 Dec 22 00:00 daily.6
drwxr-xr-x   7 root     root        4096 Dec 29 00:00 hourly.0
drwxr-xr-x   7 root     root        4096 Dec 28 20:00 hourly.1
drwxr-xr-x   7 root     root        4096 Dec 28 16:00 hourly.2
drwxr-xr-x   7 root     root        4096 Dec 28 12:00 hourly.3
drwxr-xr-x   7 root     root        4096 Dec 28 08:00 hourly.4
drwxr-xr-x   7 root     root        4096 Dec 28 04:00 hourly.5
```

Each of these directories contains a full backup of that point in time. The destination directory paths you specified as the backup and backup_script parameters are placed directly under these directories. In the example:

```
backup          /etc/          localhost/etc/
```

the */etc/* directory will initially back up into */.snapshots/hourly.0/localhost/etc/*.

Each subsequent time rsnapshot is run with the hourly command, it will rotate the *hourly.X* directories, "copying" the contents of the *hourly.0* directory (using hard links) into *hourly.1*.

When rsnapshot daily runs, it will rotate all the *daily.X* directories, then copy the contents of *hourly.5* into *daily.0*.

*hourly.0* will always contain the most recent snapshot, and *daily.6* will always contain a snapshot from a week ago. Unless the files change between snapshots, the full backups are really just multiple hard links to the same files. This is how rsnapshot uses space so efficiently. If the file changes at any point, the next backup will unlink the hard link in *hourly.0*, replacing it with a brand new file. This will now use twice the disk space it did before, but it is still considerably less space than 13 full, unique copies would occupy.

Remember, if you are using different intervals than the ones in this example, the first interval listed is the one that gets updates directly from the main filesystem. All subsequently listed intervals pull from the previous snapshots.

## Accessing Snapshots

When rsnapshot first runs, it will create the configured *snapshot_root* directory. It assigns this directory the permissions 0700 since the snapshots will probably contain files owned by all sorts of users on your system.

The simplest but least flexible solution is to disallow access to the snapshot root altogether. The root user will still have access, of course, and will be the only one who can pull backups. This may or may not be desirable, depending on your situation. For a small setup, this may be sufficient.

If users need to be able to pull their own backups, you will need to do a little extra work up front. The best option seems to be creating a container directory for the snapshot root with 0700 permissions, giving the snapshot root directory 0755 permissions, and mounting the snapshot root for the users as read-only using NFS or Samba.

Let's explore how to do this using NFS on a single machine. First, set the snapshot_root variable in *rsnapshot.conf*:

```
snapshot_root        /usr/.private/.snapshots/
```

Then, create the container directory, the real snapshot root, and a read-only mount point:

```
# mkdir /usr/.private/
# mkdir /usr/.private/.snapshots/
# mkdir /.snapshots/
```

Set the proper permissions on these new directories:

```
# chmod 0700 /usr/.private/
# chmod 0755 /usr/.private/.snapshots/
# chmod 0755 /.snapshots/
```

In */etc/exports*, add */usr/.private/.snapshots/* as a read-only NFS export:

```
/usr/.private/.snapshots/  127.0.0.1(ro)
```

 If your version of NFS supports it, include the no_root_ squash option. (Place it within the brackets after ro with a comma—not a space—as the separator.) This option allows the root user to see all the files within the read-only export.

In */etc/fstab*, mount */usr/.private/.snapshots/* read-only under */.snapshots/*:

```
localhost:/usr/.private/.snapshots/   /.snapshots/   nfs   ro   0 0
```

Restart your NFS daemon and mount the read-only snapshot root:

```
# /etc/rc.d/nfsd restart
# mount /.snapshots/
```

To test this, try adding a file as the superuser:

```
# touch /.snapshots/testfile
```

This should fail with insufficient permissions. This is what you want. It means that your users won't be able to mess with the snapshots either.

Users who wish to recover old files can go into the */.snapshots* directory, select the interval they want, and browse through the filesystem until they find the files they are looking for. NFS will prevent them from making modifications, but they can copy anything that they had permission to read in the first place.

## See Also

- man rsnapshot
- The original rsnapshot HOWTO (*http://www.rsnapshot.org/rsnapshot-HOWTO.html*)

## HACK #40 Automate Data Dumps for PostgreSQL Databases

Building your own backup utility doesn't have to be scary.

PostgreSQL is a robust, open source database server. Like most database servers, it provides utilities for creating backups. PostgreSQL's primary tools for creating backup files are pg_dump and pg_dumpall. However, if you want to automate your database backup processes, these tools have a few limitations:

- pg_dump dumps only one database at a time.
- pg_dumpall dumps all of the databases into a single file.
- pg_dump and pg_dumpall know nothing about multiple backups.

These aren't criticisms of the backup tools—just an observation that customization will require a little scripting. Our resulting script will backup multiple systems, each to their own backup file.

## Creating the Script

This script uses Python and its ability to execute other programs to implement the following backup algorithm:

1. Change the working directory to a specified database backup directory.

2. Rename all backup files ending in *.gz* so that they end in *.gz.old*. Existing files ending in *.gz.old* will be overwritten.

3. Clean up and analyze all PostgreSQL databases using its vacuumdb command.

4. Get a current list of databases from the PostgreSQL server.

5. Dump each database, piping the results through gzip, into its own compressed file.

Why Python? My choice is one of personal preference; this task is achievable in just about any scripting language. However, Python is cross-platform and easy to learn, and its scripts are easy to read.

## The Code

```
#!/usr/local/bin/python

# /usr/local/bin/pg2gz.py

# This script lists all PostgreSQL
# databases and pipes them separately
# through gzip into .gz files.

# INSTRUCTIONS
# 1.  Review and edit line 1 to reflect the location
#       of your python command file.
# 2.  Redefine the save_dir variable (on line 22) to
#       your backup directory.
# 3.  To automate the backup process fully, consider
#       scheduling the regular execution of this script
#       using cron.

import os, string

# Redefine this variable to your backup directory.
# Be sure to include the slash at the end.
save_dir = '/mnt/backup/databases/'

# Rename all *.gz backup files to *.gz.old.
curr_files = os.listdir(save_dir)
for n in curr_files:
        if n[len(n)-2:] == 'gz':
                os.popen('mv ' + save_dir + n + " " + save_dir + n + '.old')
        else:
                pass
```

```
# Vacuum all databases
os.popen('vacuumdb -a -f -z')

# 'psql -l' produces a list of PostgreSQL databases.
get_list = os.popen('psql -l').readlines()

# Exclude header and footer lines.
db_list = get_list[3:-2]

# Extract database names from first element of each row.
for n in db_list:
        n_row = string.split(n)
        n_db = n_row[0]

        # Pipe database dump through gzip
        # into .gz files for all databases
        # except template*.
        if n_db == 'template0':
                pass
        elif n_db == 'template1':
                pass
        else:
                os.popen('pg_dump ' + n_db + ' | gzip -c > ' + save_dir +
                        n_db + '.gz')
```

## Running the Hack

The script assumes that you have a working installation of PostgreSQL. You'll also need to install Python, which is available through the ports collection or as a binary package. The Python modules used are installed by default.

Double-check the location of your Python executable using:

```
% which python
/usr/local/bin/python
```

and ensure the first line of the script reflects your location. Don't forget to make the script executable using chmod +x.

On line 22 of the script, redefine the sav_dir variable to reflect the location of your backup directory. As is, the script assumes a backup directory of /mnt/backup/databases/.

You'll probably want to add the script to the pgsql user's crontab for periodic execution. To schedule the script for execution, log in as pgsql or, as the superuser, su to pgsql. Once you're acting as pgsql, execute:

```
% crontab -e
```

to open the crontab file in the default editor.

Given the following crontab file, */usr/local/bin/pg2gz.py* will execute at 4 AM every Sunday.

```
# more /var/cron/tabs/pgsql
SHELL=/bin/sh
PATH=/var/cron/tabs:/bin:/sbin:/usr/bin:/usr/sbin:/usr/local/bin

#minute    hour    mday    month    wday    command
0          4       *       *        0       /usr/local/bin/pg2gz.py
```

### See Also

- The PostgreSQL web site (*http://www.postgresql.org/*)
- The Python web site (*http://www.python.org/*)

## HACK #41   Perform Client-Server Cross-Platform Backups with Bacula

Don't let the campy name fool you. Bacula is a powerful, flexible, open source backup program.

Having problems finding a backup solution that fits all your needs? One that can back up both Unix and Windows systems? That is flexible enough to back up systems with irregular backup needs, such as laptops? That allows you to run scripts before or after the backup job? That provides browsing capabilities so you can decide upon a restore point? Bacula may be what you're looking for.

### Introducing Bacula

Bacula is a client-server solution composed of several distinct parts:

*Director*
> The Director is the most complex part of the system. It keeps track of all clients and files to be backed up. This daemon talks to the clients and to the storage devices.

*Client/File Daemon*
> The Client (or File) Daemon runs on each computer which will be backed up by the Director. Some other backup solutions refer to this as the Agent.

*Storage Daemon*
> The Storage Daemon communicates with the backup device, which may be tape or disk.

*Console*
> The Console is the primary interface between you and the Director. I use the command-line Console, but there is also a GNOME GUI Console.

Each File Daemon will have an entry in the Director configuration file. Other important entries include FileSets and Jobs. A FileSet identifies a set of files to back up. A Job specifies a single FileSet, the type of backup (incremental, full, etc.), when to do the backup, and what Storage Device to use. Backup and restore jobs can be run automatically or manually.

## Installation

Bacula stores details of each backup in a database. You can use either SQLite or MySQL, and starting with Bacula Version 1.33, PostgreSQL. Before you install Bacula, decide which database you want to use.

> FreeBSD 4.x (prior to 4.10-RELEASE) and FreeBSD 5.x (Version 5.2.1 and earlier) have a pthreads bug that could cause you to lose data. Refer to *platform/freebsd/pthreads-fix.txt* in your Bacula source directory for full details.

The existing Bacula documentation provides detailed installation instructions if you're installing from source. To install instead the SQLite version of the FreeBSD port:

```
# cd /usr/ports/sysutils/bacula
# make install
```

Or, if you prefer to install the MySQL version:

```
# cd /usr/ports/sysutils/bacula
# make -DWITH_MYSQL install
```

> Don't use the clean target with your make command, because there are some scripts in the *work* directory you'll need to use.

## Configuration Files

Bacula installs several configuration files that should work for your environment with few modifications.

**File Daemon on the backup client.** The first configuration file, */usr/local/etc/bacula-fd.conf*, is for the File Daemon. This file needs to reside on each machine you want to back up. For security reasons, only the Directors specified in this file will be able to communicate with this File Daemon. The name and password specified in the Director resource must be supplied by any connecting Director.

You can specify more than one Director { } resource. Make sure the password matches the one in the Client resource in the Director's configuration file.

The FileDaemon { } resource identifies this system and specifies the port on which it will listen for Directors. You may have to create a directory manually to match the one specified by the Working Directory.

**Storage Daemon on the backup server.** The next configuration file, */usr/local/ etc/bacula-sd.conf*, is for the Storage Daemon. The default values should work unless you need to specify additional storage devices.

As with the File Daemon, the Director { } resource specifies the Director(s) that may contact this Storage Daemon. The password must match that found in the Storage resource in the Director's configuration file.

**Director on the backup server.** The Director's configuration is by necessity the largest of the daemons. Each Client, Job, FileSet, and Storage Device is defined in this file.

In the following example configuration, I've defined the Job Client1 to back up the files defined by the FileSet Full Set on a laptop. The backup will be performed to the File storage device, which is really a disk located at *laptop.example.org*.

This isn't an optimal solution for a real backup, as I'm just backing up files from the laptop to somewhere else on the laptop. It is sufficient for demonstration and testing, though.

```
# more /usr/local/etc/bacula-dir.conf

    Director {
      Name                   = laptop-dir
      DIRport                = 9101
      QueryFile              = "/usr/local/etc/query.sql"
      WorkingDirectory       = "/var/db/bacula"
      PidDirectory           = "/var/run"
      Maximum Concurrent Jobs = 1
      Password               = "1LftflC4QtgZnWEB6vAGcOuSL3T6n+P7jeH+HtQOCWwV"
      Messages               = Standard
    }
    Job {
      Name            = "Client1"
      Type            = Backup
      Client          = laptop-fd
      FileSet         = "Full Set"
      Schedule        = "WeeklyCycle"
      Storage         = File
      Messages        = Standard
      Pool            = Default
      Write Bootstrap = "/var/db/bacula/Client1.bsr"
      Priority        = 10
```

```
    }
  FileSet {
    Name = "Full Set"
    Include = signature=MD5 {
      /usr/ports/sysutils/bacula/work/bacula-1.32c
    }

  # If you backup the root directory, the following two excluded
  #    files can be useful
  #
    Exclude = { /proc /tmp /.journal /.fsck }
  }
  Client {
    Name          = laptop-fd
    Address       = laptop.example.org
    FDPort        = 9102
    Catalog       = MyCatalog
    Password      = "laptop-client-password"
    File Retention = 30 days
    Job Retention  = 6 months
    AutoPrune      = yes
  }
  # Definition of file storage device
  Storage {
    Name       = File
    Address    = laptop.example.org
    SDPort     = 9103
    Password   = "TlDGBjTWkjTS/OHNMPF8ROacI3KlgIUZllY6NS7+gyUp"
    Device     = FileStorage
    Media Type = File
  }
```

Note that the password given by any connecting Console must match the one here.

## Database Setup

Now that you've modified the configuration files to suit your needs, use Bacula's scripts to create and define the database tables that it will use.

To set up for MySQL:

```
# cd /usr/ports/sysutils/bacula/work/bacula-1.32c/src/cats
# ./grant_mysql_privileges
# ./create_mysql_database
# ./make_mysql_tables
```

If you have a password set for the MySQL root account, add -p to these commands and you will be prompted for the password. You now have a working database suitable for use by Bacula.

## Testing Your Tape Drive

Some tape drives are not standard. They require their own proprietary software and can be temperamental when used with other software. Regardless of what software it uses, each drive model can have its own little quirks that need to be catered to. Fortunately, Bacula comes with btape, a handy little utility for testing your drive.

My tape drive is at /dev/sa1. Bacula prefers to use the non-rewind variant of the device, but it can handle the raw variant as well. If you use the rewinding device, then only one backup job per tape is possible. This command will test the non-rewind device /dev/nrsa1:

```
# /usr/local/sbin/btape -c /usr/local/etc/bacula-sd.conf /dev/nrsa1
```

## Running Without Root

It is a good idea to run daemons with the lowest possible privileges. The Storage Daemon and the Director Daemon do not need root permissions. However, the File Daemon does, because it needs to access all files on your system.

In order to run daemons with nonroot accounts, you need to create a user and a group. Here, I used vipw to create the user. I selected a user ID and group ID of 1002, as they were unused on my system.

```
bacula:*:1002:1002::0:0:Bacula Daemon:/var/db/bacula:/sbin/nologin
```

I also added this line to /etc/group:

```
bacula:*:1002:
```

The bacula user (as opposed to the Bacula daemon) will have a home directory of /var/db/bacula, which is the default location for the Bacula database.

Now that you have both a bacula user and a bacula group, you can secure the bacula home directory by issuing this command:

```
# chown -R bacula:bacula /var/db/bacula/
```

## Starting the Bacula Daemons

To start the Bacula daemons on a FreeBSD system, issue the following command:

```
# /usr/local/etc/rc.d/bacula.sh start
```

To confirm they are all running:

```
# ps auwx | grep bacula
```

```
root 63416 0.0 0.3 2040 1172 ?? Ss 4:09PM 0:00.01
    /usr/local/sbin/bacula-sd -v -c /usr/local/etc/bacula-sd.conf
```

```
root 63418 0.0 0.3 1856 1036 ?? Ss 4:09PM 0:00.00
    /usr/local/sbin/bacula-fd -v -c /usr/local/etc/bacula-fd.conf
root 63422 0.0 0.4 2360 1440 ?? Ss 4:09PM 0:00.00
    /usr/local/sbin/bacula-dir -v -c /usr/local/etc/bacula-dir.conf
```

## Using the Bacula Console

The console is the main interface through which you run jobs, query system status, and examine the Catalog contents, as well as label, mount, and unmount tapes. There are two consoles available: one runs from the command line, and the other is a GNOME GUI. I will concentrate on the command-line console.

To start the console, I use this command:

```
# /usr/local/sbin/console -c /usr/local/etc/console.conf
Connecting to Director laptop:9101
1000 OK: laptop-dir Version: 1.32c (30 Oct 2003)
*
```

You can obtain a list of the available commands with the help command. The status all command is a quick and easy way to verify that all components are up and running. To label a Volume, use the label command.

Bacula comes with a preset backup job to get you started. It will back up the directory from which Bacula was installed. Once you get going and have created your own jobs, you can safely remove this job from the Director configuration file.

Not surprisingly, you use the run command to run a job. Once the job runs, the results will be sent to you via email, according to the Messages resource settings within your Director configuration file.

To restore a job, use the restore command. You should choose the restore location carefully and ensure there is sufficient disk space available.

It is easy to verify that the restored files match the original:

```
# diff -ruN \
/tmp/bacula-restores/usr/ports/sysutils/bacula/work/bacula-1.32c \
/usr/ports/sysutils/bacula/work/bacula-1.32c
#
```

## Creating Backup Schedules

For my testing, I wanted to back up files on my Windows XP machine every hour. I created this schedule:

```
Schedule {
  Name = "HourlyCycle"
  Run = Full 1st sun at 1:05
```

```
    Run  = Differential 2nd-5th sun at 1:05
    Run  = Incremental Hourly
}
```

Any Job that uses this schedule will be run at the following times:

- A full backup will be done on the first Sunday of every month at 1:05 AM.

- A differential backup will be run on the 2nd, 3rd, 4th, and 5th Sundays of every month at 1:05 AM.

- Every hour, on the hour, an incremental backup will be done.

## Creating a Client-only Install

So far we have been testing Bacula on the server. With the FreeBSD port, installing a client-only version of Bacula is easy:

```
# cd /usr/ports/sysutils/bacula
# make -DWITH_CLIENT_ONLY install
```

You will also need to tell the Director about this client by adding a new Client resource to the Director configuration file. You will also want to create a Job and FileSet resource.

When you change the Bacula configuration files, remember to restart the daemons:

```
# /usr/local/etc/rc.d/bacula.sh restart
Stopping the Storage daemon
Stopping the File daemon
Stopping the Director daemon
Starting the Storage daemon
Starting the File daemon
Starting the Director daemon
#
```

## See Also

- The Bacula web site (*http://www.bacula.org/*)
- *http://www.onlamp.com/pub/a/onlamp/2004/01/09/bacula.html* (the original Bacula article from ONLamp)

# CHAPTER FIVE

# Networking Hacks
## Hacks 42-53

You probably spend most of your time accessing servers on the Internet or on your own network. In fact, networking has become so prevalent, it's becoming increasingly difficult to tolerate even short periods of network outages.

This chapter contains many ideas for accessing networking services when the conventional avenues seem to be unavailable. Have you ever wanted to train your system to notify you of its new network configuration when its primary link becomes unavailable? Would you like to check your email from a system that doesn't contain a preconfigured email client? How can you maintain network connectivity when your ISP's DHCP server no longer recognizes your DHCP client?

You'll also gain insight into how some of the networking services and tools we often take for granted work. Become a tcpdump guru—or at least lose the intimidation factor. Understand your DNS messages and how to troubleshoot your DNS servers. Tame your sendmail daemon.

Finally, meet two excellent open source utilities that allow you to perform routine tasks simultaneously on all of your servers.

### HACK #42 See Console Messages Over a Remote Login
View a server's console messages remotely.

As a Unix system administrator, you can do 99% of your work remotely. In fact, it is very rare indeed that you'll need to sit down in front of a server (assuming the server even has an attached keyboard! [Hack #26]).

However, one of the key functionalities you lose in remote administration is the ability to see the remote server's console. All is not lost, though. First, let's answer these questions: "What do you mean by the console, and why would you want to see it?"

## The Console

If you're physically sitting at a system, the console is the virtual terminal you see when you press Alt-F1. If you've ever logged into this particular virtual terminal, you've probably noticed that error messages appear here. These messages can be rather disconcerting when you're working at the console, especially if you're fighting your way through vi and bright white error messages occasionally overwrite your text.

If you ever find yourself in that situation, Esc-Ctrl-r will refresh your screen. Better yet, don't log into Alt-F1 when you're physically sitting at a system. Instead, log into a different terminal, say, the one at Alt-F2.

However, when you access a remote system, you can't log into a virtual terminal, and the console is considered to be a virtual terminal. (You access it by pressing Alt-F1 at the local keyboard, after all). Instead, you log into a *pseudoterminal* (also known as a *network terminal*).

Here's an example. I'm sitting at a system and have logged into the virtual terminals at Alt-F2 and Alt-F3. From Alt-F3, I've used ssh to log into the localhost. If I run the w command, I'll see this:

```
% w
12:25  up 22 mins, 3 users, load averages: 0:00, 0:00, 0:00
USER        TTY     FROM          LOGIN@  IDLE WHAT
genisis     v1      -             12:25PM    - -csh (csh)
genisis     v2      -             12:25PM    - ssh localhost
genisis     p0      localhost     12:25PM    - w
```

Notice that the virtual (or physical access to keyboard) terminals begin with a v in the TTY section. Since terminals start numbering at 0, I'm logged into the second (v1) and third (v2) virtual terminals. I'm also connected to the first pseudoterminal, p0, so I'm currently the only user logged in over the network.

In my ssh session, if I press Alt-F1, I'll access the console on my *local* system (where I am sitting), not the console on the remote system.

## Seeing Remote Console Messages

If Alt-F1 won't do it, how can you see remote console messages? A quick hack for your current session is to run this command:

```
% tail -f /var/log/messages &
```

tail shows the end of a file, much like head shows the start. In this case, the file is */var/log/messages*. This particular log contains a copy of the messages that appear on the system console. When run with the -f switch, tail will remain open, allowing you to see when new entries are added to that logfile. The trailing ampersand (&) runs the command in the background, so you'll get your prompt back if you press Enter or type in another command.

As the system writes console entries to this file, `tail` will also display to your current pseudoterminal. If you're in the middle of typing something when a log message is displayed, Ctrl-r will refresh your command prompt line so you can see where you left off typing.

## An Alternate Method

There's always more than one way to skin a cat. Since `syslog` is responsible for logfiles, you can also change its configuration file. Let's start by seeing *why* messages are sent to the console:

```
% grep console /etc/syslog.conf
*.err;kern.debug;auth.notice;mail.crit        /dev/console
# uncomment this to log all writes to /dev/console to /var/log/console.log
#console.info                                  /var/log/console.log
```

See how messages are sent to */dev/console* by default? This file also gives a hint on how to send those messages elsewhere—to a file called *console.log*. By uncommenting that `console.info` line, you can send those messages to */var/log/console.log*.

If you decide to remove that #, don't forget to create an empty logfile with the specified name and to inform `syslogd` of your changes by sending it a signal one:

```
# touch /var/log/console.log
# killall -1 syslogd
```

Now you're probably thinking, big deal. So I've sent console messages to a different filename. I still have to run that `tail -f` command to see them.

Well, how about changing that `console.info` line to this instead:

```
console.info                                  root,genisis
```

Don't forget to `killall -1 syslogd` once you save your changes.

Now when I `ssh` into that system as the user `genisis`, I don't have to remember to run the `tail` command. As long as I'm the user `genisis`, even if I become the superuser, all console messages will be sent to my terminal.

## Hacking the Hack

You may have noticed that uncommenting the `console.info` line results in messages being sent twice: once to */var/log/console.log* and once to either the original console or the specified users. If you prefer to only have messages sent to either the log or the console or user, recomment the `console.info` line and indicate in the line that originally specified */dev/console* where you want the information to go.

For example, to log *only* to a file:

```
*.err;kern.debug;auth.notice;mail.crit        /var/log/console
```

Or to log *only* to the specified users:

```
*.err;kern.debug;auth.notice;mail.crit        root,genisis
```

Again, don't forget to inform syslogd of any changes you make to */etc/syslog.conf*.

### See Also

- `man w`
- `man syslog.conf`

## Spoof a MAC Address
**#43**    Even good guys can use secret identities.

Okay, I know what you're thinking. There's never a legitimate reason to spoof any type of address, right? Even if there were, why would you bother to spoof a MAC address, other than to prove that it can be done?

Consider the following scenario. I was administrating a small network where the ISP restricted the number of IP addresses a DHCP client was allowed to receive. Their DHCP server kept track of the leased addresses by using a combination of the client's MAC address and an OS identifier. One day I needed to replace that network's external NIC. It took me a while to figure out why the new NIC refused to pick up a DHCP address from the ISP. Once the restriction was explained to me, I contemplated my available courses of action. One was to spend the afternoon listening to Musak in the hopes that I'd eventually get to speak to one of the ISP's customer service representatives. I decided my time would be better spent if I instead took 30 seconds and spoofed the old MAC address. This provided a quick solution that allowed the owner to get back online until he could make arrangements with the ISP regarding the new MAC address.

### Spoofing on FreeBSD

Before I could accomplish the spoof, I needed two pieces of information. The first was the MAC address for the old NIC. Fortunately, I record such things in a binder. However, I initially found out that information using ifconfig. In this scenario, the interface in question was called rl0:

```
% ifconfig rl0
rl0: flags=8843<UP,BROADCAST,RUNNING,SIMPLEX,MULTICAST> mtu 1500
        inet 192.168.2.12 netmask 0xffffff00 broadcast 192.168.2.255
```

```
ether 00:05:5d:d2:19:b7
media: Ethernet autoselect (10baseT/UTP)
```

The MAC address is the hex number immediately following ether.

Second, I needed to know the identifier used by the ISP's DHCP server. This was found in the DHCP lease:

```
% more /var/db/dhclient.leases | grep host
option host-name "00-05-5d-d2-19-b7-36-33"
```

Some ISPs use option host-name, while others use option dhcp-client-identifier. Choose the option in the lease that is associated with the MAC address. In this example, my identifier was the MAC address, followed by -36-33.

Armed with the information I needed, I could spoof the old MAC address onto the new NIC card. In my case, the new card was an ed0:

```
# ifconfig ed0 ether 00:05:5d:d2:19:b7

#
# ifconfig ed0 | grep ether
ether 00:05:5d:d2:19:b7
```

Note that you have to be the superuser to change these settings.

This particular change won't survive a reboot, as the NIC will give the kernel its burnt-in MAC address during the hardware probe that occurs during bootup. If you intend to reboot before sorting out the situation with the ISP, carefully add this line to */etc/rc.conf*:

```
ifconfig_ed0_alias0="ether 00:05:5d:d2:19:b7"
```

This will create an alias for ed0 that uses the desired MAC address, rather than the MAC address burnt into the physical card. Think of an alias as an alternate set of instructions an interface can give to the kernel—a kind of networking nickname.

Next, I'll edit */etc/dhclient.conf*:

```
# vi /etc/dhclient.conf
# $FreeBSD: src/etc/dhclient.conf,v 1.3 2001/10/27 03:14:37 rwatson Exp $
#
#        This file is required by the ISC DHCP client.
#        See ``man 5 dhclient.conf'' for details.
#
#        In most cases an empty file is sufficient for most people as the
#        defaults are usually fine.
#
interface "ed0" {
    send host-name "00-05-5d-d2-19-b7-36-33";
    send dhcp-client-identifier "00-05-5d-d2-19-b7-36-33";
}
```

By default, this file contains only comments; I added a section for interface ed0. When editing your own file, remember to include the opening and closing curly braces ({}). Each statement must also end in a semicolon (;). Here, I've set both the host-name and the dhcp-client-identifier options to the values expected by the ISP.

Now it's time to test that these changes did indeed work. You don't need to reboot in order to test that alias in *etc/rc.conf*. This command will do the trick:

```
# /etc/netstart
Doing stage one network startup:
Doing initial network setup:.
ed0: flags=8843<UP,BROADCAST,RUNNING,SIMPLEX,MULTICAST> mtu 1500
        inet 192.168.2.95 netmask 0xffffff00 broadcast 192.168.2.255
        ether 00:05:5d:d2:19:b7
lo0: flags=8049<UP,LOOPBACK,RUNNING,MULTICAST> mtu 16384
        inet 127.0.0.1 netmask 0xff000000
Additional routing options: ignore ICMP redirect=YES log ICMP redirect=YES
drop SYN+FIN packets=YESsysctl: unknown oid 'net.inet.tcp.drop_synfin'
.
Routing daemons:.
```

Excellent. The new NIC kept the spoofed MAC address. Now let's see how the DHCP server responds when I release and try to renew an address:

```
# dhclient -r ed0
#
```

Using -r with dhclient forces the DHCP client to give up its old address and request a new lease from the DHCP server. If this succeeds, the prompt will return without any error messages. Running ifconfig ed0 will show that the ISP's DHCP server did indeed give this interface a public IP address.

## Spoofing on NetBSD

The current version of ifconfig that ships with NetBSD does not support this functionality. To allow MAC address changes, try Dheeraj Reddy's ifconfig patch, available from *http://news.gw.com/netbsd.tech.net/%3C20030808072355.GA616%40bharati.sudheeraj.net%3E*.

You will need to apply this patch to NetBSD sources and build a new version of ifconfig. To begin, download the system sources, unpack them, and change the working directory to *src/sbin/ifconfig*. Download the patch and apply it with:

```
# patch > ifconfig.patch
```

Build a new binary with:

```
# make
```

Remember that this code is experimental and may not always work as advertised, so it is crucial that you back up the original ifconfig binary in some safe place.

When you have the new binary, run it with:

```
# ifconfig interface-name lladdr MAC-addr
```

### Spoofing with OpenBSD

The standard ifconfig that ships with OpenBSD does not contain an option to change the MAC addresses of interface cards. If you need it, you will have to build your own tool for that purpose with *sea.c*. Download it from *http://www.devguide.net/books/openbsdfw-02-ed/*

Build sea as follows:

```
# gcc -Wall -o sea sea.c -lkvm
```

Next, boot OpenBSD into single-user mode:

```
# reboot
boot> boot -s
```

Then, once in single-user mode, use sea to spoof the desired address on the specified NIC:

```
# sea interface-name MAC-addr
```

### See Also

- man ifconfig
- man dhclient.conf

## HACK #44 Use Multiple Wireless NIC Configurations

Take the pain out of configuring your laptop's wireless interface.

If you use a laptop and have remote sites that you visit regularly, configuring your wireless interface can be interesting. For example, every wireless network has a unique service set identifier (SSID). Each site that uses WEP will also require a unique encryption key. Some networks may use static IP addresses, while others may use a DHCP server.

You *could* keep a copy of each network's configuration in your wallet and reconfigure your NIC manually at each site, but wouldn't you rather automate the various network configurations and choose the desired configuration after bootup?

For the purpose of this exercise, we will assume that the wireless access points have been properly configured and activated.

## Initial Preparation

Before you can script the network configurations, you'll need to collect the information listed next. I've associated the necessary information with ifconfig's keywords where possible. You will see these keywords in the configuration script.

- ssid, the name of the wireless network
- authmode, the network's authorization mode (none, open, or shared)
- nwkey, the encryption key, in hexadecimal
- Whether to use a static IP address or dhclient to obtain dynamic IP address information
- inet, the static IP address, if necessary
- netmask, the netmask, for static network configuration
- The default gateway, for static IP configuration
- Nameservers, for static IP configuration
- The network device (wi0, an0, etc.)

You can obtain all but the final item from whoever set up the wireless access points for each site.

If you don't know the name of your network device, review the output of dmesg for networking protocol names (Ethernet, 802.11) and MAC addresses. Here's the command I use and the relevant lines from my laptop:

```
# dmesg | grep address
rl0: Ethernet address: 00:08:02:9e:df:b8
wi0: 802.11 address: 00:06:25:17:74:be
```

rl0 is the device name for the cabled Ethernet port, and wi0 is the device name for the wireless PCMCIA card.

## Preparing the Script

Here are a few notes regarding the network device configuration script:

- The script is named for the network device it controls.
- The script will live in */usr/local/etc/rc.d*. Since we do not want the script activated at bootup, the script name must *not* end in *.sh*.
- Each network device should have its own script so that the connection can be easily dropped using the argument stop.
- Each configuration will have its own section in a case construct.
- Each section's name will consist of a d (to use DHCP) or an s (to use a static IP address) followed by a location name.

- The script will accept a section name as a command line argument for configuration selection.
- In order to use WEP with DHCP, the device must be configured with the encrypted code prior to calling dhclient.
- A status section will give us current network information for the device.
- A wildcard section will print a list of the section names when given an invalid argument.

Since my network device is wi0, I'll save the script as */usr/local/etc/rc.d/wi0*. I tend to use my laptop in three locations: at home with DHCP and WEP, at home with a static IP address and WEP, and at my sister's home with DHCP and WEP. Tables 5-1 through 5-3 list the appropriate configurations.

*Table 5-1. Using DHCP and WEP in my home network*

| Option name | Value |
| --- | --- |
| section name | dhome |
| ssid | myhome |
| authmode | shared |
| nwkey | 0x123456789a |
| ip address | Use dhclient **to obtain the IP address, netmask, gateway, and nameservers** |

*Table 5-2. Using a static IP address and WEP in my home network*

| Option name | Value |
| --- | --- |
| section name | shome |
| ssid | myhome |
| authmode | shared |
| nwkey | 0x123456789a |
| ip address | 192.168.1.21 |
| netmask | 255.255.255.0 |
| gateway | 192.168.1.1 |
| name servers | 24.204.0.4, 24.204.0.5 |

*Table 5-3. Using DHCP and WEP at my sister's home*

| Option name | Value |
| --- | --- |
| section name | dsister |
| ssid | sisterhome |
| authmode | shared |
| nwkey | 0x987654321a |
| ip address | Use dhclient **to obtain the IP address, netmask, gateway, and nameservers** |

## The Code

Here is the resulting script:

```
#!/bin/sh
# /usr/local/etc/rc.d/wi0
# Configure wireless interface

# See the ifconfig(8), dhclient(8) and route(8) man pages for further
# assistance.

NIC=wi0

case $1 in
dhome)
        ifconfig ${NIC} ssid "myhome" authmode "shared" nwkey 0x123456789a
        dhclient ${NIC}
        echo ${NIC}
        ;;
shome)
        ifconfig ${NIC} inet 192.168.1.21 ssid "myhome" authmode "shared"
        nwkey 0x123456789a netmask 255.255.255.0
        route add default 192.168.1.1
        echo nameserver 24.204.0.4 > /etc/resolv.conf
        echo nameserver 24.204.0.5 >> /etc/resolv.conf
        echo ${NIC}
        ;;
dsister)
        ifconfig ${NIC} ssid "sisterhome" authmode "shared" nwkey \
            0x987654321a
        dhclient ${NIC}
        echo ${NIC}
        ;;
stop)
        [ -s /var/run/dhclient.pid ] && kill `cat /var/run/dhclient.pid` \
            && rm /var/run/dhclient.pid
        ifconfig ${NIC} remove
        echo " ${NIC} removed"
        ;;
status)
        ifconfig ${NIC}
        ;;
*)
        echo "usage: /usr/local/etc/${NIC} [dhome|shome|dsister|stop|status]"
        ;;
esac
```

Note that the stop option kills dhclient. If you will be using multiple network interfaces, you may wish to delete the line that reads:

```
[ -s /var/run/dhclient.pid ] && kill `cat /var/run/dhclient.pid` && rm \
    /var/run/dhclient.pid
```

The script should be owned by root and be readable by root only. If you create your script as a normal user, you need to change its owner. Become the superuser, and:

```
# chown root:wheel /usr/local/etc/rc.d/wi0
# chmod 700 /usr/local/etc/wi0
```

## Running the Hack

Using the script is fairly straightforward. To activate the dhome configuration (DHCP at home):

```
# /usr/local/etc/rc.d/wi0 dhome
wi0
```

To remove the wi0 interface and kill the connection:

```
# /usr/local/etc/rc.d/wi0 stop
wi0 removed
```

If I enter an erroneous argument, I'll get a list of valid arguments:

```
# /usr/local/etc/rc.d/wi0 badargument
usage: /usr/local/etc/wi0 [dhome|shome|dsister|stop|status]
```

Now you can choose an existing network configuration without having to remember any network details.

A similar script will work for cabled network devices. Simply change the device name and remove the wireless keywords (ssid, authmode, and nwkey) and values.

## Hacking the Hack

For all the geek points, you could put your wireless card in promiscuous mode (if it supports it), sniff for the available ESSIDs and their signal strengths, and choose the appropriate configuration based on that information. If you go this route, install the net/bsd-airtools port and remember to ask for permission before using someone else's resources.

## See Also

- man dhclient
- man ifconfig
- man route

## Survive Catastrophic Internet Loss
**HACK #45**

Set up your network to recover from a full Internet loss.

Someday this all too common event may happen: while you're away from your network, your connection dies. Whether the ISP drops it, the cable gets unplugged or the server behind your NAT box dies, it is gone. You are now lost at sea, not knowing what is actually going on back at home. You `ping`, `telnet`, and pray to the network gods, but nothing seems to work.

Wouldn't it be better if your network could recognize that it has lost that connection and find a way for you to get back in touch? The system that I set up did just that. All it took was a well-configured OpenBSD firewall with NAT and a short Ruby program that uses the Jabber protocol to get my attention.

### Hardware Configuration

I use OpenBSD on a 486 to make my network resistant to total connectivity failure. The computer has two network cards, one for the DSL bridge and the other for the rest of the network. In addition, I managed to find a 56k ISA modem.

Since this computer provides little more than firewall and NAT services, it's more than capable of serving a small home or business network. The DSL bridge provides the primary Internet connection with a static IP. The service through my provider is usually quite good, but there have been troubled times. The house has only one phone line, which is plugged into the 56k modem in the same computer as the DSL line. You could easily make the modem computer a different machine entirely, but I found that this 486 is quite compact and sufficient for my purposes.

### Connectivity Software

The current OpenBSD operating system (Version 3.4 as of this writing) comes with a wonderful firewall and NAT package, named Packet Filter (PF). PF works well on a day-to-day basis moving my packets from the network to the Internet. Unfortunately, it does not handle the loss of the connection to the ISP. A full discussion for configuring PF is beyond the scope of this hack, but you can find what you need from the OpenBSD PF FAQ at *http://www.openbsd.org/faq/pf/index.html*.

When the unthinkable happens and your network falls off the Internet, you may fall back to your trusty 56k modem. The idea is that the modem will dial out automatically once your main connection goes away. First, though, you need some way to detect that your connection is lost. I use a slow `ping` to the router on the other end of my DSL connection.

I run this heartbeat from cron instead of using a daemon process. It sends three pings at two-second intervals every 10 minutes—a very conservative test, especially if you are only sending to your local gateway. Here is the cron entry:

```
*/10 * * * * /usr/local/testconnect/testconnect.sh
```

The *testconnect.sh* script resembles this:

```
#!/bin/sh

# First gather data about your connection
PINGS=`ping -c 1 -i 2 [your gateway] | wc -l`

# Apply test and execute on result
if [ -f /tmp/lostconnection.lock ]
then
  echo "Lockfile in place"
else
  echo "No lockfile"
  if [ $PINGS -lt 8 ]
  then
    echo "Connection lost, commencing dialup"
    touch /tmp/lostconnection.lock
    pfctl -d
    ppp -nat internet
    ruby /usr/local/testconnect/send_new_ip.rb
  else
    echo "All is well"
  fi
fi
```

If the gateway is unavailable, then the pings will time out and generate a short ping result. By counting the number of letters (with wc -1) and applying a length test (if [ $PINGS -lt 8]), the script can tell if the pings failed. In the case of failure, the script goes through the steps to give you connectivity through alternative means and to stop it from doing it every 10 minutes if things go really wrong.

First, it creates a lockfile to ensure future runs of this script do not dial out over and over again. Second, it shuts down the current NAT interface to make way for the next step. Third, it fires up the modem and connects to my emergency ISP using a preconfigured *ppp.conf* profile called internet. Here, I enabled NAT (-nat) over PPP so that computers at my house will only notice that the service is slow. The Internet connection will still function in the same way. Finally, I run a script to alert me to the failure.

You may have noticed one flaw in this setup. Most cheap ISP services usually do not give you the same IP address when you dial into them. How do you know how to contact your reconnected gateway from the outside? Easy: have the computer tell you.

## Jabber and Ruby to the Rescue!

There are many ways a computer can contact you with its current status. I decided to use Jabber because I spend a fair amount of time with a Jabber session running. This script will notify me quickly if something untoward happens to my connection at home, such as an incident involving the vacuum cleaner.

I figured that a message from my computer with the current network configuration would provide enough information to allow me to log in remotely. The most important information is the current IP address of the backup PPP connection. I decided to create a Ruby script using the Jabber4r module to accomplish this:

```ruby
require 'jabber4r/jabber4r'

now    = `date`.chomp!
ipdata = `/sbin/ifconfig tun0`

session = Jabber::Session.bind_digest("user@jabberserver/modem", "secret")
session.new_chat_message("user@jabberserver").
    set_body("I had to dial up for internet access at #{now}.\n#{ipdata}\n")
      .send

sleep 5
session.close
```

The Ruby script grabs the current time and state of the tun0 interface, which contains the current IP address assigned by the dial-up ISP. Armed with that IP address, you can then ssh into your computer and begin to diagnose the situation.

The Jabber4r module lives at *http://jabber4r.rubyforge.org/*. You will also need the REXML module from *http://www.germane-software.com/software/rexml/*. Both of these installed without issue on top of the Ruby package that shipped with OpenBSD 3.4.

## The Last Piece

After your connection has been restored, you need to clean up. You will need to stop ppp, start PF again—hopefully with pfctl—and remove the lockfile that prevents the */tmp/testconnect.sh* script from dialing out over and over. After that, you should be back to normal, at least until the next mishap.

## See Also

- The Jabber web site (*http://www.jabber.org/*)
- The Ruby web site (*http://www.ruby-lang.org/en/*)

# Humanize tcpdump Output

**#46**   Make friends with `tcpdump`.

One of the most useful utilities in a network administrator's tool belt is
`tcpdump`. While you probably agree, I bet the very thought of wading
through a `tcpdump` sniff makes you groan. Take heart: I'll walk you through
some concrete examples that show how to zero in on the information you
need to solve the particular network problem that prompted you to consider doing a packet sniff in the first place.

You might be thinking, "Why bother? There are much nicer utilities out
there." That's true. My personal favorite happens to be `ethereal`. However,
you don't always have the luxury of working on a system that allows you to
install third-party utilities or, for that matter, even has X installed. `tcpdump` is
guaranteed to be on your BSD system. It's there, it's quick, it's dirty, and it's
darn effective if you know how to harness its power.

## The Basics

Let's start with the basics: starting a capture. Before you can capture any
packets, you need to be the superuser. You also need to have the `bpf` device
in your kernel. If you're using the GENERIC kernel, you're set. If you've created your own custom kernel **[Hack #54]**, double-check you still have that
device. In this example, my kernel configuration file is called *CUSTOM*:

```
# grep bpf /usr/src/sys/i386/conf/CUSTOM
# The 'bpf' device enables the Berkeley Packet Filter.
device     bpf    #Berkeley packet filter
```

You also need to know the names of your interfaces and which interface is
cabled to the network you wish to sniff. You can find this with `ifconfig`:

```
# ifconfig
rl0: flags=8802<UP,BROADCAST,RUNNING,SIMPLEX,MULTICAST> mtu 1500
        inet 192.168.3.20 netmask 0xffffff00 broadcast 192.168.3.255
        ether 00:05:5d:d2:19:b7
        media: Ethernet autoselect (10baseT/UTP)
rl1: flags=8802<BROADCAST,SIMPLEX,MULTICAST> mtu 1500
        inet 192.168.12.43 netmask 0xffffff00 broadcast 192.168.12.255
        ether 00:05:5d:d1:ff:9d
        media: Ethernet autoselect (10baseT/UTP)
ed0: flags=8843<UP,BROADCAST,RUNNING,SIMPLEX,MULTICAST> mtu 1500
        inet 192.168.2.95 netmask 0xffffff00 broadcast 192.168.2.255
        ether 00:50:ba:de:36:33
lp0: flags=8810<POINTOPOINT,SIMPLEX,MULTICAST> mtu 1500
lo0: flags=8049<UP,LOOPBACK,RUNNING,MULTICAST> mtu 16384
        inet 127.0.0.1 netmask 0xff000000
```

This particular system has three Ethernet (ether) cards attached to three different networks. Since I'm interested in the traffic on the 192.168.2.0 network, I'll use the ed0 interface.

To start a capture, simply specify the interface you're interested in, with the interface (-i) switch:

```
# tcpdump -i ed0
tcpdump: listening on ed0
Ctrl t
tcpdump: 24 packets received by filter, 0 packets dropped by kernel
Ctrl c
33 packets received by filter
0 packets dropped by kernel
```

You will lose your prompt for the duration of the dump, and captured packets will be displayed to your terminal (these weren't shown in this example's output). If you press Ctrl-t, you can see how many packets have been captured so far and how many have been dropped, if any. If you're dropping packets, that means packets are arriving faster than tcpdump can process them. To end your sniff, press Ctrl-c and you'll return to your prompt.

Unless you're a speed reader or have a very boring network, you'll probably prefer to send the captured packets to a file. Use the -w (write) switch to specify the name of the file you'd like to create:

```
# tcpdump -i ed0 -w dumpfile
tcpdump: listening on ed0
Ctrl t
load: 0:00  cmd: tcpdump 1458 [bpf] 0.01u 0.00s 0% 1576k
Ctrl c
56 packets received by filter
0 packets dropped by kernel
```

Note that you won't be able to read that file with a pager or editor, as it is written in a format that only tcpdump or another packet-sniffer utility can understand. Instead, use the -r (read) switch and specify the name of the file:

```
# tcpdump -r dumpfile | more
```

## Display Filters

If you try the previous examples on a moderately busy network, you'll probably remind yourself why you don't like using tcpdump. In a minute you can capture hundreds of seemingly unintelligible lines of numbers. You're wasting time and brain cells if you're wading through hundreds of lines and you're interested in only two or three of them. You can save on both of those precious resources if you spend a few minutes creating a display filter.

There's always a reason behind a packet sniff. tcpdump is a very intelligent utility, but it's not a mind reader. However, if you can convert your reason into syntax that tcpdump understands, you can create a filter that will display only *interesting* packets.

Let's say that you suspect broadcast packets are slowing down a network segment. This incantation will capture only broadcast packets:

```
# tcpdump -i ed0 broadcast
```

When you end your capture, you'll find that the number of packets received by the filter will be greater than the number of packets displayed to your screen. This means that tcpdump will still capture all packets, but will display only the packets matching your filter. This can give you a good idea of ratio. For example, if you captured 100 packets in a minute and only 4 of those packets were broadcasts, then broadcasts probably aren't an issue on that network.

Next example: a particular workstation is having problems connecting to a server. Create a filter that zeros in on the packets between those two systems, in this case, genisis and server1:

```
# tcpdump -i ed0 host genisis and server1
```

In this example, I only have to use the host keyword once, as it is assumed until I specify a different keyword. If I really like to type (which I don't), it would have been just as correct to type host genisis and host server1.

You can also fine-tune that syntax to unidirectional traffic like so:

```
# tcpdump -i ed0 src host genisis and dst host server1
```

That will show only the traffic that was created at genisis and is destined for server1. This time I had to repeat the word host, as one incantation was src host while the other was dst host.

Suppose you're interested in only ICMP traffic:

```
# tcpdump -i ed0 icmp
```

or perhaps only ARP traffic:

```
# tcpdump -i ed0 arp
```

Perhaps you're having a problem with IKE, which uses UDP port 500:

```
# tcpdump -i ed0 udp port 500
```

As you can see, tcpdump comes with many keywords that assist you in creating a display filter suited to your needs. These keywords are building blocks for more complex expressions. When you do your own combinations, you might find it easier to use the words and, or, and not. For example, this will capture all traffic on network 192.168.2.0 that is not ARP-based:

```
# tcpdump -i ed0 net 192.168.2 and not arp
```

Of course, you can find all of the keywords, along with examples, in man tcpdump. I've highlighted only the most commonly used keywords.

## More Complicated Filters

tcpdump is capable of zeroing in on any particular field in a packet. In order to harness this power, it's useful to have a picture of the various types of headers in front of you. Once you have a picture of the fields contained within the particular header you're interested in, the examples in man tcpdump will make a lot more sense.

You'll know you're creating a very specific filter if your tcpdump expression contains the name of a protocol followed by square brackets ([ ]). Let's take a look at this example from the manpage, which is designed to capture only SYN-1s, the first packet in the TCP three-way handshake. Remember that square brackets may have special meaning to the shell, so quote complex expressions to prevent weird syntax errors:

```
# tcpdump -i ed0 'tcp[13] == 2'
```

If you're familiar with the three-way handshake, you know that it involves the *flags* field of a TCP header. Let's find that particular field within the TCP header. Figure 5-1 shows the header fields of a TCP packet.

| Word | 00 01 02 03 04 05 06 07 08 09 10 11 12 13 14 15 | 16 17 18 19 20 21 22 23 24 25 26 27 28 29 30 31 |
|------|---------|---------|
| 1 | Source port | Destination port |
| 2 | Sequence number | |
| 3 | Acknowledgment number | |
| 4 | Data offset / Reserved / Flags | Window |
| 5 | Checksum | Urgent pointer |
| 6 | Options and padding ... ... Data ... ... | |

*Figure 5-1. TCP packet headers*

The number enclosed within the [ ] represents how many octets into the header a particular field occurs. Each line, or word, of a header is 4 octets long. The Flags field is after the first three words (i.e., 12 octets) and occurs one more octet in, just after the Data Offset and Reserved fields. So, this particular TCP field occurs in octet 13 and is represented by tcp[13].

Still with me? Okay, where'd the == 2 come from? For that one, you need to know the names of the flags as well as the decimal equivalents for each binary bit that represents a flag. These are listed in Table 5-4.

*Table 5-4. TCP flags and their decimal equivalents*

| Flag name | Decimal equivalent |
|-----------|--------------------|
| URG | 32 |
| ACK | 16 |
| PSH | 8 |
| RST | 4 |
| SYN | 2 |
| FIN | 1 |

Finally, you need to know that the first packet in the three-way handshake is distinguished by just the SYN flag being turned on. Since all of the other flags will be turned off and will therefore contain a value of 0, a value of 2 in this field indicates that only the SYN bit is enabled.

If math isn't your strong point, there is an alternate way to write this particular expression:

```
# tcpdump -i ed0 'tcp[tcpflags] ==tcp-syn'
```

If the particular field you're interested in happens to be the TCP flags field, the ICMP type field, or the ICMP code field, you're in luck. Those three fields are predefined, so you don't have to count how many octets in that field occurs in the header. So:

- tcp[13] is the same expression as tcp[tcpflags].
- icmp[1] is the same expression as icmp[icmpcode].
- icmp[2] is the same expression as icmp[icmptype].

Again, the manpage lists which ICMP types have predefined keywords. To specify the other types or the codes, look up the desired number from the official list at *http://www.iana.org/assignments/icmp-parameters*.

## Deciphering tcpdump Output

Okay, you've managed to capture just the packets you're interested in. Now, can you understand your results?

Let's look at some sample lines from a dumpfile. This particular dump is the first few packets from a POP3 session:

```
# tcpdump -r dumpfile
17:22:36.611386 arp who-has 192.168.2.100 tell genisis.
17:22:36.611642 arp reply 192.168.2.100 is-at 0:48:54:1e:2c:76
```

ARP packets are fairly comprehensible. In this example, my ARP table didn't contain an entry for my default gateway, 192.168.2.100. My system, genisis, sent out a request looking for that gateway. The gateway responded with its MAC address, 0:48:54:1e:2c:76.

```
17:22:36.620320 genisis..49570 > nscott11.bellnexxia.net.domain:  40816+
\A? pop1.sympatico.ca. (35)
17:22:36.628557 nscott11.bellnexxia.net.domain > genisis..49570:  40816
\1/4/4 A 209.226.175.83 (203) (DF)
```

Once ARP had sorted out the MAC address, a DNS lookup had to occur. The word domain in these lines indicate a DNS lookup request followed by a DNS reply. Let's see if we can decipher both the request and the reply.

Each starts with a timestamp, which is composed of the time and a random number, separated by a dot. Since many packets can be sent within the same second, the random number is used to differentiate between packets.

The two hosts are separated by a greater-than sign. If you can visualize it as an arrow, like -->, you can see that genisis sent that first packet to nscott11.bellnexxia.net.domain. Each hostname has an extra dot, followed by either a port number or a resolved port name. In this case, genisis used port 49570, and nscott11.bellnexxia.net used the domain port. If you come across a port name you're not familiar with, look it up in /etc/services:

```
% grep -w domain /etc/services
domain    53/tcp    #Domain Name Server
domain    53/udp    #Domain Name Server
```

The next number, 40816, is an ID number that is shared by both the DNS client (genisis) and the DNS server. The client then asked a question (?) regarding the A record for pop1.sympatico.ca. The entire packet itself was 35 bytes long.

The second packet, from the DNS server, shared the same ID number. It was also a longer packet, 203 bytes, as it contained the answer. See the 1/4/4? This means that there is one entry in the answer section, four entries in the authority section, and four entries in the additional section. (See "Understand DNS Records and Tools" [Hack #47] for an explanation of these sections.) The DNS server also sent the requested A record, which contains the requested IP address, 209.226.175.83.

Now that name resolution has succeeded, a packet can be sent to the POP3 server:

```
17:22:36.629268 genisis..49499 > 209.226.175.83.pop3: S
\2697729992:2697729992(0) win 65535 <mss 1460,nop,wscale 1,nop,nop,timestamp
2474141 0> (DF)
17:22:36.642617 209.226.175.83.pop3 > genisis..49499: S
\2225396806:2225396806(0) ack 2697729993 win 25920 <nop,nop,timestamp
\3293621409 2474141,nop,wscale 0,mss 1452> (DF)
```

This output is much easier to read if you have a picture of a TCP header handy, as the output details the information found in that header. Each line starts out as before: the timestamp, source port, >, and destination port. We then see an S, which refers to that SYN flag.

This is followed by the sequence number and, almost always, by the ack number. The only packet that doesn't have an ack number is the SYN-1, the first packet in this example. This is because a SYN-1 is the first TCP packet, so there is nothing to acknowledge yet. All other TCP packets after the SYN-1 will have an ack.

Next comes the window size. If the packet has any options, they will be enclosed within angle brackets. Finally, the IP header had the "don't fragment" flag, DF, set. This is important enough to be printed at the end of any line representing a TCP or UDP header.

### See Also

- `man tcpdump`
- *http://www.tcpdump.org/*
- *http://www.ethereal.com/*
- "TCP Protocol Layers Explained," a FreeBSD Basics column (*http://www.onlamp.com/pub/a/bsd/2001/03/14/FreeBSD_Basics.html*)
- "Examining ICMP Packets," a FreeBSD Basics column (*http://www.onlamp.com/pub/a/bsd/2001/04/04/FreeBSD_Basics.html*)

## Understand DNS Records and Tools

### #47  Demystify DNS records.

DNS is one of those network services that has to be configured carefully and tested regularly. A misconfigured DNS server can prevent the world from finding your web and mail servers. Worse, a misconfigured DNS server can allow the world to find more than just your web and mail servers.

Even if you're not a DNS administrator, you should still know some handy DNS commands. The simple truth is, if DNS isn't working, you're not going anywhere. That means no surfing, no downloading, and no email for you.

### Exploring Your ISP's DNS

On your home system, you most likely receive your DNS information from your ISP's DHCP server. Do you know where to find your primary and secondary DNS server addresses? If not, try this:

```
% more /etc/resolv.conf
search domain.org
```

```
nameserver 204.101.251.1
nameserver 204.101.251.2
```

Another method is to use the dig (domain information groper) utility. Here, I'll ask for the nameservers (ns) for the *sympatico.ca* network:

```
% dig ns sympatico.ca

; <<>> DiG 8.3 <<>> ns sympatico.ca
;; res options: init recurs defnam dnsrch
;; got answer:
;; ->>HEADER<<- opcode: QUERY, status: NOERROR, id: 2
;; flags: qr rd ra; QUERY: 1, ANSWER: 4, AUTHORITY: 0, ADDITIONAL: 4
;; QUERY SECTION:
;;        sympatico.ca, type = NS, class = IN

;; ANSWER SECTION:
sympatico.ca.                8h29m IN NS     ns5.bellnexxia.net.
sympatico.ca.                8h29m IN NS     ns6.bellnexxia.net.
sympatico.ca.                8h29m IN NS     dns1.sympatico.ca.
sympatico.ca.                8h29m IN NS     dns2.sympatico.ca.

;; ADDITIONAL SECTION:
ns5.bellnexxia.net.     23m45s IN A      209.226.175.236
ns6.bellnexxia.net.     32m47s IN A      209.226.175.237
dns1.sympatico.ca.      27m28s IN A      204.101.251.1
dns2.sympatico.ca.      22m26s IN A      204.101.251.2

;; Total query time: 2038 msec
;; FROM: genisis to SERVER: default -- 198.235.216.111
;; WHEN: Sun Nov 23 17:22:31 2003
;; MSG SIZE   sent: 30   rcvd: 182
```

**Understanding DNS entries.** dig results are divided into sections. Not surprisingly, the ANSWER SECTION answers the question asked; in this case, "What are the nameservers for *sympatico.ca*?" In DNS, each entry in the DNS database is called a *record*. The answer indicates that *sympatico.ca* has four nameservers. Their hostnames are:

- ns5.bellnexxia.net
- ns6.bellnexxia.net
- dns1.sympatico.ca
- dns2.sympatico.ca

The next section, ADDITIONAL SECTION, maps each hostname in the ANSWER SECTION to its corresponding IP address. As an end user, you're really interested in the IP addresses of your nameservers, not their names. You need the address of least *one* DNS server before you can resolve *any* name to an address.

The other thing I'd like to point out is the type of records that were returned in the output. Notice that each nameserver record had an NS. If you ever see NS in a DNS database, you know you're looking at a DNS server record. Also, all hosts, regardless of whether they also happen to be a DNS server, web server, or mail server, have an A record. An A record maps a hostname to an IP address. In other words, a DNS server has two records: the NS record indicates that it is a DNS server, and the A record lists its IP address.

Can you tell which of the four nameservers in this output is the primary nameserver? You could look at the names and try to figure it out from there. However, it is possible to find out for sure, and it's easy once you know that SOA, the start of authority record, indicates the primary nameserver. Let's ask dig to show us the SOA record:

```
% dig soa sympatico.ca
<snip banner>
;; ANSWER SECTION:
sympatico.ca.                16m18s IN SOA        dns1.sympatico.ca. dns-
admin.sympatico.ca. (
<snip>
;; AUTHORITY SECTION:
sympatico.ca.                3h22m20s IN NS       dns2.sympatico.ca.
sympatico.ca.                3h22m20s IN NS       ns5.bellnexxia.net.
sympatico.ca.                3h22m20s IN NS       ns6.bellnexxia.net.
sympatico.ca.                3h22m20s IN NS       dns1.sympatico.ca.
;; ADDITIONAL SECTION:
dns2.sympatico.ca.           8m36s IN A           204.101.251.2
ns5.bellnexxia.net.          9m55s IN A           209.226.175.236
ns6.bellnexxia.net.          18m57s IN A          209.226.175.237
dns1.sympatico.ca.           13m38s IN A          204.101.251.1

;; Total query time: 239 msec
;; FROM: genisis to SERVER: default -- 198.235.216.111
;; WHEN: Sun Nov 23 17:36:22 2003
;; MSG SIZE  sent: 30  rcvd: 228
```

Notice the answer? Looks like dns1.sympatico.ca or 204.101.251.1 is the primary nameserver. We also received an extra section, the AUTHORITY SECTION. Every query except ns will show which nameservers have the "authority" to answer your question.

You may prefer to try an any query instead of ns. This will show both the NS records and the SOA record, all in one shot.

While you're digging through your ISP's DNS information, you might want to find the name of your SMTP server. Since these servers have mail exchange (MX) records, use an mx query:

```
% dig mx sympatico.ca
<snip banner>
```

```
;; ANSWER SECTION:
sympatico.ca.               27m48s IN MX      5 smtpip.sympatico.ca.
sympatico.ca.               27m48s IN MX      5 mta1.sympatico.ca.
sympatico.ca.               27m48s IN MX      5 mta2.sympatico.ca.
sympatico.ca.               27m48s IN MX      5 mta3.sympatico.ca.

;; AUTHORITY SECTION:
sympatico.ca.               2h34m29s IN NS      dns2.sympatico.ca.
sympatico.ca.               2h34m29s IN NS      ns5.bellnexxia.net.
sympatico.ca.               2h34m29s IN NS      ns6.bellnexxia.net.
sympatico.ca.               2h34m29s IN NS      dns1.sympatico.ca.

;; ADDITIONAL SECTION:
smtpip.sympatico.ca.        28m30s IN A       209.226.175.84
mta1.sympatico.ca.          13m56s IN A       209.226.175.80
mta2.sympatico.ca.          28m30s IN A       209.226.175.81
mta3.sympatico.ca.          13m56s IN A       209.226.175.82
<snip>
```

Looks like my ISP has four SMTP servers; I'd better remember which one I'm supposed to use!

MX records always include a priority number. In this example, each mail server has a priority of 5, so they all have the same priority. Sometimes you'll see records where one mail server has a higher number than another. Always try sending your email to the server with a *lower* number—that server has a higher priority. If the priority is 0, you should always use that mail server. This bit of information is good to know if you plan to send someone an email without using a mail client [Hack #48].

## Securing DNS

Put on your administrator's hat for a moment and re-examine these dig outputs. Did you happen to notice that the nameservers live on different networks? Let's take another look at those A records for the DNS servers:

```
dns2.sympatico.ca.        8m36s IN A      204.101.251.2
ns5.bellnexxia.net.       9m55s IN A      209.226.175.236
ns6.bellnexxia.net.       18m57s IN A     209.226.175.237
dns1.sympatico.ca.        13m38s IN A     204.101.251.1
```

Two of the four nameservers live on network 204.101.252, and the other two live on network 209.226.175. This is actually a good network design. Several attacks against high-profile companies have succeeded because their DNS servers were all on the same subnet of the same network. (See this article about DNS troubles at Microsoft for an example: *http://www.findarticles.com/ cf_dls/m0FOX/3_6/75645162/p1/article.jhtml.*)

Realistically, to provide such protection, your company has to enter into an agreement with another company willing to host a copy of your DNS database. That other company may be your ISP, or perhaps a sister company. While adding redundancy, this also adds complexity and another element of trust. It's one thing to keep your own DNS servers up-to-date, fully patched, and securely configured. It's quite another to work with another administrator and assume that she has the resources to devote the same time and effort to your DNS servers.

Regardless of how the network is organized, someone has to address the issue of *zone transfers*. In DNS, your database is called a *zone*, as it really is just a portion of the globally distributed DNS database. When you need to make a change to your zone, you edit the database on the primary DNS server. However, you have to implement at least one secondary DNS server to provide redundancy. How are those changes propagated to the secondary DNS server(s)? If you guessed "via a zone transfer," you're right!

It's important to make a distinction here. Resolving a hostname is one thing. As an end user, you need that functionality in order to access Internet resources. As an administrator, you want your DNS servers to provide name resolution. Otherwise, you have to listen to a lot of unhappy end users.

However, your end users do not need to know the entire contents of your DNS database. The world at large certainly doesn't need to know the name and IP address of every host in your network. Think about that one for a moment. You probably have machines right now called finance, hr, patents, store, or admin. What tasty names those are to fire the imaginations of a malicious user!

**The two-pronged approach.** You can use a two-pronged approach to prevent your DNS servers from leaking information you'd rather not have the world see. The first approach is called *split DNS*. Run your full DNS zone within your internal network, and run a very small subset of that zone in your DMZ. That small subset is all the world sees. If you think about it for a moment, which records does the world need to know about? Probably just the record for your DNS server (the one in the DMZ, with its secondary preferably hosted at your ISP or somewhere else), the record for your web server, and the record for your SMTP server. Those are the only records that this mini-zone should contain.

The second approach is to control zone transfers tightly. The last thing you want to happen is for the DNS server in the DMZ to ask for a copy of your full internal zone. For that matter, you also don't want a user on the Internet to ask your internal DNS server for all of the records in your network.

There are multiple ways to control zone transfers, and you should implement all of them. First, read the documentation for your DNS server to see how to restrict the IP addresses that are allowed to ask for zone transfers. (The "Securing an Internet Name Server" link in this hack's "See Also" section explains how to do this for BIND.)

Second, configure your firewalls to control zone transfers. DNS is an interesting protocol, as it uses port 53 with both TCP and UDP. Your firewalls *must* allow UDP 53; if you deny this, all name resolution will stop. That is a bad thing. However, TCP 53 is used for zone transfers. You must carefully construct a firewall rule that allows TCP 53 only for the specific IP addresses of the DNS servers that need to participate in a zone transfer. Remember, you *do* want to transfer changes to your secondary servers.

Third, create guidelines to test your DNS servers periodically. Notice how complex it was to secure those nameservers. How many things could go wrong? Perhaps an OS patch or a DNS server application patch will introduce a new hole. Perhaps a change in a firewall rulebase will unwittingly reallow zone transfers. You're dealing with multiple DNS servers—probably in multiple locations—and multiple firewalls, which only increases the possibility of error. A routine testing schedule increases the chance of catching those errors before they remain for very long.

**Testing DNS.** You can use the axfr switch with dig to test your DNS servers, but I prefer the output provided by host -al. When you run this utility against your own domain name, you should see a result similar to this one:

```
% host -al sympatico.ca
rcode = 0 (Success), ancount=4
Found 1 addresses for ns5.bellnexxia.net
Found 1 addresses for ns6.bellnexxia.net
Found 1 addresses for dns1.sympatico.ca
Found 1 addresses for dns2.sympatico.ca
Trying 209.226.175.236
Server failed, trying next server: Query refused
Trying 209.226.175.237
Server failed, trying next server: Query refused
Trying 204.101.251.1
Server failed, trying next server: Query refused
Trying 204.101.251.2
Server failed: Query refused
```

Remember, host -al asks for a zone transfer. You *want* your DNS servers to refuse this request. In this example, all four DNS servers received the request, so I know they are up and working. The host utility then requested a zone transfer from each server. Note the order: the first IP address is for the first listed nameserver, and so on. This is important, especially if one of those nameservers responds with a zone transfer. I can't count the number of times I've tested DNS servers and two out of three will refuse the query, but one will allow the zone transfer. You'll know which DNS server was the culprit if you make note of the server response order.

This test is especially important if one or more of your DNS servers is hosted elsewhere. Make sure your agreement indicates that you will be regularly testing your DNS servers for misconfigurations.

### See Also

- `man dig`
- `man host`
- Implementing Split DNS (*http://www.relevanttechnologies.com/splitdns_081000.asp*)
- "Securing an Internet Name Server" (*http://www.acmebw.com/resources/papers/securing.pdf*)

# Send and Receive Email Without a Mail Client
### Learn to speak SMTP and POP3.

Contrary to popular belief, you don't have to go to the trouble of configuring an email client just because you want to check your email or send off a quick email message.

Normally when you use the `telnet` application, you use a Telnet client to attach to a Telnet server listening on port 23. Once you're connected, you can log in and do anything on that device as if you were physically there, typing at its keyboard.

The Telnet client has even more powerful capabilities than this. If you specify a port number with the `telnet` command, you will attach directly to the TCP server listening on that port. If you know which commands that server can respond to, and if the service understands plain text commands, you can talk directly to that server. This essentially means that you no longer require a client application specific to that server.

### Sending Email with telnet

Whenever you send an email, you connect to an SMTP server listening on port 25. Let's use `telnet` to see what really happens in the background and which commands the client and the SMTP server exchange. Note that in the following examples, the names and addresses have been changed to protect the innocent.

```
% telnet smtp.mycompany.com 25
Trying 1.2.3.4...
Connected to smtp.mycompany.com.
```

```
Escape character is '^]'.
220 smtp.mycompany.com ESMTP server (InterMail version x) ready Sun, 2
Nov 2003 09:54:18 -0500
mail from:<moi@mycompany.com>
250 Sender <moi@mycompany.com> Ok
rcpt to:<you@mycompany.com>
250 Recipient <you@mycompany.com> Ok
data
354 Ok Send data ending with <CRLF>.<CRLF>
This is a test message.
Not very interesting, really.
.
250 Message received: 20031102145448.QON15340.smtp.mycompany.com@[1.2.3.4]
quit
```

Let's pick apart that output. Note the 25 at the end of the telnet command. If you forget the port number, your prompt will probably hang. This is because instead of trying to connect to the SMTP service, you're trying to receive a login prompt from your ISP's mail server. If you actually do receive a login prompt, it is time to switch ISPs, as security is obviously not one of their concerns!

Next, the output indicates when you successfully connect to the SMTP service. Notice that there are very few secrets in TCP/IP-land. The SMTP server readily shows its banner, which indicates the type of SMTP application running on that server, its version and patch level, as well as the time and date you connected. We'll talk more about banners later.

After connecting to the server, I issued two SMTP commands: MAIL FROM and RCPT TO. Some SMTP servers are pickier than others and won't recognize these commands unless you say hello first. If your SMTP server complains about your lack of politeness, try typing HELO or EHLO. I know that this SMTP server accepted my commands because the responses start with 2xx and end with Ok. Responses that begin with 5xx indicate errors—you either made a typo or used the wrong command. Most SMTP servers try to be helpful by giving the syntax of the command they expect to receive.

After providing the sender and recipient email addresses, I issued the DATA command and pressed Enter. The SMTP server then asked me to type my message. To indicate I was finished, I put a dot (.) on a line by itself. The server responded with a message number, and I ended the session by typing QUIT.

Some interesting things happen if I play a bit with the SMTP commands. For example, the MAIL FROM command does not verify that the given email address is valid. This has some interesting ramifications, as I could pretend to be *santa@northpole.com*, *satan@hell.org*, or any other address my imagination could dream up. Remember this quirk when you read your email. There is no guarantee that any given email was actually sent from the email address it purports to be from.

Additionally, I'll have mixed results if I start playing with the RCPT TO address. I might start receiving error messages like this:

```
550 relaying mail to nowhere.com is not allowed
```

This is actually a good error message to receive, as SMTP relaying is considered to be a bad thing. In this particular instance, I've asked the SMTP server of *mycompany.com* to send my message to a recipient at *nowhere.com*. The server rightfully complained, as it should only be responsible for the recipients at *mycompany.com*. If I want to send a message to a recipient at *nowhere.com*, I should instead attach to *nowhere.com*'s SMTP server.

 Since you're supposed to connect to the correct SMTP server in order to send email, how can you find out the name of a recipient's SMTP server? This is a very easy matter, since a company's DNS server has to maintain an MX record for just this purpose. See "Understand DNS Records and Tools" **[Hack #47]** for details.

## Testing for Relaying

As mentioned before, relaying is considered harmful because it allows spammers to use another company's SMTP server to relay spam. If you're responsible for an SMTP server, be sure to read your SMTP documentation to see whether relaying is off by default and how to turn it off if it isn't. You can then initiate a quick telnet session to port 25 to ensure your SMTP server does indeed refuse to relay email. For example, I don't want the *mycompany.com* SMTP server to respond like this:

```
rcpt to:<beastie@unix.ca>
250 Recipient <beastie@unix.ca> Ok
```

If it does, it is willing to relay to the *unix.ca* SMTP server.

What else should you look for when you telnet to your own SMTP server? Take a careful look at your banner. Does it freely advertise that you're one or two patch levels behind? Do you really want to tell anyone who knows enough to ask which particular SMTP product you're using? If they know enough to use telnet, they probably know how to use Google to look for known vulnerabilities in that product. It's always good to know exactly what the world sees. You can then determine if you prefer to change the banner to something a little less chatty. Read the documentation for your particular product to see how to do so.

## Testing SMTP Server Availability

Finally, telnet is an invaluable troubleshooting tool. For example, if users complain that they can no longer access the mail server, your first step is to check connectivity by pinging the mail server. If the mail server responds, you can telnet to its SMTP port to verify that the SMTP service is still running.

## Reading Email with telnet

Let's move on to POP3, so we can pick up our email messages. Here I'll pick up that message I sent previously:

```
% telnet pop.mycompany.com 110
Trying 1.2.3.4...
Connected to pop.mycompany.com.
Escape character is '^]'.
+OK InterMail POP3 server ready.
user you
+OK please send PASS command
pass thecleartextpassword
+OK you is welcome here
list
+OK 1 messages
1 544
.
retr 1
+OK 544 octets
Return-Path: <moi@mycompany.com>
Received: from [1.2.3.4] by smtp.mycompany.com
        (InterMail version x) with SMTP
        id: <20031102145448.QON15340.smtp.mycompany.com@[1.2.3.4]>
        for <you@mycompany.com>; Sun, 2 Nov 2003 09:54:18 -0500
Message-Id: <20031102145448.QON15340.smtp.mycompany.com@[1.2.3.4]>
Date: Sun, 2 Nov 2003 09:57:34 -0500
From: <moi@mycompany.com>

This is a test message.
Not very interesting, really.
.
quit
+OK you InterMail POP3 server signing off.
Connection closed by foreign host.
```

Notice that you use port 110 to connect to a POP3 server. Also, the commands used by POP3 are very different than those understood by SMTP. In this session, I used the USER command to indicate my username and the PASS command for my password. Unlike SMTP, you do have to authenticate to use POP3.

Once I successfully authenticated, I used the LIST command to see how many email messages were waiting for me. I had one message, which was

544 bytes long. I then used the RETR command to display that message, including the headers as well as its contents, and typed the QUIT command to end the POP3 session.

There are several things you should be aware of regarding the POP3 protocol. The first is that every single packet—including those containing your username, password, and the contents of each email message—are sent in clear text. That means that a packet sniffer running on your network would have full access to that information.

Second, anyone who knows your email password could conceivably connect to your POP3 server and read your email. Worse, they could use the DELE command to delete your email before you had a chance to receive it.

## Security Considerations

That doesn't sound very good, does it? There are several things you can do as an end-user to protect your email. One is to use a third-party email encryption product, which will protect the contents of your email (but not your username and password) from packet sniffers. The other is to use different passwords for different functions. For example, don't use the same password to pick up email, do online banking, log into your office network, etc. And always pick a password that your friends and family won't be able to guess.

As an email administrator, you can also create a safer environment for your users. Create a different username for each user, something other than the names contained within their email addresses. For example: *moi@mycompany.com* usually indicates a username of moi. That means I could connect to the POP3 server at *mycompany.com* and try to guess the password for the user moi. However, if the administrator had given that user a username such as 12tn4g and instructed that user never to give out his username, it would be much more difficult for someone else to access his email.

## See Also

- RFC 2821, the latest SMTP RFC (including valid SMTP commands), at *http://www.ietf.org/rfc/rfc2821.txt*
- RFC 1939, the latest POP3 RFC (including valid POP3 commands), at *http://www.ietf.org/rfc/rfc1939.txt*
- The Relaying FAQ (*http://ordb.org/faq/*)
- How to Read Email Headers (*http://www.stopspam.org/email/headers.html*)

## HACK #49 Why Do I Need sendmail?

Don't be too quick to disable sendmail completely—you might still need it.

As an end user, you've probably asked yourself: "If all I'm doing is running a FreeBSD machine for personal use, why should I need to run a heavyweight MTA daemon like sendmail?"

sendmail is the standard Mail Transport Agent (MTA) on FreeBSD, as it is on most Unix systems. In fact, the majority of email passing over the Internet will probably travel through a sendmail server at some point. However, sendmail isn't the easiest software package to manage, and the configuration file syntax gives most people a headache. There are several alternative MTA packages available, but these are also industrial-strength programs suitable for demanding use.

Many modern graphical email clients, such as Netscape Mail or Evolution, can send email directly to a mail server machine across the network. So, no, you won't need an MTA on your local machine to send email. (However, you will need an MTA if you use one of the more traditional Unix mail clients, such as mail, mutt, or pine.)

Regardless of your email client, if you want to see any automatic emails the system sends—usually from the periodic scripts—then you do require an MTA. More precisely, Unix programs expect to be able to send email by piping its text into the standard input of /usr/sbin/sendmail, and have the system take care of the rest of the work for them.

> The venerable sendmail is only one of many MTAs available. Choosing another MTA does not always mean that you need to change the habits you picked up while working with sendmail. All three major BSD systems have a translator file, /etc/mailer.conf, that identifies which commands to execute when the user or another process executes sendmail, mailq, or newaliases.
>
> For example, if you install postfix, you still use the sendmail command, even though the real job is done by the commands from the postfix package. The existence of /etc/mailer.conf makes it easy to replace one MTA with another without turning the whole mail subsystem upside down.

### Closing Port 25

Since most systems aren't mail servers, you can disable the *receiving* of email. In other words, there's no reason to have sendmail listening on port 25 on any exposed interface.

Port 25 must be open on SMTP mail servers, but it does *not* have to be open in order to send an email as a client. Remember, any unnecessary open port is a potential security risk.

It is possible to close port 25 (except on the loopback interface) and still allow sendmail to run occasionally in order to process outgoing messages. Add the following line to */etc/rc.conf*:

```
sendmail_enable="NO"
```

With the release of sendmail-8.12.2 in 2002, sendmail has been split into two parts, each with a separate configuration file. These are the MTA process, which uses SMTP to copy the mail from machine to machine, and the Mail Submission Process (MSP), whose job is to read in the complete text of any new email and reliably inject it into the MTA. When programs run */usr/sbin/sendmail*, they interact with the MSP.

You can either run an MTA process locally or not run it at all, configuring the MSP to deliver straight to the MTA on your provider's smart host. In order to deliver any email, it has to pass from the MSP to an MTA. The MSP talks SMTP to the MTA to do that, which requires the MTA to be listening on port 25.

## Simple sendmail Configuration with a Local MTA

Setting sendmail_enable="NO" in */etc/rc.conf* does not turn off sendmail—use sendmail_enable="NONE" for that—but it does stop sendmail from receiving incoming email. In fact, sendmail_enable="NO" will result in starting up two sendmail processes: an MSP queue manager and an MTA process that listens on the loopback address only. Having the MTA listen only on the loopback interface means that it can be accessed only from the local machine. This is an acceptably secure compromise between having port 25 open generally and not having access to the local MTA at all.

If you want to send emails to external recipients, edit the sendmail configuration file slightly to tell it the name of your provider's email smart host:

```
# cd /etc/mail
# cp freebsd.mc `hostname`.mc
```

where `hostname` turns into the system's hostname.

Open *<hostname>.mc* in your favorite editor. Change the line that says:

```
dnl define(`SMART_HOST', `your.isp.mail.server')
```

to read:

```
define(`SMART_HOST', `smtp.yourprovider.net')
```

Replace *smtp.yourprovider.net* with the correct name of your provider's SMTP server. dnl stands for "Delete until New Line"—it's used to comment out text in *.mc* files, so this change simply uncomments an example line in the default *.mc* file. Note that in *.mc* files, the left tick (`) is different from the right tick (').

> By default, the submission port (587) is also open. This port is part of the SMTP standard, but there is very little application support at the moment, so you won't miss it if you close it. Add this line to your *hostname.mc*:
>
> ```
> FEATURE(no_default_msa)dnl
> ```

Now process the *.mc* file into a *.cf* file, and install and activate it:

```
# make
# make install
# make restart-mta
```

You don't need to make any changes to the default sendmail MSP configuration. This setup will send all messages for nonlocal users to the provider's smart host for processing. It doesn't provide any means of receiving incoming emails over the network.

## Simple sendmail Configuration Without a Local MTA

Instead of running both a sendmail MSP queue runner and a sendmail MTA process, an alternative is to use just an MSP queue runner. Don't worry about the sendmail MTA, as you're not using it. In addition to sendmail_enable="NO", add these lines to */etc/rc.conf*:

```
sendmail_submit_enable="NO"
sendmail_outbound_enable="NO"
```

You'll also need to customize the sendmail configuration slightly, this time for the MSP rather than the MTA.

```
# cd /etc/mail
# cp freebsd.submit.mc submit.mc
```

Change the last line in *submit.mc* from:

```
FEATURE(`msp', `[127.0.0.1]')dnl
```

to:

```
FEATURE(`msp', `smtp.yourprovider.net')dnl
```

where, as before, *smtp.yourprovider.net* is your ISP's mail smart host.

Then, install and activate the new configuration:

```
# make
# make install
# make restart-msp
```

Again, this will permit you to send email anywhere in the world, but not to receive incoming messages. This differs from the preceding "with MTA" configuration, in that this has to send all outgoing messages—without exception—through the provider's smart host. In return, there is no longer a sendmail process listening on port 25.

> A third alternative to send-only SMTP is ssmtp, which is available in the FreeBSD ports collection or from source at the main web site. You can find detailed instructions in Bill Moran's "Setting up to send only" article at *http:// www.potentialtech.com/wmoran/outgoing-only.html*.

### See Also

- `man sendmail`
- `man mailer.conf`
- `man rc.conf`
- The ssmtp web site (*http://packages.debian.org/testing/mail/ssmtp.html*)

## HACK #50 Hold Email for Later Delivery

Control when sendmail uses an intermittent Internet connection.

The default sendmail configuration assumes that you have a constant network connection. What if you're on a dial-up system and want to be able to work on emails without causing your modem to dial up immediately? In this scenario, you want to queue your sent messages to send later, the next time you go online.

### Configuring sendmail Queueing

Fortunately, sendmail has a "hold expensive" function designed for this purpose. To activate it, add the following lines to the */etc/mail/<hostname>.mc* file:

```
define(`confCON_EXPENSIVE', `True')dnl
MODIFY_MAILER_FLAGS(`RELAY', `+e')dnl
MODIFY_MAILER_FLAGS(`SMTP', `+e')dnl
MODIFY_MAILER_FLAGS(`ESMTP', `+e')dnl
MODIFY_MAILER_FLAGS(`SMTP8', `+e')dnl
define(`confTO_QUEUEWARN', `12h')dnl
```

The first line enables the feature. The next four lines add the letter e to the flags for each named mailer, to indicate that it is "expensive" and that email should first be queued rather than immediately delivered. The last line just extends the length of time the system will wait before it warns you that your message hasn't been delivered yet (the default is four hours).

Now just build the configuration file, install it, and restart sendmail as usual:

```
# cd /etc/mail
# make
# make install
# make restart-mta
```

The four mailers listed (RELAY, SMTP, ESMTP, and SMTP8) will handle the bulk of all transmissions over the network. The configuration of both local and remote mail systems will determine which one to use. However, if you send out all of your mail via your provider's smart host, the RELAY mailer is the best choice.

So far so good. However, you still need to make some more changes to the way sendmail runs. Queued messages will sit in the mail queue (/var/spool/ mqueue) until the next sendmail queue run. These occur every 30 minutes when using the default sendmail command-line flags. The following settings in /etc/rc.conf will suppress that default:

```
sendmail_enable="NO"
sendmail_submit_flags="-L sm-mta -bd -ODaemonPortOptions=Addr=localhost"
```

Note the deletion of -q30m from the default value of sendmail_submit_flags. Those lines assume that you don't want a sendmail process listening on port 25 on your network interface for incoming emails, which can be problematic on a transient link, such as dial-up. (See "Why Do I Need sendmail?" **[Hack #49]** for an alternate approach.)

## Configuring PPP

Having effectively prevented the system from ever flushing the mail queue, you'll now need to add a mechanism for sending all queued email when the PPP link activates. If you're running the user land ppp daemon, create /etc/ ppp/ppp.linkup with these contents:

```
papchap:
     !bg /usr/sbin/sendmail -q
```

/etc/ppp/ppp.linkup should be owned by the root user and the wheel group, and be writable only by root, although it can be readable by all.

Alternatively, add the line /usr/sbin/sendmail -q to an existing *auth-up* file. (pppd uses the shell script /etc/ppp/auth-up to run commands after the link has come up and the systems have authenticated successfully.)

If you don't have an existing */etc/ppp/auth-up*, copy it from */usr/share/examples/pppd/auth-up.sample*.

## Dealing with DNS

There is a huge gotcha in this whole discussion. sendmail makes extensive use of the DNS while it processes email. That DNS traffic will usually trigger on-demand dialing, and bringing up the PPP link—triggering an immediate queue flush—defeats the whole purpose of what you've done so far.

There are several things you can do to ameliorate this problem:

- Add DNS traffic to the dial filter in */etc/ppp/ppp.conf* if you use usermode ppp. This is effective, but leads to annoying delays waiting for DNS lookups to time out.

*0* and *1* are just the rule numbers for the dial filter set: modify these as necessary if you already have some dial filter rules.

- Run your own DNS server either just as a local cache or as the authoritative host for your local networks.
- Record the hostnames and IP numbers of your systems and your provider's mail systems in */etc/hosts*, and configure the system to use the flat files instead of DNS. (See man host.conf for FreeBSD 4.x and man nsswitch.conf for 5.x.)
- Alternatively, use other local databases to do host lookups, such as NIS or LDAP.
- Specify hostnames in the sendmail configuration using square brackets around the [*hostname*].

This last option tells sendmail not to look up MX records, which are available only from DNS; instead, it will only look up IP numbers. For example, specify your ISP's SMTP server's hostname in this line of */etc/mail/<hostname>.mc*:

```
define(`SMART_HOST', `[smtp.example.com]')dnl
```

Then, rebuild the configuration file as before.

Note that these hacks will only mitigate the DNS problem. Unfortunately, it is all but impossible to eliminate inconvenient DNS lookups.

## See Also

- `man ppp`
- `man pppd`
- `man host.conf`
- `man nsswitch.conf`

## Get the Most Out of FTP

**#51**    Get the most out of stock ftp with macros and scripts.

In this age of GUIs and feature-rich browsers, it's easy to forget how quick and efficient command-line `ftp` can be. That is, until you're logged into a system that doesn't have X installed, nor a browser, nor any fancy FTP programs. If it's really your lucky day, it won't even have any manpages. And, of course, you'll need to download something.

Perhaps you find yourself using `ftp` all the time, always going to the same FTP servers and downloading from or uploading to the same directories. Clearly, it's time for some FTP automation.

### Automating Logins

Have you ever noticed how easy it is to use FTP from a modern browser? Simply click on a hyperlink to start a download. At the command line, though, you can't even browse the FTP directory structure until you successfully log into the FTP server. Well, guess what: you *always* have to log into an FTP server. It's just that your web browser hides this little detail by doing it for you in the background.

You can achieve the same transparency for command-line `ftp` by creating a file called *.netrc* in your home directory and placing the following line in that file:

```
% more ~/.netrc
default login anonymous password genisis@istar.ca
```

This line will work for any FTP server on the Internet that accepts anonymous logins. (Most do, unless it's a private server.) When creating your own file, use your own email address as the password.

Test your change with this command:

```
% ftp ftp.freebsd.org
```

Compare your results to the FTP output in "Create an Emergency Repair Kit" **[Hack #71]**. You should receive the same banner shown there without having to first type in a username and password.

If you're a webmaster who uses FTP to upload your new files, you do have to log in first. After all, you don't want just anyone uploading files, so you require a username and password. To automate that process, add a section to your ~.netrc that reflects the name of your server and your username and password:

```
machine ftp.myserver.com
login myusername
password mypassword
```

Since you've just inserted your password into a plain text file, it's important to change the permissions on this file so that only you can read it:

```
% chmod 600 ~/.netrc
```

If you forget to change the permissions and try to access an FTP server that requires a username and password, your login attempt should fail and result in this error message:

```
ftp: Error: .netrc file is readable by others.
ftp: Remove password or make file unreadable by others.
```

To be extra safe, exclude the password line completely. When you connect to the FTP server, your username will be provided for you, but you will still be prompted for the password.

## Automating Transfers

Now, let's say that you visit *ftp.freebsd.org* on a regular basis and always access its *pub/FreeBSD/releases/i386* directory. Rather than cding every time, you can automate that process by creating an FTP macro. Add these lines to ~/.netrc:

```
macdef fbsd
bin
cd /pub/FreeBSD/releases/i386
```

Macros are defined by macdef, and the name of the macro follows. Keep the name short but useful, as a macro is supposed to be a timesaver. Once you've declared the macro, add the FTP commands you want to execute, one line at a time. This particular macro contains the bin (or binary) command. That command is useful when downloading because it ensures all files, including non-ASCII files such as applications, will download correctly. I also included a cd command to automatically take me to my usual working directory.

It's important that a macro always ends with a blank line.

There are two ways to use your macro. If you're already connected to the FTP server, type $ *macroname* at the ftp prompt:

```
ftp> $ fbsd
bin
200 Type set to I.
cd /pub/FreeBSD/releases/i386
250 "/pub/FreeBSD/releases/i386" is new cwd.
```

Note that each command in the macro will be executed, followed by its results.

The second way to run the macro is when you first invoke the ftp command:

```
% echo "$ fbsd" | ftp ftp.freebsd.org
```

Now, if you try that one, you'll notice that all of your commands will succeed. Then, your FTP session will abruptly end, and you'll receive your regular prompt back! Rather disappointing if you were planning on typing some more commands at the ftp prompt, but absolutely perfect if your intention is to script an entire FTP session.

## Scripting an Entire Session

If you already know what you want to do, and especially if you need to do it more than once, why type in everything at the ftp prompt? Suppose you want to download the latest XFree86 distribution directly from *ftp://ftp.xfree86.org/*. Consider placing this macro in *~/.netrc*:

```
macdef X
bin
bell
prompt
cd /pub/XFree86/4.3.0/source
mget *
bye
```

This macro assumes that this *~/.netrc* file already contains the line that allows anonymous logins.

The bell command, which is optional, should produce a sound after each successful file transfer. The prompt command is very important, though. By default, the FTP server expects interaction from the user. That is, when you ask to download multiple files with mget, the FTP server will wait for you to confirm every transfer by typing y. Obviously, we want to disable that behavior when we're scripting a download.

To run this macro:

```
% echo "$ X" | ftp ftp.xfree86.org
```

By default, ftp will save the downloaded files in your current working directory. If you prefer, you can specify an alternate location in your macro with the lcd (local change directory) command. For example:

```
lcd /usr/local/Xsource
```

will save the downloaded files to the */usr/local/Xsource* directory. Make sure your directory exists and put the lcd line before your mget line.

## A Better FTP?

No matter how hard you try to make the default FTP client user-friendly, it is still a very basic command, and you may find a little too primitive, especially if you use ftp often. If you would like to try a more convenient and user-friendly command-line tool, try ncftp, which is available as a port or package for FreeBSD, NetBSD, and OpenBSD.

## See Also

- man ftp
- The ncftp web site (*http://www.ncftp.com/ncftp/*)

### HACK
### #52
## Distributed Command Execution
Use tentakel for parallel, distributed command execution.

Often you want to execute a command not only on one computer, but on several at once. For example, you might want to report the current statistics on a group of managed servers or update all of your web servers at once.

## The Obvious Approach

You could simply do this on the command line with a shell script like the following:

```
# for host in hostA hostB hostC
> do ssh $host do_something
> done
```

However, this has several disadvantages:

- It is slow because the connections to the remote hosts do not run in parallel. Every connection must wait for the previous one to finish.

- Managing many sets of hosts can become a complicated task because there is no easy way to define groups of hosts (e.g., mailservers or workstations).

- The output is provided by the program that is run remotely.
- The output is hard to read because there are no marks indicating when the output for a specific host begins or ends.

## How tentakel Can Help

While you could write a shell script to address some of these disadvantages, you might want to consider tentakel, which is available in the ports collection. Its execution starts multiple threads that run independently of each other. The maximum waiting time depends on the longest running remote connection, not on the sum of all of them. After the last remote command has returned, tentakel displays the results of all remote command executions. You can also configure how the output should look, combining or differentiating the results from individual hosts.

tentakel operates on groups of hosts. A group can have two types of members: hosts or references to other groups. A group can also have parameters to control various aspects of the connection, including username and access method (rsh or ssh, for example).

## Installing and Configuring tentakel

Install tentakel from the ports collection:

```
# cd /usr/ports/sysutils/tentakel
# make install clean
```

You can instead install tentakel by hand; consult the *INSTALL* file in the distribution. A make install should work in most cases, provided that you have a working Python environment installed.

After the installation, create the configuration file *tentakel.conf* in the directory *$HOME/.tentakel/*. See the example file in */usr/local/share/doc/tentakel/ tentakel.conf.example* for a quick overview of the format.

Alternatively, copy the file into */usr/local/etc/* or */etc/*, depending on your system's policy, in order to have a site-wide *tentakel.conf* that will be used when there is no user-specific configuration. As an administrator, you may predefine groups for your users this way.

Assuming that you have a farm of three servers, mosel, aare, and spree, of which the first two are web servers, your configuration might resemble this:

```
set format="%d\n%o\n"

group webservers(user="webmaster")
    +mosel +aare
```

```
group servers(user="root")
  @webservers +spree
```

With this definition, you can use the group name servers to execute a command on all your servers as root and the group name webservers to execute it only on your web servers as user webmaster.

The first line defines the output format, as explained in Table 5-5.

*Table 5-5. tentakel output format characters*

| Character | Output |
|---|---|
| %d | The hostname |
| %o | The output of the remotely executed commands |
| \n | A newline character |

This commands tentakel to print the hostname, followed by the lines of the remote output for each server sequentially. You can enrich the format string with additional directives, such as %s for the exit status from commands. See the manpage for more information.

As you can see from the servers definition, there is no need to list all servers in each group; include servers from other groups using the @groupname notation.

On the remote machines, the only required configuration is to ensure that you can log into them from the tentakel machine without entering a password. Usually that will mean using ssh and public keys, which is also tentakel's default. tentakel provides the parameter method for using different mechanisms, so refer to the manpage for details.

## Using tentakel

To update the web pages on all web servers from a CVS repository:

```
% tentakel -g webservers "cd /var/www/htdocs && cvs update"
### mosel(0):
cvs update: Updating .
U index.html
U main.css
### aare(1):
C main.css
cvs update: Updating .
%
```

Note the use of quotes around the command to be executed. This prevents the local shell from interpreting special characters such as & or ;.

If no command is specified, tentakel invokes interactive mode:

```
% tentakel
interactive mode
tentakel(default)> use webservers
tentakel(webservers)> exec du -sh /var/www/htdocs
### mosel(0):
364k    /var/www/htdocs
### aare(0):
364k    /var/www/htdocs
tentakel(webservers)> quit
%
```

While in interactive mode, the command help prints further information.

## See Also

- man tentakel
- The tentakel web site (*http://tentakel.biskalar.de/*)

## HACK #53  Interactive Remote Administration

Monitor and interact with remote administration tasks.

Managing a large network can be a daunting task. Even with the Unix utilities available for remote administration, making changes on many systems can be taxing. Scripting tools make life easier to some extent, but some tasks require hands- and eyes-on interaction.

Several system utilities allow you to execute the same command on multiple hosts. This form of loosely coupled clustering is useful for information gathering and some monitoring purposes. However, on some occasions, you not only need to run a process on multiple hosts, but you must also observe it and interact with the process to resolve host-specific issues. An administration shell script will save typing and minimize mistakes, but it's hard to write a script that will work correctly on every machine on a diverse network.

Wouldn't it be nice if there were a program that allowed you to interact with your remote hosts while running parallel commands? Enter ClusterIt.

### Why ClusterIt?

ClusterIt is a set of tools written by Tim Rightnour, designed to place all of your network hosts at your fingertips. ClusterIt includes utilities for running a single command on all of the hosts in your cluster. It also allows automatic distribution of the tasks to any available hosts in a defined group. It uses a remote login method, such as sshd on the target hosts, so you only need to install it on the control host.

Scripts can also synchronize between task completions on different hosts. For example, you can set two hosts to compile an application and install it on the other machine. Neither host should begin the installation until the other host has finished compiling, but it is impossible to predict which host will finish first. ClusterIt defines barrier operations that can be included in a script to prevent passing a synchronization point until all hosts have caught up.

In most clustering systems for Unix, once you issue a command, you cannot interact with the hosts in the cluster individually; you only see the final output of each command run on each of the hosts. ClusterIt does not have this limitation, making it ideal for dealing with processes that need continual monitoring.

## Installation and Configuration

Install ClusterIt from the NetBSD pkgsrc collection:

```
# cd /usr/pkgsrc/parallel/clusterit
# make install clean
```

It is also available in FreeBSD's */usr/ports/parallel/clusterit*.

Before using any ClusterIt utility, you must create a list of machines in your cluster. Create the file *~/.cluster*, containing a list of host names. Be sure not to put any whitespace after GROUP:, as in this example:

```
GROUP:setB
Bester
Brust
GROUP:setOther
Clarke
Dick
Niven
Pohl
Zelazny
```

Set an environment variable to tell ClusterIt where to find the list of hosts, and set two more to specify ssh as the tool to start remote shells and terminals. Run this from the command line or add the commands to your *~.cshrc* or equivalent file [Hack #1]:

```
% export CLUSTER=$HOME/.cluster
% export RCMD_CMD=ssh
% export RLOGIN_CMD=ssh
```

Use ssh-agent or an equivalent method to prevent ClusterIt from prompting for a password every time you connect to a host. If you're unfamiliar with ssh-agent, see "What is SSH agent, and how do I use it?" at *http://security.sdsc.edu/help/ssh/agent.shtml*.

## Testing Noninteractive Commands

Now you're ready to issue commands to the cluster. You can run simple commands that require no interactivity from the command line with the dsh (distributed shell) command. Let's start by checking the version of the operating system on each of the hosts in a group:

```
% dsh -g setB uname -a
Bester: SunOS bester 5.7 Generic_106541-11 sun4u sparc
SUNW,UltraSPARC-IIi-Engine
Brust: NetBSD brust 1.6ZC NetBSD 1.6ZC (GENERIC.MP) #1: Fri Sep 26
23:33:56 EDT 2003
david@pohl:/usr/obj/usr/src/sys/arch/i386/compile/GENERIC.MP i386
```

The -g *groupname* option specifies which hosts in the cluster should run this command. Every ClusterIt command allows you to specify a list of hosts, a named group of hosts, the entire cluster, or any of those options minus a list of excluded hosts.

As you can see, not much can go wrong with the uname command. Interestingly, the two hosts that I've chosen to use for examples are running different operating systems.

## Using dvt

Many maintenance operations require different steps on machines running different operating systems. ClusterIt also includes a command called dvt (distributed virtual terminal), which allows you to interact with several hosts simultaneously or individually. This is where dvt shines!

Suppose that I want to install a Perl module on both of these example machines. First, I'll open the distributed terminals:

```
% dvt -g setB
```

Three terminal windows have opened up to my screen: one window for each of the two hosts and one control window. Anything I type in the control window goes to all of the host windows, as if I typed the same thing in each one. (I can also type within an individual host window, which will send my input only to that particular host.)

I have windows open to the hosts in the group now, but I'll need to be root to install the module.

In the control window, I'll type su. If the root password is the same on all the hosts, I can type it everywhere at once by typing in the command window. If the passwords are different on different hosts, I'll have to activate each host window in turn, typing the appropriate password in each one.

For simplicity, imagine I've already copied the module to my home directory on each host. I now need to un-tar it, run Perl on the *Makefile.PL*, run make, and run make install:

```
# tar xzvf Perl-Package-1.0.tgz && cd Perl-Package-1.0 && perl \
  Makefile.PL && make && make install
```

If I knew that this command would work without any errors, I could have used dsh instead. However, any number of differences between these two machines could cause one or both to fail to complete this process. This Perl package may not have been tested on Solaris yet, or either machine could be missing some prerequisite package.

Since each host has its own window that I can view and type into, I can monitor the progress of the installation. If either host encounters a problem, I can focus my mouse on that window and manually correct and continue the process, without interfering with the other host.

## Hacking the Hack

This technique is useful in several other situations. You can monitor a set of hosts by running ps, who, or top in several windows. You can diagnose network issues by running tcpdump on the source host, destination host, and any machines routing the packets in between the two.

An interesting way to troubleshoot networking is to have every host in your cluster ping or traceroute to the problem host. The missing route or mistyped filter rule quickly becomes obvious.

A sysadmin must troubleshoot all sorts of issues, including diagnosing name service troubles, NFS mount permissions, sysctl values, disk space, routing tables, backups, and logfiles. You can solve these problems more easily when you have a consolidated view of your systems.

## See Also

- man dvt
- man dsh
- The ClusterIt web site (*http://www.garbled.net/clusterit.html*)

# Securing the System
## Hacks 54-68

The BSDs have gained a reputation for running reliably and securely out-of-the-box. They also provide many tools for customizing a system to a particular environment's security needs.

This chapter includes several hacks that demonstrate some security mechanisms that aren't well-documented elsewhere. I've also provided some new twists on old security favorites. Everyone has heard of sudo, but are you also aware of the security pitfalls it can introduce? You're probably also well-versed in ssh and scp, but you may have yet to harness the usefulness of scponly.

You'll also find several scripts to automate some common security practices. Each provides an excellent view into another administrator's thought processes. Use their examples to fuel your imagination and see what security solutions you can hack for your own network.

### HACK #54 Strip the Kernel

Don't be shy. A kernel stripped down to the bare essentials is a happy kernel.

Picture the typical day in the life of a system administrator. Your mission, if you choose to accept it, is to achieve the impossible. Today, you're expected to:

- Increase the security of a particular server
- Attain a noticeable improvement in speed and performance

Although there are many ways to go about this, the most efficient way is to strip down the kernel to its bare-bones essentials. Having this ability gives an administrator of an open source system a distinct advantage over his closed source counterparts.

The first advantage to stripping the kernel is an obvious security boost. A vulnerability can't affect an option the kernel doesn't support. The second is a noticeable improvement in speed and performance. Kernels are loaded into memory and must stay in memory. You may be wasting precious memory resources if you're loading options you have no intention of ever using.

If you've never compiled a kernel or changed more than one or two kernel options, I can hear you groaning now. You're probably thinking, "Anything but that. Kernels are too complicated to understand." Well, there is a lot of truth in the idea that you haven't really used an operating system until you've gone through that baptism of fire known as kernel compiling. However, you may not have heard that compiling a kernel isn't all that difficult. So, grab a spare afternoon and a test system; it's high time to learn how to hack a BSD kernel.

I'll demonstrate on a FreeBSD system, but you'll find resources for other systems at the end of this hack.

Before you start, double-check that you have the kernel source installed. On an Intel FreeBSD system, it lives in */usr/src/sys/i386/conf*. If that directory doesn't exist, become the superuser and install it:

```
# /stand/sysinstall
Configure
Distributions
spacebar [ ] src to select it
spacebar [ ] sys to select it
tab to OK
```

Next, navigate into that directory structure and check out its contents:

```
# cd /usr/src/sys/i386/conf
# ls
./           GENERIC.hints   OLDCARD      gethints.awk
../          Makefile        PAE          GENERIC
NOTES        SMP
```

Two files are important: the original kernel configuration file, *GENERIC*, and *NOTES*. Note that *NOTES* is instead called *LINT* on 4.x FreeBSD systems.

## Customizing Your Kernel

Customizing a kernel is a very systematic process. Basically, you examine each line in the current configuration file, asking yourself, "Is this applicable to my situation?" If so, keep it. Otherwise, remove it. If you don't know, read *NOTES* for that option.

I always customize my kernel in several steps. First, I strip out what I don't need. Then, I use buildkernel to test my new configuration file. If it doesn't build successfully, I know I've inadvertently removed something essential. Using the error message, I go back and research that missing line.

If the build succeeds, I read through *NOTES* to see if there are any options I wish to add to the kernel. If I add anything, I'll do another buildkernel, followed by an installkernel if the build is successful. I find it much easier to troubleshoot if I separate my deletions from my additions.

Let's copy over *GENERIC* and see about stripping it down:

```
# cp GENERIC STRIPPED
# vi STRIPPED
#
# GENERIC -- Generic kernel configuration file for FreeBSD/i386
#
# For more information on this file, please read the handbook section on
# Kernel Configuration Files:
#
#    http://www.FreeBSD.org/doc/en_US.ISO8859-1/books/handbook/kernelconfig-
config.html
#
# The handbook is also available locally in /usr/share/doc/handbook
# if you've installed the doc distribution, otherwise always see the
# FreeBSD World Wide Web server (http://www.FreeBSD.org/) for the
# latest information.
#
# An exhaustive list of options and more detailed explanations of the
# device lines is also present in the ../../conf/NOTES and NOTES files.
# If you are in doubt as to the purpose or necessity of a line, check first
# in NOTES.
```

**CPU options.** The first thing you'll notice is that this file is very well commented. It's also divided into sections, making it easier to remove things such as ISA NIC, SCSI, and USB support. The first section deals with CPU type:

```
machine    i386
cpu        I486_CPU
cpu        I586_CPU
cpu        I686_CPU
ident      GENERIC
```

Whenever you come across a section you're not sure about, look for that section in *NOTES*. Here, I'll search for CPU:

```
# grep CPU NOTES
```

Your output will include a few pages worth of CPU information. The first few lines describe which CPUs belong with the I486, I586, and I686 entries.

Once you find your CPU, remove the two entries that don't apply. If you're not sure what type of CPU is installed on the system you're configuring, try:

```
# grep CPU /var/run/dmesg.boot
CPU: Intel(R) Pentium(R) III CPU        1133MHz (1138.45-MHz 686-class CPU)
acpi_cpu0: <CPU> port 0x530-0x537 on acpi0
```

Since a Pentium III is considered to be an I686_CPU, I'll remove the I486_CPU and I586_CPU lines from this system's configuration file.

The rest of the output from grep CPU NOTES contains extra lines that can be added to the kernel. Read through these to see if any apply to your specific CPU and the needs of the machine you are configuring. If so, make a note to try adding these later.

**System-specific options.** The next section contains a heck of a lot of options. If this is your first kernel, most of your research will be deciding which options you need for your particular system. I find the handbook most helpful here, as it lists the pros and cons of nearly every option. I always keep these options on all of my systems:

```
options     SCHED_4BSD       # 4BSD scheduler
options     INET             # InterNETworking
options     FFS              # Berkeley Fast Filesystem
options     COMPAT_FREEBSD4  # Compatible with FreeBSD4
options     COMPAT_43        # Compatible with BSD 4.3 [KEEP THIS!]
```

Note that that last listed option tells you to keep it. Do keep anything that contains such a comment.

The rest of the options are specific to that system's needs. For example, does it need to support IPv6? Do you wish to use softupdates or the new MAC framework? Does this system need to be an NFS server or NFS client? Does this system have a CD-ROM attached or any SCSI devices?

Does the system have multiple processors? If so, uncomment the next two lines; otherwise, you can safely remove them:

```
# To make an SMP kernel, the next two are needed
#options     SMP              # Symmetric MultiProcessor Kernel
#options     APIC_IO          # Symmetric (APIC) I/O
```

**Supported buses and media devices.** The next section deals with devices. First, we start with the buses:

```
device      isa
device      eisa
device      pci
```

If you grep device NOTES, you'll see that you can also add the agp and mca buses if your system requires them. If your system doesn't use the isa or eisa buses, you can remove those lines.

If you wish to disable floppy support on your server, removing these lines will do it:

```
# Floppy drives
device          fdc
```

Next, does your server use IDE or SCSI devices? If it uses IDE, the next section applies:

```
# ATA and ATAPI devices
device          ata
device          atadisk         # ATA disk drives
device          atapicd         # ATAPI CDROM drives
device          atapifd         # ATAPI floppy drives
device          atapist         # ATAPI tape drives
options         ATA_STATIC_ID   # Static device numbering
```

Remember, you can remove the CD-ROM, floppy, and tape lines to suit your requirements. However, keep the other lines if you use an IDE hard drive. Conversely, if your system is all SCSI, delete the ATA lines and concentrate on this section:

```
# SCSI Controllers
device          ahb         # EISA AHA1742 family
device          ahc         # AHA2940 and onboard AIC7xxx devices
<snip>
```

Keep the entries for the SCSI hardware your system is using, and remove the entries for the other devices. If your system doesn't have SCSI hardware, you can safely delete the entire SCSI section.

The same logic applies to the following RAID section:

```
# RAID controllers interfaced to the SCSI subsystem
device          asr         # DPT SmartRAID V, VI and Adaptec SCSI RAID
device          ciss        # Compaq Smart RAID 5*
device          dpt         # DPT Smartcache III, IV - See NOTES for options!
device          iir         # Intel Integrated RAID
device          mly         # Mylex AcceleRAID/eXtremeRAID
```

and for the SCSI peripherals and RAID controllers sections:

```
# SCSI peripherals
device          scbus       # SCSI bus (required)
device          ch          # SCSI media changers
<snip>

# RAID controllers
device          aac         # Adaptec FSA RAID
device          aacp        # SCSI passthrough for aac (requires CAM)
<snip>
```

**Peripheral support and power management.** The next few entries are usually keepers as it's always nice to have a working keyboard, unless you're using a headless system [Hack #26].

```
# atkbdc0 controls both the keyboard and the PS/2 mouse
device          atkbdc      # AT keyboard controller
device          atkbd       # AT keyboard
```

The next line depends on whether you're using a serial or a PS/2 mouse:

```
device          psm         # PS/2 mouse
```

You'll probably want to keep your video driver:

```
device          vga         # VGA video card driver
```

However, you'll probably remove the splash device, unless you plan on configuring a splash screen [Hack #24].

```
device          splash      # Splash screen and screen saver support
```

You'll have to choose a console driver. It can be either the default SCO driver or the pcvt driver (see the handbook for details):

```
# syscons is the default console driver, resembling an SCO console
device          sc
# Enable this for the pcvt (VT220 compatible) console driver
#device         vt
#options        XSERVER         # support for X server on a vt console
#options        FAT_CURSOR      # start with block cursor
```

The next options refer to power management on laptops, as well as laptop PCMCIA cards. Unless your server is a laptop, you can remove these:

```
# Power management support (see NOTES for more options)
#device         apm
# Add suspend/resume support for the i8254.
device          pmtimer

# PCCARD (PCMCIA) support
# Pcmcia and cardbus bridge support
device          cbb         # cardbus (yenta) bridge
#device         pcic        # ExCA ISA and PCI bridges
device          pccard      # PC Card (16-bit) bus
device          cardbus     # CardBus (32-bit) bus
```

Do you plan on using your serial and parallel ports? If not, the next section allows you to disable them:

```
# Serial (COM) ports
device          sio         # 8250, 16[45]50 based serial ports

# Parallel port
device          ppc
device          ppbus       # Parallel port bus (required)
```

```
device      lpt        # Printer
device      plip       # TCP/IP over parallel
device      ppi        # Parallel port interface device
#device     vpo        # Requires scbus and da
```

**Interface support.** Now it's time to support your system's NICs. Here's one way to find out the device names of your interfaces:

```
# grep Ethernet /var/run/dmesg.boot
rl0: Ethernet address: 00:05:5d:d2:19:b7
rl1: Ethernet address: 00:05:5d:d1:ff:9d
ed0: <NE2000 PCI Ethernet (RealTek 8029)> port 0x9800-0x981f irq 10 at
device 11.0 on pci0
```

Once you know which interfaces are in your system, remove the NICs that aren't. If your system doesn't contain any ISA or wireless NICs, you can safely remove those entire sections.

Do make note of this comment, though:

```
# PCI Ethernet NICs that use the common MII bus controller code.
# NOTE: Be sure to keep the 'device miibus' line in order to use these NICs!
device      miibus     # MII bus support
device      dc         # DEC/Intel 21143 and various workalikes
<snip>
```

Any NICs underneath that comment require that miibus entry. If you forget it, your kernel won't build. Fortunately, the error message will have the word miibus in it.

Next come the pseudodevices. If you plan on using encryption, keep the random device. You'll probably also need to keep the loop and ether devices.

If you use an analog modem to connect to your service provider, keep the ppp and tun devices. Otherwise, remove them, along with the slip device.

Several applications—including emacs, xterm, script, and the notorious telnet—require the pty device. Depending upon the use of your server, you may be able to remove that device. If it breaks needed functionality, you can always recompile it back into your kernel.

Are you planning on using memory disks? If not, you can remove md. If you're not sure, try reading man mdmfs.

If you previously removed IPv6 support with options INET6, you might as well remove these two devices as well:

```
device      gif        # IPv6 and IPv4 tunneling
device      faith      # IPv6-to-IPv4 relaying (translation)
```

The next device has some security implications, as it is required in order to run a packet sniffer such as tcpdump. However, it's also required if your system is a DHCP client. If neither applies, remove the bpf device:

```
# The `bpf' device enables the Berkeley Packet Filter.
# Be aware of the administrative consequences of enabling this!
device          bpf          # Berkeley packet filter
```

**USB support.** Does your system have any USB devices? If so, you need a host controller as well as USB bus support. First, determine which type of USB host controller you have. man uhci and man ohci describe which hardware goes with which controller. Once you've found your hardware, keep the appropriate interface entry:

```
# USB support
device          uhci         # UHCI PCI->USB interface
device          ohci         # OHCI PCI->USB interface
```

Also, don't forget to keep that USB bus line:

```
device          usb          # USB Bus (required)
```

Are you confused about the next three USB options? Fortunately, each has a manpage. Try man udbp, man ugen, and man uhid to see if any apply to your particular situation.

```
#device         udbp         # USB Double Bulk Pipe devices
device          ugen         # Generic
device          uhid         # "Human Interface Devices"
```

Next, keep the devices you have installed and remove the rest. Again, note that USB NICs need that miibus entry we saw earlier. Also, some entries require device scbus and device da. Double-check your SCSI sections. If you removed these devices earlier and need them, add them to this section.

```
device          ukbd         # Keyboard
device          ulpt         # Printer
device          umass        # Disks/Mass storage - Requires scbus and da
device          ums          # Mouse
device          urio         # Diamond Rio 500 MP3 player
device          uscanner     # Scanners
# USB Ethernet, requires mii
device          aue          # ADMtek USB ethernet
device          axe          # ASIX Electronics USB ethernet
device          cue          # CATC USB ethernet
device          kue          # Kawasaki LSI USB ethernet
```

Finally, the only option group left is Firewire support. If you need it, keep the entire section, and double-check that you have a device scbus and device da entry somewhere in your configuration file. If you don't need Firewire support, remove the entire section:

```
# FireWire support
device          firewire     # FireWire bus code
device          sbp          # SCSI over FireWire (Requires scbus and da)
device          fwe          # Ethernet over FireWire (non-standard!)
```

Whew. We finally made it through the configuration file. Congratulations! You now have a much better idea of the hardware on your system and can rest easily in the knowledge that soon no extra drivers will be wasting memory resources. Not only that, your next kernel configuration will go much more quickly as you've already researched the possibilities.

## Building the New Kernel

Now comes the moment of truth. Will the configuration file actually build? To find out:

```
# cd /usr/src
# make buildkernel KERNCONF=STRIPPED
```

Replace *STRIPPED* with whatever name you called your kernel configuration file. If all goes well, you should just get your prompt back after a period of time, which varies depending upon the speed of your CPU. If you instead get an error message, you probably forgot miibus, scbus, or da, and the message will reflect that. Add the missing line and try again.

Occasionally you'll get a kernel that just refuses to build, even when you're sure the configuration file is fine. If that's the case, try building GENERIC. If that fails, you have a hardware issue.

I once inherited a system with a flaky motherboard. I tried a few kernel compiles, which took forever before finally resulting in an error code 1. Fortunately, I use removable drives, so I simply inserted the drive into another system, successfully compiled the kernel, and then returned the drive to the flaky system for the actual kernel install.

## Keeping Track of Your Options

Once I have a successful build, I like to document what I removed from the original kernel. This is easily done:

```
# echo "These are the lines I deleted" > changes.txt \
    & diff GENERIC STRIPPED >> changes.txt
```

The diff utility will list the differences between the original and my version of the kernel configuration file. Note that I used >> to append those differences without removing my previously echoed comment. See "Apply, Understand, and Create Patches" [Hack #92] for more examples that use diff.

Before installing the kernel, read through *NOTES* to see if there are any lines you wish to add. Additionally, if you wish to take advantage of memory addresses over 4 GB, carefully read through *PAE* and its section in the handbook to see if it is appropriate for your situation.

If you add any lines, repeat the make buildkernel command when you are finished. I also like to append my additions to my *changes.txt* file:

```
# echo "And these are the lines I added" >> changes.txt \
    & diff GENERIC STRIPPED >> changes.txt
```

Note that this time it is very important I remember to append both my comment and the output of diff by using two > characters.

### Installing the New Kernel

Now, let's install the kernel:

```
# cd /usr/src
# make installkernel KERNCONF=STRIPPED
```

This process is much quicker than building the kernel. However, the kernel won't actually be loaded into memory until you reboot. Before you do that, it's always a good idea to print out the "If Something Goes Wrong" page of the FreeBSD Handbook, just in case something goes wrong. See *http://www.freebsd.org/doc/en_US.ISO8859-1/books/handbook/kernelconfig-trouble.html#KERNELCONFIG-NOBOOT*.

It's rare that a kernel will install but not boot, but it never hurts to be prepared ahead of time.

### See Also

- The Kernel Configuration section of the FreeBSD Handbook (*http://www.freebsd.org/doc/en_US.ISO8859-1/books/handbook/kernelconfig.html*)
- The "Why would I want to create my own custom kernel?" section of the OpenBSD FAQ (*http://www.openbsd.org/faq/faq5.html#Why*)
- The NetBSD Kernel FAQ (*http://www.netbsd.org/Documentation/kernel*)

## FreeBSD Access Control Lists

Unix permissions are flexible and can solve almost any access control problem, but what about the ones they can't?

Do you really want to make a group every time you want to share a file with another user? What if you don't have root access and can't create a group at will? What if you want to be able to make a directory available to a web server or other user without making the files world-readable or -writable? Root-owned configuration files often need to be edited by those without root privileges; instead of using a program like sudo (see "Sudo Gotchas" [Hack #61] and "sudoscript" [Hack #62]), it would be better just to allow certain nonowners to edit these files.

Access Control Lists (ACLs) solve these problems. They allow more flexibility than the standard Unix user/group/other set of permissions. ACLs have been available in commercial Unixes such as IRIX and Solaris, as well as Windows NT, for years. Now, thanks to the TrustedBSD project's work, ACLs are available in FreeBSD 5.0-RELEASE and beyond.

ACLs take care of access control problems that are overly complicated or impossible to solve with the normal Unix permissions system. By avoiding the creation of groups and overuse of root privileges, ACLs can keep administrators saner and servers more secure.

## Enabling ACLs

ACLs are enabled by an option in the file system superblock, which contains internal housekeeping information for the file system.

Edit the superblock with the tunefs command, which can be used only on a read-only or unmounted file system. This means that you must first bring the system into single-user mode. Make sure there aren't any active connections to the system, then shut it down:

```
# shutdown now

*** FINAL System shutdown message from root@mycompany.com ***
System going down IMMEDIATELY

Dec 11 10:28:07 genisis shutdown: shutdown by root:
System shutdown time has arrived
Writing entropy file:.
Shutting down daemon processes:.
Saving firewall state tables:.
Dec 11 10:28:10 genisis syslogd: exiting on signal 15
Enter full pathname of shell or RETURN for /bin/sh:
#
```

At the prompt, type:

```
# /sbin/tunefs -a enable /
# /sbin/tunefs -a enable /usr
# exit
```

> To see if ACLs are already set on your system, type mount.

If you use the UFS2 file system, you are done. The UFS_ACL option is enabled in the default GENERIC kernel, so reboot and enjoy. If you use UFS1, though, don't reboot yet.

To check your version of UFS, try dumpfs [mountpoint] |
grep UFS, where [mountpoint] is something like ad0s1a. mount
will list the names of your particular mount points.

## Additional UFS1 Configuration

Things are more difficult if you, like most FreeBSD 5.0 users, use UFS1.
(FreeBSD 5.1 and later come with UFS2 as the default file system.) ACLs are
built on top of extended attributes, which are not native to UFS1. To enable
extended attributes, you must add options UFS_EXTATTR and options UFS_
EXTATTR_AUTOSTART to your kernel configuration and compile and install the
new kernel [Hack #54]. Don't reboot yet; you still need to initialize the
extended attributes on each file system.

For example, to initialize extended attributes on the /var filesystem, use
extattrctl, the extended attributes control command:

```
# mkdir -p /var/.attribute/system
# cd /var/.attribute/system
# extattrctl initattr -p /var 388 posix1e.acl_access
# extattrctl initattr -p /var 388 posix1e.acl_default
```

Repeat for each filesystem on which you wish to enable ACL support. Just
replace /var with the mount point of the desired file system. After initializing the attributes with reboot, the extended attributes should be enabled.

## Viewing ACLs

Okay, you've successfully enabled ACLs. Now what? Let's start by viewing
ACLs. Looking at ACLs is simple. Files with ACLs will be designated with a
+ in the long listing provided by ls -l:

```
% ls -l acl-test
-rw-rw-r--+ 1 rob   rob   0 Apr 19 17:27 acl-test
```

Use the getfacl command to see information about the ACL:

```
% getfacl acl-test
#file:acl-test
#owner:1000
#group:1000
user::rw-
user:nobody:rw-
group::r--
group:wheel:rw-
mask::rw-
other::r--
```

The user::, group::, and other:: fields should all be familiar. They are simply the ACL representations of the standard Unix permissions system. The nobody and wheel lines, however, are new. These specify permissions for specific users and groups (in this case, the nobody user and the wheel group) in addition to the normal set of permissions.

The mask field sets maximum permissions, so an r-- mask (set with m::r) in combination with an rw- permission for a user will give the user only r-- permissions on the file.

## Adding and Subtracting ACLs

The setfacl command adds, changes, and deletes ACLs. Like chmod, only the file's owner or the superuser can use this command. You only need to use a few of its options to start manipulating ACLs.

First, a word on syntax. ACLs are specified just as they're printed by getfacl. Let's remove and reconstruct the ACL for *acl-test*:

```
% setfacl -b acl-test
% setfacl -m user:nobody:rw-,group:wheel:rw- acl-test
```

The -b option removes all ACLs, except for the standard user, group, and other lines. The -m option modifies the ACL with the specified entry (or comma-separated entries). Entries may also be abbreviated: the code here could have been shortened to u:nobody:rw-,g:wheel:rw-.

You can even use setfacl to modify traditional permissions; setting a user::rw- ACL entry is equivalent to running chmod u=rw on a file.

Removing ACLs is almost identical: setfacl -x u:nobody:rw-,g:wheel:rw- removes that ACL. You can also specify ACLs in files. The -M and -X options perform the functions of their lowercase relatives, but read their entries from a file. Consider the *acl-test* file again:

```
% cat test-acl-list
u:nobody:rw-
# this is a comment
g:wheel:rw-
% setfacl -X test-acl-list acl-test
% getfacl acl-test
#file:acl-test
#owner:1000
#group:1000
user::rw-
group::r--
mask::r--
other::r--
```

## Using ACLs with Samba and Windows

If you compile Samba with ACL support, you can edit ACLs on files shared by Samba with the native Windows ACL tools. Simply compile (or recompile) Samba with ACL support:

```
# cd /usr/ports/net/samba
# make -DWITH_ACL_SUPPORT install clean
```

You will see the Samba port configuration dialog with ACL support enabled, as shown in Figure 6-1.

*Figure 6-1. Configuring Samba with ACLs*

Once you have Samba up and running, browse to a share on an ACL-enabled file system. Right-click any file and select Properties, and you'll see something like Figure 6-2. Go to the Security tab, and you can see and change the ACL as though it were on a Windows server.

If you've been reluctant to move from a Windows server to Samba because of its lack of ACLs, you can start thinking seriously about deploying Samba and FreeBSD on your file servers.

## Setting Default ACLs

Let's consider a more advanced example. You want to make your *cool_ widgets* directory accessible to Bob, your partner in coolness, but not to the world. If you just add an ACL entry, added files won't automatically pick up

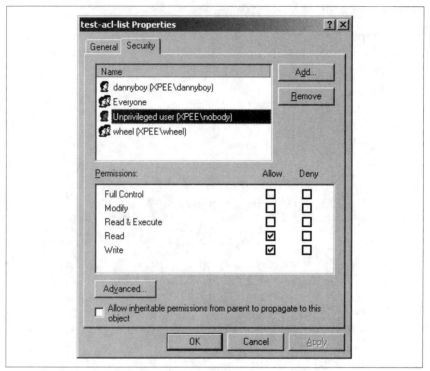

*Figure 6-2. Manipulating ACLs on FreeBSD from a Samba client*

the directory's ACL. You should instead set a *default ACL* on the directory. Any files created in the directory will inherit the default ACL.

Passing the -d option to either getfacl or setfacl will operate on the default ACL of a directory, instead of on the directory itself:

```
% mkdir cool_widgets
% chmod o-rwx cool_widgets
% ls -l
drwxr-x--- 2 rob   rob    512 Apr 19 21:21 cool_widgets

% getfacl -d cool_widgets
#file:cool_widgets
#owner:1000
#group:1000
```

Pretty boring, isn't it? Let's try to add a default ACL:

```
% setfacl -d -m u:bob:rw- cool_widgets
setfacl: acl_calc_mask( ) failed: Invalid argument
setfacl: failed to set ACL mask on cool_widgets
```

Oops. Default ACLs don't work quite like regular ACLs do. You cannot set specific entries on a default ACL until you add the generic user::, group::, and other:: entries:

```
% setfacl -d -m u::rw-,g::r--,o::---,u:bob:rw- cool_widgets
% setfacl -m u:bob:r-x cool_widgets
```

Note the nondefault r-x entry for bob on the directory. The default ACL affects files that will be created inside the directory but *not* the directory itself. An ACL entry u:bob:rw- will now be added to any file created in *cool_widgets*.

Now you have a *cool_widgets* directory whose files can be read and written by both yourself and Bob, without the use of a group. If you later decide to get rid of the default ACL, the -k option to setfacl works for directory ACLs just as the -b option does for file ACLs.

Use getfacl -d to view the new directory's default ACL.

### See Also

- man tunefs
- man extattrctl
- man getfacl
- man setfacl
- "FreeBSD Access Control Lists," as originally published on ONLamp's BSD DevCenter (*http://www.onlamp.com/pub/a/bsd/2003/08/14/freebsd_acls.html*)
- The TrustedBSD project (*http://www.trustedbsd.org/*)

## Protect Files with Flags

#56
Ever feel limited when tightening up Unix permissions? Really, there's only so much you can do with r, w, x, s, and t.

When you consider the abilities of the superuser account, traditional Unix permissions become moot. That's not very comforting if you're a regular user wishing to protect your own files or an administrator trying to protect the files on a network server from a rootkit.

Fortunately, the BSDs support a set of extended permissions known as *flags*. Depending upon your securelevel, these flags may prevent even the superuser from changing the affected file and its flags.

## Preventing File Changes

Let's start by seeing what flags are available. Table 6-1 summarizes the flags, their meanings, and their usual usage.

*Table 6-1. Extended permissions flags*

| Flag name | Meaning | Usage |
|-----------|---------|-------|
| arch | archive | Forces or prevents a backup |
| nodump | nodump | Excludes files from a dump |
| sappnd | system append | Applies to logs |
| schg | system immutable | Applies to binaries and /etc |
| sunlnk | system undeletable | Applies to binaries and /etc |
| uappnd | user append-only | Prevents changes to existing data |
| uchg | user immutable | Prevents any type of changes |
| uunlnk | user undeletable | Prevents deletion or rename |

Any user can use any flag that starts with u to protect her own files. Let's say you have an important file that you don't want to change inadvertently. That's a candidate for the uchg flag. To turn that flag on, use the chflags (change flags) command:

```
% chflags uchg important_file
% ls -lo important_file
-rw-r--r-- 1 dru wheel uchg 14 Dec  1 11:13 important_file
```

Use ls -lo to view a file's flags. (I tend to think o was the only letter left. Perhaps a mnemonic would be "Hello, *this* is why I can't modify that file!" Perhaps not.) Let's see exactly how immutable this file is now. I'll start by opening the file in vi, adding a line, and trying to save my changes:

```
Read-only file, not written; use ! to override.
```

Okay, I'll use wq! instead:

```
Error: important_file: Operation not permitted.
```

Looks like I can no longer make changes to my own file. I'll receive the same results even if I try as the superuser.

Next, I'll try to use echo to add some lines to that file:

```
% echo "test string" >> important_file
important_file: Operation not permitted.
```

Finally, I'll try moving, deleting, and copying that file:

```
% mv important_file test
mv: rename important_file to test: Operation not permitted

% rm important_file
```

```
override rw-r--r--  dru/wheel uchg for important_file? y
rm: important_file: Operation not permitted

% cp important_file test
%
```

Notice an important difference between the mv and rm commands and the cp command. Since mv and rm require a change to the original file itself, they are prevented by that unchangeable flag. However, the cp command doesn't try to change the original file; it simply creates a new file with the same contents. However, if you try ls  -lo on that new file, the uchg flag will *not* be set. This is because new files inherit permissions and flags from the parent directory. (Okay, that's not the whole story. See man  umask for more gory details.)

## Watch Your Directories

What do you think will happen if you place all of your important files in a directory and recursively set uchg on that directory?

```
% mkdir important_stuff
% cp resume important_stuff/
% chflags -R important_stuff/
% ls -lo important_stuff/
drwxr-xr-x   2 dru  wheel  uchg     512 Dec  1 11:23 ./
drwxr-xr-x  34 dru  wheel  -       3072 Dec  1 11:36 ../
-rw-r--r--   1 dru  wheel  uchg      14 Dec  1 11:13 resume
```

So far so good. That file inherited the uchg flag from the directory, so it is now protected from changes. What if I try to add a new file to that directory?

```
% cp coverletter important_stuff
cp: important_stuff/coverletter: Operation not permitted
```

Because the directory itself is not allowed to change, I can't add or remove any files from the directory. If that's what you want, great. If not, keep that in mind when playing with directory flags.

What if you change your mind and really do want to change a file? If you own the file, you can unset the flag by repeating the chflags command with the no word. For example:

```
% chflags nouchg resume
```

will allow me to make edits to my résumé. However, I won't be able to delete it from that protected directory unless I also use the nouchg flag on the *important_stuff* directory.

## Preventing Some Changes and Allowing Others

Sometimes, the uchg flag is a bit too drastic. For example, if you want to be able to edit a file but not inadvertently delete that file, use this flag instead:

```
% chflags uunlnk thesis
%
```

I can now edit that file to my heart's content. However, if I try to move or delete that file, I'll receive those Operation not permitted error messages again.

The uappnd flag is more interesting. It allows you to append changes to a file but prevents you from modifying the existing contents. This might be useful for a blog:

```
% chflags uappnd myblog
%
```

Then again, it might not. echoing comments to the end of the file works nicely. However, opening it in an editor does not. Note that this flag also prevents you from moving or deleting the file.

## Log Protection

Let's move on to the rest of the flags, which can be managed only by the superuser. sappnd, schg, and sunlnk work exactly the same as their u equivalents. So, think s for superuser and u for user.

The append flag was a bit weird for a regular user, but it is ideal for protecting the system logs. One of the first things an intruder will do after breaking into a system is to cover up his tracks by changing or deleting logs. This command will thwart those attempts:

```
# chflags -R sappnd /var/log
```

Now is a good time to mention a security truth: security is a myth. In reality, security is a process of making things more inconvenient in the hopes that a miscreant will go elsewhere. Remember, though, that inconvenience doesn't just affect the bad guys; it also affects you.

That command seems ideal because it allows logs to be appended to but not modified or deleted. That's great if you live in the world of unlimited disk space. Of course, it also just broke newsyslog, and you've just delegated yourself the joys of manual log rotation.

There's one other thing you need to consider when you start playing with the superuser flags. If your securelevel is set to 0 or -1, the superuser can unset any flag by adding no to it. If your attacker has heard of flags before and has managed to gain access to the superuser account, all of your flag setting was for naught.

Having said that, suppose you're hardening a server and want to protect the logs. Your securelevel is set at 1 or higher, and you plan on using that previous chflags command. Since you're now responsible for log rotation, you might as well start by taking stock of the contents of */var/log* before turning on that sappnd flag. Remove any unnecessary logs now, before setting the flag.

Next, edit */etc/crontab* and comment the newsyslog line so it looks like this:

```
# Rotate log files every hour, if necessary.
#0      *       *       *       *       root        newsyslog
```

Comment out any lines in */etc/syslog.conf* that refer to logs you removed.

You should also consider using something like the following script to warn you if a partition is filling up:

```
#!usr/local/bin/bash
# checkfreespace.sh
# check that a device has sufficient free space
# thanks to David Lents and Arnold Robbins for awk/gawk/nawk suggestions

# set the following variables as necessary
PARTITION="/var/log"
THRESHOLD="80"

USED=$(
    eval "df | awk -- '\$6 == ENVIRON[\"PARTITION\"]
        { printf( \"%0.d\", \$5 ) }'"
);

if [ "$USED" -ge $THRESHOLD ]
then
  echo "Used space of $USED above $THRESHOLD on $PARTITION"
else
  # disable this if running through cron
  echo "Enough free space"
fi
```

If you schedule this program through cron, it will mail any output to the user owning the cron job. Edit the two variables at the top of the script to change the partition to scan and the threshold above which the script will warn. With the variables set as shown, the script will warn if */var/log* is more than 80% full.

Remember, once you disable newsyslog, it becomes your responsibility to monitor disk space in */var/log*. You won't be able to compress or delete log files unless the superuser temporarily unsets the sappnd flag. This can be a real pain if your securelevel is 1 or higher, as the system first has to be dropped down to single-user mode. This usually isn't an option on busy systems as it will disconnect all current connections. Carefully consider the size of */var/log* and how often the system realistically can be put into single-user mode before setting this flag.

## Protecting Binaries

When a system is compromised, the attacker may install a rootkit that will try to change your system's binaries. For example, it might replace ps with a version that doesn't display the rootkit's processes. Or, it might replace a commonly used utility with another program that executes something nastier than expected.

"Use mtree as a Built-in Tripwire" [Hack #58] shows how to create your own file integrity checking program that will alert you if any of your binaries or other important files are changed. An additional layer of protection is to use chflags to prevent those files from being changed in the first place. Usually, the schg flag is used to prevent any modifications. Useful candidates for this flag are:

- */usr/bin*, which contains user programs
- */usr/sbin*, which contains system programs
- */etc*, which contains system configurations

Again, evaluate your particular scenario before implementing this flag. The protection provided by this flag usually far outweighs the inconvenience. The only time the contents of */usr/bin* or */usr/sbin* should change is when you upgrade the operating system or rebuild your world. Doing that requires a reboot anyway, so dropping to single-user mode to unset schg shouldn't be a problem.

How often do you change your configuration files in */etc*? If you typically configure a system only when it is installed and rarely make changes afterward, protect your configurations with schg. However, keep in mind that a rare configuration change may require you to drop all connections in order to implement it. Also, if you need to add more users to your system, remember to remove that flag from */etc/passwd*, */etc/master.passwd*, and */etc/group* first.

Things are a bit more problematic for a system running installed applications. Most ports install their binaries into */usr/local/bin* or */usr/X11R6/bin*. If you set the schg flag on those directories, you won't be able to patch or upgrade those binaries unless you temporarily unset the flag. You'll have to balance your need to keep your server up and running with the protection you gain from the schg flag and how often you have to patch a particular binary.

## Controlling Backups

The last two flags, arch and nodump, affect backups. The superuser can ensure a particular file or directory will always be backed up, regardless of whether the contents have been altered, by setting the arch flag.

Similarly, when using dump to back up an entire filesystem, the superuser can specify which portions of that filesystem will *not* be included by setting the nodump flag.

### See Also

- man securelevel
- man -a chflags (to view all manpages that match chflags, not just the first one)
- man newsyslog
- "Use mtree as a Built-in Tripwire" [Hack #58]

## Tighten Security with Mandatory Access Control
### HACK #57

Increase the security of your systems with MAC paranoia.

Ever feel like your Unix systems are leaking out extra unsolicited information? For example, even a regular user can find out who is logged into a system and what they're currently doing. It's also an easy matter to find out what processes are running on a system.

For the security-minded, this may be too much information in the hands of an attacker. Fortunately, thanks to the TrustedBSD project, there are more tools available in the admin's arsenal. One of them is the Mandatory Access Control (MAC) framework.

As of this writing, FreeBSD's MAC is still considered experimental for production systems. Thoroughly test your changes before implementing them on production servers.

### Preparing the System

Before you can implement Mandatory Access Control, your kernel must support it. Add the following line to your kernel configuration file:

```
options MAC
```

You can find full instructions for compiling a kernel in "Strip the Kernel" [Hack #54].

While your kernel is recompiling, take the time to read man 4 mac, which lists the available MAC modules. Some of the current modules support simple policies that can control an aspect of a system's behavior, whereas others provide more complex policies that can affect every aspect of system operation. This hack demonstrates simple policies designed to address a single problem.

## Seeing Other Users

One problem with open source Unix systems is that there are very few secrets. For example, any user can run ps -aux to see every running process or run sockstat -4 or netstat -an to view all connections or open sockets on a system.

The MAC_SEEOTHERUIDS module addresses this. You can load this kernel module manually to experiment with its features:

```
# kldload mac_seeotheruids
Security policy loaded: TrustedBSD MAC/seeotheruids (mac_seeotheruids)
```

If you'd like this module to load at boot time, add this to /boot/loader.conf:

```
mac_seeotheruids_load="YES"
```

If you need to unload the module, simply type:

```
# kldunload mac_seeotheruids
Security policy unload: TrustedBSD MAC/seeotheruids (mac_seeotheruids)
```

When testing this module on your systems, compare the before and after results of these commands, run as both a regular user and the superuser:

- ps -aux
- netstat -an
- sockstat -4
- w

Your before results should show processes and sockets owned by other users, whereas the after results should show only those owned by the user. While the output from w will still show which users are on which terminals, it will not display what other users are currently doing.

By default, this module affects even the superuser. In order to change that, it's useful to know which sysctl MIBs control this module's behavior:

```
# sysctl -a | grep seeotheruids
security.mac.seeotheruids.enabled: 1
security.mac.seeotheruids.primarygroup_enabled: 0
security.mac.seeotheruids.specificgid_enabled: 0
security.mac.seeotheruids.specificgid: 0
```

sysctl is used to modify kernel behavior without having to recompile the kernel or reboot the system. The behaviors that can be modified are known as *MIBs*.

See how there are two MIBs dealing with specificgid? The enabled one is off, and the other one specifies the numeric group ID that would be exempt if it were on. So, if you do this:

```
# sysctl -w security.mac.seeotheruids.specificgid_enabled=1
security.mac.seeotheruids.specificgid_enabled: 0 -> 1
```

you will exempt group 0 from this policy. In FreeBSD, the wheel group has a GID of 0, so users in the wheel group will see all processes and sockets.

You can also set that primarygroup_enabled MIB to 1 to allow users who share the same group ID to see each other's processes and sockets.

Note that while you can change these MIBs from the command line, you will be able to see them only with the appropriate kernel module loaded.

## Quickly Disable All Interfaces

ifconfig allows you to enable and disable individual interfaces as required. For example, to stop traffic on *ed0*:

```
# ifconfig ed0 down
```

To bring the interface back up, simply repeat that command, replacing the word down with up.

However, ifconfig does not provide a convenient method for stopping or restarting traffic flow on all of a system's interfaces. That ability can be quite convenient for testing purposes or to quickly remove a system from a network that is under attack. The MAC_IFOFF module is a better tool for this purpose. Let's load this module and see how it affects the system:

```
# kldload mac_ifoff
Security policy loaded: TrustedBSD MAC/ifoff (mac_ifoff)
# sysctl -a | grep ifoff
security.mac.ifoff.enabled: 1
security.mac.ifoff.lo_enabled: 1
security.mac.ifoff.other_enabled: 0
security.mac.ifoff.bpfrecv_enabled: 0
```

By default, this module disables all interfaces, except the loopback lo device. When it's safe to reenable those interfaces, you can either unload the module:

```
# kldunload mac_ifoff
Security policy unload: TrustedBSD MAC/ifoff (mac_ifoff)
```

or leave the module loaded and enable the interfaces:

```
# sysctl -w security.mac.ifoff.other_enabled=1
security.mac.ifoff.other_enabled: 0 -> 1
```

Perhaps you have a system whose interfaces you'd like to disable at bootup until you explicitly enable them. If that's the case, add this line to */boot/loader.conf*:

```
mac_ifoff_load="YES"
```

## See Also

- man 4 mac
- man mac_seeotheruids
- man mac_ifoff
- man sysctl
- The TrustedBSD project (*http://www.trustedbsd.org/*)
- The sysctl section of the FreeBSD Handbook (*http://www.freebsd.org/doc/en_US.ISO8859-1/books/handbook/configtuning-sysctl.html*)
- The MAC section of the FreeBSD Handbook (*http://www.freebsd.org/doc/en_US.ISO8859-1/books/handbook/mac.html*)

# HACK #58 Use mtree as a Built-in Tripwire

Why configure a third-party file integrity checker when you already have mtree?

If you care about the security of your server, you need file integrity checking. Without it, you may never know if the system has been compromised by a rootkit or an active intruder. You may never know if your logs have been modified and your ls and ps utilities replaced by Trojaned equivalents.

Sure, you can download or purchase a utility such as tripwire, but you already have the mtree utility [Hack #54]; why not use it to hack your own customized file integrity utility?

mtree lists all of the files and their properties within a specified directory structure. That resulting list is known as a *specification*. Once you have a specification, you can ask mtree to compare it to an existing directory structure, and mtree will report any differences. Doesn't that sound like a file integrity checking utility to you?

## Creating the Integrity Database

Let's see what happens if we run mtree against */usr/bin*:

```
# cd /usr/bin
```

```
# mtree -c -K cksum,md5digest,sha1digest,ripemd160digest -s 123456789 \
     > /tmp/mtree_bin
mtree: /usr/bin checksum: 2126659563
```

Let's pick apart that syntax in Table 6-2.

*Table 6-2. mtree command syntax*

| Command | Explanation |
| --- | --- |
| -c | This creates a specification of the current working directory. |
| -K | This specifies a keyword. In our case, it's cksum. |
| md5digest, sha1digest, ripemd160digest | Here, I've specified the three cryptographic checksums understood by mtree. This is how it detects file modifications: any change to a file will result in a different hash. While it may be mathematically feasible for an attacker to bypass one cryptographic hash, it's darn near impossible for her to bypass all three cryptographic hashes. |
| -s | This gives the numeric seed that is used to create the specification's checksum. Remember that seed to verify the specification. |
| > | This redirects the results to the file */tmp/mtree_bin* instead of stdout. |

If you run that command, it will perk along for a second or two, then write the value of the checksum to your screen just before giving your prompt back. That's it; you've just created a file integrity database.

Before we take a look at that database, take a moment to record the seed you used and the checksum you received. Note that the more complex the seed, the harder it is to crack the checksum. Those two numbers are important, so you may consider writing them on a small piece of paper and storing them in your wallet. (Don't forget to include a hint to remind you why you have that piece of paper in your wallet!)

Now let's see what type of file we've just created:

```
# file /tmp/mtree_bin
/tmp/mtree_bin: ASCII text
```

```
# ls -l /tmp/mtree_bin
-rw-r--r--  1 root  wheel  111503 Nov 23 11:46 /tmp/mtree_bin
```

It's an ASCII text file, meaning you can edit it with an editor or print it directly. It's also fairly large, so let's use head to examine the first bit of this file. Here I'll ask for the first 15 lines:

```
# head -n 15 /tmp/mtree_bin
#           user: dru
#        machine: genisis
#           tree: /usr/bin
#           date: Sun Nov 23 11:46:21 2003

# .
/set type=file uid=0 gid=0 mode=0555 nlink=1 flags=none
```

```
    .              type=dir mode=0755 nlink=2 size=6656 time=1065005676.0
    cc             nlink=3 size=78972 time=1059422866.0 cksum=1068582540 \
                   md5digest=b9a5c9a92baf9ce975eee954994fca6c \
                   sha1digest=a2e4fa958491a4c2d22b7f597f05885bbe8f6a6a \
                   ripemd160digest=33c74b4200c9507b4826e5fc8621cddb9e9aefe2
    Mail           nlink=3 size=72964 time=1059422992.0 cksum=2235502998 \
                   md5digest=44739ae79f3cc89826f6e34a15f13ed7 \
                   sha1digest=a7b89996ffae4980ad87c6e7c56cb207af41c1bd \
```

The specification starts with a nice summary section. In my example, the user that created the specification was dru. Note that I used the su utility to become the superuser before creating the specification, but my login shell knew that I was still logged in as the user dru. The summary also shows the system name, genisis, the directory structure in question, /usr/bin, and the time the specification was created.

The /set type=file line shows the information mtree records by default. Notice that it keeps track of each file's uid, gid, mode, number of hard links, and flags.

Then, each file and subdirectory in /usr/bin is listed one at a time. Since I used -K to specify three different cryptographic hashes, each file has three separate hashes or digests.

## Preparing the Database for Storage

Once you've created a specification, the last place you want to leave it is on the hard drive. Instead, sign that file, encrypt it, transfer it to a different medium (such as a floppy), and place it in a secure storage area.

To sign the file:

```
# md5 /tmp/mtree_bin
MD5 (/tmp/mtree_bin) = e05bab7545f7bdbce13e1bb04a043e47
```

You may wish to redirect that resulting fingerprint to a file or a printer. Keep it in a safe place, as you'll need it to check the integrity of the database.

Next, encrypt the file. Remember, right now it is in ASCII text and susceptible to tampering. Here I'll encrypt the file and send the newly encrypted file to the floppy mounted at /floppy:

```
# openssl enc -e -bf -in /tmp/mtree_bin -out /floppy/mtree_bin_enc
enter bf-cbc encryption password:
Verifying - enter bf-cbc encryption password:
```

The syntax of the openssl command is fairly straightforward. I decided to encrypt enc -e with the Blowfish -bf algorithm. I then specified the input file, or the file to be encrypted. I also specified the output file, or the resulting encrypted file. I was then prompted for a password; this same password will be required whenever I need to decrypt the database.

Once I verify that the encrypted file is indeed on the floppy, I must remember to remove the ASCII text version from the hard drive:

```
# rm /tmp/mtree_bin
```

 The ultra-paranoid, experienced hacker would zero out that file before removing it using dd if=/dev/zero of=/tmp/mtree_bin bs=1024k count=12.

I'll then store the floppy in a secure place, such as the safe that contains my backup tapes.

## Using the Integrity Database

Once you have an integrity database, you'll want to compare it periodically to the files on your hard drive. Mount the media containing your encrypted database, and then decrypt it:

```
# openssl enc -d -bf -in /floppy/mtree_bin_enc -out /tmp/mtree_bin
enter bf-cbc encryption password:
```

Notice that I used basically the same command I used to encrypt it. I simply replaced the encrypt switch (-e) with the decrypt switch (-d). The encrypted file is now the input, and the plain text file is now the output. Note that I was prompted for the same password; if I forget it, the decryption will fail.

Before using that database, I first want to verify that its fingerprint hasn't been tampered with. Again, I simply repeat the md5 command. If the resulting fingerprint is the same, the database is unmodified:

```
# md5 /tmp/mtree_bin
MD5 (/tmp/mtree_bin) = e05bab7545f7bdbce13e1bb04a043e47
```

Next, I'll see if any of my files have been tampered with on my hard drive:

```
# cd /usr/bin
# mtree -s 123456789 < /tmp/mtree_bin
mtree: /usr/bin checksum: 2126659563
```

If none of the files have changed in /usr/bin, the checksum will be the same. In this case it was. See why it was important to record that seed and checksum?

What happens if a file does change? I haven't built world on this system in a while, so I suspect I have source files that haven't made their way into /usr/bin yet. After some poking about, I notice that /usr/src/usr.bin has a bluetooth directory containing the source for a file called btsockstat. I'll install that binary:

```
# cd /usr/src/usr.bin/bluetooth/btsockstat
# make
```

```
# make install
```

```
# ls -F /usr/bin | grep btsockstat
btsockstat*
```

Now let's see if mtree notices that extra file:

```
# cd /usr/bin
# mtree -s 123456789 < /tmp/mtree_bin
. changed
        modification time expected Wed Oct  1 06:54:36 2003
                found Sun Nov 23 16:10:32 2003
btsockstat extra
mtree: /usr/bin checksum: 417306521
```

Well, it didn't fool mtree. That output is actually quite useful. I know that btsockstat was added as an extra file, and I know the date and time it was added. Since I added that file myself, it is an easy matter to resolve. If I hadn't and needed to investigate, I have a time to assist me in my research. I could talk to the administrator who was responsible at that date and time, or I could see if there were any network connections logged during that time period.

Also note that this addition resulted in a new checksum. Once the changes have been resolved, I should create a new database that represents the current state of */usr/bin*. To recap the necessary steps:

1. Use mtree -c to create the database.
2. Use md5 to create a fingerprint for the database.
3. Use openssl to encrypt the database.
4. Move the database to a removable media, and ensure no copies remain on disk.

## Deciding on Which Files to Include

When you create your own integrity database, ask yourself, "Which files do I want to be aware of if they change?" The answer is usually your binaries or applications. Here is a list of common binary locations on a FreeBSD system:

- */bin*
- */sbin*
- */usr/bin*
- */usr/sbin*
- */usr/local/bin*
- */usr/X11R6/bin*
- */usr/compat/linux/bin*
- */usr/compat/linux/sbin*

The *sbin* directories are especially important because they contain system binaries. Most ports will install to */usr/local/bin* or */usr/X11R6/bin*.

The second question to ask yourself is "How often should I check the database?" The answer will depend upon your circumstances. If the machine is a publicly accessible server, you might consider this as part of your daily maintenance plan. If the system's software tends to change often, you'll also want to check often, while you can still remember when you installed what software.

### See Also

- `man mtree`

## HACK #59  Intrusion Detection with Snort, ACID, MySQL, and FreeBSD

How the alert administrator catches the worm.

With the current climate of corporate force reductions and the onslaught of new, fast-spreading viruses and worms, today's administrators are faced with a daunting challenge. Not only is the administrator required to fix problems and keep things running smoothly, but in some cases he is also responsible for keeping the network from becoming worm food. This often entails monitoring the traffic going to and from the network, identifying infected nodes, and loading numerous vendor patches to fix associated vulnerabilities.

To get a better handle on things, you can deploy an Intrusion Detection System (IDS) on the LAN to alert you to the existence of all the nastiness associated with the dark side of the computing world.

This hack will show you how to implement a very effective and stable IDS using FreeBSD, MySQL, Snort, and the Analysis Console for Intrusion Databases (ACID). While that means installing and configuring a few applications, you'll end up with a feature-rich, searchable IDS capable of generating custom alerts and displaying information in many customizable formats.

### Installing the Software

We'll assume that you already have FreeBSD 4.8-RELEASE or newer installed with plenty of disk space. The system is also fully patched and the ports collection is up-to-date. It also helps to be familiar with FreeBSD and MySQL commands.

**Install PHP4, Apache, and MySQL.** We'll start by installing PHP4, Apache, and the MySQL client. As the superuser:

```
# cd /usr/ports/www/mod_php4
# make install clean
```

When the PHP configuration options screen appears, choose the GD Library Support option. Leave the other default selections, and choose OK.

The build itself will take a while because it must install Apache and the MySQL client in addition to PHP.

**Install MySQL-server.** You'll also need the MySQL server, which is a separate port. To ensure this port installs correctly, temporarily set the system hostname to localhost:

```
# hostname localhost
```

```
# cd /usr/ports/databases/mysql40-server
# make install clean
```

This one will also take a while.

**More installations.** There are a few other ports to install. The next three applications are used by ACID to create graphs of the output. ACID supports bar graphs (as shown in Figure 6-3), line graphs (Figure 6-4), and pie charts (Figure 6-5).

We'll need adodb, a database library for PHP:

```
# cd /usr/ports/databases/adodb
# make install clean
```

PHPlot adds a graph library to PHP so it will support charts:

```
# cd /usr/ports/graphics/phplot
# make install clean
```

JPGraph adds more support to PHP for graphs:

```
# cd /usr/ports/graphics/jpgraph
# make install clean
```

Finally, we must install ACID and Snort. Start by modifying snort's *Makefile* to include MySQL support:

```
# cd /usr/local/ports/security/snort
# vi Makefile
```

Change:

```
CONFIGURE_ARGS= --with-mysql=no
```

to:

```
CONFIGURE_ARGS= --with-mysql=yes
```

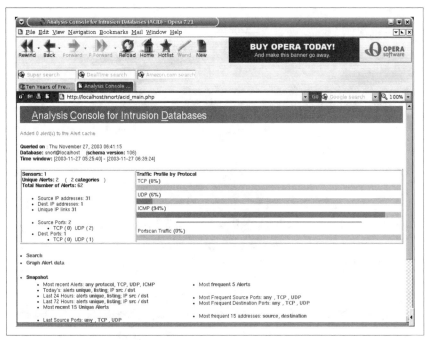

*Figure 6-3. An ACID bar graph*

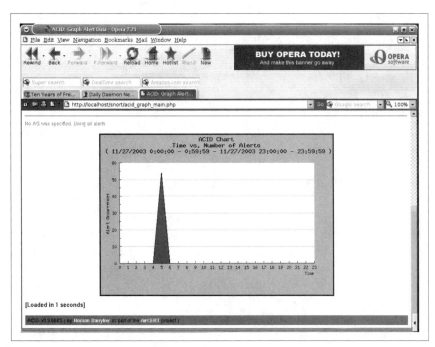

*Figure 6-4. An ACID line graph*

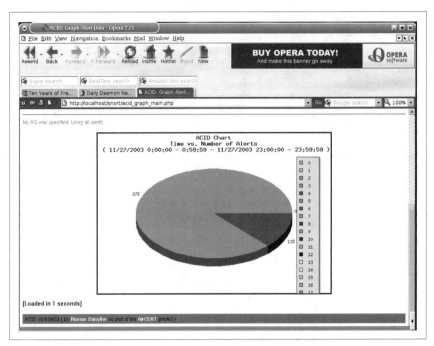

*Figure 6-5. An ACID pie chart*

Save your changes and exit.

Finally, install acid, which will also install snort using your modified *Makefile*:

```
# cd /usr/ports/security/acid
# make install clean
```

## Configuring

Now that we've installed all the necessary pieces for our IDS, it's time to configure them to work together.

**Configure Apache and PHP.** You'll need to make two changes to Apache's configuration file, */usr/local/etc/apache/httpd-conf*. First, search for #ServerName, remove the hash mark (#), and change www.example.com to your actual server name. Then, for security reasons, change ServerSignature   On to ServerSignature   Off. This prevents the server from providing information such as HTTP server type and version. Most admins who run IDSs on their networks like to keep their presence somewhat hidden, since there are exploits/tools written to defeat IDS detection.

**Configure PHP.** After installing PHP, you will notice two sample configuration files in */usr/local/etc*, *php.ini-dist* and *php.ini-recommended*. As the name suggests, the latter is the recommended PHP 4–style configuration file. It contains settings that make PHP "more efficient, more secure, and [encourage] cleaner coding." Since our focus is security, I recommend using this file.

Configuring PHP is as simple as copying the sample configuration file to */usr/local/etc/php.ini*:

```
# cd /usr/local/etc
# cp php.ini-recommended php.ini
```

**Configure MySQL.** MySQL supports several configurations. Use *my-small.cnf* or *my-medium.cnf* if you have less than 64 M of memory, *my-large.cnf* if you have 512 M, and *my-huge.cnf* if you have 1–2 G of memory. Later, if you find your system running out of swap space, you can stop mysql and copy one of the smaller *.cnf* files to fix the problem. In my example, I'll copy over *my-large.cnf*:

```
# cp /usr/local/share/mysql/my-large.cnf /etc/my.cnf
```

Next, set up the initial databases and install the server:

```
# /usr/local/bin/mysql_install_db
# /usr/local/etc/rc.d/mysql-server.sh start
```

You can use the sockstat command to confirm that the MySQL server is running. You should see MySQL listening on port 3306:

```
# sockstat | grep mysql

USER     COMMAND    PID   FD PROTO  LOCAL ADDRESS      FOREIGN ADDRESS
mysql    mysqld     16262 5  tcp4   *:3306             *:*
mysql    mysqld     16262 6  stream /tmp/mysql.sock
```

Then, set the password for the root MySQL user. You'll have to use the FLUSH PRIVILEGES command to tell MySQL to reload all of the user privileges, or the server will continue using the old (blank) password until it restarts:

```
# /usr/local/bin/mysql -u root

Welcome to the MySQL monitor.  Commands end with ; or \g.
Your MySQL connection id is 1 to server version: 4.0.16-log

Type 'help;' or '\h' for help. Type '\c' to clear the buffer.

mysql>SET PASSWORD FOR root@localhost=PASSWORD('your_password_here');
mysql>FLUSH PRIVILEGES;
Query OK, 0 rows affected (0.00 sec)
```

Then, you can create the snort database:

```
mysql>CREATE DATABASE snort;
Query OK, 1 row affected (0.00 sec)
```

Now we can create a MySQL user with sufficient permissions to access the new snort database. Do *not* use the MySQL root user! By creating a new user who has access to only one database, we've limited the damage an attacker could do if he ever gained access to this account.

MySQL uses the GRANT command to give users access to databases. You can control which types of statements the user can issue, as well as the network hosts from which the user can access MySQL. localhost is a nice, safe setting, as we only need to access the database from the local machine. Again, this restricts the damage that an attacker could do from another compromised host.

```
mysql> GRANT INSERT,SELECT ON snort.* to snort_user_here@localhost \
         IDENTIFIED BY 'snort_users_password';
Query OK, 0 rows affected (0.00 sec)

mysql> GRANT INSERT,SELECT,CREATE,DELETE on snort.* \
         to snort_user_here@localhost IDENTIFIED BY 'snort_users_password';
Query OK, 0 rows affected (0.01 sec)

mysql> FLUSH PRIVILEGES;
Query OK, 0 rows affected (0.01 sec)

mysql> quit
Bye
```

**Configure Snort.** First you'll need to download the latest sources from *http://www.snort.org* (currently v2.0.5). After unpacking, use the create_mysql file to create the necessary tables in the snort database. That's all the configuration you need; you can now simply delete the unpacked directory.

```
# tar xvfz snort-2.0.5.tar.gz
# cd snort-2.0.5/contrib
# cp create_mysql /tmp
# /usr/local/bin/mysql -p < /tmp/create_mysql snort
Enter password:          Enter the MySQL root password here

# cd /usr/local/etc
# cp snort.conf-sample snort.conf
# vi snort.conf
```

Scroll down until you reach the # output database: log, mssql, dbname=snort user=snort password=test line. Insert the following lines *beneath* it:

```
output database: log, mysql, user=mysql_user_name password=mysql_users_
    password dbname=snort host=localhost
output database: alert, mysql, user=mysql_user_name password=mysql_users_
    password dbname=snort host=localhost
```

Now page down toward the bottom of the file and select the types of rules you want to monitor for. Keep in mind that the more rules you use, the more work snort will have to do, using up CPU cycles and memory that might be better used elsewhere. For example, if you don't want to monitor X11 or Oracle on any computer on your network, comment out those rules. When you're done, save your changes and exit.

Finish by creating the snort log directory:

```
# cd /var/log
# mkdir snort
```

**Configure ACID.** Start by tightening the permissions of the configuration file:

```
# chmod 644 /usr/local/www/acid/acid_conf.php
```

 Have a good read through the Security section of */usr/local/ www/acid/README* when you're configuring ACID. It contains many good pointers to ensure your configuration is secure.

Then, change the section that contains alert_dbname = "snort_log"; to include the appropriate entries:

```
$alert_dbname   = "snort";
$alert_host     = "localhost";
$alert_port     = "";
$alert_user     = "mysql_snort_user";
$alert_password = "mysql_snort_users_password";
```

Leave the Archive parameters alone, unless you want to create a separate database for snort to store archived alert messages in. To do this, you'll need to log into MySQL, create an archive database, set the appropriate permissions, and run the mysql_create script again as described earlier. The Snort and ACID documentation describe this in more detail.

You do need to tell ACID where to find some of the libraries installed earlier. In particular, change:

```
$ChartLib_path = "";
```

to:

```
$ChartLib_path = "/usr/local/share/jpgraph";
```

## Running ACID

It's time to start Apache:

```
# /usr/local/sbin/apachectl start
/usr/local/sbin/apachectl start: httpd started
```

Then, link the ACID web directory. Of course, for security reasons, I recommend giving the link name something other than *acid*.

```
# cd /usr/local/www/
# ln -s /usr/local/www/acid /usr/local/www/snort
```

Point your web browser to *http://localhost/snort/acid_main.php* and click the Setup link. Click the Create ACID AG button to create the extended tables that ACID will use. When it finishes, you should see something similar to the following:

```
Successfully created 'acid_ag'

Successfully created 'acid_ag_alert'

Successfully created 'acid_ip_cache'

Successfully created 'acid_event'
```

Now click the Main page link to be taken to ACID's main display page. At this point you might ask, "Where are the alerts?" There aren't any—we didn't start snort!

## Running Snort

First, try starting snort manually to make sure it works. Use the -i switch to specify the network interface that will be monitoring traffic. In my case, it is xl0.

```
# cd /usr/local/etc
# /usr/local/bin/snort -c snort.conf -i xl0
database: using the "alert" facility
1458 Snort rules read...
1458 Option Chains linked into 146 Chain Headers
0 Dynamic rules
++++++++++++++++++++++++++++++++++++++++++++++++++++++++++

Rule application order: ->activation->dynamic->alert->pass->log

        --== Initialization Complete ==--

-*> Snort! <*-
Version 2.0.5 (Build 98)
By Martin Roesch (roesch@sourcefire.com, www.snort.org)
```

If snort doesn't show any errors, as depicted here, pat yourself on the back: snort is running!

Quit snort by pressing Ctrl-C, and restart it in daemon mode:

```
# /usr/local/bin/snort -c snort.conf -i xl0 -D
```

Now flip on over to the ACID display page in your web browser. You should start to see alerts coming in. Figure 6-6 shows a sample alert listing.

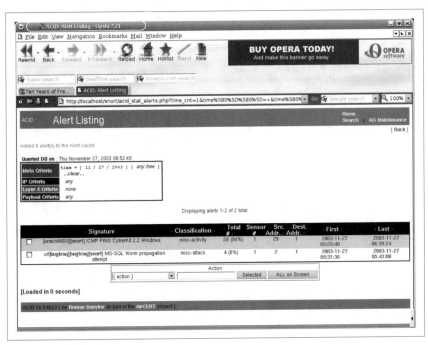

*Figure 6-6. ACID alerts*

Note that each detected signature includes a hyperlink to information about that particular type of attack. Snort also keeps track of how many packets matched that signature, the number of unique source and destination addresses, and the time frame between the first and last packet.

You can also configure your own alert groups to better organize your results, as shown in Figure 6-7.

ACID can also display each rogue packet in intimate detail, as seen in Figure 6-8.

Keep in mind that you'll probably start getting false positives, depending on the types of traffic on your network. However, these can easily be weeded out by making the appropriate changes to your */usr/local/etc/snort.conf* file and the rule files in */usr/local/share/snort*.

If you start noticing a bunch of alerts that look like Figure 6-9, it's a good indication that some nodes on your network are infected with a virus or worm.

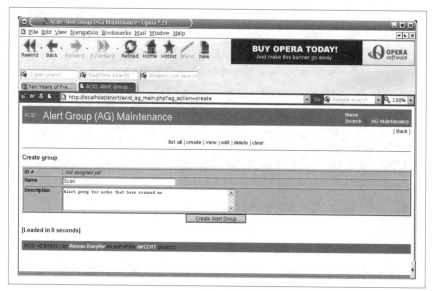

Figure 6-7. ACID alert groups

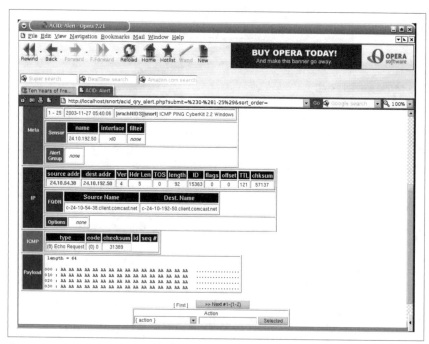

Figure 6-8. An ACID packet in detail

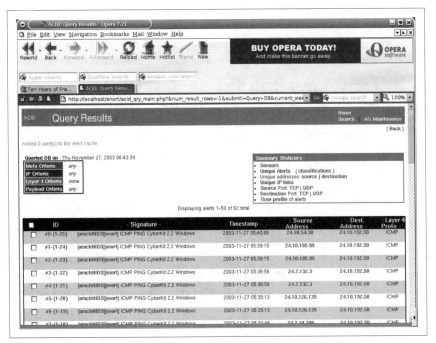

*Figure 6-9. Suspicious Snort alerts*

## Hacking the Hack

Snort and ACID have many additional features. For example, you can use your favorite mail transfer agent, such as Sendmail or Postfix, to send out email alerts, and you can create an archive database to store alerts generated by snort. There's even a snort plug-in for the Big Brother System and Network Monitor that can alert you when 30 or more alerts are generated.

You can also add additional security to MySQL, Snort, and ACID by creating a nonprivileged snort user and locking down the */usr/local/www/acid* directory with the use of a properly configured *.htaccess* file. Configuration of these features goes beyond the scope of this hack, but I encourage you to read all the documentation included with these applications, as well as the documentation at each application's home page, to find out how you can tailor them to suit your needs.

## See Also

- The MySQL Reference Manual (*http://www.mysql.com/documentation/index.html*)
- The Snort web site (*http://www.snort.org/*)

- The Analysis Console for Intrusion Databases (ACID) web site (*http://www.cert.org/kb/acid/*)
- The Big Brother Network and System Monitor web site (*http://bb4.com/*)

## HACK #60   Encrypt Your Hard Disk

Keep your secrets secret by keeping everything secret.

People often store sensitive information on their hard disks and have concerns about this information falling into the wrong hands. This is particularly relevant to users of laptops and other portable devices, which might be stolen or accidentally misplaced.

File-oriented encryption tools like GnuPG are great for encrypting particular files that will be sent across untrusted networks or stored on disk. But sometimes these tools are inconvenient, because the file must be decrypted each time it is to be used; this is especially cumbersome when you have a large collection of files to protect. Any time a security tool is cumbersome to use, there's a chance you'll forget to use it properly, leaving the files unprotected for the sake of convenience.

Worse, readable copies of the encrypted contents might still exist on the hard disk. Even if you overwrite these files (using `rm -P` before unlinking them), your application software might make temporary copies that you don't know about or that have been paged to swapspace. Even your hard disk might have silently remapped failing sectors with data still in them.

The solution is simply never to write the information unencrypted to the hard disk. Rather than taking a file-oriented approach to encryption, consider a block-oriented approach—a virtual hard disk that looks just like a normal hard disk with normal filesystems, but which encrypts and decrypts each block on the way to and from the real disk.

NetBSD includes the encrypting block device driver cgd(4) to help you accomplish this task; the other BSDs have similar virtual devices that, with somewhat different commands, can achieve the same thing. This hack concentrates on NetBSD's cgd.

### The Cryptographic Disk Device

To the rest of the operating system, the cgd(4) device looks and behaves like any other disk driver. Rather than driving real hardware directly, it provides a logical function layered on top of another block device. It has a special configuration program, cgdconfig, to create and configure a cgd device and point it at the underlying disk device that will hold the encrypted data. You can stack several logical block devices together; cgd(4) on top of vnd(4) is handy for making an encrypted volume in a regular file without repartitioning, or you can make an encrypted raid(4).

Once you have a cgd configured, you can put a disklabel on it to divide it up into partitions, make filesystems or enable swapping to those partitions, or mount and use those filesystems, just like any other new disk.

Roland C. Dowdeswell wrote the cgd driver. It first appeared in NetBSD-current after the 1.6 release branch. As a result, it is not in the 1.6 release series; it will be in the 2.0 release and, in the meantime, many people are using it with -current.

In order to use cgd, ensure that you have the line:

```
pseudo-device          cgd     4     # cryptographic disk devices
```

in your kernel configuration file; otherwise, build and install a new kernel. You'll also need a running system, as the NetBSD installer currently doesn't support installing new systems directly into a cgd.

## Preparing the Disk

First, decide which filesystems you want to move to an encrypted device. You need to leave at least the small root filesystem (at /) unencrypted in order to load the kernel and run init, cgdconfig, and the rc.d scripts that configure your cgd. In this example, we'll encrypt everything except /.

We are going to delete and remake partitions and filesystems, and will require a backup to restore the data. So, make sure you have a current, reliable backup stored on a different disk or machine. Do your backup in single-user mode, with the filesystems unmounted, to ensure you get a clean dump. Make sure you back up the disklabel of your hard disk as well, so you have a record of the original partition layout.

With the system in single-user mode, / mounted as read-write, and everything else unmounted, delete all the data partitions you want to move into cgd.

Then, make a single new partition in all the space you just freed up, say, wd0e. Set the type for this partition to ccd. (There's no code specifically for cgd, but ccd is very similar. Though it doesn't really matter what it is, it will help remind you that it's not a normal filesystem.) When finished, label the disk to save the new partition table.

## Scrubbing the Disk

We've removed the partition table information, but the existing filesystems and data are still on disk. Even after we make a cgd device, create filesystems, and restore our data, some of these disk blocks might not yet be overwritten and might still contain our data in plain text. This is especially likely if the filesystems are mostly empty. We want to scrub the disk before we go further.

We could use dd to write */dev/zero* over the new wd0e partition, but this will leave our disk full of zeros, except where we later write encrypted data. We might not want to give an attacker any clues about which blocks contain real data and which are free space, so we want to write noise into all the disk blocks. We'll create a temporary cgd, configured with a random, unknown key.

First, we make a parameters file to tell cgd to use a random key:

```
# cgdconfig -g -k randomkey -o /tmp/wd0e-rnd aes-cbc
```

Then, we use that file to configure a temporary cgd:

```
# cgdconfig cgd0 /dev/wd0e /tmp/wd0e-rnd
```

> If this seems to get stuck, it may be that */dev/random* doesn't have enough entropy for cgdconfig. Hit some keys on the console to generate entropy until it returns.

Now we can write zeros into the raw partition of our cgd (this device will be cgdxd on NetBSD/i386 and cgdxc on most other platforms):

```
# dd if=/dev/zero of=/dev/rcgd0d bs=32k
```

The encrypted zeros will look like random data on disk. This might take a while if you have a large disk. Once finished, unconfigure the random-key cgd:

```
# cgdconfig -u cgd0
```

## Creating the Encrypted Disk Device

The cgdconfig program, which manipulates cgd devices, uses parameters files to store such information as the encryption type, key length, and a random password salt for each cgd. These files are very important and must be kept safe—without them, you will not be able to decrypt the data!

We'll generate a parameters file and write it into the default location (make sure the directory */etc/cgd* exists and is mode 600):

```
# cgdconfig -g -V disklabel -o /etc/cgd/wd0e aes-cbc 256
```

This creates a parameters file describing a cgd using aes-cbc encryption, a key verification (-V) method of disklabel, and a key length of 256 bits. Remember, you'll want to save this file somewhere safe later.

Now it's time to create our cgd, for which we'll need a passphrase. This passphrase must be entered every time the cgd is opened, usually at each reboot, and it is from this passphrase that the encryption key used is derived. Make sure you choose something you won't forget and others won't guess.

The first time we create the cgd, there is no valid disklabel, so the validation mechanism we want to use later won't work. We override it this one time:

```
# cgdconfig -V re-enter cgd0 /dev/wd0e
```

This will prompt twice for a matching passphrase.

Now that we have a new cgd, we need to partition it and create filesystems. Recreate your previous partitions with all the same sizes, although the offsets will be different because they're starting at the beginning of this virtual disk. Remember to include the -I argument to disklabel, because you're creating an initial label for a new disk.

Then, use newfs to create filesystems on all the relevant partitions. This time your partitions will reflect the cgd disk names:

```
# newfs /dev/rcgd0h
```

## Modifying Configuration Files

We've moved several filesystems to another disk, and we need to update */etc/fstab* accordingly. Each partition will have the same letter but will be on cgd0 rather than wd0. So, you'll have */etc/fstab* entries that are similar to these:

```
/dev/wd0a     /      ffs    rw,softdep     1 1
/dev/cgd0b    none   swap   sw             0 0
/dev/cgd0b    /tmp   mfs    rw,-s=132m     0 0
/dev/cgd0e    /var   ffs    rw,softdep     1 2
/dev/cgd0f    /usr   ffs    rw,softdep     1 2
/dev/cgd0h    /home  ffs    rw,softdep     1 2
```

Note that */tmp* should be a separate filesystem, either mfs or ffs, inside the cgd, so that your temporary files are not stored in plain text in the / filesystem.

Each time you reboot, you're going to need your cgd configured early, before fsck runs and filesystems are mounted.

Put the following line in */etc/cgd/cgd.conf*:

```
cgd0     /dev/wd0e
```

and the following line into */etc/rc.conf*:

```
cgd=YES
```

You should now be prompted for cgd0's passphrase whenever rc starts.

## Restoring Data

Next, mount your new filesystems, and restore your data into them. It often helps to have /tmp mounted properly first, as restore can use a fair amount of space when restoring a large dump.

To test your changes to the boot configuration, unmount the filesystems and unconfigure the cgd, so when you exit the single-user shell, rc will run as it does on a clean boot. Now you can bring the system up to multiuser and make sure everything works as before.

## Hacking the Hack

Here are some other things you might consider doing, for extra hack value:

- Use two separate cgds: one with a random key just for swap and one like the cdg in this hack.

- Use multiple cgds for different kinds of data, e.g., one mounted all the time and others mounted only when needed.

- Use a cgd configured on top of a vnd made from a file on a remote network file server (NFS, SMBFS, CODA, etc.) to safely store private data on a shared system.

- Build a kernel with a special minimized, embedded ramdisk root image containing init, cgdconfig, your parameters file, and any other required tools. Boot that image from removable media (such as a USB flash device) that you carry securely on your person, and remount / from the cgd on the hard disk. This can help defend against someone tampering with the kernel or cgdconfig binary in the unencrypted portion of the hard disk and using it to steal your passphrase.

## Final Thoughts and Warnings

Prevent cryptographic disasters by making sure you can always recover your passphrase and parameters file. Protect the parameters file from disclosure, perhaps by storing it on removable media as just mentioned, because the salt it contains helps protect against dictionary attacks on the passphrase.

Keeping the data encrypted on your disk is all very well, but what about other copies? You already have at least one other such copy (the backup we used during this setup), and it's not encrypted. Piping dump through a file-based encryption tool such as gpg can be one way of addressing this issue, but make sure you can decrypt it to restore after a disaster.

Like any form of software encryption, the cgd key stays in kernel memory while the device is configured and may be accessible to privileged programs and users, such as kmem grovelers. Running your system with an elevated securelevel is highly recommended.

Once the cgd volumes are mounted as normal filesystems, their accessibility is just like any other file. Take care of file permissions, and ensure that your running system is protected against application and network security attacks.

Avoid using suspend and resume, especially for laptops with a BIOS suspend-to-disk function. If an attacker can resume your laptop with the key still in memory or read it from the memory image on disk later, the whole point of using cgd is lost.

### See Also

- man cgd
- man cgdconfig
- man disklabel
- The Encrypting Disk Partitions (using gdbe) section of the FreeBSD Handbook (*http://www.freebsd.org/doc/en_US.ISO8859-1/books/handbook/ disks-encrypting.html*)

 ## Sudo Gotchas

**#61** Be aware of these limitations when configuring sudo.

sudo is a handy utility for giving out some, but not all root privileges to users of Unix and Unix-like systems. sudo has some limitations and gotchas, however.

 On FreeBSD, build sudo from the ports collection in */usr/ ports/security/sudo*.

### Limitations of sudo

Tools like sudo exist because the standard Unix privilege model is monolithic. That is, you are either root, with all the privileges and dangers attendant, or you aren't, in which case you lack the ability to affect the system in significant ways. sudo is a workaround of this model. As such, there are limits to what it can achieve, and many of these limitations show up in interactions with the shell. For example:

```
% sudo cd /some/protected/dir
Password:
sudo: cd: command not found
```

Because a process cannot affect the environment of its parent, cd can't be implemented as a program external to the shell. The command is therefore built into the shell itself. sudo can confer privilege only on programs, not pieces of programs. So, the only way to cd to a protected directory using sudo is to execute the shell itself with sudo:

```
% sudo bash
# cd /some/protected/dir
# pwd
/some/protected/dir
```

A workaround is to write a script like the following:

```
#!/usr/local/bin/bash
cd /some/protected/dir;/bin/ls
```

If you enable access to this command in */usr/local/etc/sudoers*, authorized users will be able to ls the contents of a protected directory. This won't allow you to cd to a protected directory, but it will allow you to do work in one.

Another possibility is to allow the user to run a restricted shell, for example, bash -r. This is not a good general solution, though, since most such shells are *very* restrictive. For example, bash -r disallows use of cd!

Another interaction between the shell and sudo involves I/O redirection.

```
% sudo echo "secret stuff"  > /some/protected/dir/secret
bash: /some/protected/dir/secret: Permission denied
```

The problem here is that the bash shell does the I/O direction, not the echo command. This time there is a workaround, however:

```
% echo "secret stuff" | sudo tee -a  /some/protected/dir/secret \
    > /dev/null
% sudo cat /some/protected/dir/secret
secret stuff
```

Here we use sudo to run tee with the -a (append) switch, which dumps the I/O stream coming from stdin to a file. We throw away the stdout stream since we just want the file. Now sudo can confer privilege on the *program* tee, and we get the desired result, although it's a bit awkward.

The same problem exists when trying to redirect stdin. In this case, we can use the similar, but less unusual, expedient of sudo cat to get at the data.

The following interaction is not really a limitation, but more of a wart:

```
% sudo cat /some/protected/dir/secret | wc | sudo tee \
    /some/protected/dir/count > /dev/null
Password:Password:
```

Here we have no cached credentials, so sudo prompts us for our password. But since there are two sudo commands in the pipeline, we get two password prompts, one right after the other. When we enter our password and press Return, nothing happens—our cursor stays put on the next line. We are actually at the second password prompt, but there is no indication of this. Entering our password again will get us out of the mysteriously hung pipeline.

## sudo Configuration Gotchas

sudo is very flexible. The */usr/local/etc/sudoers* file has rich semantics to implement a nearly infinite set of policies that can range from very open to very restrictive. Of course, open policies are easier to understand and implement than the restrictive ones, because there are so many ways to subvert many seemingly restrictive policies.

The earlier examples of sudo limitations assumed that all the commands used were authorized for our use in the *sudoers* file. However, both cat and tee are dangerous commands that could allow a user to easily take control of a system. (Consider sudo tee /etc/spwd.db < myevilspwd.db.) This underlines the generic risk of enabling commands with sudo. It is difficult to analyze all the possible ways a particular command could be misused to subvert a closed security policy. The more commands you enable with sudo, the harder this task becomes. In general, beware of commands that are capable of modifying files, such as editors, dd, cat, and tee, or those that allow shells to be run from within them, such as emacs and vi.

> vim provides an rvim variant that disallows shell escapes. This variant is installed to */usr/local/bin/rvim* when you build the port */usr/ports/editors/vim*.

You can try restricting what arguments can be given to dangerous commands, but beware of alternate methods for supplying those arguments. For example, the following configuration entry recently came up on the sudo-users mailing list:

```
Cmnd_Alias     PASSWD  = /usr/bin/passwd, !/usr/bin/passwd root
```

This works great if the user types passwd root:

```
% sudo passwd root
Sorry, user test is not allowed to execute '/usr/bin/passwd root' as root on
****.
```

Consider, though:

```
% sudo passwd -l root
Changing local password for root
New Password:
```

Oops! The addition of the -l flag causes the pattern in the *sudoers* file not to match the equivalent command.

The moral is: to restrict parameters in *sudoers*, you must disallow *all permutations* of arguments and switches that you deem undesirable.

man sudoers warns about another danger:

> It is generally not effective to "subtract" commands from ALL using the '!' operator. A user can trivially circumvent this by copying the desired command to a different name and then executing that. For example:
>
>     bill        ALL = ALL, !SU, !SHELLS
>
> Doesn't really prevent bill from running the commands listed in SU or SHELLS since he can simply copy those commands to a different name, or use a shell escape from an editor or other program. Therefore, these kind of restrictions should be considered advisory at best (and reinforced by policy).

## Shell Access with sudo

Authorizing shell access with sudo obviously opens your security policy to the largest possible extent, since any available command can then be run in the root-enabled shell. This may be exactly what you want, but you also lose sudo's audit trail, since subsequent commands issued from the shell are not logged.

One way to allow shell access to trusted users without losing the audit trail is to use sudoscript [Hack #62].

## See Also

- man sudo
- man sudoers
- man passwd
- The sudo web site (*http://www.courtesan.com/sudo/*)
- The Sudo-users mailing list archive (*http://www.sudo.ws/pipermail/sudo-users/*)

### H A C K   sudoscript
### #62
sudo can help enforce strict security policies, but what about situations in which you don't want to restrict what commands your users run?

Maybe you're looking for a way to keep track of what your sysadmin team does as root, so you can quickly find out what happened when something goes wrong. Even if you're the only administrator, it's possible to make a bad error as root without realizing it. An audit trail allows you to go back and see exactly what you did type during that 3:00 AM hacking session.

As mentioned in "Sudo Gotchas" [Hack #61], giving access to a shell with sudo means that you lose your audit trail the moment the root shell executes. One answer to this problem is sudoscript.

Another scenario where sudoscript is useful is one similar to the situation that caused me to write sudoscript in the first place. I was a sysadmin in a small startup whose engineers all had the root password. The IT crew all used sudo, but they had tried without success to convince the engineers to use it. Upon investigation, I discovered that the principal reason for this was the prohibition on running shells with sudo.

> In fact, the sysadmins used the "everything-but-shells" method the sudoers manpage warns against [Hack #61].

It quickly became clear that I wasn't going to be able to argue that sudo, as implemented, was equivalent to having a root shell; positions had hardened long before I showed up. So, I wrote sudoscript to bring these engineers back into the IT department's supported circle. It worked, and having the audit trail saved my bacon several times.

## sudoscript Overview

sudoscript is a pair of Perl scripts. One is called sudoshell, or just ss. Contrary to its name, sudoshell is not a shell like tcsh or bash. Instead, it is a frontend script that uses authorization from sudo to run as root and runs script(1) on a FIFO (named pipe) managed by the second script. That script is a daemon, called sudoscriptd. It takes data from the FIFO opened by sudoscript and tags it with the user's name, PID, and a timestamp before writing it to a log file. This log file, */var/log/sudoscript*, is managed by the daemon and rotated if its size exceeds 2 MB. The effect of all this is a root shell that saves its terminal input and output in a log file.

> FreeBSD provides sudoscript in the ports collection in */usr/ ports/security/sudoscript*. Download OpenBSD and NetBSD ports from *http://egbok.com/sudoscript/*.

## Is sudoscript Secure?

The answer is yes and no. The answer is "yes" because sudoscript doesn't confer any privilege of its own; it relies on sudo for that. For that reason, programming or architecture errors in sudoscript (which I have worked hard to avoid) shouldn't increase the security risk to a system. The user of sudoscript already has the privilege to do anything at all on the system.

The answer is "no" if you expect the audit trail provided by sudoscript to be bulletproof. It isn't. For one thing, an xterm will produce a shell that is not audited. Additionally, the FIFO that the scripts use must be writable by the effective user running it. If that effective user is root, then of course there are many, many ways to avoid the audit trail. Simply killing the daemon (but *not* sudoshell) would do the trick nicely, for example.

The moral is: don't give sudoscript to users you don't trust with root. If you have to give it to such users, though, it is probably better than nothing.

## Using sudoscript

Build sudoscript from source in the ports tree or install it from a binary package. (Note that both are misnomers with respect to sudoscript, since it is pure Perl. These mechanisms install the scripts and supporting files.) If you want to enable only root shells, sudoscript configuration is easy. Add an entry like the following to */usr/local/etc/sudoers*:

```
Cmnd_Alias      SS    = /usr/local/bin/sudoshell, /usr/local/bin/ss
```

You can then grant sudoscript access to chosen users through the usual mechanisms. For example:

```
%wheel          ALL=SS
joe             joesbox=SS
```

Now when a user runs ss:

```
% ss
The sudoscriptd doesn't appear to be running!
Would you like me to start it for you? (requires root sudo privilege)? yes
This will be a one-off startup of the daemon. You may have
to arrange for it to be started when the system starts, if that's
what you want. See the INSTALL file in the distribution for details.
sudoscriptdwaiting for the daemon ..done
Script started, output file is
        /var/run/sudoscript/ssd.test_root_1667/test1667.fifo
#
```

The *INSTALL* file mentioned lives in */usr/local/share/doc/sudoscript-version/*, along with lots of other documentation.

As shown in the example, sudoshell will start sudoscriptd if it isn't running already. You probably want to add sudoscriptd to the system startup, which you can do by renaming */usr/local/rc.d/sudoscriptd.sh.sample* to */usr/local/rc.d/sudoscriptd.sh*. Unfortunately, this script isn't a true rc-style startup script in the manner of SysV init, in that it doesn't have start and stop targets; however, this will change in the next release. (As of this writing, sudoscript is at Version 2.1.1.)

> The impatient can modify the startup script using "Create Your Own Startup Scripts" [Hack #86].

sudoscript can enable shells as users other than root. This could be handy for auditing activity of the dba user, for instance. If you want to use this feature, you must also add a Unix group called ssers. If this group exists when sudoscriptd starts, it will make some changes to the files in */var/run/ sudoscript* (where the FIFOs live) to accomodate group access to those files. This has security implications in that anyone in the ssers group will have access to the FIFOs being used by any other concurrent user of sudoscript. Both the user that will run ss *and* the user ss will enable must be in the ssers group.

To get nonroot shells to work, you also have to change your *sudoers* entries like so:

```
Host_Alias    DBBOXES    = db1,db2,db3
Cmnd_Alias    SS         = /usr/local/bin/sudoshell, \
                           /usr/local/bin/ss
Cmnd_Alias    SSASDBA    = /usr/local/bin/sudoshell -u dba, \
                           /usr/local/bin/ss -u dba

%wheel        ALL=SS
joe           joesbox=SS
datamonkey    DBBOXES=(dba) SSASDBA
```

Once the ssers group and the preceding entries in are place:

```
% id
uid=1004(datamonkey) gid=1004(datamonkey) groups=1004(datamonkey), 92(ssers)
% ss -u dba
Password:
Script started, output file is
        /var/run/sudoscript/ssd.datamonkey_dba_2223/datamonkey2223.fifo
bash-2.05b$ id
uid=1005(dba) gid=1005(dba) groups=1005(dba), 92(ssers)
```

## The sudoscript Log File

The sudoscript log file lives in */var/log/sudoscript*. It contains entries like the following:

```
Mon Dec 22 00:32:19 New logger for datamonkey with pid 2223
Mon Dec 22 00:32:19 datamonkey:2223 Script started on Mon Dec 22 00:32:19
    2003
Mon Dec 22 00:32:25 datamonkey:2223 bash-2.05b$ id
Mon Dec 22 00:32:25 datamonkey:2223 uid=1005(dba) gid=1005(dba)
```

```
                 groups=1005(dba), 92(ssers)
  Mon Dec 22 00:49:09 datamonkey:8603 bash-2.05b$ vi .bashrc

  (Tons and tons of garbage)

  Mon Dec 22 00:49:54 datamonkey:8603 bash-2.05b$ exit
  Mon Dec 22 00:49:54 datamonkey:8603
  Mon Dec 22 00:49:54 datamonkey:8603 Script done on Mon Dec  22 00:49:54 2003
  Mon Dec 22 00:49:54 logger (datamonkey,8603) caught signal. Exiting
```

This looks pretty bad! The problem is that the `script` command faithfully
stores all the input and output in the shell, including all the escape codes
that the terminal emulator turns into things like cursor movement and
screen refreshes. The problem is particularly acute when the user enters a
full screen editor, such as vi. There are two approaches to this problem that
help turn the gibberish into useful data. First, this sed script from *Unix
Power Tools*, Third Edition (O'Reilly) will remove simple escape codes from
script output.

```
#!/bin/sh
# Public domain.

# Put CTRL-M in $m and CTRL-H in $b.
# Change \010 to \177 if you use DEL for erasing.
eval `echo m=M b=H | tr 'MH' '\015\010'`

exec sed "s/$m\$//
:x
s/[^$b]$b//
t x" $*
```

Run the previous output through this script. You'll see something like:

```
Mon Dec 22 00:32:19 New logger for datamonkey with pid 2223
Mon Dec 22 00:32:19 datamonkey:2223 Script started on Mon Dec 22 00:32:19
    2003
Mon Dec 22 00:32:25 datamonkey:2223 bash-2.05b$ id
Mon Dec 22 00:32:25 datamonkey:2223 uid=1005(dba) gid=1005(dba)
        groups=1005(dba), 92(ssers)
Mon Dec 22 00:49:09 datamonkey:8603 bash-2.05b$ vi .bashrc

(Still tons of garbage)

Mon Dec 22 00:49:54 datamonkey:8603 ESC[Mon Dec 22 00:49:54 datamonkey:8603
bash-2.05b$ exit
Mon Dec 22 00:49:54 datamonkey:8603
Mon Dec 22 00:49:54 datamonkey:8603 Script done on Mon Dec  22 00:49:54 2003
Mon Dec 22 00:49:54 logger (datamonkey,8603) caught signal. Exiting
```

That's a more intelligible version of the output, but the vi session is still
scrambled. We can take advantage of the fact that we probably are running

the same terminal emulator as the user. If we snip out just the vi session from the log and then cat it to the screen, we get:

```
This is a normal line in a file
Why does this look so bad??

~
~
.. many more ~ lines..
~
~
~
:q
```

That's recognizable as a vi screen. In fact, our screen has been updated several times, once for every time the screen was refreshed in the original session. The final display shows the final state of the vi session.

Why not clean this up in the logging daemon? Because information is invariably lost when you do that kind of thing. It's better to clean up *after* the log file is written. In case you filter out something important, you still have the original log to fall back on.

## See Also

- man sudoscript
- man sudoscriptd
- man sudoshell
- The sudoscript web site (*http://egbok.com/sudoscript/*)
- The Sudoscript-user mailing list subscription link (*http://lists.sourceforge. net/mailman/listinfo/sudoscript-user*)
- The Problem of PORCMOLSULB (*http://egbok.com/sudoscript/ PORCMOLSULB.html*)

### HACK #63 Restrict an SSH server

Control your ssh scripts by placing them in a jail.

Using SSH increases the security of file transfers and network logins. Many network tasks, however, don't really need the shell associated with a user account—remote backups, for example. After all, a shell brings with it commands and an entry point into a system's directory structure. That's somewhat scary when you consider that many of your SSH tasks are scripted.

Configuring a restricted SSH shell such as scponly can mitigate this risk. Not only does it provide noninteractive (read *scripted*) logins into the SSH server, it limits the set of available commands. Additionally, it provides a chroot option, allowing you to restrict the scponly user account to its own directory structure.

## Installing scponly

Before installing this port, read through the available options in its *Makefile*:

```
# cd /usr/ports/shells/scponly
# more Makefile
```

Depending on the scripts you plan on using, consider disabling wildcard processing (which can help prevent accidents like rm -R *). You can also enable rsync support, which is ideal if you're using rsnapshot for backups [Hack #35]. If you want to restrict the account to its own directory, preventing your scripts from accessing anything else on the SSH server, include the chroot option.

Once you've chosen your desired options, pass them to the make command. Here I'll enable chroot support:

```
# make -DWITH_SCPONLY_CHROOT install
```

> If you include the chroot option, do *not* use the clean target at the end of your make command. make clean will remove the *work/* directory, which contains a script that will set up the chroot for you.

Toward the end of the installation, you'll see this message:

```
Run following script to setup chroot cage:
/usr/ports/shells/scponly/work/scponly-3.8/setup_chroot.sh
```

Before running this script, choose a new name for the user account you wish to restrict. The script will abort if you use an existing user account.

Here I'll create a chroot for an account named backup:

```
# cd work/scponly-3.8/
# chown +x setup_chroot.sh
# ./setup_chroot.sh
Next we need to set the home directory for this scponly user.
please note that the user's home directory MUST NOT be writable
by the scponly user. this is important so that the scponly user
cannot subvert the .ssh configuration parameters.

for this reason, an "incoming" subdirectory will be created that
the scponly user can write into. if you want the scponly user to
automatically change to this incoming subdirectory upon login, you
can specify this when you specify the user's home directory as
follows:

set the home dir to /chroot_path//incoming
```

when scponly chroots, it will only chroot to chroot_path and
afterwards, it will chdir to incoming.
enter the home directory you wish to set for this user:
**/usr/home/rembackup/**
Install for what username? **backup**
ls: /lib/libnss_compat*: No such file or directory
creating  /usr/home/rembackup/incoming directory for uploading files

## Testing the chroot

The script will have created the following directory structure for you:

```
# ls -l /usr/home/rembackup
total 10
drwxr-xr-x  2 root    wheel  512 Jan 22 12:37 bin/
drwxr-xr-x  2 root    wheel  512 Jan 22 12:38 etc/
drwxr-xr-x  2 backup  wheel  512 Jan 22 12:38 incoming/
drwxr-xr-x  2 root    wheel  512 Jan 22 12:37 lib/
drwxr-xr-x  7 root    wheel  512 Jan 22 12:37 usr/

# ls -l /usr/home/rembackup/bin/
total 1868
-rwxr-xr-x  1 root  wheel   88808 Jan 22 12:37 chmod*
-rwxr-xr-x  1 root  wheel   14496 Jan 22 12:37 echo*
-rwxr-xr-x  1 root  wheel   72240 Jan 22 12:37 ln*
-rwxr-xr-x  1 root  wheel  567772 Jan 22 12:37 ls*
-rwxr-xr-x  1 root  wheel   73044 Jan 22 12:37 mkdir*
-rwxr-xr-x  1 root  wheel  437684 Jan 22 12:37 mv*
-rwxr-xr-x  1 root  wheel   80156 Jan 22 12:37 pwd*
-rwxr-xr-x  1 root  wheel  439812 Jan 22 12:37 rm*
-rwxr-xr-x  1 root  wheel   69060 Jan 22 12:37 rmdir*

# ls -l /usr/home/rembackup/usr/bin/
total 48
-rwxr-xr-x  1 root  wheel   7016 Jan 22 12:37 chgrp*
-rwxr-xr-x  1 root  wheel   7688 Jan 22 12:37 groups*
-rwxr-xr-x  1 root  wheel   7688 Jan 22 12:37 id*
-rwxr-xr-x  1 root  wheel  22616 Jan 22 12:37 scp*

# ls -l /usr/home/rembackup/usr/sbin/
total 8
-rwxr-xr-x  1 root  wheel  7016 Jan 22 12:37 chown*
```

There you have it; these are the only commands that account can use during an SSH session.

You can also verify that the specified user account was created for you. I'll check for that backup account:

```
# grep backup /etc/master.passwd
backup:*:1015:1015::0:0:User \
&:/usr/home/rembackup//incoming:/usr/local/sbin/scponlyc
```

Notice that the account is restricted to the scponlyc shell. The trailing c indicates that this is a chroot.

## Now What?

Now that you have a restricted account, test it with one of your SSH scripts. Don't forget to set up your authentication method. Either set a password on the account or configure key-based authentication.

You can use this hack in conjunction with "Secure Backups Over a Network" **[Hack #38]** and "Automate Remote Backups" **[Hack #39]**.

## See Also

- man scponly
- The scponly home page (*http://www.sublimation.org/scponly/*)

## HACK #64 Script IP Filter Rulesets

One firewall ruleset isn't always enough.

As a firewall administrator, you know that it takes a bit of creative genius to create a ruleset that best reflects your network's security needs. Things can get more interesting if those needs vary by time of day. For example, you may need to allow Internet access between business hours but ban it during the evening hours. This is easy to do with two rulebases, a couple of scripts, and trusty old cron.

### Limiting Access with IP Filter

I have a FreeBSD firewall/router guarding my home network. I also happen to have a daughter who would spend her life online if she were allowed. There's a simple solution to restricting her access to the Internet to certain times of the day without having to use a proxy.

I use FreeBSD's IP Filter as my firewall software. My normal set of firewall rules, */etc/ipf.rules*, allows unrestricted access to the Internet. Here's the section of that rulebase that controls my daughter's access:

```
# ------------------------comment area begin--------------------------
# Internal Interface: ed0
# Allow internal traffic to flow freely.
# ------------------------ comment area end --------------------------
pass in  on ed0 all
pass out on ed0 all
```

Note that this is not my entire rulebase, just the section controlling the interface, ed0, connected to the portion of the network containing my daughter's computer.

Also note that I did not use the normal pass in quick on ed0 all or pass out quick on ed0 all. This is because the use of the word quick in IP Filter tells the program not to look any further for rules applying to the flow of traffic on an interface. If that were the case, this hack would not work.

I saved a copy of my unrestricted rulebase as */etc/ipf.rules.allow* for safekeeping. This will be my first rulebase.

```
# cp /etc/ipf.rules /etc/ipf.rules.allow
```

I next edited a copy of the original rulebase file, */etc/ipf.rules*, to block Natasha's computer (IP 10.0.0.3) from accessing the outside world while still allowing her to do homework:

```
# ------------------------comment area begin----------------------------
# Internal Interface: ed0
# Allow internal traffic to flow freely.
# ------------------------ comment area end ----------------------------
pass in  on ed0 all
pass out on ed0 all

# ------------------------block Natasha's computer----------------------
block in  on ed0 from any to 10.0.0.3
block out on ed0 from any to 10.0.0.3
```

I saved this rule file as */etc/ipf.rules.block*, my second rulebase. This second ruleset will effectively block her from surfing and using the usual plethora of messaging programs.

## Switching Rules on a Schedule

To implement these restrictions at a specific time, I wrote a small script:

```
#!/bin/sh

# copy the restrictive rules to the default ipfilter rulebase
cp /etc/ipf.rules.block /etc/ipf.rules

# cause ipfilter to re-read and apply the new rulebase
/sbin/ipf -Fa -f /etc/ipf.rules
```

Notice that this is a very simple Bourne shell script. As the comments state, it copies the second, restrictive rulebase to the rulebase used by IP Filter. It then tells IP Filter to reread and apply the newly copied rulebase.

I saved this script as */usr/local/bin/block.sh* and made it executable:

```
# chmod 751 /usr/local/bin/block.sh
```

From there, I used cron to schedule the restriction. First, I open up the crontab editor:

```
# crontab -e
```

and then add the line:

```
# minute, hour, all days, all weeks, on these days, script to run
   0       21    *          *             0-4             /usr/local/bin/block.sh
```

which will effectively shut down access to the outside world starting at 9:00 PM, Sunday through Thursday (i.e., school nights).

To allow access to the Internet in the morning, I need another script:

```
#!/bin/sh

# copy the non-restrictive rules to the default ipfilter rulebase
cp /etc/ipf.rules.allow /etc/ipf.rules

# cause ipfilter to re-read and apply the new rulebase
/sbin/ipf -Fa -f /etc/ipf.rules
```

This script is very similar to the first one, except that it copies over the non-restrictive rulebase. I saved this file as */usr/local/bin/allow.sh* and made it executable:

```
# chmod 751 /usr/local/bin/allow.sh
```

Once again, I launched crontab -e to add the following line:

```
# minute, hour, all days, all weeks, on these days, script to run
   0       7     *          *             1-5             /usr/local/bin/allow.sh
```

This will allow access to resume at 7:00 AM, Monday to Friday. Obviously there are no restrictions on the weekends.

## Hacking the Hack

While I've successfully used this hack at home for several years, it is easy to see how the same logic could apply to schedule multiple rulebases to suit any network's needs. This gives an administrator much more flexible control over traffic, without the overhead of additional firewall software.

## See Also

- man crontab
- The IP Filter HOWTO (*http://www.obfuscation.org/ipf/*)

# Secure a Wireless Network Using PF

**Protect your private wireless network from unauthorized use.**

The abundance of 802.11 wireless networks has raised an important question. How can you secure a wireless network so that only recognized systems can use it?

Wireless Encryption Protocol (WEP) and MAC access lists offer some protection against unauthorized users; however, they can be difficult to maintain. With OpenBSD's PF, we can maintain tables of recognized clients and update those tables with a single shell command. Known clients can access the Internet; unknown clients will only ever see a web page informing them that this is a private network.

For this hack, we will use dhcpd, PF, and Apache.

## DHCP Configuration

We'll use a simple DHCP configuration in */etc/dhcpd.conf* like this:

```
shared-network GUEST-NET {
        max-lease-time 300;
        default-lease-time 120;

        option     domain-name-servers 192.168.0.1;
        option     routers 192.168.0.1;

    subnet 192.168.0.0 netmask 255.255.255.0 {
        range 192.168.0.101 192.168.0.254;
    }
}
```

In this case, we're using the subnet 192.168.0.0/24. Our firewall and NAT gateway is 192.168.0.1, and it's also configured as the DNS server for our network.

We've allocated a range of IP addresses (192.168.0.101 to 192.168.0.254) for distribution on a first-come, first-served basis to any host that requests an address via DHCP. Anybody that connects to our network will be able to request a valid IP address in that range. The security will come from our PF configuration.

## PF Configuration

OpenBSD has an excellent FAQ on PF, along with an example of how to write a ruleset for a home or small office network. We'll use this example as a template.

We'll start with the sample PF configuration that allows any host on the internal interface (represented by the macro $int_if) full access to the Internet. Then, we will modify the rules in /etc/pf.conf so that only authorized hosts have access and set up a web server to respond to requests from unauthorized hosts. We will also allow unauthorized hosts direct access to our DNS server, to simplify our rules and to avoid more complex split-horizon DNS configuration.

First, let's create the table for authorized hosts and macros for the web server and the DNS server:

```
auth_server = "127.0.0.1 port 8080"
dns_server  = "192.168.0.1"
table <authorized_hosts> { 192.168.0.1, 192.168.0.11 };
```

These lines go near the top of /etc/pf.conf, before any queue, NAT, or filter rules.

We've initialized the table to contain the addresses of our NAT gateway and one other host, 192.168.0.11, a statically configured box we'd like to have access to as well. While PF has a ruleset loaded, we can add a host to the table on the fly:

```
# pfctl -t authorized_hosts -Tadd 192.168.0.101
```

We can also delete a host:

```
# pfctl -t authorized_hosts -Tdelete 192.168.0.102
```

and list all the authorized hosts:

```
# pfctl -t authorized_hosts -Tshow
```

Now we need to modify the filter rules so only our authorized hosts have access. These rules allow any host on our network to have access:

```
pass in  on $int_if from $int_if:network to any          keep state
pass out on $int_if from any          to $int_if:network keep state
```

We'll change them like this to use our table:

```
pass in  on $int_if from <authorized_hosts> to any keep state
pass out on $int_if from any to <authorized_hosts> keep state
```

Right after those rules, we'll add the following rules to allow unauthorized hosts to access our web server and DNS server:

```
pass in  on $int_if proto tcp from !<authorized_hosts> to $auth_server
pass in  on $int_if proto {tcp, udp} from any to $dns_server port domain \
    keep state
```

Now any host in the authorized_hosts table will have full access to the Internet. Any other hosts will only be able to lookup names and reach the web server. We'll add some simple rules so unauthorized users will see a rejection page if they try to go to any web site.

In the NAT section, we'll add this rule:

```
rdr on $int_if proto tcp from !<authorized_hosts> to any port www -> \
    $auth_server
```

This rule redirects any unknown host attempting to access a remote machine on the www port to the web server that will return the rejection page. We could install a web server on the firewall box or on some separate machine. In my case, I'll run Apache on the firewall, listening at 127.0.0.1 and port 8080, so it won't be confused with any other web servers I'm running.

## Apache Configuration

Apache is installed by default with OpenBSD, so we'll reconfigure it to listen on port 8080 of the gateway (with IP address 127.0.0.1) and return the same page for every URL requested. (Apache is also available in the FreeBSD ports collection and NetBSD packages collection.)

First, we'll enable Apache with the httpd_flags parameter in */etc/rc.conf*. Next, we need to edit Apache's configuration file, */var/www/conf/httpd.conf*. Find the Listen directive and add 127.0.0.1:8080. Next, create a VirtualHost entry like this:

```
<VirtualHost 127.0.0.1:8080>
  ServerAdmin none
  DocumentRoot /var/www/auth
  ErrorDocument 404 /index.html
</VirtualHost>
```

This tells Apache to listen to the appropriate port and IP address. For every incoming request, Apache will try to serve a page beneath the given directory. Any time it can't find a page, it will serve the *index.html* page instead.

We don't have either yet, so create the directory */var/www/auth* and place an *index.html* like this in it:

```
<html>
  <head>
    <title>Unauthorized -- This is a private network</title>
  </head>
  <body>
    <h1>Unauthorized</h1>
    <p>This is a private network and you are not authorized to use
      it.</p>
  </body>
</html>
```

## Putting it All Together

Start or restart dhcpd, pf, and Apache like this, where *[interfaces]* is the list of interfaces on which you provide DHCP:

```
# kill `cat /var/run/dhcpd.pid`; dhcpd -q [interfaces]
# pfctl -f /etc/pf.conf
# apachectl stop && apachectl start
```

Congratulations! When a new host connects to your network, it should request an address with DHCP. If so, it will receive an address in the range of 192.168.0.101 to 192.168.0.254. If the assigned address is not already in the authorized_hosts table, any time that host attempts to load a web page it will receive your Unauthorized page. The firewall will silently discard any packets destined for any other ports outside of your network.

If you want to allow a new host to use your network, just use pfctl to add it to the table. To make the change permanent, add the address or a range of addresses to the table definition in */etc/pf.conf*, or even create an external file listing allowed addresses. See the PF FAQ section on tables for more.

## Security Concerns

This technique only controls the ability of hosts on your network to route packets through your firewall. It will not protect other hosts on the same subnet from unauthorized access, so they should have reasonable local firewall rules. A wise approach might be to build a firewall with three interfaces: one external and two internal. One internal subnet would host your regular machines, and the other subnet would allow guest access with this technique, separating the subnets with additional PF rules.

## Hacking the Hack

Running the web server on the firewall is a simple approach. However, you can redirect to another host, such as a dedicated authentication server. For simplicity, this server should not be on the $int_if:network subnet; if it is, the redirection becomes more complicated. The PF FAQ has a section devoted to port forwarding in this manner.

I used Apache because it is installed by default with OpenBSD and because its configuration is trivial in this case. Almost any HTTP server will do the job, though.

## See Also

- OpenBSD's PF FAQ (*http://www.openbsd.org/faq/pf/*)
- NoCat.net's NoCatAuth, authentication software for open wireless nodes (*http://nocat.net/*)

# Automatically Generate Firewall Rules
## #66

Easily protect any FreeBSD workstation with a fully configured firewall.

You know the importance of being protected by a firewall. You know where to look in the manpages for details. Given enough time and trouble, you could write a firewall configuration for any situation. They're all reasonably similar, though, so why not generate the configuration by answering a few questions?

That's the purpose of the IPFilter setup script: to generate configuration rules for typical SOHO firewalls using FreeBSD and IPFilter. Even novice users can retain the full benefits of a firewall without first having to learn syntax. In fact, with this script, you should be able to set up a typical firewall with no FreeBSD configuration knowledge at all.

Even if you're not a novice user, this is a great script to refer friends to as they discover FreeBSD. Now you can rest easy in the thought that your friends are protected—and you didn't even have to find the time to show them how to set up their systems.

## What the Script Does

The script uses a simple question and answer text interface. It has four main parts:

*Network settings and IPFilter firewall and IPNAT configuration*
> This configures internal and external network card interface IP address settings either manually or via DHCP. It creates stateful firewall rules on the external network interface and configures NAT to provide Internet connection sharing on the internal network interface.

*ADSL PPPOE configuration*
> This prompts for a login name, password, and Ethernet NIC to generate the */etc/ppp/ppp.conf* file. It then inserts the required PPP variables in */etc/rc.conf*. This starts userland PPP at bootup.

*DHCP server configuration*
> This checks for the installation of the ISC DHCP server. If it's not installed, the script offers to install the latest version from the ports system or via a precompiled package.

> Once installed, the script will configure the DHCP server by prompting for the addresses of the ISP's DNS servers, the address of the internal NIC to use as the default gateway, and the IP address range and subnet mask to use for the internal LAN.

*Serial console setup*
> Answer "yes" to this section of the script if you plan on running the firewall headless [Hack #26].

## Installation

The easiest way to install the script is to download it to the system that will become the firewall. I prefer the fetch command:

```
% fetch http://www.roq.com/bsd/ipfilterscript.tar.gz
```

If networking isn't configured on that system yet, you can copy the file from another device, such as a USB flash key:

```
# mount -t msdos /dev/da0s1 /mnt
# cp /mnt/ipfilterscript.tar.gz /tmp/
```

Once you have the script, extract it and run it:

```
# tar -zxf ipfilterscript.tar.gz
# ./ipfilter.pl
######################################################################
1: Would you like to setup PPPoE DSL connection (Choose 1)
2: Setup IP configuration, Firewalling and NAT (Choose 2) or
3: Setup a DHCP server (Choose 3 and hit enter)
4: Setup serial console support
5: Exit
######################################################################
```

If you use ADSL with PPPoE, choose 1 and press Enter. If you have ADSL but use it with a static IP, instead choose 2, which combines IP configuration, Firewalling, and NAT setup. Choosing 3 will install and configure a DHCP server. First, however, configure your network, as the script will attempt to download and install the DHCP server.

## Example Usage

For this example, I will choose 2 for IP configuration. The script lists my three Ethernet cards, rl0, xl0, and rl0, two of which I haven't configured.

```
rl0: flags=8843<UP,BROADCAST,RUNNING,SIMPLEX,MULTICAST> mtu 1500
        inet6 fe80::202:44ff:fe36:8259%rl0 prefixlen 64 scopeid 0x1
        inet 10.0.0.5 netmask 0xff000000 broadcast 10.255.255.255
        ether 00:02:44:36:82:59
        media: Ethernet autoselect (10baseT/UTP)
        status: active
xl0: flags=8802<BROADCAST,SIMPLEX,MULTICAST> mtu 1500
        options=3<RXCSUM,TXCSUM>
        ether 00:50:da:89:bc:9f
        media: Ethernet 10baseT/UTP (10baseT/UTP <half-duplex>)
rl1: flags=8802<BROADCAST,SIMPLEX,MULTICAST> mtu 1500
        ether 00:02:44:04:14:2c
        media: Ethernet autoselect (10baseT/UTP)
        status: no carrier
lo0: flags=8049<UP,LOOPBACK,RUNNING,MULTICAST> mtu 16384
        inet6 ::1 prefixlen 128
        inet6 fe80::1%lo0 prefixlen 64 scopeid 0x4
```

```
                inet 127.0.0.1 netmask 0xff000000
#####################################################################
  Choose your external Nic, eg "fxp0" . If you are firewalling for a PPPoE
  / ADSL setup use "tun0"
#####################################################################
```

At the moment, I have only one Ethernet card plugged into something. Only rl0 has active status, so it is plugged into my ADSL modem. I'll configure it with a static IP address by typing in rl0 and pressing Enter. The script now asks for my internal network card, which is rl1.

```
#####################################################################
  choose your internal Nic, eg "rl0"
#####################################################################
rl1
#####################################################################
  Internal nic IP, Recommended "192.168.1.1" . Hit "ENTER" for recommended
  defaults
#####################################################################
```

Now the script needs to know the IP address of the gateway device, behind which all of my internal machines live. The defaults are fine, so I can simply press Enter for the next few questions.

```
Setting Internal nic IP to 192.168.1.1
#####################################################################
  Internal nic Netmask, Just hit enter for 255.255.255.0
#####################################################################
Setting Internal nic Netmask to 255.255.255.0
```

When asked for my external IP, I type it in manually since I am setting up a static IP connection:

```
#####################################################################
  External nic IP, or type "DHCP" for DHCP, for connections like ADSL type
  "NONE" for no dhclient on external nic
#####################################################################
10.6.1.2
Setting External nic IP to 10.6.1.2
#####################################################################
  External nic netmask, eg 255.255.255.0
#####################################################################
255.255.255.254
Setting External Netmask to 255.255.255.254
#####################################################################
Do you want to enter a gateway default IP address? if you ISP provided
you with a default gateway choose Yes Y/N, default = no
y
What is your gateway IP for your firewall machine to route to, (eg:
111.1.1.1)
10.6.1.1
#####################################################################
  Do you want statefull firewall or just allow everything and rely on
```

```
IPNAT to protect you, I recommend firewalling :)
Choose: "y" for statefull firewall or "n" for allow everything
######################################################################
 y
######################################################################
Do you want to forward any ports from the firewall to a internal host ip?
 n
######################################################################
Do you want IP Filter to log denied packets? Y/N, default = yes
 y
#### Denied packets will be logged to /var/log/firewall.log ####
######################################################################
Do you want to install a /etc/ipfrestart script so you can easily reset
your rules? Handy if you are trying out new rulesets. Y/N, default = yes
 y
######################################################################
Do you want ftp active mode supprt? when ftping out behind a basic NAT
firewall, active mode ftp wont work.
This is because normal active mode ftp actually initiates a FTP
connection from the server back to YOU! and requires more then basic nat
to work.
The day FTP is gone and fully replaced by something more secure like
SSH's sftp will be a day when the internet is large degree more secure.
Choose: "y" to switch on active ftp support (recommended) or "n"
 y
Going to write the data to these files
/etc/rc.conf
/etc/ipf.rules
/etc//etc/ipnat.rules
/etc/newsyslog.conf

hit ctrl+c to abort
All done, type "reboot" for changes to take effect

######################################################################
Settings for internal machines behind the firewall:
Gateway: 192.168.1.1
Netmask: 255.255.255.0
DNS: (Your ISPS DNS)
Clients IP: 192.168.1.2 or higher
######################################################################
```

Finally, the script writes the necessary information to the required configuration files. When I reboot, the system is fully configured to access the ISP and provide NAT and DHCP services to the internal LAN, and it will protect all packets through its firewall.

## See Also

- The IPFilterscript web site (*http://www.roq.com/bsd/*)
- The IPFilter web site (*http://coombs.anu.edu.au/~avalon/*)

# Automate Security Patches

## #67  Keep up-to-date with security patches.

We all know that keeping up-to-date with security patches is important. The trick is coming up with a workable plan that ensures you're aware of new patches as they're released, as well as the steps required to apply those patches correctly.

Michael Vince created `quickpatch` to assist in this process. It allows you to automate the portions of the patching process you'd like to automate and manually perform the steps you prefer to do yourself.

## Preparing the Script

quickpatch requires a few dependencies: `perl`, `cvsup`, and `wget`. Use `which` to determine if you already have these installed on your system:

```
% which perl cvsup wget
/usr/bin/perl
/usr/local/bin/cvsup
wget: Command not found.
```

Install any missing dependencies via the appropriate port (*/usr/ports/lang/ perl5*, */usr/ports/net/cvsup-without-gui*, and */usr/ports/ftp/wget*, respectively).

Once you have the dependencies, download the script from *http://roq.com/ projects/quickpatch* and untar it:

```
% tar xzvf quickpatch.tar.gz
```

This will produce an executable Perl script named `quickpatch.pl`. Open this script in your favorite editor and review the first two screens of comments, up to the `#Stuff you probably don't want to change` line.

Make sure that the `$release` line matches the tag you're using in your cvs-supfile **[Hack #80]**:

```
# The release plus security patches branch for FreeBSD that you are
# following in cvsup.
# It should always be a long the lines of RELENG_X_X , example RELENG_4_9
$release='RELENG_4_9';
```

The next few paths are fine as they are, unless you have a particular reason to change them:

```
# Ftp server mirror from where to fetch FreeBSD security advisories
$ftpserver="ftp.freebsd.org";
# Path to store patcher program files
$patchdir="/usr/src/";
```

```
# Path to store FreeBSD security advisories
$advdir="/var/db/advisories/";
$advdirtmp="$advdir"."tmp/";
```

If you're planning on applying the patches manually and, when required, rebuilding your kernel yourself, leave the next section as is. If you're brave enough to automate the works, make sure that the following paths accurately reflect your kernel configuration file and build directories:

```
# Path to your kernel rebuild script for source patches that require kernel
#rebuild
$kernelbuild="/usr/src/buildkernel";
#$kernelbuild="cd /usr/src ; make buildkernel KERNCONF=GENERIC && make
#installkernel KERNCONF=GENERIC ; reboot";
# Path to your system recompile scipt for patches that require full
# operating system recompile
$buildworld="/usr/src/buildworld";
#$buildworld="cd /usr/src/ ; make buildworld && make installworld ; reboot";
#Run patch command after creation, default no
$runpatchfile="0";
# Minimum advisory age in hours. This is to make sure you don't patch
# before your local cvsup server has had a
# chance to recieve the source change update to your branch, in hours
$advisory_age="24";
```

Review the email accounts so the appropriate account receives notifications:

```
# Notify email accounts, eg: qw(billg@microsoft.com root@localhost);
@emails = qw(root);
```

## Running the Hack

Run the script without any arguments to see the available options:

```
# /.quickpatch.pl
# Directory /var/db/advisories/ does not exist, creating
# Directory /var/db/advisories/tmp/ does not exist, creating
Quickpatch - Easy source based security update system
"./quickpatch.pl updateadv" to download / update advisories db
"./quickpatch.pl patch" or "./quickpatch.pl patch > big_patch_file" to
create patch files
"./quickpatch.pl notify" does not do anything but email you commands of what
it would do
"./quickpatch.pl pgpcheck" to PGP check advisories
```

Before applying any patches, it needs to know which patches exist. Start by downloading the advisories:

```
# ./quickpatch.pl updateadv
```

This will connect to *ftp://ftp.freebsd.org/pub/FreeBSD/CERT/advisories* and download all of the advisories to */var/db/advisories*. The first time you use this command, it will take a while. However, once you have a copy of the advisories, it takes only a second or so to compare your copies with the FTP site and, if necessary, download any new advisories.

After downloading the advisories, see if your system needs patching:

```
# ./quickpatch.pl notify
#
```

If the system is fully patched, you'll receive your prompt back. However, if the system is behind in patches, you'll see output similar to this:

```
# ./quickpatch.pl notify
###########################################################################
####### FreeBSD-SA-04%3A02.shmat.asc
####### Stored in file /var/db/advisories/tmp/FreeBSD-SA-04%3A02.shmat
####### Topic: shmat reference counting bug
####### Hostname: genisis - 20/2/2004 11:57:30
####### Date Corrected: 2004-02-04 18:01:10
####### Hours past since corrected: 382
####### Patch Commands
cd /usr/src
# patch < /path/to/patch
### c) Recompile your kernel as described in
<URL:http://www.freebsd.org/handbook/kernelconfig.html> and reboot the
system.
/usr/src/buildkernel
## Emailed root
```

It looks like this system needs to be patched against the "schmat reference counting bug." While running in notify mode, quickpatch emails this information to the configured address but neither creates nor installs the patch.

To create the patch, use:

```
# ./quickpatch.pl patch
#########################################################
####### FreeBSD-SA-04%3A02.shmat.asc
####### Stored in file /usr/src/FreeBSD-SA-04%3A02.shmat
####### Topic: shmat reference counting bug
####### Hostname: genisis - 21/2/2004 10:41:54
####### Date Corrected: 2004-02-04 18:01:10
####### Hours past since corrected: 405
####### Patch Commands
cd /usr/src
# patch < /path/to/patch
### c) Recompile your kernel as described in
#<URL:http://www.freebsd.org/handbook/kernelconfig.html> and reboot the
#system.
/usr/src/buildkernel

# file /usr/src/FreeBSD-SA-04%3A02.shmat
/usr/src/FreeBSD-SA-04%3A02.shmat: Bourne shell script text executable
```

This mode creates the patch as a Bourne script and stores it in */usr/src*. However, it is up to you to apply the patch manually. This may suit your purposes if you intend to review the patch and read any notes or caveats associated with the actual advisory.

## Automating the Process

One of the advantages of having a script is that you can schedule its execution with cron. Here is an example of a typical cron configuration for quickpatch.pl; modify to suit your own purposes. Remember to create your logging directories and touch your log files before the first run.

```
# Every Mon, Wed, and Fri at 3:05 do an advisory check and download any
# newly released security advisories
5  3  *  *  1,3,5   root  /etc/scripts/quickpatch.pl updateadv > \
    /var/log/quickpatch/update.log 2>1

# 20 minutes later, check to see if any new advisories are ready for use
# and email the patch commands to the configured email address
25 3  *  *  1,3,5   root   /etc/scripts/quickpatch.pl notify >> \
    /var/log/quickpatch/notify.log 2>&1

# 24 hours later patch mode is run which will run the patch commands if
# no one has decided to interfere.
25 3  *  *  2,4,6   root  /etc/scripts/quickpatch.pl patch >> \
    /var/log/quickpatch/patch.log 2>&1
```

## See Also

- The quickpatch.pl web site (*http://roq.com/projects/quickpatch*)
- The FreeBSD Security Advisories page (*http://www.freebsd.org/security/index.html#adv*)

# HACK #68 Scan a Network of Windows Computers for Viruses

> Even after educating your users to use discretion regarding downloads and emails, you can still experience occasional problems with viruses.

Regardless of the size of your network, the cost of annual subscriptions for antivirus software can quickly become a pain in the...checkbook. Using FreeBSD's strength as a network server, how hard could it be to hack an easier and cheaper way to administer the antivirus battle?

The solution I found uses a combination of FreeBSD and ClamAV and Sharity-Light, both of which are found in the ports collection. As seen in "Access Windows Shares Without a Server" **[Hack #19]**, Sharity-Light can mount

Windows shares. Once the shares are mounted, ClamAV will scan them for viruses.

## Preparing the Windows Systems

For the systems you wish to virus scan, share their drives as follows:

1. Open My Computer and right-click on the drive you wish to share.
2. Select Sharing from the list of options that appear.

> If Sharing is not available, you will need to activate file sharing in the Network setting in Control Panel. Use Help if you're unsure of where to find this setting.

3. In the Sharing tab of the Properties window, assign a name to the new share. I'll use cdrive in this example. Choose a name that is both useful to you and not already in use. (If a share already exists, click on New Share.)
4. Unless your network is completely closed to the outside world, click on Permissions and limit the access to your user. You should only need read access for scanning purposes.
5. If you need further assistance, search for "sharing" in Windows Help. (Click on the Start button and select Help.)

Once you've configured the Windows systems for sharing, it's time to prepare the FreeBSD system.

## Preparing the FreeBSD System

Install and configure Sharity-Light [Hack #19]. Remember to edit /etc/hosts to reflect the NetBIOS names of the Microsoft systems.

Then, create a mount point. Since I'll be automating the process later on with a script, I need only one mount point. For now, I'll test the required steps using one system:

```
# mkdir /mnt/winshare
# shlight //winbox1/cdrive /mnt/winshare -U algould -P pwd
Using port 1653 for NFS.
```

Here, I've mounted the cdrive share located on winbox1 to the /mnt/winshare mount point. This particular share has a username and password.

## Installing and Running the Virus Scanner

ClamAV is a GPL antivirus application that can be used alone or as a daemon in conjunction with mail server tools such as milter or pop3vscan (both are available in the ports collection). Although ClamAV can detect and remove files that have been contaminated with viruses, it does not disinfect these files.

First, install ClamAV from the ports system:

```
# cd /usr/ports/security/clamav
# make install clean
```

The ClamAV port installs several executables, including clamd, clamdscan, clamscan, freshclam, and sigtool. Each of these commands has a manpage, as does *clamav.conf*, the configuration file.

For the purposes of this project, we will be using only clamscan and freshclam. Since we will not be activating clamd, we do not need to change the configuration file.

To update ClamAV's virus database, execute freshclam:

```
# freshclam
Current working dir is /usr/local/share/clamav
Checking for a new database - started at Tue Dec 30 14:55:43 2003
Connected to clamav.elektrapro.com.
Reading md5 sum (viruses.md5): OK
viruses.db is up to date.
Reading md5 sum (viruses2.md5): OK
Downloading viruses.db2 ........... done
Database updated (containing in total 11983 signatures).
Database updated from clamav.elektrapro.com.
```

Once you've updated the virus definitions, use clamscan to scan for viruses. You don't need to be the superuser, but you must be able to read the files and directories that you're scanning. Here's what happens when I scan an arbitrary file in my home directory:

```
% clamscan todo.txt
todo.txt: OK

----------- SCAN SUMMARY -----------
Known viruses: 11982
Scanned directories: 0
Scanned files: 1
Infected files: 0
Data scanned: 0.00 Mb
I/O buffer size: 131072 bytes
Time: 0.241 sec (0 m 0 s)
```

One file scanned and no viruses found—good. When we scan the Windows share, however, we will want to scan directories recursively (using the -r option) and log the resulting report to a file (using the -l *filename* option).

To scan the Windows share mounted at */mnt/winshare* and save the scan report to */var/log/clamscan.log*, execute:

```
# clamscan -l /var/log/clamscan.log -r /mnt/winshare
```

At this point, thousands of filenames fly by the console, ending in a report similar to the one shown earlier, which is saved to */var/log/clamscan.log*. clamscan will create the report file if it does not exist. If the report file exists, it will append the new report to the existing file. You can review the report with any text editor.

By default, clamscan only reports that a file has been infected—it is up to you to remove the virus.

## Automating the Process

Scanning a single share is nice, but it would be even better to scan all of the computers in the network at night. Since I can mount and scan a share without being prompted for additional information, I can automate these commands in a script.

I want each Windows system to be mounted, scanned, and unmounted in turn, and I want each system to have its own scan report log. Since I also want to put the report logs in a *clamscan* directory in */var/log*, I need to create the directory. While I'm at it, I'll create the script file and make it readable and executable only by root:

```
# mkdir /var/log/clamscan
# touch /root/scanscript
# chmod u+x,go-rwx /root/scanscript
```

Next, I'll use my favorite editor to add the commands to */root/scanscript*:

```
# more /root/scanscript
#! /bin/sh
# /root/scanscript
# Sequentially mount Windows shares, scan them for viruses and unmount them.

# update virus databases
freshclam

# winbox1
shlight //winbox1/cdrive /mnt/winshare -U algould -P pwd
clamscan -l /var/log/clamscan/winbox1 -r /mnt/winshare
unshlight /mnt/winshare
```

```
# winbox2
shlight //winbox2/cdrive /mnt/winshare -U algould -P pwd
clamscan -l /var/log/clamscan/winbox2 -r /mnt/winshare
unshlight /mnt/winshare

# winbox3
shlight //winbox3/cdrive /mnt/winshare -U algould -P pwd
clamscan -l /var/log/clamscan/winbox3 -r /mnt/winshare
unshlight /mnt/winshare
```

Now I can execute the script at will or schedule its execution using cron.

> As with any antivirus scanning policy, execute the script
> when users will be least affected and the scanned computers
> are up and running.

## See Also

- man `clamscan`
- man `freshclam`
- man `clamd`
- man `clamdscan`
- man `clamav.conf`
- man `sigtool`
- The Sharity-Light README and FAQ (*/usr/local/share/doc/Sharity-Light/*)
- The Sharity-Light web site (*http://www.obdev.at/products/sharity-light/*)
- The ClamAV web site (*http://clamav.elektrapro.com/*)

# Going Beyond the Basics
## Hacks 69-76

As a hacker, you're always pushing the envelope, trying new things, and going beyond the documentation. This chapter contains hands-on demonstrations from real-life users who push the envelope with their systems.

Have you ever wondered what modifications a web or mail administrator makes to her servers? Maybe you're curious about what policies other administrators use to implement bandwidth control? How do busy administrators manage the log data from a server farm?

Perhaps you've contemplated using the Expect scripting language. However, there's a good chance you've never thought of using eesh, a totally undocumented but useful scripting utility.

This chapter also includes two hacks on the emergency repair process, as many users prefer to hope that they'll never need an emergency repair kit. Instead, learn to overcome your fear of the inevitable and master the art of repairing before the emergency.

### HACK #69    Tune FreeBSD for Different Applications
Know how to tune and what to tune on your FreeBSD system.

As an administrator, you want to tune your server systems so they work at peak efficiency. How do you know what to tune? The answer depends heavily upon the system's function. Will the system perform a lot of small network transactions? Will it perform a small number of large transactions? How will disk operations factor in?

How you answer these and other questions determines what you need to do to improve the performance of your systems. This hack starts with general optimizations and then looks at function-specific tunables.

## Optimizing Software Compiling

A good place to start is with software compiling, as you want to compile software and updates as efficiently as possible. Whenever you compile, your compiler makes assumptions about your hardware in order to create binaries. If you have an x86-compliant CPU, for example, your compiler will create binaries that can run on any CPU from a 386 onward. While this allows portability, it won't take advantage of any new abilities of your CPU, such as the extended MMX, SSE, SSE2, or 3DNow! instruction sets. This is also why using precompiled binaries on your system is a surefire way to reduce your overall performance.

To ensure that software will be compiled efficiently, update your compiler flags in */etc/make.conf*. This file does not exist on new systems, but you can copy it from */usr/share/examples/etc/defaults/make.conf*.

Start by editing the CPUTYPE= line to reflect your CPU type; you'll find supported types listed as comments just before this line. While this will take advantage of your CPU's features, the disadvantage is that your compiled binaries may not run on different CPU types. However, if all of your systems run the same CPU platform, any optimizations you make to shared binaries will affect all of your systems equally well.

Next, change the CFLAGS line to CFLAGS= -O2 -pipe -funroll-loops. The -pipe option can significantly decrease the amount of time it takes to compile software, by using pipes to communicate between compiler processes instead of temporary files, but at the expense of using slightly more memory. The -funroll-loops saves one CPU register that would otherwise be tied up in tracking the iteration of the loop, but at the expense of making a slightly larger binary.

> The *make.conf* file also contains a line for CXXFLAGS. These options are similar to the CFLAGS options but apply to C++ code.

## Kernel Optimizations

In your kernel configuration, add the following line after the machine i386 line:

```
makeoptions    COPTFLAGS="-O2 -pipe -funroll-loops -ffast-math"
```

This is similar to the CLAGS option in */etc/make.conf*, except that it optimizes kernel compilation.

> See "Strip the Kernel" **[Hack #54]** for instructions on how to strip and compile a kernel.

You can also add this line:

```
TOP_TABLE_SIZE=number
```

where *number* is a prime number that is at least twice the number of lines in */etc/passwd*. This statement sets the size of the hash that top uses.

Set the following option if you have an AMD K5/K6/K6-2 or Cyrix 6x86 chip. It enables cache write allocation for the L1 cache, which is disabled by default for these chips.

```
options         CPU_WT_ALLOC
```

This option will disable NFS server code, so include it when you know that you will not be acting as an NFS server:

```
options         NFS_NOSERVER
```

Another way of saving kernel memory is to define the maximum number of swap devices, as shown in the next example. Your kernel needs to allocate a fixed amount of bitmapped memory so that it can interleave swap devices. I set the number to 1 on my workstation and 2 on my servers. If I need to add more to a server, I can easily create another partition.

```
options         NSWAPDEV=number
```

If you plan on compiling all your requisites into the kernel (NIC driver, IPF/IPFW, etc.) and won't be loading any of these options as modules, you can include this line to skip module compiling. This saves significantly on the time taken to compile a kernel (sometimes reducing it by two-thirds).

```
makeoptions     MODULES_OVERRIDE=""
```

By default, all kernel options are compiled as modules. This allows you to use kldload to load a module even though it isn't specified in your kernel configuration file.

The advantage of MODULES_OVERRIDE is the decrease in kernel compilation time. The disadvantage is that you'll need to recompile your kernel if you ever need to add additional functionality, since you will have lost the ability to load the kernel module separately.

## Optimizing Network Performance

Most modern network cards and switches support the ability to auto-negotiate the communication speed. While this reduces administration, it comes at the cost of network throughput. If your switch, server, or workstation is set to use auto-negotiation, it will stop transferring network traffic every few moments to renegotiate its speed.

If your network driver supports it, you can set network speed with `ifconfig` at runtime or in */etc/rc.conf* at boot time. Here is an example:

```
% grep fxp0 /etc/rc.conf
ifconfig_fxp0="inet x.x.x.x netmask x.x.x.x media 100BaseTX mediaopt
    full-duplex"
```

 Read the manpage for your NIC driver to see whether it supports `mediaopt`. For example, if your NIC is `rl0`, read `man 4 rl`.

Next, you can enable `DEVICE_POLLING` in your kernel, which changes the method by which data travels from your network card to the kernel. Without this setting, frequent interrupt calls may never free the kernel. This is known as *livelock* and can leave your machine unresponsive. Those of us unfortunate enough to be on the wrong side of certain denial-of-service attacks know about this.

The `DEVICE_POLLING` option causes the kernel to poll the network card at certain predefined times, during idle loops, or on clock interrupts. This allows the kernel to decide when it is most efficient to poll a device for updates and for how long, and ultimately results in a significant increase in performance.

To take advantage of `DEVICE_POLLING`, you need to compile two options into your kernel: `options DEVICE_POLLING` and `options HZ=1000`. The latter option slows the clock interrupts to 1,000 times per second, which prevents the kernel from polling too often.

Once you've recompiled your kernel, you'll still need to enable the feature. Add this line to */etc/sysctl.conf*:

```
kern.polling.enable=1
```

The `DEVICE_POLLING` option does not work with SMP-enabled kernels by default. If you are compiling an SMP kernel with `DEVICE_POLLING`, first remove the following lines from */usr/src/sys/kern/kern_poll.c*:

```
#ifdef SMP
#include "opt_lint.h"
#ifndef COMPILING_LINT
#error DEVICE_POLLING is not compatible with SMP
#endif
#endif
```

## Optimizing Mail Servers

Mail servers typically have a very large number of network connections, during which they transfer a small amount of data for a short period of time before closing the connection. In this case, it is useful to have a large number of small network buffers.

Network connections have two buffers, one for sending and one for receiving. The size of the buffer dictates how quickly data will funnel through the network and, in the event of a network delay, how much data can back up the server for that connection before there is a problem. Having a network buffer that is too small will cause a data backlog as the CPU waits for the network to clear, which causes greater CPU overhead. Having a network buffer that is too large wastes memory by using the buffer inefficiently. Finding a balance is the key to tuning.

I find that multiplying the number of *established* connections by 32 leaves me with room to breathe in the event that I see an abnormally high surge of traffic. I've come to this number over time through trial and error. So, if you expect to have a peak of 128 servers sending you mail, having 8,192 network buffer clusters would be good ($128 \times 2$ per connection $\times 32$). Also, remember that connections can take up to two full minutes or more to close completely. If you expect more than 128 emails in any given two-minute period, increase the number accordingly.

Another important value to control is the maximum number of sockets. Start with the same number of sockets as there are network buffers, and then tune as appropriate.

You can find out how many network buffer clusters are in use with the command netstat -m. You can specify the values you want in */boot/loader.conf*. For example:

```
kern.ipc.nmbclusters=8192
kern.ipc.maxsockets=8192
```

As with any performance tuning, monitor your system after making changes. Did you go overboard or underestimate what you would need? Always check and adjust accordingly.

## Optimizing File Servers

File servers generally have longer-lived and less frequent network connections than those on mail servers. They usually transfer larger files.

To determine the optimal number of network buffer clusters, consider how many clients you have. Multiplying the number of network buffers by two is good practice, though some admins prefer to multiply by four to accommodate multiple file transfers. If you have 128 clients connecting to the file server, set the number of network buffer clusters to 1,024 ($128 \times 2$ per connection $\times 4$).

## Optimizing Web Servers

If you have more than one element on your web page (for example, multiple images or frames), expect web browsers to make multiple connections to your web server. It's common to see four connections per page served. Also count any database or network connections made in server-side scripting.

Web servers go through periods of highs and lows. While you might serve 100 pages per minute on average, at your low you might serve 10 pages per minute and at peak over 1,000 pages per minute. At a peak of 1,000 pages per minute, your clusters and sockets should be around 16,384 (1,000 pages ×2 per connection × 4 connections × 2 for growth).

## See Also

- man tuning
- man gcc (the GCC manpage, which explains CPU compiling optimizations)
- man ifconfig
- "Tuning FreeBSD for different applications" (*http://silverwraith.com/ papers/freebsd-tuning.php*)
- "Optimizing FreeBSD and its kernel" (*http://silverwraith.com/papers/ freebsd-kernel.php*)
- Notes on tuning Apache servers at *http://www.bolthole.com/uuala/ webtuning.txt*

## Traffic Shaping on FreeBSD
## #70  Allocate bandwidth for crucial services.

If you're familiar with your network traffic, you know that it's possible for some systems or services to use more than their fair share of bandwidth, which can lead to network congestion. After all, you have only so much bandwidth to work with.

FreeBSD's dummynet may provide a viable method of getting the most out of your network, by sharing bandwidth between departments or users or by preventing some services from using up all your bandwidth. It does so by limiting the speed of certain transfers on your network—also called *traffic shaping*.

### Configuring Your Kernel for Traffic Shaping

To take advantage of the traffic shaping functionality of your FreeBSD system, you need a kernel with the following options:

```
options IPFIREWALL
options DUMMYNET
options HZ=1000
```

dummynet does not require the HZ option, but its manpage strongly recommends it. See "Tune FreeBSD for Different Applications" **[Hack #69]** for more about HZ and "Strip the Kernel" **[Hack #54]** for detailed instructions about compiling a custom kernel.

The traffic-shaping mechanism delays packets so as not to exceed the transfer speed limit. The delayed packets are stored and sent later. The kernel timer triggers sending, so setting the frequency to a higher value will smooth out the traffic by providing smaller delays. The default value of 100 Hz will trigger sends every 10 milliseconds, producing bursty traffic. Setting HZ=1000 will cause the trigger to happen every millisecond, resulting in less packet delay.

## Creating Pipes and Queues

Traffic shaping occurs in three stages:

1. Configuring the pipes
2. Configuring the queues
3. Diverting traffic through the queues and/or pipes

Pipes are the basic elements of the traffic shaper. A pipe emulates a network link with a certain bandwidth, delay, and packet loss rate.

Queues implement weighted fair queuing and cannot be used without a pipe. All queues connected to a pipe share the bandwidth of that pipe in a certain configurable proportion.

The most important parameter of a pipe configuration is its bandwidth. Set the bandwidth with this command:

```
# ipfw pipe 1 config bw 120kbit/s
```

This is a sample command run at the command prompt. However, as the hack progresses, we'll write the actual dummynet policy as rules within an ipfw rulebase.

This command creates pipe 1 if it does not already exist, assigning it 120 kilobits per second of bandwidth. If the pipe already exists, its bandwidth will be changed to 120 Kbps.

When configuring a queue, the two most important parameters are the pipe number it will connect to and the weight of the queue. The weight must be in the range 1 to 100, and it defaults to 1. A single pipe can connect to multiple queues.

```
# ipfw queue 5 config pipe 1 weight 20
```

This command instructs dummynet to configure queue 5 to use pipe 1, with a weight of 20. The weight parameter allows you to specify the ratios of bandwidth the queues will use. Queues with higher weights will use more bandwidth.

To calculate the bandwidth for each queue, divide the total bandwidth of the pipe by the total weights, and then multiply each weight by the result. For example, if a 120 Kbps pipe sees active traffic (called *flows*) from three queues with weights 3, 2, and 1, the flows will receive 60 Kbps, 40 Kbps, and 20 Kbps, respectively.

If the flow from the queue with weight 2 disappears, leaving only the flows with weights 3 and 1, those will receive 90 Kbps and 30 Kbps, respectively. (120 / (3+1) = 30, so multiply each weight by 30.)

The weight concept may seem strange, but it is rather simple. Queues with equal weights will receive the same amount of bandwidth. If queue 2 has double the weight of queue 1, it has twice as much bandwidth. Queues that have no traffic are not taken into account when dividing traffic. This means that in a configuration with two queues, one with weight 1 (for unimportant traffic) and the other with weight 99 (for important business traffic), having both queues active will result in 1%/99% sharing, but if there is no traffic on the 99 queue, the unimportant traffic will use all of the bandwidth.

## Using Masks

Another very useful option is to create a mask by adding mask *mask-specifier* at the end your config line. Masks allow you to turn one flow into several flows; the mask will distinguish the different flows.

The default mask is empty, meaning all packets fall into the same flow. Using mask all would make all connections significant, meaning that every TCP or UDP connection would appear as a separate flow.

When you apply a mask to a pipe, each of that pipe's flows acts as a separate pipe. Yet, each of those flows is an exact clone of the original pipe, in that they all share the same parameters. This means that the three active flows from our example pipe will use 360 Kbps, or 120 Kbps each.

For a queue, the flows will act as several queues, each with the same weight as the original one. This means you can use the mask to share a certain bandwidth equally. For our example with three flows and the 120 Kbps pipe, each flow will get a third of that bandwidth, or 40 Kbps.

This hack assumes that you will integrate these rules in your firewall configuration or that you are using ipfw only for traffic shaping. In the latter case, having the `IPFIREWALL_DEFAULT_TO_ACCEPT` option in the kernel will greatly simplify your task.

In this hack, we sometimes limit only incoming or outgoing bandwidth. Without this option, we would have to allow traffic in both directions, traffic through the loopback interface, and through the interface we will not limit.

However, you should consider disabling the `IPFIREWALL_DEFAULT_TO_ACCEPT` option, as it will drop packets that your policy does not specifically allow. Additionally, enabling the option may cause you to accept potentially malicious traffic you hadn't considered. The example configurations in this hack were tested with an `ipf`-based firewall that had an explicit deny rule at the end.

When integrating traffic shaping into an existing `ipfw` firewall, keep in mind that an `ipfw pipe` or `ipfw queue` rule is equivalent to "ipfw accept after slow down..." if the sysctl `net.inet.ip.fw.one_pass` is set to 1 (the default). If the sysctl is set to 0, that rule is just a delay in a packet's path to the next rule, which may well be a deny or another round of shaping. This hack assumes that the default behavior of the pipe and queue commands is to accept or an equivalent action.

## Simple Configurations

There are several ways of limiting bandwidth. Here are some examples that assume an external interface of ed0:

```
# only outgoing gets limited
ipfw pipe 1 config bw 100kbits/s

ipfw add 1 pipe 1 ip from any to any out xmit ed0
```

To limit both incoming and outgoing to 100 and 50 Kbps, respectively:

```
ipfw pipe 1 config bw 100kbits/s
ipfw pipe 2 config bw 50kbits/s

ipfw add 100 pipe 1 ip from any to any in  recv ed0
ipfw add 100 pipe 2 ip from any to any out xmit ed0
```

To set a limitation on total bandwidth (incoming plus outgoing):

```
ipfw pipe 1 config bw 100kbits/s

ipfw add 100 pipe 1 ip from any to any in  recv ed0
ipfw add 100 pipe 1 ip from any to any out xmit ed0
```

In this example, each host gets 16 Kbps of incoming bandwidth (outgoing is not limited):

```
ipfw pipe 1 config bw 16kbits/s mask dst-ip 0xffffffff

ipfw add 100 pipe 1 ip from any to any in recv ed0
```

## Complex Configurations

Here are a couple of real-life examples. Let's start by limiting a web server's outgoing traffic speed, which is a configuration I have used on one of my servers. The server had some FreeBSD ISO files, and I did not want it to hog all the outgoing bandwidth. I also wanted to prevent people from gaining an unfair advantage by using download accelerators, so I chose to share the total outgoing bandwidth equally among 24-bit networks.

```
# pipe configuration, 2000 kilobits maximum
ipfw pipe 1 config bw 2000kbits/s

# the queue will be used to enforce the /24 limit mentioned above
ipfw queue 1 config pipe 1 mask dst-ip 0xffffff00

# with this mask, only the first 24 bits of the destination IP
# address are taken into consideration when generating the flow ID

# divert outgoing traffic from the web server (at 1.1.1.1)
ipfw add queue 1 tcp from 1.1.1.1 80 to any out
```

Another real-life example involves limiting incoming traffic by department. This configuration limits the incoming bandwidth for a small company behind a 1 Mbps connection. Before this was applied, some users were using peer-to-peer clients and download accelerators, and they were hogging almost all the bandwidth. The solution was to implement some weighted sharing between departments and let the departments take care of their own hogs.

```
# Variables we will use
# External interface
EXTIF=fxp0

# My IP address
ME=192.168.1.1

# configure the pipe, 95% of total incoming capacity
ipfw pipe 1 config bw 950kbits/s

# configure the queues for the departments
# departments 1 and 2 heavy net users
ipfw queue 1 config pipe 1 weight 40
ipfw queue 2 config pipe 1 weight 40

# accounting, they shouldn't use the network a lot
ipfw queue 3 config pipe 1 weight 5

# medium usage for others
ipfw queue 4 config pipe 1 weight 20
```

```
# incoming mail (SMTP) to this server, HIGH priority
ipfw queue 10 config pipe 1 weight 100

# not caught by the previous categories - VERY LOW bandwidth
ipfw queue 11 config pipe 1 weight 1

# classify the traffic
# only incoming traffic is limited, outgoing is not affected.
ipfw add 10 allow ip from any to any out xmit via $EXTIF

# department 1
ipfw add 100 queue 1 ip from any to 192.168.0.16/28 in via $EXTIF

# department 2
ipfw add 200 queue 2 ip from any to 192.168.0.32/28 in via $EXTIF

# accounting
ipfw add 300 queue 3 ip from any to 192.168.0.48/28 in via $EXTIF

# mail
ipfw add 1000 queue 10 ip from any to $ME 25 in via $EXTIF

# others
ipfw add 1100 queue 11 ip from any to any in via $EXTIF
```

The incoming limit is set to 95% of the true available bandwidth. This will allow the shaper to delay some packets. If this were not the case and the pipe had the same bandwidth as the physical link, all of the delay queues for the pipe would have been empty. The extra 5% of bandwidth on the physical link fills the queues. The shaper chooses packets from the queues based on weight, passing through packets from queues with a higher weight before packets from queues with lower weight.

 dummynet can limit incoming or outgoing bandwidth in multiple ways. Pairing it with well thought out ipfw rules can produce good results when your requirements are not extremely complex. However, keep in mind that dummynet cannot guarantee bandwidth or quality of service.

## See Also

- man dummynet
- man ipfw
- man ipf
- "Using Dummynet for Traffic Shaping on FreeBSD" (*http://www.bsdnews.org/ 02/dummynet.php*)

## Create an Emergency Repair Kit

The Boy Scout and system administrator motto: "Be prepared!"

As a good administrator, you back up on a regular basis and periodically perform a test restore. You create images [Hack #23] of important servers so you can quickly recreate a system that is taken out of commission.

Are you prepared if a system simply refuses to boot?

Some parts of your drives are as important as your data, yet few backup programs back them up. I'm talking about your partition table and your boot blocks. Pretend for a moment that these somehow become corrupted. The good news is that your operating system and all of your data still exist. The bad news is that you can no longer access them.

Fortunately, this is recoverable, but only if you've done some preparatory work *before* the disaster. Let's see what's required to create an emergency repair kit.

### Inventory of the Kit

When you install a system, particularly a server, invest some time preparing for an emergency. On a FreeBSD system, your kit should include:

- The original install CD (or two floppies containing *kern.flp* and *mfsroot.flp* or one floppy containing *boot.flp*)
- A floppy containing additional drivers, *drivers.flp*
- A fixit floppy, *fixit.flp* (or a CD containing the live filesystem; this will be the second, third, or fourth CD in a set, but *not* the first CD)
- A printout of your partition table, */etc/fstab*, and */var/run/dmesg.boot*

Place these items in an envelope and store it in a secure location with your backup tapes. Make a note on the envelope of the system to which this kit should apply, along with the version of the operating system. Ideally, you should have two copies of both your emergency kit and backup media. Store the second copy off-site.

### Preparing the Floppies

Regardless of how you install a system, take a few minutes to download the *\*.flp* files found in the *floppies* directory. This is especially important if you use cvsup to upgrade a system, as you can go months or years without the installation CD-ROM or floppy media. Your aim is to test these floppies on your system *before* a disaster strikes. The last thing you want to be doing in an emergency is scurrying around creating floppies only to find that an essential driver is missing.

Here, I'll connect to the main FreeBSD FTP server and download the files for an i386, 5.1-RELEASE system:

```
# ftp ftp.freebsd.org
Trying 62.243.72.50...
Connected to ftp.freebsd.org.
<snip banner>
220
Name (ftp.freebsd.org:dlavigne6): anonymous
331 Guest login ok, send your complete e-mail address as password.
Password:
ftp> cd pub/FreeBSD/releases/i386/5.1-RELEASE/floppies
250 CWD command successful.
ftp> binary
200 Type set to I.
ftp> mget *.flp
mget boot.flp [anpqy?]? a
Prompting off for duration of mget.
<snip transfer of five files>
ftp> bye
221 Goodbye.
```

I find it convenient to create a *floppies* directory with subdirectories for each version of FreeBSD I have running in my network. I then download the appropriate *.flp* files to the appropriate subdirectory so they are available when I wish to create an emergency repair kit for a new system.

Once you have all five files, you can decide which ones you'll need for your particular system. To perform an emergency repair, you'll need some way to load your version of the operating system into memory so you can access the utilities on the fixit floppy and restore whatever damage has happened to your own operating system. There are several ways to load an operating system.

The first approach is to boot directly from the install CD-ROM, assuming it is bootable and your BIOS supports this. If this is your scenario, you don't need *boot.flp*, *kern.flp*, or *mfsroot.flp*.

If booting from the CD-ROM isn't an option, you can use either *boot.flp* or both *kern.flp* and *mfsroot.flp*. *boot.flp* is basically the contents of the other two floppies placed onto one floppy. The kicker is that you need a floppy capable of holding 2.88 MB of data.

Depending upon your hardware, you may or may not need *drivers.flp*. If the installer detected all of your hardware, you won't need this floppy. Otherwise, you will. Finally, if you don't have a CD containing the live filesystem, you'll need *fixit.flp*, as this floppy contains the actual repair utilities.

Use dd to transfer these files to floppies. Repeat this for each *.flp* file you require, using a different floppy for each file:

```
# dd if=fixit.flp of=/dev/fd0
```

Label each floppy with its name and version of FreeBSD and write protect the floppies.

## The Rest of the Kit

Before testing your floppies, print some important system information—you won't remember all of these details in an emergency. First, you'll want a copy of your filesystem layout:

```
# more /etc/fstab
# Device          Mountpoint          FStype     Options     Dump  Pass#
/dev/ad0s1b       none                swap       sw          0     0
/dev/ad0s1a       /                   ufs        rw          1     1
/dev/ad0s1e       /tmp                ufs        rw          2     2
/dev/ad0s1f       /usr                ufs        rw          2     2
/dev/ad0s1d       /var                ufs        rw          2     2
/dev/acd0         /cdrom              cd9660     ro,noauto   0     0
proc              /proc               procfs     rw          0     0
linproc           /compat/linux/proc  linprocfs  rw          0     0
/dev/fd0          /floppy             msdos      rw,noauto   0     0
```

Here, I've just sent the output to a pager for viewing. Depending upon how printing is set up on your system, redirect that output either directly to lpr or to a file that you can send to a printer.

Notice that all of my hard drive partitions start with */dev/ad0s1*. The name of your hard drive is needed in order to view the partition table, or what FreeBSD calls the disklabel:

```
# bsdlabel ad0s1
# /dev/ad0s1:
8 partitions:
#         size    offset  fstype  [fsize bsize bps/cpg]
  a:    524288         0  4.2BSD   2048 16384 32776
  b:   1279376    524288  swap
  c:  30008097         0  unused      0     0 # "raw" part, don't edit
  d:    524288   1803664  4.2BSD   2048 16384 32776
  e:    524288   2327952  4.2BSD   2048 16384 32776
  f:  27155857   2852240  4.2BSD   2048 16384 28512
```

Once you have a printout of your disklabel, complete your kit by printing the contents of */var/run/dmesg.boot*. This file contains your startup messages, including the results of the kernel probing your hardware.

## Testing the Recovery Media

Now you're ready to test that your kit works before sealing the envelope and sending it off for secure storage. First, boot the system using either your CD-ROM or the emergency floppies. Once the kernel has loaded and probed your hardware, the screen will ask: Would you like to load kernel modules from the driver floppy? If you choose yes, you will be asked to insert the *drivers.flp* floppy and will be presented with a list of modules to choose from:

```
cd9660.ko
if_awi.ko
if_fwe.ko
if_sk.ko
if_sl.ko
if_sn.ko
<snip>
```

Taking a look at those modules, aren't you glad you're testing your kit *before* an emergency? While the modules don't have the most descriptive names, it's easy to find out what each module represents if you have access to a working system. For example, the modules that begin with if are interfaces. To see what type of interface if_awi.ko is:

```
% whatis awi
awi(4)        - AMD PCnetMobile IEEE 802.11 PCMCIA wireless network driver
```

You can whatis each name; just don't include the beginning if or the trailing .ko. If you do need any of these drivers, save yourself some grief and write yourself a note explaining which drivers to choose off of the *drivers.flp*. The lucky bloke who has to repair the system will thank you for this bit of homework.

Once you exit from this menu, you'll be prompted to remove the floppy. You'll then be presented with the sysinstall Main Menu screen. Choose Fixit from the menu and insert *fixit.flp*. You should be prompted to press Alt F4, and you should then see a Good Luck! screen with a Fixit# prompt. Excellent, your floppy is good and your repair kit is complete. Type exit to return to the menu and exit your way out of the install utility.

If this had been an actual emergency, you'd definitely want to read the next hack [Hack #72].

## See Also

- man bsdlabel
- The Emergency Restore Procedure section of the FreeBSD Handbook (*http://www.freebsd.org/doc/en_US.ISO8859-1/books/handbook/backup-basics.html*)

## Use the FreeBSD Recovery Process
### HACK #72
Learn how to use your emergency repair kit before the emergency.

Now that you have an emergency repair kit, it's worth your while to do a dry run so you know ahead of time what options will be available to you. You may even decide to modify your kit as a result of this test.

Let's go back to that sysinstall Main Menu screen **[Hack #71]** and see what happens when you choose Fixit. You'll be presented with the following options:

```
Please choose a fixit option
    There are three ways of going into "fixit" mode:
    - you can use the live filesystem CDROM/DVD, in which case there will be
      full access to the complete set of FreeBSD commands and utilities,
    - you can use the more limited (but perhaps customized) fixit floppy,
    - or you can start an Emergency Holographic Shell now, which is
      limited to the subset of commands that is already available right now.


    X Exit        Exit this menu (returning to previous)
    2 CDROM/DVD   Use the "live" filesystem CDROM/DVD
    3 Floppy      Use a floppy generated from the fixit image
    4 Shell       Start an Emergency Holographic Shell
```

If you choose the Shell option, you'll find that they weren't kidding when they warned you'd be limited to a subset of commands. Nearly all of the commands you know and love will result in a *not found* error message. This is why you went to the trouble of either creating that *fixit* floppy or purchasing/burning a CD-ROM/DVD that contains the live filesystem.

## Using the fixit Floppy

Let's see what you can repair with the *fixit* floppy. When you choose that option, follow the prompts: insert the floppy, then press Alt F4. Do make note of the message you receive:

```
+----------------------------------------------------------------------+
| You are now running from FreeBSD "fixit" media.                      |
| -------------------------------------------------------------------- |
| When you're finished with this shell, please type exit.              |
| The fixit media is mounted as /mnt2.                                 |
|                                                                      |
| You might want to symlink /mnt/etc/*pwd.db and /mnt/etc/group        |
| to /etc/ after mounting a root filesystem from your disk.            |
| tar(1) will not restore all permissions correctly otherwise!         |
|                                                                      |
| Note: you might use the arrow keys to browse through the             |
| command history of this shell.                                       |
+----------------------------------------------------------------------+

Good Luck!

Fixit#
```

It's not a bad idea to create those symlinks now, before you forget. You'll have to mount your root slice first, so refer to your *etc/fstab* printout for the proper name of that slice. In this example, / is on *dev/ad0s1a*. I'll mount it with the read-write option:

```
Fixit# mount -o rw /dev/ad0s1a /mnt
Fixit#
```

If your command is successful, you'll receive the prompt back. A quick ls through /mnt should convince you that you now have access to the hard disk's root filesystem.

If your command is not successful, run fsck_ffs until the filesystem is clean, then mount the filesystem:

```
Fixit# fsck_ffs /dev/ad0s1
** /dev/ad0s1
** Last Mounted on /mnt
** Phase 1 - Check blocks and Sizes
** Phase 2 - Check Pathnames
** Phase 3 - Check Connectivity
** Phase 4 - Check Reference Counts
** Phase 5 - Check Cyl groups
821 files, 27150 used, 99689 free (985 frags, 12338 blocks, 0.8%
fragmentation)
Fixit# mount -u -o rw /dev/ad0s1 /mnt
```

Now for those symlinks:

```
Fixit# ln -f -s /mnt/etc/*pwd.db /etc
Fixit# ln -f -s /mnt/etc/group /etc
```

Note that you need to include the force (-f) switch when you make your symbolic (-s) links. You need to overwrite the existing link that links mnt2, or the fixit floppy, to /etc. You instead want to link the files on your hard drive (/mnt) to /etc.

You'll also notice that while in the Fixit# prompt, the up arrow will recall history, but tab completion does not work.

At that Fixit# prompt, you have two command sets available to you. The first is that limited command set that comes with the sysinstall utility. Note that these are the only commands available at that holographic shell prompt:

```
Fixit# ls stand
-sh*             gunzip*          route*
[*               gzip*            rtsol*
arp*             help/            sed*
boot_crunch*     hostname*        sh*
camcontrol*      ifconfig*        slattach*
cpio*            minigzip*        sysinstall*
dhclient*        mount_nfs*       test*
dhclient-script* newfs*           tunefs*
etc/             ppp*             usbd*
find*            pwd*             usbdevs*
fsck_ffs*        rm*              zcat*
```

The second command set is on the floppy itself, mounted as *mnt2*:

```
Fixit# ls mnt2/stand
bsdlabel*    dd*          fixit_crunch*    mount_cd9660*    sleep*
cat*         df*          ftp*             mount_msdosfs*   swapon*
chgrp*       disklabel*   kill*            mv*              sync*
chmod*       dmesg*       ln*              reboot*          tar*
chown*       echo*        ls*              restore*         telnet*
chroot*      ex*          mkdir*           rm*              umount*
clri*        expr*        mknod*           rmdir*           vi*
cp*          fdisk*       mount*           rrestore*        view*
```

You'll also find a minimal set of notes in:

```
Fixit# ls stand/help
```

One of the first things you'll notice, especially if you try to read one of those help documents, is the lack of a pager. You won't have any luck with more or less. However, cat and view are available for viewing files. If you've never used view before, remember to type :q to quit the viewer.

Also note that all of the restore utilities are on hand, unless you've used pax as your backup utility.

## Using the Live Filesystem

Let's pause here for a moment and compare the fixit floppy to the live filesystem. There's one CD marked as live in a purchased set. If you burn your own ISO images, the second image for your release will contain the live filesystem. For example, here is the listing for *ftp://ftp.freebsd.org/pub/FreeBSD/ISO-IMAGES/5.1-RELEASE/*:

```
5.1-RELEASE-i386-disc1.iso     630048 KB     06/05/03    00:00:00
5.1-RELEASE-i386-disc2.iso     292448 KB     06/05/03    00:00:00
5.1-RELEASE-i386-miniinst.iso  243488 KB     06/05/03    00:00:00
CHECKSUM.MD5                         1 KB     06/05/03    00:00:00
```

disc1.iso is the install CD, and disc2.iso is the live filesystem CD.

There are several advantages to using the live filesystem. First, you don't have to make any floppies. In fact, your entire kit can be as simple as this one CD and your printouts specific to that system. Second, the CD is bootable, so you can reach that Fixit# prompt in under a minute.

Third, you have the entire built-in command set available to you. When you enter the Fixit screen, you'll see the same welcome message as before. This time, it is the CD that is mounted as */mnt2*, which is really a link to */dist*:

```
Fixit# ls -l /mnt2
lrwxr-xr-x  1 root  wheel  5 Dec  8 08:22 /mnt2@ -> /dist
```

```
Fixit# ls /dist
.cshrc       boot/         etc/         root/         tmp/
.profile     boot.catalog  floppies/    rr_moved/     usr/
COPYRIGHT    cdrom.inf     mnt/         sbin/         var/
bin/         dev/          proc/        sys@
```

A quick ls /dist/bin and ls /dist/sbin will display all of the commands that come with a FreeBSD system. There isn't a limited command set with the live filesystem.

### Emergency Repair

Now that I've shown you the various ways to enter the Fixit facility, you're probably wondering what you should be doing at that prompt. FreeBSD is quite robust and is usually capable of booting your hard drive to some sort of prompt. However, if the disk fails completely or is somehow incapable of booting to a prompt, the fixit facility is one of your options.

From here, you can run fsck on your various filesystems, which may fix the problem. You can see which filesystems are still mountable, allowing you to assess the extent of the damage. If some files were damaged, you can restore those files from backup.

If it turns out that the drive is damaged beyond repair, you can rest easy in the fact that you have a printout of your hardware and partitioning scheme, a floppy containing any necessary drivers, and a backup of all of your data. Above all, you were prepared.

### See Also

- The Backup Basics section of the FreeBSD Handbook (*http://www.freebsd. org/doc/en_US.ISO8859-1/books/handbook/backup-basics.html*)

### HACK #73 Use the GNU Debugger to Analyze a Buffer Overflow

You don't have to be a programmer to use a debugger.

As an end user, you may not realize that you have the ability to analyze security exploits. After all, the organization that distributes your operating system of choice or the provider of a given application will deal with security issues and make updates available.

However, keep in mind that Security Officers apply the same tools and techniques that end users use for debugging programs. Knowing how to analyze a problem will help you to troubleshoot any misbehaving process in a Unix environment.

## An Example Exploit

Analyzing a malfunctioning process starts with basic information, such as error messages and return values. Sometimes those aren't enough, though. Some error messages are unclear. In the case of security vulnerabilities, there may not be an error code or return value, because the program may crash or misbehave silently.

The BSDs provide several tools to analyze a program's execution. You can monitor system calls with ktrace and resources with fstat. You can run a debugger such as GDB, the GNU Debugger, and watch your operating system's internal operation.

In some cases, a program must run in a particular environment, which may make it difficult to analyze due to the limitations of some tools. For example, a telnetd advisory from 2001 (*http://www.cert.org/advisories/CA-2001-21.html*) affected most Unix operating systems. This particular vulnerability came to light when a group called TESO released an example exploit for it.

On Unix systems, telnetd runs as root, so that once the system authenticates the user, the process has the privileges required to set the user ID of the login shell to that of the user who logged in. This means that a remote entity who can cause telnetd to misbehave by sending it carefully designed input could execute processes as root on your system.

On most Unix systems, telnetd does not run as a standalone daemon. Since logins are relatively infrequent (on the system timescale compared to thousands of interrupts per second), the inetd service starts telnetd as needed.

This is a simple example of the data stream sufficient to crash vulnerable telnetds using perl and nc (netcat):

```
% perl -e 'print "\377\366"x512' | nc testhost telnet
```

This was the example I used to diagnose the problem and test the fix. If you run this command against an impervious Telnet daemon, you'll see the following output:

```
% perl -e 'print "\377\366"x512' | nc testhost telnet
```

[Yes]

[Yes]

[Yes]

The [Yes] message will repeat 512 times because the characters you sent, \377\366, represent the Telnet protocol's "ARE YOU THERE" control message, and you asked the question 512 times.

If you run this command against a vulnerable telnetd, the output can vary. In some cases, your connection may close before you get 512 [Yes] responses because telnetd crashed. In other cases, you may receive seemingly random output from portions of the telnetd memory space. These both indicate that the program did something it was not supposed to, due to the specific input you gave it.

## Using the GNU Debugger

In order to fix the problem, we need to find out where the executable did something incorrectly. We would like to run the program under the control of GDB, but we cannot start telnetd from the command line the way we usually would when debugging most executables. Normally, GDB is invoked in one of three ways.

First, to run a program and debug it, type:

```
% gdb programname
GNU gdb 5.3nb1
Copyright 2002 Free Software Foundation, Inc.
GDB is free software, covered by the GNU General Public License, and you
are welcome to change it and/or distribute copies of it under certain
conditions.
Type "show copying" to see the conditions.
There is absolutely no warranty for GDB.  Type "show warranty" for details.
This GDB was configured as "i386--netbsdelf"...(no debugging symbols found).
..
(gdb) run
```

> If this is your first time using gdb, type help at the (gdb) prompt. Type quit when you are finished using the debugger.

Second, to examine the core file of a program that has already crashed, use:

```
% gdb programname programname.core
```

Third, to examine a program that is already running, type:

```
% gdb programname processid
```

In the case of telnetd, we cannot use the first method, because inetd must start telnetd in order to attach it to a network socket and operate properly. We cannot use the second method, because processes that run with root privileges do not leave core files, since the program's memory image could contain sensitive data.

That leaves the third method. Attaching to a running process is problematic because telnetd isn't running until someone connects. We'll need to modify our attack script:

```
% perl -e 'sleep 30; print "\377\366"x512' |  nc testhost telnet
```

Now nc opens a socket to the testhost, inetd spawns a telnetd in response, and perl waits for 30 seconds before sending the attack string.

In another terminal, on the testhost, we say:

```
% ps -ax | grep telnetd
27857 ?? S       0:00.05 telnetd
27859 pd S+      0:00.02 grep telnetd

% gdb /usr/libexec/telnetd 27857
GNU gdb[...]
Attaching to program `/usr/libexec/telnetd', process 27857
```

From here we can allow telnetd to crash and observe the exact type of error that caused the crash. If we've built telnetd with debugging information, GDB will even display the line of source code the program was executing when it crashed. Now we can use our favorite debugging techniques and either insert debugging messages or use GDB and set breakpoints and watchpoints to discover at what point the program went off course. We can then determine what changes to make to correct the error and prevent the exploit.

If you're not a programmer, you can save the information and send it to the developers.

## Hacking the Hack

We were fortunate in this example because we had details of the exploit. That made it easy to experiment and try different approaches. In many cases, however, you won't know the details of an exploit, and you may only know that there is a problem because of error messages in your logs.

You can use tcpdump to capture the traffic on the relevant port. Once you can correlate the timestamp of the log's error message with some of your tcpdump traffic, you can take the data sent in an attack and create a Perl script to resend it. You can then apply the techniques already described to analyze and correct the problem.

## See Also

- man ktrace
- man fstat
- man gdb

- The Netcat web site; see the *Read Me* file (*http://www.atstake.com/research/tools/network_utilities*)
- The "Debugging with GDB" tutorial (*http://www.delorie.com/gnu/docs/gdb/gdb_toc.html*)

## HACK #74 Consolidate Web Server Logs

Automate log processing on a web farm.

As the administrator of multiple web servers, I ran across a few logging problems. The first was the need to collect logs from multiple web servers and move them to one place for processing. The second was the need to do a real-time `tail` on multiple logs so I could watch for specific patterns, clients, and URLs.

As a result, I wrote a series of Perl scripts collectively known as `logproc`. These scripts send the log line information to a single log host where some other log analysis tool can work on them, solving the first problem. They also multicast the log data, letting you watch live log information from multiple web servers without having to watch individual log files on each host. A primary goal is never to lose log information, so these scripts are very careful about checking exit codes and such.

The basic model is to feed logs to a program via a pipe. Apache supports this with its standard logging mechanism, and it is the only web server considered in this hack. It should be possible to make the system work with other web servers—even servers that can only write logs to a file—by using a named pipe.

I've used these scripts on production sites at a few different companies, and I've found that they handle high loads quite well.

### logproc Described

Download logproc from *http://www.peterson.ath.cx/~jlp/software/logproc.tar.gz*. Then, extract it:

```
% gunzip logproc.tar.gz
% tar xvf logproc.tar
% ls -F logproc
./    ../    logserver.bin/    webserver.bin/

% ls -F logserver.bin
./    apache_rrd*    cleantmp*    logwatch*    mining/
../    arclogs*    collect*    meter*

% ls -F webserver.bin
./    ../    batcher*    cleantmp*    copier*
```

As you can see, there are two parts. One runs on each web server and the other runs on the log server.

The logs are fed to a process called batcher that runs on the web server and writes the log lines to a batch file as they are received. The batch file stays small, containing only five minutes' worth of logs. Each completed batch file moves off to a holding area. A second script on each web server, the copier, takes the completed batch files and copies them to the centralized log host. It typically runs from cron. On the log host, the collect process, also run from cron, collects the batches and sorts the log lines into the appropriate daily log files.

The system can also monitor log information in real time. Each batcher process dumps the log lines as it receives them out to a multicast group. Listener processes can retrieve those log lines and provide real-time analysis or monitoring. See the sample logwatch script included with logproc for details.

## Preparing the Web Servers

First, create a home directory for the web server user. In this case, we'll call the user www. Make sure that www's home directory in */etc/master.passwd* points to that same location, not to */nonexistent*. If necessary, use vipw to modify the location in the password file.

```
# mkdir ~www
# chown www:www ~www
```

Next, log in as the web server user and create a public/private SSH keypair:

```
# su www
% ssh-keygen -t dsa
```

Create the directories used by the log processing tools, and copy the scripts over:

```
% cd ~www
% mkdir -p bin logs/{work,save}/0 logs/tmp logs/work/1

% cp $srcdir/logproc/webserver.bin/* bin/
```

Examine those scripts, and edit the variables listed in Table 7-1 to reflect your situation.

*Table 7-1. Variables and values for logproc's web server scripts*

| Script | Variable | Value |
| --- | --- | --- |
| batcher | $loguser | The name of the web server user |
| | $mcast_if | The name of the interface that can reach the log host |
| | $logroot | The home directory of the web server user |

*Table 7-1. Variables and values for logproc's web server scripts (continued)*

| Script | Variable | Value |
|---|---|---|
| cleantmp | $logroot | The home directory of the web server user |
| copier | $loghost | The name of the host where the logs will collect |
| | $logroot | The home directory of the web server user |
| | $loghost_logroot | The directory on the collector host where the logs will be collected |
| | $loghost_loguser | The user on the log host who owns the logs |
| | $scp_prog | The full path to the scp program, plus any additional options |
| | $ssh_prog | The full path to ssh, plus any options |

Then, make sure you have satisfied all of the dependencies for these programs:

```
# perl -wc batcher; perl -wc cleantmp; perl -wc copier
```

The only dependency you likely won't have is IO::Socket::Multicast. Install it via the */usr/ports/net/p5-IO-Socket-Multicast* port on FreeBSD systems or from the CPAN site (*http://www.cpan.org/*).

Next, configure *httpd.conf* to log to the batcher in parallel with normal logging. Note that the batcher command line must include the instance (site, virtual, secure) and type (access, error, ssl) of logging:

```
LogFormat "%h %l %u %t \"%r\" %>s %b \"%{Referer}i\" "%{User-Agent}i\" \
    \"%{Cookie}i\" %v" full
CustomLog "|/home/www/bin/batcher site access" full
ErrorLog  "|/home/www/bin/batcher site error"
```

You can adjust the LogFormat directive as necessary to log the information you or your log summarization software needs.

Finally, restart Apache and verify that the batchers are creating batches:

```
# apachectl configtest
# apachectl graceful
# cd $wwwhome/logs/
# ls tmp        Should list error log files for each batcher instance
# ls work/0     Should list the working batches for each batcher instance
# ls save/0     Verify that batches have moved into the save directory after a
                five-minute batch interval
# ls work/0     and that new batches are currently being created
```

## Preparing the Log Host

Start by creating a log user to receive the logs, complete with a home directory. Become the log user and copy the public key from the web server into

*~log/.ssh/authorized_keys2*. Then, as the log user, create the directories the log collection tools use:

```
# su log
% cd ~log
% mkdir -p bin web/{work,save}/{0,1} web/tmp web/{current,archive}
```

## Testing the Configuration

From a web server (as the web server's user), ssh to the log host manually to verify the configuration of the authorized_keys2:

```
# su www
% ssh loghost -l loguser date
```

> If your command fails, check that the permissions on that file are set to 600.

Then, run copier manually to verify that the log files actually make it to the log server. Watch your run output on the web server, then check that *save/0* on the log server contains the newly copied logs.

Once you're satisfied with these manual tests, schedule a cron job that copies and cleans up log files. These jobs should run as the web server user:

```
# crontab -e -u www

---------------------------- cut here ----------------------------
# copy the log files down to the collector host every 15 minutes
0,15,30,45 * * * * /home/www/bin/copier

# clean the tmp directory once an hour
0 * * * * /home/www/bin/cleantmp
---------------------------- cut here ----------------------------
```

Finally, wait until the next copier run and verify that the batches appear on the log host.

## Configuring Scripts on the Log Host

You should now have several batches sitting in *save/0* in the log tree. Each batch contains the log lines collected over the batch interval (by default, five minutes) and has a filename indicating the instance (site, virtual, secure), type (access, error, ssl), web server host, timestamp indicating when the batch was originally created, and PID of the batcher process that created each batch.

Now, install the log processing scripts into *bin/*:

```
# cp $srcdir/collector/{arclogs,cleantmp,collect} bin/
```

Edit them to have valid paths for their new location and any OS dependencies, as shown in Table 7-2.

*Table 7-2. Variables and values for logproc's log host scripts*

| Script | Variable | Value |
|---|---|---|
| arclogs | $logroot | The location of the logs |
| | $gzip_prog | The full path to the gzip binary |
| cleantmp | $logroot | The location of the logs |
| collect | $logroot | The location of the logs |
| | $gzip_prog | The full path to the gzip binary |

Again, make sure all dependencies are satisfied:

```
# perl -wc arclogs; perl -wc cleantmp; perl -wc collect
```

If you don't have Time::ParseDate, then install it from the */usr/ports/devel/ p5-Time-modules* port on FreeBSD or from CPAN.

Run collect manually as the log user to verify that the log batches get collected and that log data ends up in the appropriately dated log file. Once you're satisfied, automate these tasks in a cron job for the log user:

```
# crontab -e -u log

--------------------------- cut here ---------------------------
# run the collector once an hour
0 * * * * /home/log/bin/collect

# clean the tmp directory once an hour
0 * * * * /home/log/bin/cleantmp
--------------------------- cut here ---------------------------
```

Wait until the next collect run and verify that the batches are properly collected.

Compare the collected log files with the contents of your old logging mechanism's log file on the web servers. Make sure every hit makes it into the collected log files for the day. You might want to run both logging mechanisms for several days to get a good feel that the system is working as expected.

## Viewing Live Log Data

The log server programs provide additional tools for monitoring and summarizing live log data. On a traditional single web server environment, you can always tail the log file to see what's going on. This is no longer easy to do, because the logs are now written in small batches. (Of course, if you have multiple web servers, multiple tail processes would have to run on each web server.)

The batcher process helps with this by multicasting the logs out to a multicast group. Use the logwatch tool on the log server to view the live log data:

```
% cd ~log/bin
% ./logwatch
<lines of log data spew out here>
```

On a high-volume web site, there is likely to be too much data to scan manually. logwatch accepts arguments to specify which type of log data you want to see. You can also specify a Perl regular expression to limit the output.

The meter script watches the log data on the multicast stream, in real time, and summarizes some information about the log data. It also stores information in an RRDTool (*http://www.rrdtool.org/*) database.

The *mining* directory contains a checklog script that produces a "top ten clients" and "top ten vhosts" report. Alternatively, you can feed the collected log files to your existing web server log processing tools.

### See Also

• The logproc web site (*http://www.peterson.ath.cx/~jlp/software/logproc.tar.gz*)

## HACK #75   Script User Interaction

Use an expect script to help users generate GPG keys.

There are occasions when you can take advantage of Unix's flexibility to control some other tool or system that is less flexible. I've used Unix scripts to update databases on user-unfriendly mainframe systems when the alternative was an expensive mainframe-programming service contract. You can use the same approach in reverse to let the user interact with a tool, but with a constrained set of choices.

The Expect scripting language is ideal for creating such interactive scripts. It is available from NetBSD pkgsrc as *pkgsrc/lang/tcl-expect* or *pkgsrc/lang/tk-expect*, as well as from the FreeBSD ports and OpenBSD packages collections. We'll use the command-line version for this example, but keep in mind that expect-tk allows you to provide a GUI frontend to a command-line process if you're willing to write a more complex script.

In this case, we'll script the generation of a GPG key. Install GPG from either *pkgsrc/security/gnupg* or the appropriate port or package.

### The Key Generation Process

During the process of generating a GPG key, the program asks the user several questions. We may wish to impose constraints so that a set of users ends up with keys with similar parameters. We could train the users, but that would not guarantee correct results. Scripting the generation makes the process easier and eliminates errors.

First, let's look at a typical key generation session:

```
% gpg --gen-key
gpg (GnuPG) 1.2.4; Copyright (C) 2003 Free Software Foundation, Inc.
This program comes with ABSOLUTELY NO WARRANTY.
This is free software, and you are welcome to redistribute it
under certain conditions. See the file COPYING for details.

Please select what kind of key you want:
   (1) DSA and ElGamal (default)
   (2) DSA (sign only)
   (4) RSA (sign only)
Your selection? 4
What keysize do you want? (1024) 2048
Requested keysize is 2048 bits
Please specify how long the key should be valid.
         0 = key does not expire
      <n>  = key expires in n days
      <n>w = key expires in n weeks
      <n>m = key expires in n months
      <n>y = key expires in n years
Key is valid for? (0) 0
Key does not expire at all
Is this correct (y/n)? y

You need a User-ID to identify your key; the software constructs the user id
from Real Name, Comment and Email Address in this form:
    "Heinrich Heine (Der Dichter) <heinrichh@duesseldorf.de>"

Real name:
```

Let's pause there to consider the elements we can constrain.

You probably want to specify the cryptographic algorithm and key length for all users consistently, based on your security and interoperability requirements. I'll choose RSA signing and encryption keys, but GPG doesn't provide a menu option for that. I'll have to create the signing key first and then add the encryption subkey.

## A Simple Script

Here's an expect script that would duplicate the session shown so far:

```
#!/usr/pkg/bin/expect -f

set timeout -1
spawn gpg --gen-key
match_max 100000
expect "(4) RSA (sign only)"
expect "Your selection? "
```

```
send "4\r"
expect "What keysize do you want? (1024) "
send "2048\r"
expect "Key is valid for? (0) "
send -- "0\r"
expect "Key does not expire at all"
expect "Is this correct (y/n)? "
send -- "y\r"
expect "Real name: "
```

The script begins by setting timeout to infinite, or -1, so expect will wait forever to match the provided input. Then we spawn the process that we're going to control, gpg --gen-key. match_max sets some buffer size constraints in bytes, and the given value is far more than we will need.

After the initial settings, the script simply consists of strings that we expect from the program and strings that we send in reply. This means that the script will answer all of the questions GPG asks until Real name: , without waiting for the user's input.

Note that in several places we expect things besides the prompt. For example, before responding to the Your selection? prompt, we verify that the version of GPG we have executed still has the same meaning for the fourth option, by expecting that the text of that menu choice is still RSA (sign only). If this were a real, production-ready script, we should print a warning message and terminate the script if the value does not match our expectations, and perhaps include a check of the GPG version number. In this simple example, the script will hang, and you must break out of it with Ctrl-c.

## Adding User Interaction

There are several ways of handling the fields we do want the user to provide. For the greatest degree of control over the user experience, we could use individual expect commands, but here we will take a simpler approach. Here's some more of the script:

```
interact "\r" return
send "\r"
expect "Email address: "
interact "\r" return
send "\r"
expect "Comment: "
interact "\r" return
send "\r"
expect "Change (N)ame, (C)omment, (E)mail or (O)kay/(Q)uit? "
interact "\r" return
send "\r"
expect "Enter passphrase: "
interact "\r" return
send "\r"
```

```
expect "Repeat passphrase: "
interact "\r" return
send "\r"
```

The interact command allows the user to interact directly with the spawned program. We place a constraint that the user's interaction ends as soon as the user presses the Enter key, which sends the carriage return character, \r. At that point, the interact command returns and the script resumes. Note that we have to send the \r from the script; expect intercepted the carriage return and GPG did not see it.

## Handling Incorrect Input

Again, a correct script would have a more complex flow of execution and allow for cases where the spawned program rejects the user's input with an error message. For example, the Real Name field must be more than five characters long. If a user types less than five characters, GPG will prompt him to retype his username. However, the expect script just shown will not accept the new user input, because it is now waiting for the Email address: prompt.

Alternatively, we could replace these three lines:

```
interact "\r" return
send "\r"
expect "Email address: "
```

with:

```
interact -o "Email address: " return
send_user "Email address: "
```

Instead of stopping interaction when the user presses return, we stop interaction when the program outputs the Email address: prompt. That's the difference between interact and interact -o; the former stops interaction based on input from the user, and the latter on output from the program. This time, we don't need to send the carriage return, because the user's keypress is passed through to GPG. However, we do need to echo the prompt, because expect has consumed it. This method lets GPG handle the error conditions for us:

```
Real name: abc
Name must be at least 5 characters long
Real name: abcde
Email address:
```

## Hacking the Hack

After GPG receives the information it needs to generate the key, it might not be able to find enough high-quality random data from the system. The script ought to handle that by spawning a process to generate more system activity, such as performing a lot of disk activity by running a find across the entire disk.

After generating the signing key, the script could spawn a new instance of GPG with the --edit-key option, to generate the desired RSA encryption key.

Although the final script may end up executing three processes, the whole process is seamless to the user. You can hide even more of the guts by using expect's log_user setting to hide the output of the programs at points where the user does not need to see them.

You can use a script like this in conjunction with any Unix command-line program. By combining expect with telnet or ssh, you can control non-Unix systems, thereby leveraging the flexibility of Unix into a non-Unix domain. This even works with programs for which you do not have source code, such as control utilities for commercial databases or application software.

In the case of GPG, we do have source code, so we *could* modify the program, but writing an expect script is easier. A carefully designed expect script may not require changes when a new version of GPG is released. Source code changes to GPG would require integration with any new version of GPG.

### See Also

- man expect
- The expect web site, which includes sample scripts (*http://expect.nist.gov/*)
- *Exploring Expect*, by Don Libes, the author of expect (*http://www.oreilly.com/catalog/expect/*)

## HACK #76    Create a Trade Show Demo

Use an undocumented utility to showcase your window manager and applications.

I frequently represent NetBSD at trade shows. It's challenging to attract attention because there are many booths at a show—people will walk by quickly unless something catches their eye. You also need to balance eye-candy with functionality so that you can attract and keep a visitor's attention. I needed an enticing demo to run on one of the computers in the booth.

I wanted to show off several applications, such as office productivity tools, video, and games, and have music playing, but there's only so much screen real estate. Cramming all of those things on the screen at once would clutter the screen, and the point would be lost.

Most X window managers have some concept of virtual desktops, separate work spaces that you can flip between. For example, Enlightenment (*pkgsrc/wm/enlightenment*) not only has the concept of virtual desktops, but as an added bonus for the trade show environment offers a nice sliding effect as you transition from one desktop to the next.

## Introducing eesh

Normally in Enlightenment, to switch from one virtual desktop to the next, you move the mouse pointer to the edge of the screen and then push past it, or you use a key sequence to move to an adjacent desktop. For an unattended demo, we need to automate this process. Enlightenment provides an undocumented utility called eesh that can control most aspects of the Enlightenment window manager. You can write scripts to move windows, resize them, or flip between desktops.

Note that eesh isn't a friendly utility; it doesn't even produce a prompt when you run it. Type help for the menu or exit to quit:

```
% eesh
help
Enlightenment IPC Commands Help
commands currently available:
use "help all" for descriptions of each command
use "help <command>" for an individual description

actionclass              active_network           advanced_focus   sfa
autosave                 background               border
button                   button_show              colormod
configpanel              copyright                current_theme    tc
cursor                   default_theme            dialog_ok        dok
dock                     dump_mem_debug           exit             q
focus_mode       sf      fx                       general_info
geominfo_mode    sgm     goto_area         sa     goto_desktop     sd
group            gc      group_info        gl     group_op         gop
help             ?       imageclass               internal_list    il
list_class       cl      list_remember            list_themes      tl
module                   move_mode         smm    nop
```

Unfortunately, the eesh utility seems to be untested. It sometimes behaves inconsistently by not accepting commands until you enter them a second time or by withholding output until you press Enter again. As an example, there are actually more commands than those indicated in the help listing. Look in the Enlightenment source's *ipc.c* file for a complete list.

## Discovering Commands

We'll start our script by making sure that Enlightenment is configured the way we want for our demo. We want six work spaces (3 by 2) to display our programs. Within eesh, try the following commands:

```
num_areas ?
Number of Areas: 2 2
```

```
help num_areas
Enlightenment IPC Commands Help : num_areas (sna)
--------------------------------
Change the size of the virtual desktop
Use "num_areas <width> <height>" to change the size of the virtual desktop.
Example: "num_areas 2 2" makes 2x2 virtual destkops
Use "num_areas ?" to retrieve the current setting
```

```
num_areas 3 2
```

Now we have the number of areas we want. areas is the Enlightenment name for virtual desktops, since Enlightenment also supports multiple desktops, but that's different. Now we'd like our screen to display the first area, so that the programs our script runs will open there:

```
goto_area 0 0
```

If your terminal wasn't on the first area, it just moved off the screen. Use the mouse to return to that area.

eesh also lets us write commands on the command line with the -e (execute command) flag:

```
% eesh -e "goto_area 0 0"
```

## Sample Scripts

Now we know enough to write a simple demo script:

```
#!/bin/sh

eesh -e "num_desks 1"
eesh -e "num_areas 3 2"
sleep 1
eesh -e "goto_area 0 0"

# Configure the default gqmpeg playlist to play your desired music
gqmpeg

# Show an interesting avi file.
xanim -geometry +50x+10 netbsd3.avi &

# Give the programs time to start, to make sure they
# open on the correct area.
# Also, lets people watching see what started up.
sleep 3
eesh -e "goto_area 1 0"

# Word Processing
abiword sampledoc.abw &
sleep 2
eesh -e "goto_area 2 0"
```

```
# Spreadsheet
gnumeric samplesheet.gnumeric &
sleep 2
eesh -e "goto_area 0 1"

# A lively game
battleball &
sleep 2
eesh -e "goto_area 1 1"

# Web Browsing (of a local hierarchy, in case you don't have net
# connectivity at a trade show)
firebird file://index.html &
sleep 3
eesh -e "goto_area 2 1"
sleep 1

# Insert your favorite application here
# Leave screen back at page 1.
eesh -e "goto_area 0 0"
```

When you run the script, the screen will slide around to the various areas and pause a few seconds between program launches. We have most of the things we wanted: music, video, and applications. The next step is to keep it moving. Try the following script:

```
#!/bin/sh
while [ 1 ]
do
        eesh -e "goto_area 0 0"
        sleep 2
        eesh -e "goto_area 1 0"
        sleep 2
        eesh -e "goto_area 2 0"
        sleep 2
        eesh -e "goto_area 0 1"
        sleep 2
        eesh -e "goto_area 1 1"
        sleep 2
        eesh -e "goto_area 2 1"
        sleep 2
done
```

To stop the moving display, you have to get your keyboard focus into the xterm where the script is running so that you can press Ctrl-c. That can be difficult, but we'll address it shortly.

## More Complex Scripts

For a complex demonstration, you can have different sets of these scripts that visit different sets of areas. You can also change the delay so that complex areas display for a longer period. I also made a script that clears all of the viewing areas. That way, when visitors to the booth play around with the machine, I can easily reset to a clean state and then start the demo again.

Since many of the utilities you'll demonstrate don't create *.pid* files, I find it easiest to use pkill, the "kill process by name" utility. (FreeBSD provides killall.)

I'll also leave you with two example scripts that show how to extract information about Enlightenment's current settings for use in a more complex script.

The first script is retitle:

```
#!/bin/sh

WIN=`eesh -ewait "set_focus ?" | sed 's/^focused: //' `
xterm -geometry 47x7+227+419 -fn -*-courier-*-o-*-*-34-*-*-*-*-*-*-* -e \
/home/david/bin/retitle2 $WIN
```

The second is retitle2:

```
#!/bin/sh
WIN=$1
echo "enter new title:"
read TITLE
eesh -e "win_op $WIN title $TITLE"
```

With these scripts and e16keyedit, you can bind a key combination to change the title of any window. This makes it much easier to keep track of xterms, if you prefer task-oriented titles.

Now back to the control issue. When I first wrote this demo, I used a switch wired to a serial port to start and stop the demo so that keyboard focus did not matter. However, wiring switches is more work than configuring software, so I found a better way.

The e16keyedit utility, written by Geoff "Mandrake" Harrison and Carsten "Raster" Haitzler (the primary developers of Enlightenment), allows you to bind function keys and Meta keys to run programs or perform the same functions that you can with eesh. Using e16keyedit, you can define function keys to set up the demo, clean up the demo, and start and stop the area rotations. Since the function keys can be bound to work anywhere within Enlightenment, keyboard focus no longer matters. You're ready to give a fantastic demo!

e16keyedit is not part of the main Enlightenment distribution. Download it from SourceForge (*http://sourceforge.net/project/showfiles.php?group_id=2*).

## See Also

- The Enlightenment web site (*http://www.enlightenment.org/*)

# CHAPTER EIGHT

# Keeping Up-to-Date
## Hacks 77-88

One of the distinguishing characteristics of the BSDs is the ease with which you can keep your operating system source and installed software up-to-date. In fact, each of the BSDs provides multiple alternatives, allowing users to choose the approaches that best match their time and bandwidth requirements.

This chapter provides a plethora of ways to maintain an updated system. While many are written from the FreeBSD perspective, don't let that stop you from hacking your own customized NetBSD or OpenBSD solutions. In fact, this chapter concludes with one user demonstrating how to enjoy the benefits of the BSD ports and packages collections on Mac OS X!

 **HACK** **Automated Install**
**#77** If you're responsible for installing multiple systems, hopefully you've discovered the art of automating installs.

Most operating systems have some sort of scripting mechanism that allows you to predefine the answers to the questions asked by the install program. Once you've started the actual install, you can leave and return to a fully installed system. The alternative is to sit there, answering every prompt when it appears. No, thank you!

Even as a home user, it's well worth your while to spend a few minutes customizing the install script that comes with FreeBSD. Try this hack once and you'll never want to sit and watch an install again.

### Preparing the Install Script

Before installing any system, you need to know the following:

- The IP settings and hostname of the host you're installing
- The FreeBSD name of that host's NIC

- Which distributions, or parts of the OS, to install
- Your desired partitioning scheme
- Which packages (applications) to install

Of course, it's always a good idea to record this information and include it with the documentation for the system.

FreeBSD's install mechanism lives in */stand/sysinstall*. Not surprisingly, man sysinstall describes all of the scriptable bits of this program. I'll go over some useful parameters, but you'll definitely want to skim through the manpage to see if there are additional parameters suited to your particular environment.

FreeBSD also comes with a commented, ready-to-customize install script, located in */usr/src/usr.sbin/sysinstall/install.cfg*. Copy this file, then edit the copy in your favorite editor. Start by inserting your own network settings:

```
# This is the installation configuration file for my test machine,
# crate.cdrom.com.
# It is included here merely as a sort-of-documented example.
#
# $FreeBSD: src/usr.sbin/sysinstall/install.cfg,v 1.11 2001/09/06 10:04:27
murray Exp $

# Turn on extra debugging.
debug=yes

###############################
# My host specific data
hostname=crate.cdrom.com
domainname=cdrom.com
nameserver=204.216.27.3
defaultrouter=204.216.27.228
ipaddr=204.216.27.230
netmask=255.255.255.240
###############################
```

Replace the example network information with the name and IP settings associated with the specific host you'd like to install. If you're using DHCP to obtain this information, fill in the hostname line and replace the other lines with:

```
tryDHCP=YES
```

Next, replace the name of the NIC and the path to the FTP site. In this example, the NIC is rl0 and I'm using the default FTP site:

```
###############################
# Which installation device to use
_ftpPath=ftp://ftp.freebsd.org/pub/FreeBSD/
netDev=rl0
mediaSetFTP
###############################
```

Next come the desired distributions. (See man sysinstall for more details.)
Include them all on the one dists= line, separated by a space:

```
################################
# Select which distributions we want.
dists=bin doc games manpages dict compat4x ports src sbase ssys Xbin Xcfg \
    Xdoc Xlib Xman Xset Xfnt Servers/XS3V Xfsrv
distSetCustom
################################
```

> Note that distSetCustom allows you to customize which dis-
> tributions to install. If you'd like to install the works, use
> distSetEverything and don't specify any dists=.

The partitioning scheme section is very important. If you don't want to use
the default scheme which uses the entire disk, read this section of the
manpage carefully.

Also, the default file gives examples for three disks. Make sure you remove
the examples and replace them with your own partitioning scheme.

The following example is the equivalent of choosing a for "all," followed by
a for "auto defaults":

```
###########################################################
# Set the parameters for the partition editor
# ad = IDE, da = SCSI
disk=ad0
partition=exclusive
diskPartitionEditor

###########################################################
# - All sizes are expressed in 512 byte blocks!
# - "Size in MB" = sectors * 512 / 1024 / 1024
# - "Number of blocks" = xsize in mb * 1024 * 1024 / 512
# The non-zero value after the mountpoint means enable soft updates

# 256MB UFS ad0s1a
ad0s1-1=ufs 524288 /

# 240MB SWAP ad0s1b
ad0s1-2=swap 491520 none

# 256MB UFS ad0s1d
ad0s1-3=ufs 524288 /var

# 256MB UFS ad0s1e
ad0s1-4=ufs 524288 /tmp
```

```
# Rest of FreeBSD partition ad0s1f
ad0s1-5=ufs 0 /usr

diskLabelEditor

# runs diskLabelCommit diskPartitionWrite
installCommit
```

Finally, list which applications you would like to install. List each package on its own line, followed by the packageAdd command:

```
# Install some packages at the end.
package=fetchmail-6.2.0
packageAdd
package=pine-4.55
packageAdd
package=lynx-2.8.5d14
packageAdd
```

The FreeBSD package list (*ftp://ftp.freebsd.org/pub/FreeBSD/releases/i386/5.1-RELEASE/packages/All*) has the exact names of each available package. Replace *i386/5.1-RELEASE* with your platform and desired operating system version.

## Test-Drive

Now that you've created a customized version of *install.cfg*, prepare a freshly formatted *UFS* floppy:

```
# fdformat -f 1440 /dev/fd0
# bsdlabel -w /dev/fd0 fd1440
# newfs /dev/fd0
```

Once the floppy is ready, copy *install.cfg* onto it.

On a test system, start the install process either by booting from a FreeBSD CD-ROM/DVD or with the two install floppies. When you receive the sysinstall Main Menu screen, choose Load Config. Insert the floppy containing your customized *install.cfg* and press OK. Once the configuration file has been loaded, you'll receive the message You may remove the floppy from floppy drive unit A.

While this is meant to be an unattended install, you should be present during your first test install. This will give you the opportunity to ensure that your script runs smoothly, without hanging at any portion of the install. If it does hang, check your *install.cfg* for a typo in that section.

Once the install is complete, you'll return to the sysinstall Main Menu. At this point, you can either configure the system interactively by choosing Configure or use a prepared post-configuration script, as found in */usr/doc/en_US.ISO8859-1/articles/pxe/post*.

> *install.cfg* is not responsible for post-install configuration.

Once you're happy with your floppy, label it with your operating system version. Store it where you can find it the next time you're ready to install a version of that operating system.

### See Also

- `man sysinstall`
- */usr/src/usr.sbin/sysinstall/install.cfg* (the sample installation configuration file)

 ### FreeBSD from Scratch

For those who prefer to wipe their disks clean before they upgrade their systems.

Have you ever upgraded your system with make world? If you have only one system on your disks, you may run into a problem: if the installworld fails partway through, you may end up with a broken system that might not even boot. It's also possible that the installworld will run smoothly, but the new kernel will not boot.

What if you're like me and believe in the "wipe your disks when upgrading systems" paradigm? Reformatting ensures there is no old cruft left lying around. It also means you have to recompile or reinstall all your ports and packages and then redo all your carefully crafted configuration tweaks.

FreeBSD From Scratch solves all these problems. The strategy is simple: use a running system to install a new system under an empty directory tree, mounting new partitions in that tree as appropriate. Many config files can copy straight across, and mergemaster can take care of those that cannot. You can perform arbitrary post-configuration of the new system from within the old system, up to the point where you can chroot to the new system.

This upgrade has three stages, where each stage either runs a shell script or invokes make:

*stage_1.sh*
> Creates a new bootable system under an empty directory, merges or copies as many files as are necessary, and then boots the new system

*stage_2.sh*
> Installs your desired ports

*stage_3.mk*

Does post-configuration for software installed in the previous stage

From now on, whenever you feel like an update is in order, simply toggle the partitions you want to wipe and reinstall.

> While compiling the ports during stage two, the system will not be available for its usual duties. If you run a production server, consider the downtime caused by stage two. If time is an issue, consider using precompiled packages instead of ports.

## Stage One: System Installation

This hack uses several scripts and configuration files that you can download from the original document's site (listed in this hack's "See Also" section). Also, if you keep your docs up-to-date with cvsup, the scripts and original document can be found in */usr/doc/en_US.ISO8859-1/articles/fbsd-from-scratch*.

The script for stage one is *stage_1.sh*. When run with exactly one argument:

```
# ./stage_1.sh default
```

it will read its configuration from *stage_1.conf.default* and write a log to *stage_1.log.default*.

You'll need to customize *stage_1.conf.default* to match your idea of the perfect system. I have tried to comment all of the sections you should adapt. In addition to the customized sections, the configuration script must provide four shell functions:

- create_file_systems
- create_etc_fstab
- copy_files
- all_remaining_customization

Before you run *stage_1.sh*, make sure you have completed the usual tasks in preparation for make installworld/installkernel:

- Configure your kernel config file.
- Complete make buildworld.
- Complete make buildkernel KERNCONF=*whatever*.

The *stage_1.sh* script will stop at the first command that fails, so you cannot overlook errors. It will also stop if you use an unset environment variable, which is probably due to a typo.

Answer no or press Enter when mergemaster asks if whether should delete */var/tmp/temproot.stage1*. This directory contains some files that must be copied to the new system later.

```
*** Comparison complete
Do you wish to delete what is left of /var/tmp/temproot.stage1? [no] no
```

After that, it will list the files it installed:

```
*** You chose the automatic install option for files that did not
    exist on your system.  The following were installed for you:
    /newroot/etc/defaults/rc.conf

    ...
    /newroot/COPYRIGHT

(END)
```

Type q to quit the pager. Then, you'll have to deal with *login.conf*:

```
*** You installed a login.conf file, so make sure that you run
    '/usr/bin/cap_mkdb /newroot/etc/login.conf'
    to rebuild your login.conf database

Would you like to run it now? y or n [n]
```

The answer does not matter, since we will run cap_mkdb in either case.

You can download the author's *stage_1.conf.default*, which you'll need to modify substantially. The comments should give you enough information regarding what to change.

Pay attention to the newfs commands. While you cannot create new filesystems on mounted partitions, the script will happily erase any unmounted partitions. This can be enough to ruin your day, so be sure to modify the device names to match your scenario.

Running this script installs a system that, when booted, provides inherited users and groups, firewalled Internet connectivity over Ethernet and PPP, correct time zone settings and NTP, and more minor configurations, such as */etc/ttys* and */etc/inetd.conf*.

Other areas of configuration will not work until stage two completes. For example, we have copied files to configure printing and X11. Printing, however, needs applications not found in the base system. Similarly, X11 will not run before we have compiled the server, libraries, and programs.

## Stage Two: Ports Installation

It is possible to install precompiled packages at this stage instead of compiling ports. In this case, *stage_2.sh* will be nothing more than a scripted list of pkg_add commands.

I install my favorite ports via the downloadable *stage_2.sh* script. You can run it multiple times safely, as it will skip all ports that are already installed. It also supports the dry run option (-n), which will show what would be done. Run it like *stage_1.sh*, with exactly one argument to denote a config file:

```
# ./stage_2.sh default
```

This example will read the list of ports from *stage_2.conf.default*.

The actual list of ports consists of lines with two or more space-separated words: the category and the port, optionally followed by an installation command that will compile and install the port. By default, this is make install. Most of the time, it suffices to name only the category and port. You can fine-tune some ports by specifying make variables, as found in the port's *Makefile*:

```
www mozilla make WITHOUT_MAILNEWS=yes WITHOUT_CHATZILLA=yes install
mail procmail make BATCH=yes install
```

In fact, you can specify arbitrary shell commands, so you are not restricted to simple make invocations:

```
java linux-sun-jdk14 yes | make install
news inn-stable CONFIGURE_ARGS="--enable-uucp-rnews --enable-setgid-inews" \
    make install
```

Note that the line for news/inn-stable includes an example of a one-shot shell variable assignment to CONFIGURE_ARGS. The port's *Makefile* will use this as an initial value and augment some other essential args.

The difference between specifying a make variable on the command line (as in the last example) and the following:

```
news inn-stable make CONFIGURE_ARGS="--enable-uucp-rnews \
    --enable-setgid-inews" install
```

is that the latter will *override* instead of *augment*.

 Be careful that your ports do not use an interactive install; they should not try to read from stdin. If they do, they will read the next line or lines from your list of ports and get confused. If *stage_2.sh* mysteriously skips a port or stops processing, this is likely the reason.

Finally, this script will create a log file named *LOGDIR/category+port* for each port it installs.

When you download the *stage_2.sh* script, you may want to
modify these variables at the beginning of the script to reflect
your environment:

```
DBDIR="/var/db/pkg"
PORTS="/usr/ports"
LOGDIR="/home/root/setup/ports.log"; mkdir -p \
    ${LOGDIR}
```

## Stage Three: Post-Configuration

You installed your beloved ports during stage two, but some ports require a
little bit of configuration. This is the job of stage three, the post-
configuration stage. I have chosen to implement stage three as a *Makefile*
because this allows easy selection of what you want to configure simply by
running:

```
# make -f stage_3.mk target
```

As with *stage_2.sh*, make sure you have *stage_3.mk* available after booting
the new system, either by putting it on a shared partition or by copying it
somewhere on the new system.

Automating the installation of a port may prove difficult if it is interactive
and does not support make BATCH=YES install. For a few ports, the interaction is nothing more than typing yes when asked to accept some license. If
such input is read from the standard input, we simply pipe the appropriate
answers to the installation command, usually make install. This is how I
dealt with *java/linux-sun-jdk14* in the previous example.

This strategy, however, does not work for *editors/staroffice52*, which
requires that X11 is running. The installation procedure involves a fair
amount of clicking and typing, so it cannot be automated like other ports
can. However, the following workaround does the trick for me. First, I created a *staroffice* package on the old system with:

```
# cd /usr/ports/editors/staroffice52
# make package
===> Building package for staroffice-5.2_1
Creating package /usr/ports/editors/staroffice52/staroffice-5.2_1.tbz
Registering depends:.
Creating bzip'd tar ball in
'/usr/ports/editors/staroffice52/staroffice-5.2_1.tbz'
```

During stage two, I used pkg_add to add this package:

```
# pkg_add /usr/ports/editors/staroffice52/staroffice-5.2_1.tbz
```

## Upgrading Configuration Files

Be aware of upgrade issues for config files. In general, you do not know when and if the format or contents of a config file changes. A new group may be added to */etc/group*, or */etc/passwd* may gain another field. Simply copying a config file from the old to the new system may be enough most of the time, but in these cases it is not. Unfortunately, `mergemaster` is available only for base system files, not for anything installed by ports. All you can do is be alert, especially when the major version number bumps. All actively maintained software programs are prime candidates for config file scrutiny. To detect such silent changes, I keep a copy of the modified config files in the same place where I keep *stage_3.mk* and compare the result with a make rule. For example, I examine Apache's *httpd.conf* in target `config_apache` with:

```
# ... automated httpd.conf modifications here ...
@if ! cmp -s /usr/local/etc/apache2/httpd.conf httpd.conf; then \
    echo "ATTENTION: the httpd.conf has changed. Please examine if"; \
    echo "the modifications are still correct. Here is the diff:"; \
    diff -u /usr/local/etc/apache2/httpd.conf httpd.conf; \
fi
```

If the `diff` is innocuous, I can make the message go away with `cp /usr/local/etc/apache2/httpd.conf  httpd.conf`. See "Apply, Understand, and Create Patches" **[Hack #92]** for more on this strategy.

The downloadable *stage_3.mk* will give you an idea of how to automate all reconfiguration.

### See Also

- "FreeBSD From Scratch" (includes links to the scripts) at *http://www.freebsd.org/doc/en_US.ISO8859-1/articles/fbsd-from-scratch/article.html*

 ## Safely Merge Changes to /etc

**#79**  Use a three-way merge to deal with upgraded configuration files.

Even though you probably run `cvsup` on a daily basis, you likely run `make world` only a few times a year, whenever a new version of the OS is released. The steps required to upgrade your system are well documented and fairly straightforward. That is, it's easy until it's time to run `mergemaster`.

`mergemaster` is an important step, as it integrates changes to */etc*. For example, occasionally a core utility such as Sendmail will require a new user or group in */etc/passwd*. Problems can occur if those changes aren't integrated.

If you've used mergemaster before, you know it's not the most user-friendly utility out there. Misinterpret a diff, and you might lose your configuration file changes or, worse, miss a necessary change. You might even end up blowing away your own users in /etc/passwd—not the most convenient way to start off a new upgrade.

## Initial Preparations

An alternative is to use etcmerge (/usr/ports/sysutils/etcmerge). This utility does most of the work for you. Unlike the two-way diff used by mergemaster, this utility can compare the changes between three sets of edits:

- The /etc from your original version of FreeBSD
- Any changes you've made to /etc since then
- The /etc for your new version of FreeBSD

> Before any upgrade, you definitely want a fresh, tested backup of all of your data, including /etc.

Once you've installed etcmerge, ensure you have a backup copy of /etc:

```
# tar czvf etc.tgz /etc
```

Here, I've saved a copy only to the local hard drive. Be sure to copy it to another location as well, just to be safe: to another system, a removable media, or even your email account.

The next step is to locate a copy of /etc that is original to your current operating system and save it to /var/db/etc. (This is a good step to add to your regime when you install a new system.) Assuming this isn't a fresh install and you've made changes to /etc, you can get the original, unmodified /etc for your operating system version at http://people.freebsd.org/~eivind/etc/.

Here, I've downloaded the 5.1-RELEASE version and untarred it to the correct place:

```
# tar -C /var/db -zxvpf etc-5.1-RELEASE.tar.gz
# ls /var/db/etc/
```

So, now you have a copy of the original /etc, as well as your own customized /etc. You'll receive the /etc for a newer version of FreeBSD once you've changed your cvs-supfile to reflect the newer tag [Hack #80].

For example, I'm currently running 5.1-RELEASE, so my custom supfile contains this line:

```
*default tag=RELENG_5_1_0_RELEASE
```

When I'm ready to upgrade to 5.2, I'll change that line to reflect the new tag:

```
*default tag=RELENG_5_2_0_RELEASE
```

My next cvsup will grab the sources for the new operating system version.

> None of the changes to /usr/src will be integrated until you make buildworld and make installworld as per the instructions in the handbook. Simply downloading the changes does not upgrade your operating system.

Once cvsup has finished downloading all of the changes, take the time to read /usr/src/UPDATING, which lists all of the known gotchas for this release. For example, there may be mandatory options for the kernel process of the upgrade, certain stages may require a reboot before the next stage works, or perhaps directory structures such as /etc have seen major changes.

Once you've made your necessary preparations, ensure these steps have succeeded before using etcmerge:

- make buildworld
- make buildkernel
- make installkernel
- make installworld

## Using etcmerge

Now that you have a new world, use etcmerge to integrate any changes to /etc. As per its manpage, start with the initialization step:

```
# etcmerge init
```

The script will perk along for a moment or two before producing a screen full of lines that start with ETCMERGE. Here's the beginning of that output:

```
ETCMERGE: >>>    Finding classes of files
ETCMERGE: >>>    Working from
ETCMERGE: >>>    Active:    /etc
ETCMERGE: >>>    Reference: /var/db/etc
ETCMERGE: >>>    New:       /root/etc-work/200401191624/etc-new
```

Note the name of the directory in the last line. It contains the working files that are ready for your review.

You'll then receive lines for different classes—see man etcmerge for a description of each conflict class. Here's a sample output from a system I recently upgraded:

```
ETCMERGE: >>>> Class 7:     3 conflict(s)
```

A class 7 conflict means a file existed for all three versions of /etc. Any differences will appear with diff-style markers. This particular system has three files containing conflicts. Their names are in the file called 7.conflicts:

```
# more /root/etc-work/200401191624/7.conflicts
./manpath.config
./pwd.db
./spwd.db
```

The etc-merged subdirectory contains copies of those files with the differences marked. Look there and examine each file listed as containing conflicts:

```
# cd /root/etc-work/200401191624/etc-merged
# vi manpath.config
```

> Don't send pwd.db or spwd.db to an editor—these are the database versions of your password files. Instead, use diff to see if the conflict is because you've added users or because FreeBSD has added a new user:
>
> ```
> # diff etc-new/master.passwd /etc/master.passwd
> ```
>
> Remove the two .db lines from 7.conflicts manually so etcmerge is aware that you've resolved the conflicts to your password databases.

As you review your own files, the angle bracket markers indicate which lines have changed. Next to each angle bracket marker is the name of the file containing the conflicting lines. For example, if the name of the file includes the /etc-new directory, the lines in question belong to the new version of the file. Once you've decided which version of the lines you wish to keep, remove the angle bracket lines as well as the unwanted version of the lines.

Once you're finished your edits, this command will integrate them:

```
# etcmerge install
/etc/mail/aliases: 24 aliases, longest 10 bytes, 246 bytes total
Install done - removing copies of old /etc/ and old reference.
Done.
#
```

Congratulations! You've successfully upgraded your operating system while maintaining your customizations to /etc.

## See Also

- "Apply, Understand, and Create Patches" [Hack #92]
- man mergemaster
- man etcmerge

- man build
- The makeworld section of the FreeBSD Handbook, which includes directions for using mergemaster (*http://www.freebsd.org/doc/en_US.ISO8859-1/ books/handbook/makeworld.html*)

## Automate Updates

FreeBSD provides many tools to make software upgrades as painless as possible. In fact, the entire process is fully scriptable. Simply choose the pieces you want and how up-to-date you want to be.

End users and administrators alike share a desire to keep their operating systems and applications as up-to-date as possible. However, if you're an operating systems veteran, you're well aware that this desire doesn't always translate into foolproof, easy execution. For example, do you have to scour the far corners of the Internet to find the latest updates? Once you find them, is it possible to upgrade safely without overwriting the dependencies required by other applications?

### Assembling the Pieces

The cvsup process provides the latest updates to the FreeBSD operating system, ports collection, and documents collection. You no longer have to scour the Internet looking for the latest sources. Simply run cvsup!

Since our intention is to script the whole process, install the *cvsup-without-gui* port:

```
# cd /usr/ports/net/cvsup-without-gui
# make install clean
```

If you've never used cvsup before, take the time to read its section in the FreeBSD Handbook so you have an overview of how the process works.

When the install finishes, copy */usr/share/examples/cvsup/cvs-supfile* to a location that makes sense to you (e.g., */root* or */usr/local/etc*). Use the comments in that file and the instructions in the handbook to customize the file so it reflects your closest mirror, operating system (tag), and what you would like to update.

Here's my *cvs-supfile*. It uses a Canadian mirror and updates all sources, ports, and documents on a FreeBSD 5.1-RELEASE system:

```
# more /root/cvs-supfile
#use the Canadian mirror
*default host=cvsup.ca.freebsd.org

#keep these lines as-is!
*default base=/usr/local/etc/cvsup
*default prefix=/usr
```

```
#this is a 5.1-RELEASE system
*default tag=RELENG_5_1_0_RELEASE

#keep this line as-is!
*default release=cvs delete use-rel-suffix compress

#update all src, ports, and docs
src-all
ports-all tag=.
doc-all tag=.
```

 If you want to specify which source, ports, and docs to install, see the handbook for directions on creating a *refuse* file.

If your *cvs-supfile* includes the `ports-all  tag=.` line, install portupgrade. This port will not only keep track of which ports need upgrading, it will also track dependencies and automate the entire application upgrade process:

```
# cd /usr/ports/sysutils/portupgrade
# make install clean
```

We can also take advantage of the `fastest-cvsup` port. As the name implies, it looks for the fastest cvsup mirror:

```
# cd /usr/ports/sysutils/fastest-cvsup
# make install clean
```

## An Example Dry Run

With the necessary pieces in place, let's run them from the command line to see how they work. First, use cvsup to download any changes to the operating system, software, or documents tree:

```
# cvsup -L2 /root/cvs-supfile
Parsing supfile "/root/cvs-supfile"
Connecting to cvsup.ca.freebsd.org
Connected to cvsup.ca.freebsd.org
Server software version: SNAP_16_1f
Negotiating file attribute support
Establishing collection information
Establishing multiplexed-mode data connection
Running
Updating collection src-all/cvs
Updating collection ports-all/cvs
<snip downloaded sources>
Updating collection doc-all/cvs
<snip downloaded sources>
Shutting down connection to server
Finished successfully
```

The -L2 switch turns on verbosity. Substitute */root/cvs-supfile* with the location of your customized *cvs-supfile*.

> It's rare for *src* to change. When it does, it is usually due to a security patch. If you notice changes to *src*, go to *http:// www.freebsd.org/security/#adv* to see if the security incident affects you and how to apply the patch if it does.

Once cvsup is complete, integrate the changes to the ports and the documents trees. This will take care of the document changes:

```
# cd /usr/doc
# make install
```

> You need the docproj-nojadetex port **[Hack #89]** for this command to succeed.

For the ports, first update your ports index:

```
# cd /usr/ports
# make index
Generating INDEX-5 - please wait.. Done.
```

An alternative is to instead run portsdb -Uu. Note that if you've created a *refuse* file, either command will produce a screen or two of error messages. You can safely ignore these.

Once your ports tree is up-to-date, see if any of your installed applications need upgrading:

```
# portversion -l "<"
[Updating the pkgdb <format:bdb1_btree> in /var/db/pkg ...
256 packages found (-0 +1) . done]
ghostscript-gnu        <
gimp-print             <
linux-sun-jdk          <
p5-MIME-Base64         <
subversion             <
xmlcatmgr              <
```

The -l "<" flag tells portversion to list only the ports matching that pattern (which represents ports that need upgrading). This particular system has 256 installed ports. I've added one (+1) new port since my last cvsup, and six packages need upgrading.

To perform the actual upgrade:

```
# portupgrade -arR
```

-a means to upgrade all ports requiring an upgrade. -rR is *very important*—it will ensure that the upgrade takes care of all dependencies properly.

I've only scratched the surface of all of these utilities. Spend some time reviewing the resources at the end of this hack to ensure you're getting the most out of your upgrade process.

## Automating the Process

Once you have a few dry runs under your belt and are happy with your results, create a shell script to automate the process. You can start out with something as simple as a Bourne script that strings together the desired commands and switches. Here, the only new command I've introduced is fastest-cvsup. I've also added an else statement to terminate the script if there is a problem with cvsup—for example, if the network connection fails.

```
# more /root/bin/mycustomupgrade.sh
#!/bin/sh
# script to automate cvsup of latest src, ports, and doc
# then rebuilds doc and ports trees
# then checks for and upgrades out-of-date software
# when finished, prints date and time

# use fastest_cvsup to find fastest Canadian or US mirror
# store the results in $SERVER to be passed to cvsup command
# substitute /root/cvs-supfile with path to custom cvs-supfile
# terminate the script if a connection is not available to
# the cvsup server

if SERVER=`fastest_cvsup -q -c ca,us`
then
  echo "Running cvsup"
  cvsup -L2 -h $SERVER /root/cvs-supfile
else
  echo "There's a problem!" 1>&2
  exit 1
fi

echo "Updating docs"
cd /usr/ports
make install

echo "Updating ports index"
cd /usr/ports
make index

echo "The following ports need upgrading"
portversion -l "<"
```

```
echo "Upgrading ports"
portupgrade -arR

echo "Finished at `/bin/date`."
exit
```

Don't forget to make your script executable with chmod +x and to test it to ensure all of the steps execute as desired. On some of my systems, I'm really picky about which software updates to apply, so I don't include the portupgrade -arR command in my script. This allows me to review which ports need upgrading so I can manually upgrade the ones I deem necessary.

### See Also

- man portversion
- man portupgrade
- man fastest-cvsup
- The cvsup section of the FreeBSD Handbook (*http://www.freebsd.org/doc/en_US.ISO8859-1/books/handbook/cvsup.html*)
- The CVS tags section of the FreeBSD Handbook (*http://www.freebsd.org/doc/en_US.ISO8859-1/books/handbook/cvs-tags.html*)
- "portupgrade," from the FreeBSD Basics column (*http://www.onlamp.com/pub/a/bsd/2003/08/28/FreeBSD_Basics.html*)

 **HACK**
**#81**
## Create a Package Repository

Combine the advantages of compiling from source and installing packages.

We saw in "Tune FreeBSD for Different Applications" **[Hack #69]** that compiling applications from source, i.e., by making their ports, has several advantages. You can tune */etc/make.conf* to take advantage of your architecture. You can also customize the installation by passing various arguments to make.

However, if you're responsible for maintaining software on multiple machines, do you always want to install from source? If your systems run similar hardware, why not create your own customized packages on one machine and make them available to your other systems via a package repository?

Creating your own custom packages allows you to retain all the benefits of make. Even better, the resulting package installs the desired software very quickly. This can be a real time-saver when you maintain multiple systems.

 The experienced hacker may prefer to use */usr/ports/devel/distcc* to provide multiple builds.

## Creating Custom Packages

Pick a machine in your network to contain the package repository, and install the ports collection on that system. The rest of your systems won't need the ports collection, which saves their disk space for other purposes.

On the system containing the ports collection, create a directory to store the packages:

```
# mkdir /usr/ports/packages
```

Then, decide which packages you'd like to create. I'll start with Exim. Before creating the package, I'll search through the port's *Makefile* to see if there are any make options:

```
# grep WITH /usr/ports/mail/exim/Makefile
#WITH_TCP_WRAPPERS=    yes
#WITH_MYSQL=           yes
#WITH_SASLAUTHD=       yes
#WITHOUT_TLS=          yes
#WITHOUT_PERL=         yes
#WITHOUT_PAM=          yes
<snip>
```

This particular port has dozens of tweakables. After a more careful read-through of the *Makefile*, I've chosen to use WITHOUT_IPV6 and WITH_SASLAUTHD.

Next, I need to determine if there are any dependencies:

```
# grep DEP /usr/ports/mail/exim/Makefile
LIB_DEPENDS=    iconv.3:${PORTSDIR}/converters/libiconv
RUN_DEPENDS=    ${LOCALBASE}/sbin/eximon:${PORTSDIR}/mail/exim-monitor
LIB_DEPENDS+=   db4.0:${PORTSDIR}/databases/db4
LIB_DEPENDS+=   db41.1:${PORTSDIR}/databases/db41
LIB_DEPENDS+=   db-4.2.2:${PORTSDIR}/databases/db42
RUN_DEPENDS+=   ${LOCALBASE}/sbin/saslauthd:${PORTSDIR}/security/
                cyrus-sasl2-saslauthd
RUN_DEPENDS+=   ${LOCALBASE}/sbin/pwcheck:${PORTSDIR}/security/cyrus-sasl
LIB_DEPENDS+=   pq.3:${PORTSDIR}/${POSTGRESQL_PORT}
```

Yup. Lots of those as well. This means I'll pass an extra argument to make to ensure the package also creates packages for each dependency. Once I know the desired make arguments, I create the package:

```
# cd /usr/ports/mail/exim
# make package -DWITHOUT_IPV6 -DWITH_SASLAUTHD DEPENDS_TARGET=package
```

Notice that I used make package rather than the usual make install. I then included my two make options. I ended the command with the DEPENDS_TARGET=package option. (I found this argument on a mailing list as the result of a Google search.) If you're building *any* package that has dependencies, remember to include that option.

make package does two things. First, it creates and stores the package in a subdirectory of */usr/ports/packages*. In this example, that subdirectory will be *mail*. Second, it installs the port on the local machine, if necessary. If you don't want to keep the application installed on the machine acting as the package repository, simply type make deinstall after creating the package.

## Creating the NFS Share

Once you've populated */usr/ports/packages* with the packages required by your network, set up an NFS mount to share the package repository. The easiest way to do this is with stand/sysinstall. On the machine holding the packages:

    # /stand/sysinstall

Choose Configure, then Networking, and then NFS server. You should see the following message:

    Operating as an NFS server means that you must first configure an
    /etc/exports file to indicate which hosts are allowed certain kinds of
    access to your local file systems. Press [ENTER] now to invoke an editor
    on /etc/exports

Unless you've changed your default editor, */etc/exports* will open in vi. The default file contains some example syntax; see man exports for additional tips.

I added this line to reflect my network settings:

    /usr/ports/packages -network 192.168.2.0 -mask 255.255.255.0

Once you've saved your changes, initialize and start the NFS server:

    # /etc/rc.d/nfsd rcvar
    # /etc/rc.d/nfsd start

Then, ensure the NFS server is listening for requests:

    # sockstat | grep nfs
    root    nfsd    3973    tcp4*:2049    *:*

Next, you'll need to create an NFS client on each machine that will use the package repository. This time, in /stand/sysinstall, choose NFS client instead of NFS server. There are no prompts, so just select the box. Once you've exited the utility, type:

    # nfsiod -n 4

This will optimize the performance of the NFS client.

Then, check to see if you can access your package repository. In my example, the machine containing the packages has an IP address of 192.168.2.12 and the local machine has a mount point called */packages*:

```
# mkdir /packages
# mount 192.168.2.12:/usr/ports/packages /packages
# ls /packages
All     Latest    ipv6              mail    security    sysutils
```

These various subdirectories contain the Exim package and its dependencies. To get an idea of which packages are available, use ls /packages/All.

It's also a good idea to try a test installation of a package:

```
# pkg_add /packages/mail/exim-4.30.tbz
```

Don't forget to unmount the NFS share when you're finished:

```
# umount /packages
```

### See Also

- man exports
- man nfsiod

## Build a Port Without the Ports Tree

While the ports tree is one of the most useful FreeBSD directory structures, you may have systems where it's not appropriate to maintain the entire ports structure.

On some of your systems, disk space may be an issue. The ports tree tarball itself is a 21 MB download. Once untarred, it will occupy around 500 MB of disk space. That space will continue to grow as you install ports since, by default, source files download into */usr/ports/distfiles*.

Does this mean that installing packages is your only alternative? Packages are convenient, but since they are precompiled, you don't have the option of providing your own make arguments to optimize the install for your environment.

One alternative is the anonymous CVS system. Even a minimal install of FreeBSD includes the cvs command. This allows you to check out only the particular port skeleton you need. You'll still have the convenience of the ports collection without actually having to install it.

### Connecting to Anonymous CVS

The first time you use cvs, create an empty CVS password file, as CVS will complain if this file is missing:

```
# touch ~root/.cvspass
```

Then, ensure your present working directory is */usr*:

```
# cd /usr
```

**Build a Port Without the Ports Tree**

> When using cvs to maintain your ports, be sure you are in */usr*.
> cvs downloads the requested files to your current working
> directory and will overwrite any files of the same name.

Then, use the cvs login command to connect to a CVS server. There are five
FreeBSD anonymous CVS servers; see the Handbook reference at the end of
this hack for their names and passwords. Use the setenv command to specify the server to log into:

```
# setenv CVSROOT :pserver:anoncvs@anoncvs.at.FreeBSD.org/home/ncvs
# cvs login
Logging in to :pserver:anoncvs@anoncvs.at.freebsd.org:2401/home/ncvs
CVS password: anoncvs
#
```

Once you've successfully logged in, you'll receive your normal prompt back.
You'll remain connected to the CVS server until you explicitly log off. In the
meantime, you now have the ability to issue commands either on the CVS
server or on your own system.

## Checking Out Port Skeletons

Let's assume you have a minimum install and don't have an existing */usr/
ports* directory structure. To install a port, you need the *Mk* and *Templates*
directories as well as the port's *Makefile*.

Use the cvs checkout command to retrieve the necessary files from the CVS
server:

```
# cvs checkout -A -P -l ports/Mk
cvs server: Updating ports/Mk
U ports/Mk/bsd.emacs.mk
U ports/Mk/bsd.gnome.mk
U ports/Mk/bsd.gnustep.mk
U ports/Mk/bsd.java.mk
U ports/Mk/bsd.kde.mk
U ports/Mk/bsd.openssl.mk
U ports/Mk/bsd.port.mk
U ports/Mk/bsd.port.post.mk
U ports/Mk/bsd.port.pre.mk
U ports/Mk/bsd.port.subdir.mk
U ports/Mk/bsd.python.mk
U ports/Mk/bsd.ruby.mk
U ports/Mk/bsd.sites.mk

# cvs checkout -A -P -l ports/Templates
cvs server: Updating ports/Templates
U ports/Templates/README.category
U ports/Templates/README.port
```

```
U ports/Templates/README.top
U ports/Templates/config.guess
U ports/Templates/config.sub
#
```

Since you're in the *usr* directory, cvs will create */usr/ports* for you and will populate the *Mk* and *Templates* subdirectories with their sets of files. It's interesting to note how little disk space this bare-minimum ports tree requires:

```
# du -h /usr/ports | tail -n1
418K    ports
```

That's a pretty big difference from 500 MB!

## Finding a Port and Its Dependencies

Next, decide which port you'd like to install. The only disadvantage to not having the entire ports structure is that you need an alternate method of discovering the name of the port you'd like to install. For example, in order to install lynx, I need to know that it is in the *www* subdirectory and that there are three different versions of lynx to choose from. The easiest way to discover this information is to use the search utility at *http://www.freshports.org*.

Once you find the port you're looking for, it will indicate the name of its directory. In my example, *lynx-2.8.5d17* lives in *www/lynx-current*.

Now it's a simple matter of checking out that port's skeleton:

```
# cvs checkout -A -P -l ports/www/lynx-current
cvs server: Updating ports/www/lynx-current
U ports/www/lynx-current/Makefile
U ports/www/lynx-current/distinfo
U ports/www/lynx-current/pkg-descr
U ports/www/lynx-current/pkg-plist
```

Next, check the port's *Makefile* to see if there are any dependencies:

```
# grep DEPENDS /usr/ports/www/lynx-current/Makefile
LIB_DEPENDS=    intl.5:${PORTSDIR}/devel/gettext
```

As it stands right now, this port will not install, as I don't have the ports skeleton for the dependency *devel/gettext*. So, I'll download that port skeleton and double-check that *that* port doesn't have any dependencies:

```
# cvs checkout -A -P -l ports/devel/gettext
<snip output>
# grep DEPENDS /usr/ports/devel/gettext/Makefile
#
```

Okay, it looks like all dependencies are there. I'm ready to build the port:

```
# cd /usr/ports/www/lynx-current
# make install clean
```

> If disk space is an issue, instead use make install distclean, which will delete the source from /usr/ports/distfiles once the build successfully completes.

That's it. As long as you remember to look for dependencies before you issue your make install command, your minimal ports structure should work as flawlessly as the full ports collection.

Don't forget to use cvs logout when you're finished retrieving the files you need from the CVS server.

### See Also

- man cvs
- The AnonCVS section of the FreeBSD Handbook, which includes the names of the BSD CVS servers (*http://www.freebsd.org/doc/en_US. ISO8859-1/books/handbook/anoncvs.html*)

## Keep Ports Up-to-Date with CTM

**#83**   Keep your ports up-to-date without using cvsup.

If you have a slow Internet connection, it can take a while to download the ports tree; the current tarball is over 21 MB in size. Once you have the ports collection, keeping up-to-date with cvsup might not be such an attractive option if it involves tying up your phone line.

Perhaps bandwidth isn't the problem. Perhaps you're just looking for an alternative way to stay current, without having to install and configure cvsup. After all, why install additional software if you can achieve the same results using commands that come with the base system?

Regardless of which category you fall into, CTM may be what you're looking for.

CTM was originally CVS Through Email, meaning you could receive the changes you usually receive through cvsup via email. (In the case of numerous changes, you'd receive several, smaller mails instead of one monolithic message.) This can be a cheaper alternative to cvsup if you're charged for the amount of time you are connected to the Internet.

However, it's even easier to retrieve these changes with ftp. FreeBSD maintains several CTM servers that contain the changes, or deltas, to the FreeBSD source and the ports collection. This hack will concentrate on keeping your ports up-to-date using ftp and the CTM servers.

## Using ftp and ctm to Stay Current

Let's start with a system that doesn't have the ports collection installed. First, I'll create an empty *ports* directory for ctm to work with:

```
# mkdir /usr/ports/
# cd /usr/ports
```

Then, instead of downloading and untarring the ports tree tarball, I'll ftp into a CTM server and download the latest ports tree delta. The Handbook's section on CTM includes the addresses of the CTM mirrors.

```
# ftp ftp.freebsd.org

<snip banner and login>

ftp> cd pub/FreeBSD/development/CTM/ports-cur
ftp> ls

<snip most of long listing>

-rw-r--r--  1 110   root    22332066 Jan 23 08:46 ports-cur.5100xEmpty.gz
-rw-r--r--  1 110   root       67953 Jan 24 00:43 ports-cur.5101.gz
-rw-r--r--  1 110   root       14256 Jan 24 16:51 ports-cur.5102.gz
```

Look toward the end of the listing for the large file closest to the present date. It will have the word xEmpty in its name. That file is your starting delta. Download that and any subsequent deltas.

```
ftp> get ports-cur.5100xEmpty.gz
ftp> get ports-cur.5101.gz
ftp> get ports-cur.5102.gz
ftp> quit
```

 Your first ftp transfer will be the largest and longest, as you are downloading the elements necessary to build the ports tree structure. Subsequent sessions will be very quick.

Note the *.gz* extension; leave the files compressed. CTM will still work, and you'll save disk space.

Save your deltas to */usr/ports*, and remain in this directory when you use the ctm command.

Now that you have your starting deltas, apply them with ctm:

```
# ctm ports-cur.5100xEmpty.gz
ctm: warning: .ctm_status not found
<snip long output>
```

The first time you use ctm, it will complain about a missing *.ctm_status* file. Don't worry; it will create it for you. After a few seconds, it will send a lot of output to stdout. Once the command has finished, you'll have a fully installed version of the ports tree.

That *.ctm-status* file will tell you the delta number of that ports tree:

```
# more .ctm-status
ports-cur 5100
```

Then, simply apply any subsequent deltas in ascending order. This will correctly incorporate all of the changes to the ports tree.

```
# ctm ports-cur.5101.gz
# ctm ports-cur.5102.gz
# more .ctm-status
ports-cur 5102
```

That's it. Whenever you want to update your ports tree, ftp into your CTM mirror, download the deltas containing a higher number than your current version, and apply them in order.

It's up to you whether to keep the compressed versions of the files you download. Once you've successfully applied a delta—as indicated by *.ctm-status*—you no longer need to store that delta file. However, if download speed or time is an issue, consider keeping a copy of that large starting delta, just in case you ever want to recreate your ports tree from scratch.

## Hacking the Hack

If you're too lazy or forgetful to ftp for changes periodically, consider receiving them automatically via email. Changes occur once or twice a day. Subscribe to the ctm-ports-cur mailing list to receive them (*http://lists.freebsd.org/mailman/listinfo/ctm-ports-cur/*).

Complete the online subscription form, and reply to the email that asks you to confirm your subscription.

However, *do not* subscribe to that mailing list until you've configured your system to handle those emails. Basically, you want the system to intercept those CTM updates instead of sending them directly to your mailbox. There are two ways to do this: either create a sendmail alias or create a procmail recipe. See man ctm_rmail for detailed instructions.

It's also a good idea to verify the PGP signatures before applying those updates. You can find detailed instructions for this, as well as for using ctm_rmail to handle incoming deltas, in this message from the ctm-users mailing list: *http://lists.freebsd.org/pipermail/ctm-users/2003-October/000039.html*.

## See Also

- `man ctm_rmail`
- The CTM section of the FreeBSD Handbook (*http://www.freebsd.org/doc/ en_US.ISO8859-1/books/handbook/ctm.html*)

 ## Navigate the Ports System

**#84** Use built-in commands to keep abreast of the FreeBSD ports collection.

What first attracted me to FreeBSD—and what has definitely kept my attention since—is the ports collection. Over 10,000 applications are a mere make install clean away. For a software junkie like myself, it is indeed Nerdvana to no longer scour the Internet for software or fight my way through dependency hell just to convince an application to install.

Admittedly, it's easy to get lost in a sea of ports. How do you choose which application best suits your needs? How do you keep track of which ports have been installed on your system? How do you make sure you don't inadvertently delete a dependency? Read on to see how to get the most out of the built-in utilities for managing ports.

### Finding the Right Port

You know you want to install some software to add functionality to your system. Wouldn't it be great if you could generate a list of all the ports that are available for your specific need? Well, you can, and it's almost too easy with the built-in port search facility. In this example, I'll look for ports dealing with VPN software:

```
% cd /usr/ports
% make search key=vpn | more
Port:      poptop-1.1.4.b4_2
Path:      /usr/ports/net/poptop
Info:      Windows 9x compatible PPTP (VPN) server
Maint:     ports@FreeBSD.org
Index:     net
B-deps:     expat-1.95.6_1 gettext-0.12.1 gmake-3.80_1 libiconv-1.9.1_3
R-deps:
<snip>
```

I snipped the results for brevity as this command gives the details of each port associated with VPNs. The format of the output is quite useful, as it gives the name of the port itself, its location in the ports tree, a brief description, the address of the maintainer, as well as the build and run dependencies.

If you're only interested in seeing how many ports are available, pipe the results to grep instead of more:

```
% make search key=vpn | grep Port
Port:          poptop-1.1.4.b4_2
Port:          pptpclient-1.3.1
Port:          ike-scan-1.2
Port:          openvpn-1.5.0
Port:          tinc-1.0.2
Port:          vpnd-1.1.0
```

Perhaps you'd prefer to know their locations:

```
% make search key=vpn | grep Path
Path:          /usr/ports/net/poptop
Path:          /usr/ports/net/pptpclient
Path:          /usr/ports/security/ike-scan
Path:          /usr/ports/security/openvpn
Path:          /usr/ports/security/tinc
Path:          /usr/ports/security/vpnd
```

What if you already know the name of the port you want to install but aren't sure what versions are available? Use search  name= instead. For example, this command will search for all ports with netscape in their names:

```
% make search name=netscape | grep Port
Port:          pt_BR-netscape7-7.02
Port:          netscape-remote-1.0_1
Port:          netscape-wrapper-2000.07.07
Port:          netscape-communicator-4.78
Port:          netscape-navigator-4.78
Port:          linux-netscape-communicator-4.8
Port:          linux-netscape-navigator-4.8
Port:          netscape7-7.1
```

If you find the search facility useful, it is a good idea to update your ports index periodically. Become the superuser and issue the following command (it may take a while, so don't execute it if you're in a hurry):

```
# cd /usr/ports
# make index
```

Finally, if you really want to fine-tune your search results, spend a few moments reading the examples in */usr/ports/Tools/scripts/README.portsearch*.

## Dealing with Installed Ports

You've spent a few months installing software and trying out new applications. How do you keep track of all of that software and all of those dependencies? pkg_info is your friend.

My favorite pkg_info switch is definitely -x. (There's not really a mnemonic for this switch; I tend to think of it as "give me version x.") If I stack it with any other switch, I don't need to know the full name (including the complete version number) of a port. For example:

```
% pkg_info -xc lynx
```

will show the one-line comment (-c) of every application that starts with lynx, regardless of the version number. Besides saving memory cells for other purposes, it's an excellent way to find out if you have more than one version of lynx installed.

After installing a port, it's useful to see if there were any messages, as these often contain configuration instructions:

```
% pkg_info -xD xmms
Information for xmms-esound-1.2.8_2:

Install notice:
Xmms supports Gzipped and uncompressed skins.  If you would like to use
Zip format skins you will need to ensure archivers/unzip is installed.
```

How many times have you installed a port and had no clue regarding the name of the executable, much less the names and locations of any configuration files or documentation? Thank goodness for -L, the file-listing flag:

```
% pkg_info -xL lynx | more
Information for lynx-2.8.4.1d:

Files:
/usr/local/man/man1/lynx.1.gz
/usr/local/bin/lynx
/usr/local/etc/lynx.cfg.default
/usr/local/share/doc/lynx/CHANGES
<snip>
```

Depending upon the application, the listing may be quite long. A judicious pipe to grep bin, grep man, or grep doc may better suit your purposes.

## Checking Dependencies Before Uninstalling

Before uninstalling an application, it is always a good idea to see if any other packages require that application as a dependency. For example, you've typed pkg_info | more and see the application ORBit-0.5.17. You think to yourself, "I don't remember installing, or even ever using, this application. Where did it come from? Maybe I should just get rid of it." This command will clear up your mini-mystery:

```
% pkg_info -xR ORBit
Information for ORBit-0.5.17_1:

Required by:
bonobo-1.0.22
```

```
flashplugin-mozilla-0.4.10_4
<snip>
```

Since the snipped output took up most of a page, it looks like this application is useful after all. Don't worry; if you did try to uninstall that application, pkg_delete would refuse since it is required by those other applications. However, it is always nice to be aware of these things ahead of time.

 If you really do want to force the uninstall of an application, use -F (force) with pkg_delete.

## Checking the Disk Space Your Ports Use

What happens if you go a little install-crazy and end up with more applications than disk space? Use the -s (size) switch to determine how much space an application uses. Send the output either to a pager:

```
% pkg_info -as | more
```

or to a file that you can read at your leisure:

```
% pkg_info -as > sizes
```

You'll then have an idea of which applications are using the most space so that you can decide which ones are worth uninstalling. Remember, you also have the comment and dependencies switches to help you decide.

Yet another way to find out what software you have installed is to use pkg_version:

```
% pkg_version | more
```

This will list each installed application, in alphabetical order. You'll note that each application is followed by one of the three symbols in Table 8-1.

Table 8-1. pkg_version symbols

| Symbol | Meaning |
| --- | --- |
| = | The application is up-to-date. |
| < | There is a newer version of the application available. |
| > | Your index may be out-of-date. |

So, to determine which applications require upgrading:

```
% pkg_version -l "<"
```

Note that you need to place quotes around the less-than sign or your shell will complain about a missing name for your redirect. If you don't receive any output, congratulations! All of your applications are up-to-date. If you do receive some output, you know which applications require an upgrade.

Alternately, this command will show all applications that are out-of-date:

```
% pkg_version -L "="
```

See man pkg_version if you didn't catch the difference between -l and -L.

If you prefer a more verbose output than =, >, or <, try this command:

```
% pkg_version -v | more
```

If for some reason you're not using cvsup to keep your ports tree up-to-date, you can still check your installed ports against the latest ports tree:

```
% pkg_version -v ftp://ftp.freebsd.org/pub/FreeBSD/branches/-current \
    /ports/INDEX | more
```

### See Also

- */usr/ports/README*
- man pkg_info
- man pkg_delete
- man pkg_version
- man ports
- The Installing Packages and Ports section of the FreeBSD Handbook (*http://www.freebsd.org/doc/en_US.ISO8859-1/books/handbook/ports.html*)

## Downgrade a Port

**#85** It doesn't happen often, but occasionally portupgrade will upgrade a port to a newer version that doesn't sit well with your system.

It can be very frustrating when an application that was working just fine an hour ago suddenly stops working after an upgrade. Now what?

At first glance, the solution isn't obvious. Because ports don't contain revision labels, you can't just cvsup back to an earlier version. However, the commits or changes to each port are tracked in the CVS repository. You *could* learn the syntax of the cvs command and use it to connect to the CVS repository, manually review the port's commit history, find an earlier version that worked on your system, check out that version, and rebuild the port. Whew! There must be an easier way.

That's what Heiner Eichmann thought when he created portdowngrade. His script does all of the work for you; you only need to choose which version of the port to use.

## Using portdowngrade

Installing portdowngrade is easy enough:

```
# cd /usr/ports/sysutils/portdowngrade
# make install clean
```

A few moments later, you'll have the script and an informative manpage. To run the script, simply specify which port you'd like to downgrade. Here, I'll demonstrate an arbitrary port:

```
# portdowngrade apinger
portdowngrade 0.1 by Heiner Eichmann
Please note, that nothing is changed in the ports tree
unless it is explicitly permitted in step 6!

Seeking port apinger ... found: net/apinger

Step 1: Checking out port from CVS repository
CVS root directory: :pserver:anoncvs:anoncvs@anoncvs.FreeBSD.org/home/ncvs

Step 2: Reading the port history from the CVS repository

Step 3: Analyzing the port history from the CVS repository

Step 4: Load port version numbers and present results
Keys: <space> : next page                    d : details
             p : previous page
      <enter> : leave presentation and downgrade if wanted

number      date            portversion  comment
    1   2003/11/05 15:39:39              Fix whitespace.
    2   2003/06/07 11:43:13              Fix breakage.
    3   2003/06/04 09:49:31              Add startup script for apinger.
    4   2003/05/07 11:37:52              Change maintainer email to my @FreeBSD.
    5   2003/03/28 03:41:45              Update to 0.6.1
    6   2003/02/21 13:14:34              De-pkg-comment.
    7   2003/01/02 17:54:17              Update to 0.6
    8   2002/10/14 14:02:52              upgrade to 0.5
    9   2002/10/05 19:06:00              Upgrade to 0.4.1.
   10   2002/07/19 23:02:53              Update to 0.3
   11   2002/07/18 12:55:14              Alarm Pinger (apinger) is a little tool
```

Here are the first four of six steps run by portdowngrade. It has logged into the CVS server, found the desired port, and presented you with its commit history. This particular port has had 11 revisions and number 1 is the latest.

At this point, the script pauses for user input. I'm going to go back a few revisions to Version 4:

```
Total lines: 11. Command: press enter
Enter version number to change port to (0: exit): 4

Step 5: Checking out chosen date of the port from the CVS repository

Step 6: Modifying the port
Port: net/apinger
at : 2003/05/07 11:37:52
Type 'yes' to bring the port to the state of the date above
or 'no' to exit without changing anything. Note, that this only changes
the port, not the installed software! yes or no: yes

The port has been set to the selected version. Install it if you wish.
If you have portupgrade installed, you should run portsdb -Uu now,
to see the changes in the ports database. In any case
portupgrade -f apinger will install the changed port.
Note: if you run cvsup, the port
is changed back to the chosen label!
#
```

When I typed yes, I chose to change the port version in the ports tree. The downgrade won't actually take place until I run portupgrade -f apinger. Note the use of the -f flag to force the reinstallation of an installed port. Since this port has changed in my tree, the reinstallation will overwrite my previously installed version.

```
# portupgrade -f apinger
[Updating the pkgdb <format:bdb1_btree> in /var/db/pkg ... - 288
packages found (-0 +2) .. done]
---> Downgrading 'apinger-0.6.1_1' to 'apinger-0.6.1' (net/apinger)
<snip build output>
===> Registering installation for apinger-0.6.1
===> Cleaning for apinger-0.6.1
---> Cleaning out obsolete shared libraries
[Updating the pkgdb <format:bdb1_btree> in /var/db/pkg ... - 288
packages found (-0 +1) . done]
```

## Preventing Automated Re-Upgrades

You'll notice that the next time you run your cvsup process [Hack #80], your downgraded port will appear as needing upgrading. If you've totally automated the process, it may re-upgrade to that new, buggy version.

It's easy to prevent that from happening. In fact, you can prevent automated upgrading of any port by using the HOLD_PKGS array in *pkgtools.conf*. Start by copying the sample configuration file to the real configuration file:

```
# cp /usr/local/etc/pkgtools.conf.sample /usr/local/etc/pkgtools.conf
```

Then, open */usr/local/etc/pkgtools.conf* in your favorite editor and search for this section:

```
# HOLD_PKGS: array
# This is a list of ports you don't want portupgrade(1) to upgrade,
# portversion(1) to suggest upgrading, or pkgdb(1) to fix.
# You can use wildcards ("ports glob" and "pkgname glob").
# -f/--force with each command will override the held status.
# e.g.:
#   HOLD_PKGS = [
#     'bsdpan-*',
#     'x11*/XFree86*',
#   ]

HOLD_PKGS = [
  'bsdpan-*',
]
```

Simply follow the syntax to add the packages you want to keep as is:

```
HOLD_PKGS = [
  'bsdpan-*',
  'apinger-*',
]
```

## See Also

- man cvs
- man portdowngrade
- The portdowngrade home page (*http://portdowngrade.sourceforge.net*)

## Create Your Own Startup Scripts

#### #86   Ensure your favorite installed applications start at boot time.

Some ports are nice enough to create their own startup scripts in */usr/local/etc/rc.d* when you install them. Unfortunately, not all ports do. You may wonder why you're not receiving any email, only to discover a week later that your mail server didn't start at your last bootup!

In those cases, you'll have to write your own startup script. Fortunately, that's easy.

### Was a Script Installed?

Every port comes with a packing list of installed executables, files, and manpages. To see if a particular port will install a startup script, search its *pkg-plist* for the word rc. Here, I'll check the packing lists for the stunnel and messagewall ports:

```
% grep -w rc /usr/ports/security/stunnel/pkg-plist
etc/rc.d/stunnel.sh.sample
```

```
% grep -w rc /usr/ports/mail/messagewall/pkg-plist
%
```

Use the -w switch so grep searches for the full word rc, not just words containing those two characters. If there isn't a startup script, as is the case for messagewall, you'll just get your prompt back.

If the startup script ends with *.sample*, you'll need to copy it to a new file without that extension. This is often the case with applications that expect you to change the sample configuration file to suit your system's requirements.

Also, note the relative path. The packing list knows that, by default, the files installed by a port will start with the prefix */usr/local*. That is, in the previous example, you'll find stunnel's startup script in */usr/local/etc/rc.d*, not in */etc/rc.d*.

> The converse is also true. If you *don't* want an installed application starting itself at boot time, either remove the *.sh* extension from its startup script or use chmod -x to make it nonexecutable.

## Creating Your Own Startup Script

Suppose you'd like to have messagewall start automatically at boot time. That means you'll need to write a script. Fortunately, you don't have to reinvent the wheel, as all startup scripts follow the same pattern. If you've installed some applications, you most likely already have startup scripts populating */usr/local/etc/rc.d*. If you don't, use the template startup script from the Handbook:

```
#!/bin/sh
echo -n ' FooBar'

case "$1" in
start)
        /usr/local/bin/foobar
        ;;
stop)
        kill -9 `cat /var/run/foobar.pid`
        ;;
*)
        echo "Usage: `basename $0` {start|stop}" >&2
        exit 64
        ;;
esac

exit 0
```

This script starts a generic application named foobar. When you copy the template, copy it to */usr/local/etc/rc.d* with the name of the application followed by a *.sh* extension. In my case, I'll call the file */usr/local/etc/rc.d/messagewall.sh*.

Next, replace the word foobar with the name of the application. Change these three lines to reflect the application's name:

```
echo -n ' Messagewall'

/usr/local/bin/messagewall

kill -9 `cat /var/run/messagewall.pid`
```

Remember to double-check the location of that executable, as some ports instead install to */usr/local/sbin* or */usr/X11R6/bin*:

```
% which messagewall
/usr/local/bin/messagewall
```

Occasionally, a port will install its main binary with an odd executable name. For example, the executable for netcat is not netcat. In that case, searching the packing list will reveal all:

```
% grep bin /usr/ports/net/netcat/pkg-plist
bin/nc
```

Just remember that there's a */usr/local* in front of that *bin/nc*.

## Testing the Script

Once you've saved your changes, make the script executable with chmod +x. Then, see if it works:

```
# /usr/local/etc/rc.d/messagewall.sh
 MessagewallUsage: messagewall.sh {start|stop}
```

```
# /usr/local/etc/rc.d/messagewall.sh start
<snip startup messages>
```

Pay attention if you receive any error messages. Often they indicate a typo in the application's configuration file. Address those and ensure you can successfully start the application.

Once the application successfully starts, make sure you can stop it:

```
# /usr/local/etc/rc.d/messagewall.sh stop
<snip error message regarding PID>
```

Some applications, like this one, don't record their PID in */var/run*, so your script will produce an error instead of stopping the application. Most of these applications take over your prompt when you start them, so you can simply return to the terminal (or background process if you started it as such) and press Ctrl-c to end the process. This isn't the cleanest of procedures, but it is effective nonetheless.

## Hacking the Hack

If you're using FreeBSD 5.1 or higher, you might want to experiment with writing your own scripts using the new *rc.d* structure inherited from Net-BSD. As of this writing, */etc/rc.d*, or the collection of system scripts, uses this structure. In the future, */usr/local/etc/rc.d* will likely migrate to this scripting style.

The new structure adds other commands, such as `status` and `reload`, so your scripts can do more than `start` and `stop`.

When writing your own scripts, add these lines to your template:

```
. /etc/rc.subr

name="foo"
command="/usr/local/bin/${name}"
pidfile="/var/run/${name}.pid"

your stuff here

load_rc_config $name
run_rc_command "$1"
```

The first line is mandatory, as it calls the needed subroutines. Your script will also require the last two lines. Next come three variables that every script should include. There are dozens of other useful variables, so read through the scripts in */etc/rc.d/* for ideas.

I also find NetBSD's packages list useful (see *ftp://ftp.netbsd.org/pub/ NetBSD/packages/pkgsrc/README-all.html*). If you select a port and click on its *history* then *files*, you can look for existing scripts. These scripts are written in the NetBSD *rc.d* style, so you'll have lots of examples to browse.

> *Don't* include the `rcvar=` variable in your local scripts. This is for system daemons that can be enabled and disabled using *rc.conf* variables.

## See Also

*   `man rc.subr`
*   The startup scripts section of the FreeBSD Handbook (*http://www.freebsd.org/ doc/en_US.ISO8859-1/books/handbook/configtuning-starting-services.html*)

## Automate NetBSD Package Builds
### #87   Use a sandbox to build applications that play nicely within your network.

Many NetBSD users are responsible for multiple systems running on different architectures. Instead of rebuilding the same package on machine after machine, it's often desirable to build packages for all of these machines from the most powerful one, delivering the appropriate binary packages across the network. However, problems can arise when not all machines run the same version of NetBSD or when you want different optimizations or build settings on each box.

The solution to this dilemma is simple: create a sandbox with the version of NetBSD used in the target machine and build the necessary binary packages inside it. This sounds easy, but it can be a very tedious and error-prone task. It is even more complex if you want to automate periodic package rebuilding. Fortunately, that's our final goal in this hack.

To simplify things, I assume that you have a relatively fast desktop machine running NetBSD-current, where you will build binary packages, and a server machine running the stable version of NetBSD (1.6.2 at the time of this writing).

### Installing pkg_comp

pkg_comp (also known as Package Compiler) can simplify the creation of these sandboxes: it handles any version of NetBSD inside a chroot jail and automates the build process of binary packages inside it. Its only restriction is that both the builder and the destination machine share the same architecture.

Let's begin by installing pkg_comp on the builder machine (make sure you have Version 1.15 or greater):

```
# cd /usr/pkgsrc/pkgtools/pkg_comp
# make install && make clean
```

After installation, spend some time reading man 8 pkg_comp and getting familiar with its structure because you will be using it as a reference guide during the configuration. Also ensure that your kernel configuration file contains file-system NULLFS. (See man 4 options for more information.)

### Configuration Variables

Now you are ready to set up pkg_comp. The configuration file tells pkg_comp how to create the sandbox. Type the following commands to create and edit a sample configuration file:

```
# pkg_comp maketemplate
# vi /root/pkg_comp/default.conf
```

You will notice lots of variable definitions. All you need to do is set some values; pkg_comp handles everything else. For our purposes, you need to know only some of these variables (see Table 8-2) and change them to suit your system.

*Table 8-2. pkg_comp variables*

| Variable | Usage |
| --- | --- |
| DESTDIR | Gives the location of the sandbox. This needs lots of disk space, as it will store a complete NetBSD system. In this example, use */var/chroot/pkg_comp/default*. |
| DISTRIBDIR | The location of NetBSD installation sets, whether downloaded from the FTP site or built using build.sh. pkg_comp. The */binary/sets* string will be appended to the value you provide. The resulting directory should contain the files listed in the SETS and SETS_X11 variables. In this example, use */home/NetBSD/NetBSD-1.6.2/i386*. |
| NETBSD_RELEASE | Specifies the version of NetBSD to unpack in the sandbox. This version must be compatible with pkgtools/libkver. If you leave it set to no, pkg_comp assumes the builder system and the sandboxed system are the same version. In this example, its value is 1.6.2. |
| REAL_SRC | Provides the location of pkgsrc distfiles. In this example, use */home/NetBSD/distfiles*. |
| REAL_PACKAGES | Identifies the destination of binary packages. In this example, use */home/NetBSD/packages/1.6.2*. |
| REAL_PKGSRC | Locates the pkgsrc tree in your system. In this example, use */usr/pkgsrc*. |
| REAL_DISTFILES | Gives the location of the NetBSD source tree in your system. In this example, use */usr/src-1.6*. Because we are building for 1.6.2 and the builder is running current, this will *not* be */usr/src*. |
| SETS | Lists the NetBSD sets to be extracted inside the sandbox. Do not change the default value. |
| SETS_X11 | Lists the X11R6 sets to be extracted inside the sandbox. Set this to no if you do not want to build packages for the X Window System, but avoid modifying the default list. In this example, set it to no, since I assume you do not have the X Window System installed on the server. |
| REAL_PKGVULNDIR | The location of the *pkg-vulnerabilities* file in your system. In this example, use */usr/pkg/share*. If you are not using audit-packages, then set USE_AUDIT_PACKAGES to no. The use of audit-packages is strongly encouraged because it won't install packages that have known security problems. |

Now is the time to enable compile-time optimizations for the packages you are going to build. As you modify the CFLAGS and CXXFLAGS variables, keep in mind that the configuration file is a shell script. Remember to quote your values properly.

## Initializing and Using the Sandbox

After setting your values and creating all of the referenced directories, it's time to initialize the sandbox. It is as easy as typing:

```
# pkg_comp makeroot
```

When this command finishes, the sandbox is ready to build packages for your server. In this example, the packages will linked against 1.6.2 libraries using any specified optimizations.

Suppose you want binary packages for Apache and screen. Compile them with the following call to pkg_comp:

```
# pkg_comp build www/apache misc/screen
```

This will place *apache-1.3.29.tgz* and *screen-4.0.2.tgz*—as well as their dependencies—under */home/NetBSD/packages/1.6.2/All*. They're now suitable for transferring to the destination machine. Install them with pkg_add.

If you do not need to build more packages using pkg_comp, you can safely free the space used by the sandbox with the command shown next. Note that this removes only the sandbox, not binary packages:

```
# pkg_comp removeroot
```

## Automating the Process

We can go one step further and configure pkg_comp to create the sandbox, build a predefined set of packages for your server, and remove the sandbox when finished, all automatically. This takes only a single command with pkg_comp's automatic mode.

To enable automatic mode, re-edit the configuration file, */root/pkg_comp/ default.conf*, and define the AUTO_PACKAGES variable. This variable takes the list of packages you want to build for your server. In this example:

```
AUTO_PACKAGES="misc/screen www/apache"
```

That's it for the configuration side. To check if this works, make sure the sandbox does not exist, and execute pkg_comp's automatic mode:

```
# pkg_comp removeroot
# pkg_comp auto
```

After a while, you will find binary packages for screen and Apache in your package repository, just as in the earlier example.

If the list of packages is extensive, the build will take a long while, which may not be desirable in some environments (for example, in cases when you need to shut down the builder during the night). This is not a problem: if you stop the automatic process with Ctrl-c at any point, you can resume it later by issuing:

```
# pkg_comp auto resume
```

To finish the automation, configure a cron job to rebuild your package set automatically once a week. Edit root's crontab to add the line:

```
# crontab -e
0       3       *       *       *       /usr/pkg/sbin/pkg_comp auto
```

### Hacking the Hack

I've shown the most basic usage of pkg_comp in this hack. If you found it useful, there are many more things to learn, and the manpage is a good starting point.

Here are some other ideas to try:

- Configure a cron job to rebuild all the packages you need for your own machine, so that you can easily restore them at any point with pkg_add.
- Create two configuration files with different names.
- Enable GCC 3 with extensive optimizations.

### See Also

- man pkg_comp
- man pkg_add

# HACK #88 Easily Install Unix Applications on Mac OS X

Do you miss FreeBSD's wonderful ports system on Mac OS X? Thanks to the DarwinPorts project, software installation is a breeze.

Many Mac users often seem a little surprised when I tell them I run XChat and other Unix applications on Mac OS X alongside native Aqua applications (such as Safari, Finder, and iPhoto). What they don't realize is that it's simple to install such applications thanks to the Fink and DarwinPorts projects. This hack is dedicated to installing and using DarwinPorts.

This hack assumes you have a basic understanding of *Terminal.app* and the underlying Unix bits of Mac OS X. You also need to have the Developer Tools installed.

### Installing DarwinPorts

Before you can use DarwinPorts, you must install the build system and the actual ports tree. The easiest way to accomplish this is by using CVS. Before checking the project out of CVS, you'll need to decide where you'd like it to exist on your hard drive. I usually use ~/*work*.

Open *Terminal.app* (or an xterm if you have X11 installed), and change to the directory where you'll install DarwinPorts. Then type the following commands at the prompt (when the server asks for a password, just press Return):

```
% alias dcvs cvs -d \
    :pserver:anonymous@anoncvs.opendarwin.org:/Volumes/src/cvs/od
% dcvs login
% dcvs co -P darwinports
```

You should now see a bunch of output scrolling past in the terminal window. If you do, good; the project is checking out of CVS and onto your hard disk. If you don't, double-check the three commands just shown to make sure you typed everything correctly. Once you've fetched the project, it's time to install it.

Run `ls` in the terminal window; you should see a *darwinports* directory. `cd` to it and rerun `ls`:

```
% cd darwinports
% ls
CVS  Makefile  README  README.fr  base  doc  dports  www
```

At this point, it's a very good idea to read the *README* file.

The next step is to build and install the applications that will allow you to install various ports. From the *darwinports* directory:

```
% sudo -s
<enter your password>
# make && make install && make clean
```

By default, DarwinPorts uses */opt/local* as its prefix. To change that to something else, edit */etc/ports/ports.conf*.

Next, open */etc/ports/sources.conf* and change the `file://` line to point to the proper location on your system. For example:

```
file:///Users/jim/work/darwports/dports
```

Now that everything is configured, add the directory containing Darwin-Ports binaries to your shell's path. If you're using `tcsh` (the default shell on Mac OS X 10.2 and earlier), add the following to your ~/*.cshrc* file:

```
set path = ($path /opt/local/bin)
```

If you're using bash, as Mac OS X 10.3 does, add the following line to your ~/*.bashrc* file:

```
export PATH=$PATH:/opt/local/bin
```

In order for your shell to recognize the new path, either start a new shell or source your configuration file:

```
% source ~/.cshrc
$ source ~/.bashrc
```

## Finding Ports to Install

Before you can install a port, you'll need to make sure it exists in the ports tree. This can be done in one of two ways. The first is using port search, which is very simple to use. For example, to look for xchat:

```
% port search xchat
irc/xchat      1.8.11  IRC client with gtk and text interfaces
irc/xchat2     2.0.1   IRC client for gtk2
```

The alternative is to use the web-based interface found on the DarwinPorts web site. You can view by category and search from this interface, but because the *PortIndex* file it uses isn't always up-to-date, you may have better luck with the port command.

## Installing Ports

Now that we've found something to install, it's time to learn how to install it. If you've ever worked with the FreeBSD ports collection, this section should look very familiar to you.

Sticking with XChat as our example, we have two options. We can install the xchat port, which uses GTK+ version 1, or the xchat2 port, which uses GTK+ Version 2. For the sake of example, we'll choose xchat2.

There are also two ways to install the port. The first way is to change to the port's directory and run port install:

```
% cd /path/to/darwinports/dports/irc/xchat2
% sudo -s
<enter your password>
# port install && port clean
```

The second method can be run from anywhere on the filesystem:

```
% sudo -s
<enter your password>
# port install xchat2 && port clean xchat2
```

As long as you have your path set properly and the port you're trying to install is in the *PortIndex*, installation should proceed normally.

## Updating the Ports Tree

Since the ports developers frequently add new ports and update existing ports, you'll want to keep your ports tree up-to-date. Doing so is fairly simple:

```
% cd /path/to/darwinports
% cvs -q up -Pd
```

If you notice changes to the base directory, you'll want to rebuild the DarwinPorts base system as well. This is done using the same commands used to install it initially:

```
% cd /path/to/darwinports
% sudo -s
<enter your password>
# make && make install && make clean
```

As you'd expect, the port command has other options, such as uninstall, fetch, extract, and build, to name a few. Check the port manpage for a full explanation of each option and more information.

At the time of writing, there are over 750 ports in the DarwinPorts tree and that number is growing daily. If your favorite application isn't already available in the ports tree, you can either create a port of it or join the Darwin-Ports mailing list and request that someone else create a port of it.

## See Also

- man port
- *http://www.bsdnews.org/01/darwinports.php* (the original article on BSDnews)
- The DarwinPorts web site (*http://darwinports.opendarwin.org/*)
- The DarwinPorts web interface to the ports collection (*http://darwinports. opendarwin.org/ports/*)
- The DarwinPorts mailing list (*http://www.opendarwin.org/mailman/listinfo/ darwinports/*)
- The Fink web site (*http://fink.sourceforge.net/*)

# Grokking BSD

## Hacks 89-100

Heinlein fans will recognize the word grok as the Martian word for "to be one with" or "thorough understanding." Indeed, you will sometimes feel like a stranger in a strange land when learning Unix. As any Unix guru can attest, however, the rewards far outweigh the initial learning curve.

This final chapter is a hodgepodge of useful and sometimes amusing tidbits. A sure sign you're on the right road to grokking BSD is when you're able to see both the usefulness and the quirky humor that is inherent in all Unix systems.

### HACK #89  How'd He Know That?

Make the most of your available resources.

Unless you've achieved Unix guru status, you probably find yourself asking "how did he know that?" whenever you're around other Unix users or read a really cool snippet in a book. Here's a little secret: he probably had to look it up. As I tell my students, "No one knows everything. Make sure the one thing you do know is where to go to get the information you need."

### Online Resources

If you're using FreeBSD, there is no shortage of well-written documentation. If you haven't already, bookmark the FreeBSD Documentation page at *http://www.freebsd.org/docs*.

There you'll find hyperlinks to the four handbooks, the FAQ, how-to articles, online manpages, as well as other sources of information. There's a very good chance that someone else has already documented what you want to do.

## Keeping Offline Resources Up-to-Date

Online resources are great, but what if you don't always have access to an Internet connection? If you installed the doc distribution, you already have most of those resources on your hard drive. You'll find the handbooks, FAQ, and articles in */usr/share/doc*. That directory contains symlinks so you can quickly navigate to the desired resource.

> If you haven't installed the doc directory structure, you can do so through /stand/sysinstall. Enter Configuration, then Distributions, and use your spacebar to select doc.

The online resources receive daily updates, so be sure to update your docs when you use cvsup. Make sure your *cvsup* file includes this line:

```
doc-all tag=.
```

> If you're not using cvsup [Hack #80] yet, you have no idea what you're missing!

As cvsup retrieves the latest docs, it will write them to */usr/doc*. This will *not* overwrite or update existing files in */usr/share/doc*. Also, if you've ever poked about */usr/doc*, you probably noticed that the resources themselves are written in SGML, making them a bit hard to read (unless you enjoy wading through tags).

How do you merge in those new changes? It's going to require a conversion of SGML to HTML. To achieve that, first install the docproj-nojadetex port:

```
# cd /usr/ports/textproc/docproj-nojadetex
# make install clean
```

Then:

```
# cd /usr/doc
# make install clean
```

This will merge all of the changes into the HTML files in */usr/share/doc*. If you add this step to your cvsup routine, your offline resources will always be up-to-date.

## What Did the Manpage Forget to Say?

Have you ever read a manpage and been unclear on how a certain switch worked? Perhaps you thought you understood the syntax until you tried it out and only managed to produce syntax error messages? Even more maddeningly, you might scour the Internet for concrete examples only to find endless links to the same manpage!

When this happens to me, I consider the program's source as a possible answer. If you're thinking, "I'm not a programmer; I couldn't read source code if my life depended on it," don't just skip to the next hack. You can still read comments, and most source in the FreeBSD core is very well commented.

Here's an example. I was reading through man mac_portacl, which indicates that the rule MIB takes this syntax:

```
idtype:id:protocol:port[,idtype:id:protocol:port,...]
```

but didn't give a specific example of a working rule. Since this particular MAC policy doesn't do anything until you successfully create a rule, I was looking for a more concrete example of an effective rule. And, since this module is fairly new, there weren't any tutorials or how-tos on the Internet. So, before hitting the mailing lists, I took a peek at the source.

To locate any C source file, use the locate command. Pass it the name of what you're looking for, followed by a .c. For example:

```
% locate mac_portacl.c
/usr/src/sys/security/mac_portacl/mac_portacl.c
```

You must have src installed in order for this to work, and, as indicated, it will only find source code written in C. Happily, that's most of the FreeBSD core. You can use /sys/sysinstall to install all of the src distributions. If disk space is an issue or it's not appropriate to install source on the system you're logged into, you can read the source online at *http://minnie.tuhs.org/ FreeBSD-srctree/FreeBSD.html*.

If you have src installed but don't see any results or do receive an error message that your database is too small, update the database and try again:

```
% su
Password:
# /usr/libexec/locate.updatedb
>>> WARNING
>>> Executing updatedb as root. This WILL reveal all filenames
>>> on your machine to all login users, which is a security risk.
# exit
```

Once you've located the source file, skim through its comments:

```
% grep '*' /usr/src/sys/security/mac_portacl/mac_portacl.c | tail +30
```

Here, I told grep to search for an asterisk (*), since C comments always include one. If you forget to enclose the asterisk within single quotes (' '), you won't receive any results, as it is also a shell wildcard. You may want to adjust tail +30 for your own purposes. Source code begins with anywhere from 25 to 40 lines of copyright and licensing comments. Here I've told `tail` to ignore the first (+) 30 lines of comments.

In this particular case, the comments included the example I hoped for:

```
* # sysctl security.mac.portacl.rules="uid:425:tcp:80,uid:425:tcp:79"
*
* This ruleset, for example, permits uid 425 to bind TCP ports 80 (http)
* and 79 (finger).  User names and group names can't be used directly
* because the kernel only knows about uids and gids.
```

Your mileage will vary, but source is definitely another resource at your disposal.

### See Also

- `man hier` (includes a description of the contents of */usr/share/doc/*)
- `man tail`

## Create Your Own Manpages

As a Unix administrator, the one word of sage advice you can give to any user that is guaranteed to solve any problem is RTFM.

What's an administrator to do when informed by a user that there is no manpage to read? Perhaps the application in question is a custom application or script, or perhaps it's a third-party program that didn't come with a manpage. Why not create the missing manual yourself?

### Manpage Basics

Creating a manpage isn't all that difficult. After all, a manpage is simply a text file—more specifically, a gzipped text file sprinkled with `groff` macros. (I'm quite sure `groff` gets its name from the choking sound you make as you try to decipher *its* manpage.) For `man` to do its magic, which starts with being able to *find* the page, the manpage must live in a directory `manpath` can see.

Not surprisingly, `manpath`'s configuration file, */etc/manpath.config*, contains those paths:

```
% grep MAP /etc/manpath.config
# MANPATH_MAP        path_element        manpath_element
MANPATH_MAP          /bin                /usr/share/man
MANPATH_MAP          /usr/bin            /usr/share/man
MANPATH_MAP          /usr/local/bin      /usr/local/man
MANPATH_MAP          /usr/X11R6/bin      /usr/X11R6/man
```

Basically, manpages to programs that come with the system live in */usr/share/man*, third-party applications use */usr/local/man*, and X applications use */usr/X11R6/man*. If you `ls` any of these directories, you'll find directory names that go from *man1* to *man9*. If you're rusty on the function of each manpage section, run:

```
% whatis intro
intro(1)                        - introduction to general commands (tools and
                                  utilities)
intro(2)                        - introduction to system calls and error numbers
intro(3)                        - introduction to the C libraries
intro(4)                        - introduction to devices and device drivers
intro(5)                        - introduction to file formats
intro(6)                        - introduction to games
intro(7)                        - miscellaneous information pages
intro(8)                        - introduction to system maintenance and
                                  operation commands
intro(9)                        - introduction to system kernel interfaces
```

To read a specific section, specify the number between the command and the page, as in man 7 foo.

## Creating a Manpage

You can whip up a nicely formatted manpage by knowing only three groff commands, as shown in Table 9-1.

*Table 9-1. groff commands*

| Command | Usage |
|---------|-------|
| .\" | A comment |
| .TH | The title |
| .SH NAME | The only required section |

The easiest way to convince yourself of this is to take a few minutes to type out the following custom manpage. When you're finished, save it as */usr/local/man/man1/boss.1* (as the root user) and view it with man boss. That way, you'll be able to compare those formatting sequences with how the results are displayed on your screen.

```
.\" Manpage for boss.
.\" Contact admin@mycompany.com to correct errors or omissions.
.TH man 1 "04 January 2004" "1.0" "boss man page"
.SH NAME
boss \- man page for boss
.SH SYNOPSIS
boss
.SH DESCRIPTION
The boss is an ornery creature that can be
appeased with doughnuts and the occasional afternoon
off for golf.
.SH OPTIONS
The boss does not take any options.
```

```
.SH SEE ALSO
doughnut(1), golf(8)
.SH BUGS
No known bugs at this time.
.SH AUTHOR
Dru Lavigne (dlavigne6@sympatico.ca)
```

 If you wish, compress your manpage with gzip /usr/local/
man/man1/boss.1.

If you take the time to view this listing, you'll find it looks like any manpage. In fact, it's an excellent idea to take a look at several manpages before you create your own. This will give you an idea of how you'd like your custom page to appear.

Notice first that the lines that began with .\" don't appear anywhere in the formatted manpage, as they are comments. The information in the title (.TH) line appears at the very top and bottom of the manpage. The .SH lines appear nicely bolded, and the following lines are indented for you. Remember that SH. NAME is mandatory, but you can create as many .SH sections as you wish.

As you read other manpages, you'll see that SYNOPSIS, DESCRIPTION, OPTIONS, EXAMPLES, DIAGNOSTICS, ENVIRONMENT, SEE ALSO, HISTORY, and BUGS are quite common. You'll also get an idea of what type of text belongs in each section.

## Getting Fancier

If you want to include fancier formatting in your manpage, find an existing manpage that has the desired format. Then, instead of opening the manpage with man, send it to zmore. (Remember, you won't be able to read gzipped manpages directly with more.)

For example, if I want to include switches, I'd borrow from a manpage with switches. ls springs to mind. So I'll read through:

```
% zmore /usr/share/man/man1/ls.1.gz
```

and compare it to man ls. In this manpage, the switches occur in the DESCRIPTION section and the first switch is -A. The switch itself is in bold text and the switch description is indented with the characters . and .. covered over with white. The formatting sequences to achieve this are:

```
.BL -tag -width indent
.It Fl A
List all entries except for
.Pa \&.
and
.Pa .. .
```

If you're curious as to the exact meaning of each formatting sequence, you'll find them scattered throughout man 7 groff. If you don't have the time to be curious, simply find the section that does what you want and add it to your own manpage. Save your results, then see if it worked by sending your custom manpage to man.

## Printing Manpages

It's often desirable to print certain manpages. If you've ever tried sending a manpage directly to a printer, you probably found that the results weren't what you were expecting. However, you can use groff to convert the manpage to something more printer-friendly. PostScript is usually your best bet, and you're in luck, as groff knows how to convert to PostScript.

First, it's not a bad idea to get the exact location of the source of the manpage. Continuing with ls as an example:

```
% man -w ls
/usr/share/man/cat1/ls.1.gz (source: /usr/share/man/man1/ls.1.gz)
```

Note that you're interested in the source, not in the location that includes the word cat.

Once you know the location, use zcat to open the compressed file, pipe the results to groff, and redirect the groff output to a PostScript file:

```
# zcat /usr/share/man/man1/ls.1.gz | groff > ls.ps
# file ls.ps
ls.ps: PostScript document text conforming at level 3.0
```

Note that the default invocation of groff assumes that you wish to convert a manpage to PostScript, so you need no additional switches.

## Hacking the Hack

If you'd like to publish your manpages on a local web site, groff can also convert to HTML—see man 1 groff for details.

If you prefer to convert to PDF, consider installing GNU GhostScript from your ports or packages collection. Once installed, read man 1 gs for more details.

## See Also

* man manpath
* man 7 groff (the groff formatting commands—look for the Request Short Reference section)
* man 7 mdoc (a mini-tutorial that includes a template for creating manpages)

## Get the Most Out of Manpages

#91

Now that you know how to create your own manpages, you'll want to know how to get the most out of your manpage viewing.

Since most documentation on Unix systems lives within manpages, it pays to know how to get the most out of your manpage-reading experience. How do you make sure you're aware of all of the manpages installed on a system? How do you zero in on the information you need, without having to read an entire manpage? Yes, it's a great experience to read all of man tcsh at least once in your life, but you don't want to do that when you're only interested in a certain shell variable.

### Finding Installed Manpages

You may have noticed that, by default, whatis [Hack #13] doesn't find custom manpages or those installed by third-party applications. Not only is this inconvenient, but it can also prevent your users from getting the most out of the applications installed on a system.

Remember /etc/manpath.config from "Create Your Own Manpages" [Hack #90]?

```
% grep MAP /etc/manpath.config
# MANPATH_MAP     path_element          manpath_element
MANPATH_MAP       /bin                  /usr/share/man
MANPATH_MAP       /usr/bin              /usr/share/man
MANPATH_MAP       /usr/local/bin        /usr/local/man
MANPATH_MAP       /usr/X11R6/bin        /usr/X11R6/man
```

The makewhatis command actually creates the whatis database and, by default, makewhatis reads only /usr/share/man. It'll skip any manpages in /usr/local/man and /usr/X11R6/man, because it doesn't know they exist!

To gather in those missing manpages, pass these extra directories to makewhatis:

```
# makewhatis /usr/local/man /usr/X11R6/man
#
```

The superuser can run this command at any time, say, after installing new software. If you're a forgetful or appropriately lazy superuser, consider adding this as a regular cron job.

Now users will be aware of all of the manpages on the system.

### Navigational Tricks

There's nothing worse than wading through dozens of pages of information that are irrelevant to your question. Why wade when you can zero in on the information you want? When you read a manpage, man sends the text to your default pager—a program designed for speedy navigation.

FreeBSD 4.1 replaced the more pager with less. less is chock-full of useful and configurable navigation tricks, so this is a case where less really is more.

 Even though your *.cshrc* file and man man show more as your default pager, remember more is now really less.

less even comes with its own help system containing an itemized list of all of its neat tricks. Whenever you're in a manpage—or, for that matter, in any file you've sent to a pager—simply type h to see the help screen.

I won't repeat that help here, but Table 9-2 shows some navigational keys to get you moving around.

*Table 9-2. less navigation keys*

| Key | Behavior |
| --- | --- |
| Enter | Scrolls down one line |
| y | Scrolls up one line (think "yikes, I missed it!") |
| Spacebar | Scrolls down one page |
| b | Scrolls up (back) one page |
| g | Goes to the beginning of the manpage |
| q | Quits the pager (so you don't have to read the whole manpage) |

## Customizing less

It's well worth your time to experiment with how less formats its output. For example, when you open a manpage, the prompt at the bottom of your screen indicates how many bytes of that manpage you've read. If you type -m, you'll change to the short prompt, a single colon (:). -M changes to the long prompt, which displays the line range you're currently viewing.

If you really want to know what line you're on, try -N. Read up on -P to create your own custom prompt string.

You can also configure how many lines you scroll, also known as the window size. Here I'll change the window size to 10 lines:

```
-z
Scroll window size: 10
Scroll window size is 10 lines  (press RETURN)
```

Now when I press my spacebar, I'll scroll down 10 lines instead of the entire screen.

If you experiment with the dozens of options listed in help, you'll find that they only last for the contents of the current manpage. If you find options you like, make them permanent by adding them to your ~/.cshrc file. Here I'll permanently configure the -M, or long, prompt and a window size of 10:

```
setenv LESS Mz10
```

Note that I've simply created a string of desired options, minus the switch indicator (-). I'll also have to change the line setenv PAGER more to setenv PAGER less, so that applications that honor my pager choice will use less instead of more. To test your changes, force the shell to reread its configuration file, then open up a manpage:

```
% source ~/.cshrc
% man man
```

That manpage should now have a customized prompt and window.

## Searching Text

Now that you can move around, you'll want to search for the information you need. After all, you're usually looking for something specific when you read a manpage. Fortunately, less provides an easy-to-use search feature. Press /, the forward slash. Your prompt will change to / while less waits for you to type in a search string of one or more words.

 Consider adding I to the less configuration in your .cshrc file to enable case-insensitive searching. Without it, searching for /long format in man ls will skip the desired section, as it is entitled The Long Format.

Press Enter once you've typed in a search string, and less will take you to the first occurrence of that string. Repeatedly pressing n will scroll you through the next occurrences. Press N to scroll back through your search results. If you change your mind and want to search for something else, press /.

Suppose you're reading or searching along and find an interesting bit you'll want to refer to again. Mark your current position with:

```
m
mark: a
```

Here I've marked my position with the letter a. I'll then carry on with reading the results of the rest of my search. To return to that position, I simply type a single quote and the position marker ('a). You can mark as many as 26 positions (one for each lowercase letter).

You can also use two single quotes ('') to toggle back and forth between two positions. For example, I may be in man systat and can't believe the display includes a pigs option. So I do a search for /pigs and read up on that type of display. ' ' will bring me back to the original line that piqued my curiosity. Another ' ' will put me back at my search result.

### See Also

- manpath
- man man
- man makewhatis
- man less

## Apply, Understand, and Create Patches
#### Sometimes only the little differences matter.

Despite all your best efforts, eventually you'll end up with multiple versions of a file. Perhaps you forgot to keep your *.vimrc* in sync between two machines [Hack #10]. Alternatively, you may want to see the changes between an old configuration file and the new version. You may even want to distribute a bugfix to a manpage or program.

Sending the entire changed file won't always work: it takes up too much space and it's hard to find exactly what changed. It's often easier and usually faster to see only the changes (see "Automate Updates" [Hack #80] for a practical example). That's where diff comes in: it shows the differences between two files.

As you'd expect, applying changes manually is tedious. Enter patch, which applies the changes from a diff file.

### Finding Differences

Suppose you've shared a useful script with a friend and both of you have added new features. Instead of printing out both copies and marking differences by hand or, worse, trying to reconcile things by copying and pasting from one program to another, use diff to see only the differences between the two programs.

For example, I've customized an earlier version of the *copydotfiles.pl* script from "Customize User Configurations" [Hack #9] to run on Linux instead of FreeBSD. When it came time to unify the programs, I wanted to see the changes as a whole. diff requires two arguments, the source file and the destination. Here's the cryptic (at first) result:

```
$ diff -u copydotfiles.pl copydotfiles_linux.pl
--- copydotfiles.pl        2004-02-23 16:09:49.000000000 -0800
+++ copydotfiles_linux.pl        2004-02-23 16:09:32.000000000 -0800
```

```
@@ -5,8 +5,8 @@
 #     - change ownership of those files
 # You may wish to change these two constants for your system:

-use constant HOMEDIR => '/usr/home';
-use constant SKELDIR => '/usr/share/skel';
+use constant HOMEDIR => '/home';
+use constant SKELDIR => '/etc/skel';

 use strict;

@@ -19,8 +19,8 @@
 {
     for my $dotfile (@ARGV)
     {
-        my $source = catfile( SKELDIR(),       'dot' . $dotfile );
-        my $dest   = catfile( $user->{homedir},       $dotfile );
+        my $source = catfile( SKELDIR(),       $dotfile );
+        my $dest   = catfile( $user->{homedir}, $dotfile );

        if (-e $dest)
        {
```

This output reveals only three changes. Linux and FreeBSD keep user home directories and skeleton configuration files in different directories. Fortunately, this only involved changing two constants at the top of the file.

> The -u flag produces unified output, mingling the source and destination lines. It's not the default, but it's the easiest to read and to explain. Count yourself lucky if you never run across the alternatives.

As you may have guessed from the name, only the differences appear. Each of the two files has a separate marker at the leftmost column. Let's look at that header again:

```
--- copydotfiles.pl        2004-02-23 16:09:49.000000000 -0800
+++ copydotfiles_linux.pl  2004-02-23 16:09:32.000000000 -0800
```

The first line marks the source file, the FreeBSD version. We're marking changes against that file. diff will mark lines that have changed from that file with a leading minus (-) character. The second line marks the destination file, the Linux version. Lines that have changed in this file appear with a leading plus (+) character.

diff produces output that you can apply to the first file to produce the second file. That is, you should remove (or subtract) all of the lines with the leading minus character and add all of the lines with the leading plus character to produce the destination file.

The rest of the output consists of *hunks*. Each hunk also has a header:

```
@@ -5,8 +5,8 @@
```

This indicates that the hunk starts on line 5 of the source file and affects eight lines. It also starts on the fifth line of the destination file and affects eight lines—a simple substitution. In general, you can ignore this unless you're working on something really detailed.

The actual lines of the file are more important. Pay close attention to the leading characters.

```
#     - change ownership of those files
# You may wish to change these two constants for your system:

-use constant HOMEDIR => '/usr/home';
-use constant SKELDIR => '/usr/share/skel';
+use constant HOMEDIR => '/home';
+use constant SKELDIR => '/etc/skel';

use strict;
```

Again, this is a simple substitution. Since diff only works on lines, it has no way of indicating that only the value of the constants has changed.

## Applying Patches

By redirecting this output to a file, I can produce a patch file. Though anyone who can read diff output could apply those changes manually, it's much easier to use the patch program, especially if the file I'm patching has had other changes in the meantime. As long as those changes do not overlap, patch will work magically well.

Suppose I'd written:

```
$ diff -u copydotfiles.pl copydotfiles_linux.pl > dotfiles.patch
```

Now anyone who wants to apply the changes from the latter file to the former file can apply the patch. Copy the *dotfiles.patch* file into the same directory as *copydotfiles.pl* and use the command:

```
$ patch < dotfiles.patch
patching file copydotfiles.pl
```

If you're lucky, the patch will apply with little fanfare. If you're unlucky, things may have moved around in your file since the creation of the patch. In that case, patch may warn about some fuzz. If I rearrange a couple of lines in the first hunk that aren't actually changed in the patch, I might see a message such as:

```
$ patch < dot.patch
patching file copydotfiles.pl
Hunk #1 succeeded at 7 with fuzz 2 (offset 2 lines).
```

If I were really unlucky, I'd have had changes in the lines the patch also changed. patch tries as hard as it can to massage patches, but sometimes it just can't resolve things. You'll see output like this in those cases:

```
$ patch < dot.patch
patching file copydotfiles.pl
Hunk #1 succeeded at 7 with fuzz 2 (offset 2 lines).
Hunk #2 FAILED at 21.
1 out of 2 hunks FAILED -- saving rejects to file copydotfiles.pl.rej
```

In this case, it's up to you, the user, to resolve any changes. patch has actually created two new files, *copydotfiles.pl.orig* and *copydotfiles.pl.rej*. The first contains the file before any patching attempt; the second contains the hunks patch could not apply.

Fortunately, the original file does contain the hunks that could apply without conflicts. In this case, it's easier to open the *copydotfiles.pl.rej* file to apply the changes manually.

```
***************
*** 21,28 ****
    {
        for my $dotfile (@ARGV)
        {
-           my $source = catfile( SKELDIR( ),       'dot' . $dotfile );
-           my $dest   = catfile( $user->{homedir},       $dotfile );

            if (-e $dest)
            {
--- 21,28 ----
    {
        for my $dotfile (@ARGV)
        {
+           my $source = catfile( SKELDIR( ),       $dotfile );
+           my $dest   = catfile( $user->{homedir}, $dotfile );

            if (-e $dest)
            {
```

This format is a little harder to read than the unified format, but it's reasonably straightforward. The top half comes from the source file in the patch and represents lines 21 through 28 of the original file. Again, the leading minus character represents lines to remove. The bottom half comes from the destination file in the patch, also lines 21 through 28. This contains two lines to add.

Looking in *copydotfiles.pl* around those lines, it turns out that the first line containing SKELDIR( ) has changed subtly, thus causing the conflict:

```
    {
        for my $dotfile (@ARGV)
        {
```

```
my $source = catfile( SKELDIR( ),      "dot$dotfile" );
my $dest   = catfile( $user->{homedir},      $dotfile );

if (-e $dest)
{
```

I have two options: I could edit the file directly, making the modifications as seen in either the source file or the destination file of the patch, or I could ignore this hunk if the local modifications are better than those of the patch.

In this case, the patch is clearly an improvement. Since it's only two lines, I'll just make the changes directly. Otherwise, I could revert the changes in my local file and try to reapply the rejected hunks.

## Creating Patches

It's often handy to create patches from normal files, as in the previous example, when sharing code or text with another user. It's also useful to see the differences between configuration files when upgrading an application. Knowing how to read a diff between your version of *httpd.conf* and *httpd. conf.default* can save you hours of debugging time.

What if you want to find differences between entire directories, though? Suppose you want to see the changes between two versions of a program. If you can't upgrade to the new version right away but want to see if there's a patch available that you can apply, use diff on the directories themselves. Be sure to pass the recursive flag (-r) if you want to compare files in subdirectories:

```
$ diff -ur sdl/trunk SDL_Perl-2.1.0 > sdl_trunk.patch
```

If that's not appropriate and you want to patch only a couple of files at a time, run diff multiple times. Append the output to a combined patch. patch is smart enough to recognize the start of file markers:

```
$ diff -u sdl/trunk/CHANGELOG SDL_Perl-2.1.0/CHANGELOG >> \
    sdl_textfiles.patch
$ diff -u sdl/trunk/README SDL_Perl-2.1.0/README >> \
    sdl_textfiles.patch
$ diff -u sdl/trunk/INSTALL SDL_Perl-2.1.0/INSTALL >> \
    sdl_textfiles.patch
```

Finally, if you need to create a patch for a file that doesn't exist, use the null file flag (-n) with */dev/null* as the source:

```
$ diff -un /dev/null SDL_Perl-2.1.0/LICENSE >> \
    sdl_textfiles.patch
```

This will create the file when someone applies the patch. You could also touch the file in the source directory.

## Revision Control

Life's much easier when you're working with revision control. Someday, you may find yourself patching source code or text files in core BSD. Modify the code in your tree, make sure it works, and then use cvs diff -u to generate patches to mail to the appropriate development list.

Subversion, the likely successor to CVS, generates the right kind of patches without the -u flag—simply use svn  diff. There is a FreeBSD port and a NetBSD package for Subversion. You can also download binary packages and source for most operating systems from *http://subversion.tigris.org/*.

Once you're used to using patches to keep track of file differences, you may find yourself tempted to keep all important files under version control. Hey, why not?

### See Also

- man diff
- man patch
- "CVS homedir," Joey Hess's Linux Journal article on keeping his home directory in CVS (*http://www.linuxjournal.com/article.php?sid=5976*)

## Display Hardware Information

**HACK #93**

If you're new to FreeBSD, you may be wondering where to find information about your system's hardware and the resources it uses.

You've probably noticed that your FreeBSD system didn't ship with a Microsoft-style Device Manager. However, it does have plenty of useful utilities for gathering hardware information.

### Viewing Boot Messages

When you boot your system, the kernel probes your hardware devices and displays the results to your screen. You can view these messages, even before you log in, by pressing the scroll lock key and using your up arrow to scroll back through the message buffer. When you're finished, press scroll lock again to return to the login or command prompt.

You can type dmesg any time you need to read the system message buffer. However, if it's been a while since bootup, it's quite possible that system messages have overwritten the boot messages. If so, look in the file */var/run/dmesg.boot*, which contains the messages from the latest boot. This is an ASCII text file, so you can send it to a pager such as more or less.

You may find it more convenient to search for something particular. For example, suppose you've added sound support to your kernel by adding device pcm to your kernel configuration file. This command will show if the PCM device was successfully loaded by the new kernel:

```
% grep pcm /var/run/dmesg.boot
pcm0: <Creative CT5880-C> port 0xa800-0xa83f irq 10 at device 7.0 on pci0
pcm0: <SigmaTel STAC9708/11 AC97 Codec>
```

In this example, the kernel did indeed probe my Creative sound card at bootup.

## Viewing Resource Information

Sometimes you just want to know which devices are using which system resources. This command will display the IRQs, DMAs, I/O ports, and I/O memory addresses in use:

```
% devinfo -u
Interrupt request lines:
    0 (root0)
    1 (atkbd0)
    2 (root0)
    3 (sio1)
    4 (sio0)
    5 (rl0)
    6 (fdc0)
    7 (ppc0)
    8 (root0)
    9 (acpi0)
    10 (pcm0)
    11 (rl1)
    12 (psm0)
    13 (root0)
    14 (ata0)
    15 (ata1)
DMA request lines:
    0-1 (root0)
    2 (fdc0)
    3 (ppc0)
    4-7 (root0)
I/O ports:
    0x0-0xf (root0)
    0x10-0x1f (acpi_sysresource0)
    0x20-0x21 (root0)
<snip>
I/O memory addresses:
    0x0-0x9ffff (root0)
    0xa0000-0xbffff (vga0)
    0xc0000-0xcbfff (orm0)
```

```
0xcc000-0xfbffffff (root0)
0xfc000000-0xfdffffff (agp0)
0xfe000000-0xffffffff (root0)
```

Alternately, use devinfo -r if you prefer to see your listing by device.

If you're unsure what a device is, use the whatis command. For example, in my listing, ppc0 uses IRQ 7 and DMA 3. To find out what ppc0 is:

```
% whatis ppc
ppc(4)          Parallel Port Chipset driver
```

Don't include the trailing number when using the whatis command.

## Gathering Interface Statistics

There are several ways to gather network interface information. One of the handiest is the -i switch to netstat:

```
% netstat -i
```

| Name | Mtu | Network | Address | Ipkts | Ierrs | Opkts | Oerrs | Coll |
|------|-----|---------|---------|-------|-------|-------|-------|------|
| rl0* | 1500 | <Link#1> | 00:05:5d:d2:19:b7 | 0 | 0 | 0 | 0 | 0 |
| rl1* | 1500 | <Link#2> | 00:05:5d:d1:ff:9d | 0 | 0 | 0 | 0 | 0 |
| ed0 | 1500 | <Link#3> | 00:50:ba:de:36:33 | 15247 | 0 | 11301 | 0 | 78 |
| ed0 | 1500 | 192.168.2 | genisis. | 15091 | - | 11222 | - | - |
| lp0* | 1500 | <Link#4> | | 0 | 0 | 0 | 0 | 0 |
| lo0 | 16384 | <Link#5> | | 179 | 0 | 179 | 0 | 0 |
| lo0 | 16384 | your-net | localhost | 179 | - | 179 | - | - |

This command shows all interfaces, both physical and virtual. This particular system has three network interface cards: rl0, rl1, and ed0. The first two interfaces are shut down, as indicated by the * after the device name. These three are Ethernet cards, as indicated by their MAC addresses. (This is also an excellent way to find all of the MAC addresses on your system).

The ed0 interface and loopback interface (lo0) have each been configured with a hostname and an IP address, as indicated by the Network column. If you're only interested in seeing interfaces configured with an IPv4 address, add the -f (family) switch:

```
% netstat -i -f inet
```

| ed0 | 1500 | 192.168.2 | genisis. | 15091 | - | 11222 | - | - |
| lo0 | 16384 | your-net | localhost | 179 | - | 179 | - | - |

## Viewing Kernel Environment

You can also find hardware information by using kenv to view your kernel environment. kenv will dump several screens worth of information, so use grep when possible to zero in on the information you want. For example, to view IRQ information:

```
% kenv | grep irq
hint.ata.0.irq="14"
```

```
hint.ata.1.irq="15"
hint.atkbd.0.irq="1"
hint.ed.0.irq="10"
hint.fdc.0.irq="6"
hint.ie.0.irq="10"
hint.le.0.irq="5"
hint.lnc.0.irq="10"
hint.pcic.1.irq="11"
hint.ppc.0.irq="7"
hint.psm.0.irq="12"
hint.sio.0.irq="4"
hint.sio.1.irq="3"
hint.sio.2.irq="5"
hint.sio.3.irq="9"
hint.sn.0.irq="10"
```

If you're unsure what is using a listed IRQ, use whatis to look up the second word (the one after hint). For example, this will show what is using my IRQ 12:

```
% whatis psm
psm(4)      - PS/2 mouse style pointing device driver
```

I actually prefer the output of kenv to that of devinfo. Here, I'll search for the I/O addresses used by my COM ports:

```
% kenv | grep port | grep sio
hint.sio.0.port="0x3F8"
hint.sio.1.port="0x2F8"
hint.sio.2.port="0x3E8"
hint.sio.3.port="0x2E8"
```

To see which devices are disabled:

```
% kenv | grep disabled
hint.sio.2.disabled="1"
hint.sio.3.disabled="1"
```

BSD gives the first com port the number zero, so it looks like I have COM3 and COM4 disabled on this system.

## See Also

- man dmesg
- man devinfo
- man netstat
- man kenv

## Determine Who Is on the System
#### #94
As a system administrator, it pays to know what's happening on your
systems.

Sure, you spend time reading your logs, but do you take advantage of the
other information-gathering utilities available to you? Silently, in the background, your system tracks all kinds of neat information. If you know
enough to peek under the system hood, you can get a very good view of
what is occurring on the system at any given point in time.

> For the experienced hacker, the output from these com-
> mands may suggest interesting scripting possibilities.

### Who's on First?

Have you ever needed to know who logged into a system and for how long?
Use the users command to see who's logged in now:

```
% users
dru biko
```

Perhaps you prefer to know who is on which terminal. Try who. Here, the H
includes column headers and the u shows each user's idle time:

```
% who -Hu
NAME            LINE    TIME          IDLE  FROM
dru             ttyv1   Jan 25 08:59  01:00
biko            ttyv5   Jan 25 09:57  .
dru             ttyp0   Jan 25 09:58  00:02 (hostname)
```

Feel free to experiment with who's switches to find an output that suits your
needs. Here, dru and biko have logged in physically at this system's keyboard using virtual terminals 1 and 5. dru has also logged in over the first
psuedoterminal (over the network) from the specified hostname.

To find out what everyone is doing, use w:

```
% w
10:07AM  up  1:20, 9 users, load averages: 0.02, 0.02, 0.09
USER            TTY     FROM              LOGIN@  IDLE WHAT
dru             v1      -                 8:59AM  1:08 pine
biko            v5      -                 9:57AM   - w
dru             p0      hostname          9:58AM   4 -csh (csh)
```

> If you're just interested in that first line of output, use
> uptime.

Notice that as a regular user, I was easily able to find out who is logged in, where they are, and what they're currently doing. If you don't want regular users knowing what commands other users are currently running, see "Tighten Security with Mandatory Access Control" [Hack #57].

## When Did That Happen?

You're not limited to finding out what's happening at this particular moment. Use lastlogin to see the most recent time at which each of your users logged in:

```
% lastlogin
dru        ttyv1                    Sun Jan 25 08:59:36 2004
biko       ttyv5                    Sun Jan 25 09:57:18 2004
dlavigne   ttyv6                    Sat Jan 24 09:48:32 2004
dru        ttyp0    hostname        Sun Jan 25 09:58:50 2004
rembackup  ttyp0    hostname        Fri Jan 23 01:00:00 2004
```

For a slightly different output, last can show who is still logged in:

```
% last | grep still
dru        ttyp0    hostname        Sun Jan 25 09:58    still logged in
dru        ttyv1                    Sun Jan 25 08:59    still logged in
biko       ttyv5                    Sun Jan 25 09:57    still logged in
```

Do you need a record of system shutdowns or reboots? The /var/log/wtmp database holds this information. Use last to view the desired statistics:

```
% last reboot
reboot     ~                        Tue Jan 20 15:37
reboot     ~                        Tue Nov 25 07:24
reboot     ~                        Sun Aug  3 09:05
wtmp begins Tue Jul  1 15:27:26 EDT 2003

% last shutdown
shutdown   ~                        Wed Dec 24 22:14
wtmp begins Tue Jul  1 15:27:26 EDT 2003
```

## Details, Details

Another option to consider is enabling system accounting, which maintains a database of extremely detailed statistics of every process and subprocess that has been executed on a system.

```
# touch /var/account/acct
# accton /var/account/acct
```

Note that the accton command will fail if you don't specify the name of the accounting log or if that log doesn't already exist. Also, in a queer case of logic, typing accton *with no arguments* really turns accounting off.

Once accounting is enabled, use `lastcomm` to view the contents of */var/account/acct*:

```
% lastcomm
lastcomm    -   dlavigne    ttyv6    0.00 secs Sun Jan 25 11:33
man         -   dlavigne    ttyv6    0.00 secs Sun Jan 25 11:33
sh          -   dlavigne    ttyv6    0.00 secs Sun Jan 25 11:33
sh          -F  dlavigne    ttyv6    0.00 secs Sun Jan 25 11:33
less        -   dlavigne    ttyv6    0.00 secs Sun Jan 25 11:33
col         -   dlavigne    ttyv6    0.00 secs Sun Jan 25 11:33
groff       -   dlavigne    ttyv6    0.00 secs Sun Jan 25 11:33
grotty      -   dlavigne    ttyv6    0.00 secs Sun Jan 25 11:33
troff       -   dlavigne    ttyv6    0.08 secs Sun Jan 25 11:33
tbl         -   dlavigne    ttyv6    0.00 secs Sun Jan 25 11:33
zcat        -   dlavigne    ttyv6    0.00 secs Sun Jan 25 11:33
cron        -F  root        _        0.00 secs Sun Jan 25 11:33
sh          -   operator    _        0.00 secs Sun Jan 25 11:33
sh          -   operator    _        0.00 secs Sun Jan 25 11:33
dd          -   operator    _        0.00 secs Sun Jan 25 11:33
mv          -   operator    _        0.00 secs Sun Jan 25 11:33
mv          -   operator    _        0.00 secs Sun Jan 25 11:33
mv          -   operator    _        0.00 secs Sun Jan 25 11:33
rm          -   operator    _        0.00 secs Sun Jan 25 11:33
jot         -   operator    _        0.00 secs Sun Jan 25 11:33
accton      -   root        ttyv0    0.00 secs Sun Jan 25 11:32
```

This comes from a quiet system one minute after enabling accounting. A cron job happened to be running at the time, hence the operator lines. The user dlavigne6 also opened up a manpage during that period. Note all of the processes involved before man actually started.

> This command can also show you which processes ended abnormally. Search for the D flag, which indicates that the process dumped core:
>
> ```
> % lastcomm | grep -w "D"
> ```

Depending upon your security requirements, you may not want users to have access to such detailed information. After all, `lastcomm` will show every process run by every user. Tightening permissions will fix that:

```
# chmod 600 /var/account/acct
# su dlavigne
% lastcomm
lastcomm: /var/account/acct: Permission denied
```

Also, if you're planning on using `lastcomm` as an extra audit trail, consider changing this file's flags [Hack #56]. You'll also want to have plenty of disk space on the filesystem holding the database.

Finally, to enable system accounting when the system boots, add this line to */etc/rc.conf*:

```
accounting_enable="YES"
```

## See Also

- man users
- man who
- man w
- man lastlogin
- man last
- man lastcomm

### H A C K  Spelling Bee
### #95  For those who edit their text at the command line.

Like most computer users, you probably find yourself spending a fair bit of time typing, whether responding to email, navigating the web, or working on that résumé or thesis. How often do you find yourself looking at a word, wondering if you've spelled it correctly? How often do you rack your brain trying to find a more interesting or descriptive word?

You've probably discovered that Unix doesn't come with a built-in dictionary or thesaurus. Sure, you can install a feature-rich GUI office suite, but what alternatives are there for users who prefer less bloat on their systems or are accessing systems from the command line?

### Quick Spellcheck

If you're in doubt about the spelling of a word, try using look. Simply include as much of the word as you're sure about. For example, if you can't remember how to spell "bodacious" but you're pretty sure it starts with "boda":

```
% look boda
bodach
bodacious
bodaciously
```

If you don't have access to a GUI, see "Use Multiple Screens on One Terminal" **[Hack #12]**.

I find look especially helpful with suffixes. It's very handy if you can't remember when to use "ly", "ally", or "ily". For example:

```
% look mandator
mandator
mandatorily
mandatory
```

## Creating a Dictionary or Thesaurus

look is a useful spellchecker, but it won't show you the meanings or synonyms of a word. Accordingly, I found myself spending a fair bit of time at *http://dictionary.reference.com/*. While there, I noticed a pattern. Whatever word I searched for was appended to the URL as *search?q=<myword>*. Whenever I used the dictionary, the URL started with *dictionary*, which changed to the word *thesaurus* whenever I did a thesaurus lookup. That suggested to me that it would be very easy to generate my own custom lookup utility, so I started out with these two scripts:

```
% more ~/bin/dict
#!/bin/sh
# script to look up the definition of word from dictionary.reference.com
# replaces $1 with user's search string
# or gives error message if user forgets to include search string
if test $1
then
    w3m "http://dictionary.reference.com/search?q="$1""
else
    echo "Don't forget to include the word you would like to search for"
    exit 1
fi
```

```
% more ~/bin/thes

#!/bin/sh
# script to find the synonym of word from thesaurus.reference.com
# replaces $1 with user's search string
# or gives error message if user forgets to include search string
if test $1
then
    w3m "http://thesaurus.reference.com/search?q="$1""
else
    echo "Don't forget to include the word you would like to search for"
    exit 1
fi
```

Recognize those positional parameters we saw before in "Find Things" [Hack #13]? When I use either script, I include the word that I would like to look up.

The utility I chose to grab the results is the command-line browser w3m, which can be built from */usr/ports/www/w3m*. If you have already installed another command-line browser, such as lynx or links, specify your browser in your own script. Don't forget to make your script executable with chmod +x. Then, to look up the meaning of a word:

```
% dict palladium
```

Or, to find its synonyms and antonyms:

```
% thes brusque
```

 If you're not stuck at the command line, Mozilla-based browsers allow you to create similar shortcuts. See Asa Dotzler's article on custom keywords at *http://www.mozilla.org/docs/end-user/keywords.html*.

## Improved Dictionary

Well, that's a fair start—my browser now automagically takes me to the correct section of an online dictionary or thesaurus whenever I'm curious about a particular word. However, what if I want to forgo using a browser altogether? FreeBSD comes with the fetch utility specifically to retrieve web information. Why not use it to retrieve the results?

Before editing my scripts, I tried various invocations of fetch at the command line until I had achieved my desired results. I started out by replacing w3m with fetch (note that I had to supply a word, in this case test, as I was at the command line, not within a script):

```
% fetch "http://dictionary.reference.com/search?q=test"
```

This worked, but it resulted in a file called *search?q=<myword>*, where *<myword>* was the word I had supplied as the parameter. After a while, my home directory would be full of hundreds of files starting with *search?q*.

So, I specified the name of a file to which to write the results:

```
% fetch -o results "http://dictionary.reference.com/search?q=test"
```

Now, regardless of the number of times I use my script, I'll only have one file called *results*. There's a problem with that file, though. It's an HTML file, so unless I enjoy wading through HTML tags in order to read my results, I have to open up that file in a browser. That sorta defeats my goal of not using a browser.

So, I went out on the Web looking for an HTML-to-ASCII converter. I tried out several before settling on a Perl script called html2txt.

I then tried piping the *results* file to the converter:

```
% fetch -o results "http://dictionary.reference.com/search?q=test" \
    | html2txt results
```

```
Cannot open HTML source file : results, Error No such file or directory
Receiving results: 21791 bytes
```

That's when I hit a timing issue. It takes a few seconds for fetch to retrieve the file, so html2txt complains when the shell asks for it to work on that (as of yet) nonexistent file. To solve that, I asked the shell to wait until after fetch was finished by using && instead of | :

```
% fetch -o results "http://dictionary.reference.com/search?q=test" \
        && html2txt results
```

To finish off my command, I ask for the ASCII-fied file to be opened up in a pager so I can view the results:

```
% fetch -o results "http://dictionary.reference.com/search?q=test" \
        && html2txt results && more results.txt
```

Note that this particular converter creates an ASCII file with the same name, but with a *.txt* extension.

## Become a Crossword Champion

Did you know that your system has a built-in crossword-puzzle solver? You may never have to leave a square empty again if you remember this little trick.

Consider a word that resembles:

    t _ _ _ k _ _ _r

This one-liner will show your possibilities, allowing you to choose the word that matches the clue definition:

```
% grep -wi 't...k...r' /usr/share/dict/words/
thickener
trickster
trinketer
truckster
```

Here, grep searched through the dictionary words installed on your system. (This is the same file that look searches.) Use single quotes for your search phrase, and replace each blank square in your crossword with a ..

## See Also

- man fetch
- The Perl HTML-to-text converter at *http://www.ftls.org/en/examples/perl-tools/html2txt.shtml*
- "Wanna Cheat at Crosswords?" (*http://www.osxfaq.com/tips/unix-tricks/week23/friday.ws*)

# Leave on Time

Use your terminal's built-in timers and schedulers.

You know how it is. You sit down in front of a keyboard and quickly become absorbed in your work. At some point you remember to look up, only to notice that everyone else is gone for the day. If that doesn't describe you, I bet you can think of at least one person it does describe.

## Don't Forget to Leave

Fortunately the `leave` command can save you from the embarrassment of forgetting important appointments. Use it at any time by typing:

```
% leave
When do you have to leave?
```

There are three ways to respond to that question:

- Press Enter to abort.
- Type *hhmm*, where *hh* represents the hour and *mm* represents the minute.
- Type *+number*, where *number* represents how many hours or minutes from now you'd like to leave.

For example, to leave at 5 PM:

```
% leave 500
Alarm set for Tue Dec 30 17:00:00 EST 2003. (pid 50097)
```

leave 1700 will achieve the same results.

Or, to leave in 45 minutes:

```
% leave +45
Alarm set for Tue Dec 30 9:52:00 EST 2003. (pid 50108)
```

Be sure to include the + if you're not specifying an actual time.

You can then carry on with your day. Five minutes before it's time to leave, your terminal will beep and display this message:

```
You have to leave in 5 minutes.
```

You'll receive another warning one minute before the set time, then every minute thereafter. leave definitely works for the procrastinator and those who always need to do just one more thing before leaving. The only way to end the incessant nagging is to log out or `killall leave` (but please don't take that last command literally!).

Consider placing */usr/bin/leave* in */usr/share/skel/dot.cshrc* [Hack #9].

## Creating Terminal Sticky Notes

leave is nice for scheduling your own departure, but what if you want to schedule the execution of commands? I bet you're thinking "use at or cron." Have you ever tried the scheduler built into tcsh?

While sched can execute any command at a given time, you can also use it as a reminder system. I use it as a terminal sticky-note system that won't clutter up my monitor. For example, it's 9:00, I've just logged in, and I'm mulling over my to-do list for the day. As I mentally review my list, I type the following:

```
% sched 11:55 echo Lunch with Robyn today.
% sched 2:30 echo Reminder: project due by 4:30.
% sched 5:00 echo Go home!!!
```

Now at any point in the day I can review my to-do list:

```
% sched

1      11:55    echo Lunch with Robyn today.
2      2:30     echo Reminder: project due by 4:30.
3      5:00     echo Go home!!!
```

As each appointed time arrives, the desired reminder will appear on my terminal.

To remove an item from your to-do list, simply type sched -#, where # represents the number of that item in the schedule. Logging out of your shell will also remove all items from your list since sched is a shell command.

## Saving Your Schedule

What if you plan on logging out during the day? You certainly don't want to recreate your schedule every time you log in. It's a simple matter to save the schedule. Place this line in your ~/.logout file:

```
sched > schedule
```

This will send the output of sched to a file in your home directory called *schedule*, saving any items in your to-do list to the specified file when you log out.

Unfortunately, there's no simple way to pipe that list back into sched when you log back in. This has to do with how the C shell handles its built-in commands. You would think that:

```
% sched < schedule
```

would reverse the process, but it doesn't. If you really miss your shell sending you reminders at their appointed times, consider locking your terminal [Hack #7] instead of logging out during the day.

---

## See Also

- `man leave`
- `man tcsh`

 **Run Native Java Applications**

Until recently, running Java applications on FreeBSD meant using the Linux compatibility mode.

Linux programs can sometimes be problematic on FreeBSD. Java™ uses threading very heavily, and that's probably the poorest-emulated part of Linux binary compatibility. Some Java applications or class libraries just don't work correctly under Linux emulation. Native versions of the Java distribution had restrictive licenses, and it required a great deal of work to download and compile them. Fortunately, the FreeBSD Foundation has negotiated a FreeBSD Java license with Sun Microsystems. This hack demonstrates how to configure the FreeBSD version of Java.

 What about native Java on NetBSD or OpenBSD? At the time of writing, neither system had a native Java port. You can run Java on a Linux emulator or via Tomcat.

### Choosing Which Java Port to Install

The first requirement for running Java applications is a Java Virtual Machine (JVM) and the associated runtime support libraries. There are several Java Runtime Environments (JREs) or Java Development Kits (JDKs) available in ports.

 A JRE contains everything necessary for an end user to run Java applications. A JDK contains all that, plus various extra bits required for developing, compiling, and debugging Java code.

The main criteria for choosing a port are:

- Which version of Java do you need?
- Do you want to run FreeBSD native code or Linux code run under emulation?
- Do you prefer to run a precompiled binary or compile it yourself from source code?

Unless you have a specific requirement for an earlier version, choose the latest stable release, which, as of this writing, is Java 1.4.2. The native version, found in */usr/ports/java/jdk14*, will give you the best performance, but you will have to compile it yourself. That is more easily said than done: compiling the JDK requires a great deal of disk space and CPU power, as well as a working copy of the 1.4.2 JDK. The first time you compile, you will have to install one of the Linux JDKs, such as the recommended */usr/ports/java/linux-sun-jdk14*, but once you have a working native JDK, you can use it to compile any updates and uninstall the Linux version.

> You can install several Java versions simultaneously without them interfering with each other. Each will install into its own subdirectory of */usr/local*.

If you need a precompiled native version, choose one of the Diablo Java 1.3.1 ports. These use the same code base as the */usr/ports/java/jdk13* port, and they're certified, licensed, and released through the sponsorship provided by the FreeBSD Foundation (*http://www.freebsdfoundation.org/downloads/java.shtml*).

Diablo JDK 1.4 and JRE 1.4 versions are under development, but not yet available.

The Diablo Java packages are standard FreeBSD packages, so you can install them via pkd_add. However, you're better off installing from the Diablo ports, as that will provide you with the correct dependencies.

For example, to install the Latte Diablo JRE 1.3.1 port, visit *http://www. freebsdfoundation.org/cgi-bin/download.cgi?package=diablo-jre-1.3.1-0.tar.bz2*. Read and accept the license terms, and save the downloaded file as */usr/ports/distfiles/diablo-jre-1.3.1-0.tar.bz2*. Then:

```
# cd /usr/ports/java/diablo-jre13
# make install
```

## Running Java Applications

Starting up any Java application means running a Java Virtual Machine, which in turn loads a named Java class. That class is the entry point for the program. The JVM always requires the CLASSPATH environment variable to contain a list of *.jar* archives that store all of the Java classes required by the application. You can provide extra arguments to the JVM—to limit its use of memory or other system resources, for example—and the application itself may take further command-line arguments.

## Standalone Java Applications

Many Java applications provide a shell script to set up the environment and to execute the JVM with the appropriate arguments. A typical example is ant (see */usr/ports/devel/apache-ant*), the Java equivalent to make.

The installation process edits the script that will become */usr/local/bin/ant* to use the Java version used when building the port. However, you can override the default Java version within the script by setting the JAVA_HOME environment variable:

```
% setenv JAVA_HOME=/usr/local/jdk14
```

## Javavmwrapper

Given the wide variety of JVMs available under FreeBSD, adding code to all Java application wrapper scripts or otherwise configuring standalone Java applications to use the correct JVM could become a maintenance nightmare. Fortunately, the */usr/ports/java/javawmwrapper* port provides the */usr/local/bin/javavm* script, which all applications can run to discover the site's default JVM. javavm's configuration file, */usr/local/etc/javavms*, contains a list of installed JVMs in the order of their preference. Installing or removing a JVM through ports will modify this file. You can also edit it by hand.

## Applets

In the case of a Java applet, the web browser starts the JVM and downloads and runs the applet from the Web. Applets run in a special sandbox that denies them access to most of the local system, except for the browser window.

Java support in web browsers derived from Netscape (including Mozilla, Firebird, and Galeon) uses a plug-in that comes standard with the JDK. For the native JDK 1.4.2, the plug-in is */usr/local/jdk1.4.2/jre/plugin/i386/ns610/libjavaplugin_oji.so*. To make this plug-in available to web browsers, create a symlink to this file from */usr/X11R6/lib/browser_plugins*:

```
# cd /usr/X11R6/lib/browser_plugins
# ln -s /usr/local/jdk1.4.2/jre/plugin/i386/ns610/libjavaplugin_oji.so .
```

Launch a web browser and type about:plugins into the location bar. You should see an entry for the "Java(TM) Plug-in," which claims to handle about 30 MIME types, all variants on application/x-java-*something*.

If you're using a Linux web browser under emulation, install the plug-in from one of the Linux Java versions.

## Servlets

A servlet is all or part of a web application written in Java. It runs through a servlet container application, which abstracts out all of the common server-side functionality. Tomcat (*/usr/ports/www/jakarta-tomcat41*) and Jetty (*/usr/ports/www/jetty*) are two examples of these applications.

The servlet container application runs in much the same way as standalone Java applications.

## Java WebStart

WebStart is a web-based mechanism for downloading and updating Java applications. Use the Preferences menu item in javaws to control the JVM that will run the WebStart-ed applications. Unlike applets, the downloaded applications run independently of the web browser. You don't need to download them again each time they run. They also have full access to the underlying system. The javaws application is a standard part of Java 1.4 or above. It lives in *${JAVA_HOME}/jre/javaws/javaws*.

## See Also

- FreeBSD Foundation's Java downloads (*http://www.freebsdfoundation.org/downloads/java.shtml*)

### HACK   Rotate Your Signature
### #98   End your email communications with a short witticism.

We all seem to know at least one geek friend or mailing-list poster whose emails always end with a different and humourous bit of random nonsense. You may be aware that this is the work of her *~/.signature* file, but have you ever wondered how she manages to rotate those signatures?

While there are several utilities in the ports collection that will randomize your signature, it is easy enough to roll your own signature rotator using the fortune program and a few lines of shell scripting.

### If Your Mail Program Supports a Pipe

Your approach will vary slightly, depending on whether your particular mail user agent (MUA) supports pipes. If it does, it's capable of interpreting the contents of a file as command output, just like when you use a pipe (|) on the command line.

I use pine, which supports both static signature files and signatures that come from the piped output of a signature rotation program.

When configuring pine, choose Setup from the main menu, then C for the configuration editor. Find the signature-file option and give it this value:

```
.signature |
```

The pipe character tells pine to process that filename as a program instead of inserting its contents literally.

Also enable the signature-at-bottom option found in the Reply Preferences to ensure your signature is placed at the bottom of your emails, even when replying to an email.

Next, create a file called ~/.signature containing these lines:

```
echo "Your random fortune:"
/usr/games/fortune -s
```

This isn't quite a shell script: I don't have to include the #!/bin/sh line or use chmod +x to set the file as executable. However, pine will execute those two lines whenever I compose or reply to an email, adding something like this to the bottom of the email:

```
Your random fortune:
"Right now I'm having amnesia and deja vu at the same time."
                -- Steven Wright
```

I also included the short switch (-s) to fortune, as it's bad Netiquette to end an email with a long signature.

If you try a few test messages, you'll see that every email receives a different, random signature.

Depending upon your audience, you may wish to filter further the fortunes to use as signatures. You'll find the available fortunes in /usr/share/games/fortune. If your friends are Trekkies, modify the fortune line in your ~/.signature like so:

```
/usr/games/fortune -s startrek
```

If they tend to be cynical, try murphy instead.

## Pipeless Signature Rotation

Some MUAs, such as Mozilla's mailer, don't support pipes. You'll know yours doesn't if your test message produces no fortune. Fortunately, there's another option.

Create a file as before, but this time make it a Bourne script. I'll save mine in ~/*bin* and make it executable using chmod +x:

```
#!/bin/sh
echo "Your random fortune:" > $HOME/.signature
/usr/games/fortune -s >> $HOME/.signature
```

This script does two things. It echoes the first line to the ~/.*signature* file, then appends the results of the fortune program to the same file.

To configure Mozilla to use this signature file, open the Mail & News-groups window, and choose Mail & Newsgroups Account Settings from the Edit menu. Select the "Attach this signature" option from the main menu, and use the Choose button to give the location of ~/.*signature*.

What do you think will happen when I compose an email? Since Mozilla only understands literal signature files, it will faithfully reproduce the current contents of ~/.*signature*. If I haven't run my script yet, that file doesn't exist. If I have run the script, the resulting file remains the same until the script runs again.

This is different from pine, which has the capability of executing the commands found in my signature file. Since Mozilla can't, you'll have to remember to run the script manually before you compose an email or schedule its periodic execution using cron. This may be a little disappointing if you want every recipient to receive a unique signature, or not a big deal if you send only one or two emails a day and aren't a stickler for randomness.

### Hacking the Hack

Hmm, what would happen if .*signature* were a named pipe connected to a program that provided a random signature on every read? There are many possibilities here.

### See Also

- man fortune

## Useful One-Liners

Unix allows an amazing miscellany of one-liner command combinations.

Unix is amazing. Only your imagination limits the usefulness of the built-in commands. You can create your own commands and then pipe them together, allowing one utility to work on the results of another.

If you're like me, you've run across dozens of useful combinations over the years. Here are some of my favorite one-liners, intended to demonstrate useful ideas as well as to prime your pump for writing your own one-liner hacks.

## Simultaneously Download and Untar

Have you ever downloaded an extremely large archive over a slow connection? It seems to take forever to receive the archive and forever to untar it. Being impatient, I hate not knowing how many of the archived files are already here. I miss the ability to work on those files while the rest of the archive finishes its slow migration onto my system.

This one-liner will decompress and untar the files as the archive downloads, without interfering with the download. Here's an example of downloading and untarring the ports collection:

```
# tail -f -b=1m ports.tar.gz | tar -zxvf ports.tar.gz
ports/
ports/Mk/
<snip>
```

Here I've asked `tail` to stream up to one megabyte of the specified file as it is received. It will pipe those bytes to the `tar` utility, which I've directed to decompress (`-z`) and to extract (`x`) the specified file (`f`) while displaying the results verbosely (`v`).

To use this command, download the archive to where you'd like to untar it—in this example, */usr*. Simply replace the filename *ports.tar.gz* with the name of your archive.

## When Did I Change That File?

Do you ever need to know the last modification date of a file? Consider a long listing:

```
% ls -l filename
-rw-r--r--  1 dru  wheel  12962 Dec 16 18:01 filename
```

If you count the fields, the sixth (Dec), seventh (16), and eighth (18:01) fields all contain part of the modification date. However, there's whitespace separating those fields, which makes it difficult to determine their exact character positions. Fortunately, awk doesn't mind variable whitespace, so this one-liner will always work:

```
% echo filename was last modified on `/bin/ls -l filename \
    | awk '{print $6, $7, $8}'`
filename was last modified on Dec 16 18:01
```

Here I've asked echo to repeat a string as well as the results of a command contained within single quotes. The first half of that command is simply `ls -l filename`. I've piped the output of that command to awk, which will print the sixth ($6), seventh ($7), and eighth ($8) fields of the long listing. Note that the awk action is enclosed between '{ }'.

While this is a useful one-liner, it is fairly awkward to type as needed. However, if you replace filename with a positional parameter [Hack #13], you have a very handy script. I'll call mine when:

```
% more ~/bin/when
#!/bin/sh
# script to list date of a file's last modification
# replaces $1 with specified filename
# or gives error message if user forgets to include filename
if test $1
then
    echo $1 was last modified on `/bin/ls -l $1| awk '{print $6, $7, $8}'`
else
    echo "Don't forget the name of the file you're interested in"
    exit 1
fi
```

Once you've made your script executable, use when filename to find the date of a file's most recent modification.

## Finding Symlinks

If you ever need to find symbolic links, you're in luck. find's -type l or link option serves just this purpose. Start with this invocation:

```
% find /etc -type l -ls
25298    0 lrwxrwxrwx    1 root           wheel                 23 Apr  7
2003 /etc/termcap -> /usr/share/misc/termcap
25299    0 lrwxrwxrwx    1 root           wheel                 13
Apr  7 2003 /etc/rmt -> /usr/sbin/rmt
25301    0 lrwxrwxrwx    1 root           wheel                 12
Apr  7 2003 /etc/aliases -> mail/aliases
25305    0 lrwxr-xr-x    1 root           wheel                 36
Oct 26 09:08 /etc/localtime -> /usr/share/zoneinfo/America/Montreal
```

Well, that worked, but the output is downright ugly. Let's pipe the results to our good friend awk to display only the last three fields. If you count them, those are fields 11 through 13:

```
% find /etc -type l -ls | awk '{print $11, $12, $13}'
/etc/termcap -> /usr/share/misc/termcap
/etc/rmt -> /usr/sbin/rmt
/etc/aliases -> mail/aliases
/etc/localtime -> /usr/share/zoneinfo/America/Montreal
```

Aah, much better. If you ever plan on needing to find symlinks, it's well worth saving this in a shell script similar to the when script shown previously.

## Making cron More User-Friendly

Are you always forgetting the meanings of the various fields in a crontab? It would probably be a lot easier if your crontab began like this:

```
# minute (0-59),
# |     hour (0-23),
# |       |       day of the month (1-31),
# |       |         |       month of the year (1-12),
# |       |         |         |       day of the week (0-6 with 0=Sunday).
# |       |         |         |         |       commands
   3       2         *         *       0,6     /some/command/to/run
```

To achieve that, type those lines into a text file, say *~/cronheader*. (Be patient, we're getting to the one-liner.) Then, open up your crontab editor:

```
% crontab -e
```

Unless you've changed your default editor, this will open up your crontab using vi. Place your cursor at the beginning of the file, and type the following:

```
!!more /usr/home/dru/cronheader
```

The !! tells vi to insert the output of the specified command. Be sure to give the full pathname to your file. vi will insert its contents for you once you press Enter. When you're finished, type :wq as usual to exit the editor.

## See Also

- man tail
- man tar
- man cut
- man awk

## Fun with X

**100**

Use the utilities that come with the core X distribution.

There are so many GUI utilities, available either as part of your favorite Window Manager or as a separate installation, that you can forget that the core X distribution also provides several useful and lightweight programs. Do you need to monitor console messages, manage your clipboard, send pop-up messages, or create and view screenshots? Before you hit the ports collection, give the built-in utilities a try.

### Seeing Console Messages

In "See Console Messages Over a Remote Login" [Hack #42], we saw how to redirect console messages. If you're using an X session, the xconsole utility fulfills this purpose. To start this utility, simply type its name into an xterm or use the Run command provided by your window manager.

By default, only the superuser can start xconsole. A regular user will instead receive a Couldn't open console message. This is a safety precaution on multiuser systems, preventing regular users from viewing system messages. If you're the only user who uses your system, remove the comment (#) from this line in */etc/fbtab*:

```
#/dev/ttyv0     0600     /dev/console
```

If you spend a lot of your time at an X session, consider adding xconsole to your ~/.*xinitrc* file so it will start automatically (see "Customize User Configurations" [Hack #9]).

## Managing Your Clipboard

If you do a lot of copying and pasting, xclipboard is another excellent candidate for automatic startup. This utility stores each of your clipboard selections as a separate entity, allowing you to scroll through them one at a time in a simple GUI window. In addition to the Next and Prev buttons, a Delete button lets you remove unwanted items and a Save button allows you to save all of your items as a file.

## Sending Pop-up Messages

Do you find yourself starting a command that takes a while to execute, continuing your work in an X session, then returning periodically to the original terminal or xterm to see how that command is perking along? Wouldn't it be easier to send yourself a pop-up message once the command completes?

For example, suppose I want to know when the script from "Automate Updates" [Hack #80] finishes. I could execute that script as follows:

```
#~/bin/mycustomupgrade.sh && xmessage -nearmouse cvsup is complete.
```

When the upgrade completes, a pop-up message with the text cvsup is complete. will appear in my X session near my mouse. That message will disappear once I click on the Okay button.

If you're in the habit of using su -1 to provide a new login when you become the superuser, you'll find that the preceding command will fail to send you a pop-up menu. (I'm assuming you're logged in as a regular user when you start your X session. You should be!) Instead, you'll receive this error message:

```
Xlib: connection to ":0.0" refused by server
Xlib: No protocol specified
Error: Can't open display: :0.0
```

This has to do with the X authorization process. If I start my X session as the user dru and use su to execute a command, I'm still logged in as dru, so I'm allowed to send a message to my display. However, if I use su -1 to execute the command, I'm no longer logged in as dru but as root. The X server refuses to let another user interfere with my display, which is a good thing.

A quick workaround is to not use su -1 when sending pop-up messages to your regular user account. An alternative is to understand the X authorization process. You can then use this knowledge to enable the superuser to send a message to any user on any display.

**Understanding X authorization.** Your X server uses a token known as an *MIT magic cookie* to provide authorization. When you start your X session, the server creates and stores this unique cookie in *~/.Xauthority*. You can view it at any time using this command:

```
% xauth list
genisis/unix:0  MIT-MAGIC-COOKIE-1  7e7bc20f9413469a7376e2e5c91aa6f1
```

Take note that you're the only user with access to this file:

```
% ls -l ~/.Xauthority
-rw-------  1 dru  wheel   101 Feb 18 13:28 .Xauthority
```

Always keep in the back of your mind, though, that file ownership does not matter to the superuser. For example, if I need to send an important message to the user dru, I can ssh into the system she's working on and become the superuser. Then:

```
# cp ~dru/.Xauthority .
```

I now have a copy of dru's magic cookie. However, before I can use it, I'll first have to change my display. Since I sshed into a terminal, I currently don't have one:

```
# echo $DISPLAY
DISPLAY: Undefined variable.
```

I don't want just any display, I want the display dru is currently using. I can find the name of her display by reading her magic cookie:

```
# xauth list
genisis/unix:0  MIT-MAGIC-COOKIE-1  7e7bc20f9413469a7376e2e5c91aa6f1
```

The name of her display is genisis/unix:0, where genisis represents the hostname of the system. I'll now attach to that display and send my message:

```
# setenv DISPLAY genisis/unix:0
# xmessage -nearmouse Time to go home, Dru...
(prompt hangs until dru responds by pressing the "Okay" button)
```

This cheat works on any system to which you have superuser access. Technically, you can execute any command X understands in a user's X session once you have his cookie and display. Do remember to use your superuser powers for good, though.

## Taking Screenshots

Have you ever needed to send a user a screenshot? There are ports available for this purpose, but the built-in X command xwd will suffice. Creating a screenshot is a simple matter of:

```
% xwd -out screenshot.xwd
```

The command will appear to hang as it waits for you to click your mouse on the portion of the screen you'd like to capture. Use the -root switch to capture the entire screen and save yourself a click.

You can view and manipulate the resulting file with most third-party image editors, including xv and gimp. For quick viewing, though, nothing beats the built-in xwud:

```
% xwud -in screenshot.xwd
```

Your results won't seem that impressive if you use xwud immediately, as your screen still probably looks like your screenshot. When you're finished viewing the screenshot, press Ctrl-c.

## See Also

- man xconsole
- man xclipboard
- man xauth
- man xwd
- man xwud

# Index

## Symbols

(`) (backticks) vs. single quote ('), 50
! (bang) character, retrieving previously
    issued commands, 4
.\" (comment) groff command, 375
# (hash mark) for comments in
    code, 98
(') (single quote) vs. backticks (`), 50

## A

Access Control Lists (ACLs), 225–231
    adding/subtracting, 228
    enabling, 226
    setting default ACLs, 229–231
    viewing, 227
access, limiting with IP Filter, 272–274
accounting (system), enabling, 391–393
accton command, 391
ACID (Analysis Console for Intrusion
    Databases)
    adding more security to, 255
    alerts, 253–255
    configuring, 251
    installing, 246
    running, 251
ack numbers in packets, 189
addresses, MAC, spoofing, 172–175
adduser command, 36
    Blowfish and, 117
adodb (database library for PHP),
    installing, 246
ADSL PPPoE configuration, 279–281

alerts, ACID, 253–255
anonymous CVS, 347
antivirus software, 286–290
Apache servers
    configuring, 248
    consolidating logs, 313
    installing, 246
    starting, 251
    tuning, 296
APG (Automated Password
    Generator), 128
    improving, 129–131
    installing, 129
appending changes to files, 234
applets, Java, 401
arch flag, 232, 237
archives
    compressed, 142
        without intermediate files, 145
    creating portable POSIX
        archives, 144–148
    downloading and untarring, 405
    multivolume, resources for, 147
    rooted, 146
ARP packets, 187
attaching/detaching screen sessions, 47
attributes of files, preserving when
    copying, 145
authorized/unauthorized
    hosts, 276–278
auto completion, 2
    working around, 5
autologout after inactivity, 23

We'd like to hear your suggestions for improving our indexes. Send email to *index@oreilly.com*.

intervals of backups, specifying, 154
Intrusion Detection Systems
        (IDSs), 245–256
IP Filter
    automatically generating firewall
        rules, 279–282
    limiting access with, 272–274
    switching rules on schedule, 273
IP NAT configuration, 279
IPFIREWALL_DEFAULT_TO_
        ACCEPT option, 299
ipfw command, 297, 298

## J

Jabber4r Ruby module, 182
Java applets, 401
Java applications, running on
        FreeBSD, 399–402
Java Development Kits (JDKs), 399
Java Runtime Environments (JREs), 399
Java Virtual Machines (JVMs), 399
JAVA_HOME environment
        variable, 401
javavmwrapper port, 401
javaws application, 402
JDKs (Java Development Kits), 399
Jetty (Java servlet), 402
JPGraph, installing, 246
JREs (Java Runtime Environments), 399
JVMs (Java Virtual Machines), 399

## K

kenv command, 388
kernel environment, viewing, 388
kernels
    adding SMB support to, 141
    building new, 224
    configuring for traffic shaping, 296
    customizing, 217–224
    installing, 225
    optimizing, 292
    stripping, 216–225
    supporting MAC (Mandatory Access
        Control), 237–240
keys, GPG, generating, 318–322
kldload command, 238
kldunload command, 238

## L

Langille, Dan, viii
laptops
    backing up, 162–168
    configuring wireless interfaces
        for, 175–179
    encrypting hard disks, 256–261
    power management support for, 221
last command, 391
last modification dates of files,
        finding, 405
lastcomm command, 392
lastlogin command, 391
leave command, 397
Lents, David, xii, 235
less pager
    customizing, 379
    vs. more pager, 379
Libes, Don, 322
limiting files, 81
line feeds (duplicate), removing, 64
live filesystems, using, 308
live log data, viewing, 317
livelock and kernel optimizations, 294
loader.conf file, 97, 99
    password protection, 103
loader.rc file, 97
locate command, 373
lock command, 22
log files for sudoscript, 267–269
log hosts
    configuring scripts on, 316
    consolidating web server
        logs, 313–318
    logproc and, 314
    preparing, 315
    variables/values for
        log host scripts, 317
        web server scripts, 314
logging out of login shell, 32
logging servers, setting up, 109
login banner, removing, 111–114
.login file, 31
login prompt, changing, 113
.login.conf file, 31
logins
    automating, using ftp, 206
    lastlogin command, 391

# Colophon

Our look is the result of reader comments, our own experimentation, and feedback from distribution channels. Distinctive covers complement our distinctive approach to technical topics, breathing personality and life into potentially dry subjects.

The image on the cover of *BSD Hacks* is a pitchfork. A pitchfork (also known as a garden or spading fork) is a versatile agricultural hand tool. It can be used for a range of tasks, including aerating soil, pitching hay, and mixing compost. In addition to its practical uses, the pitchfork is also symbolic; for example, it is often included in depictions of the Devil, and it is a central feature of Grant Wood's *American Gothic*. A pitchfork can have two, three, or four curved prongs, but most pitchforks manufactured today (such as the one depicted in the cover image) have four.

Genevieve d'Entremont was the production editor and copyeditor for *BSD Hacks*. Reg Aubry proofread the book. Matt Hutchinson and Claire Cloutier provided quality control. Judy Hoer wrote the index.

Hanna Dyer designed the cover of this book, based on a series design by Edie Freedman. The cover image is a photograph from the Stockbyte Work Tools CD. Emma Colby produced the cover layout with QuarkXPress 4.1 using Adobe's Helvetica Neue and ITC Garamond fonts.

David Futato designed the interior layout. This book was converted by Joe Wizda to FrameMaker 5.5.6 with a format conversion tool created by Erik Ray, Jason McIntosh, Neil Walls, and Mike Sierra that uses Perl and XML technologies. The text font is Linotype Birka; the heading font is Adobe Helvetica Neue Condensed; and the code font is LucasFont's TheSans Mono Condensed. The illustrations that appear in the book were produced by Robert Romano and Jessamyn Read using Macromedia FreeHand 9 and Adobe Photoshop 6. This colophon was written by Genevieve d'Entremont.